Responsible Tourism

Concepts, Theory and Practice

FSC

MIX
Paper from
responsible sources
www.fsc.org   FSC® C018575

To Susan, for her unfailing support throughout our
forty years (so far) together.

Responsible Tourism

Concepts, Theory and Practice

Edited by

David Leslie

www.cabi.org

CABI is a trading name of CAB International

CABI	CABI
Nosworthy Way	875 Massachusetts Avenue
Wallingford	7th Floor
Oxfordshire, OX10 8DE	Cambridge, MA 02139
UK	USA
Tel: +44 (0)1491 832111	Tel: +1 800 552 3083 (toll free)
Fax: +44 (0)1491 833508	Fax: +1 (0)617 395 4051
E-mail: info@cabi.org	E-mail: cabi-nao@cabi.org
Website: www.cabi.org	

A catalogue record for this book is available from the British Library, London, UK.

Library of Congress Cataloging-in-Publication Data

Responsible tourism : concepts, theory and practice / edited by David Leslie.
 p. cm.
 Includes bibliographical references and index.
 ISBN 978-1-84593-987-8 (alk. paper)
 1. Sustainable tourism. I. Leslie, David.
 G156.5.S87R47 2012
 910.68'4--dc23

                                    2012013387

ISBN-13: 978 1 84593 987 8

Commissioning editor: Sarah Hulbert
Editorial assistant: Alexandra Lainsbury
Production editor: Shankari Wilford

Typeset by Columns Design XML Ltd, Reading, UK.
Printed and bound in the UK by the MPG Books Group.

Contents

Contributors   vii

Preface   ix

Acknowledgements   xi

1   Introduction   1
      David Leslie

PART 1: Responsible Tourism and Responsibilities

2   The Responsible Tourism Debate   17
      David Leslie

**3   International Transport and Climate Change: Taking Responsibility
      Seriously**   43
      Hugh Somerville

4   The Consumers of Tourism   54
      David Leslie

PART 2: The Central Tenets of Tourism

5   Destination Communities and Responsible Tourism   72
      Dallen J. Timothy

6   Environmental Performance   82
      Ralf Buckley

7   The Politics of Tourism and Poverty Reduction   90
      Anita Pleumarom

8   **Governance and Responsible Tourism**   107
    C. Michael Hall

PART 3: Responsible Tourism in Action?

9   **Adventure Tours: Responsible Tourism in Practice?**   119
    Jacqueline Holland

10 **Responsible Wildlife Tourism in Africa**   130
    Anna Spenceley and Andrew Rylance

11 **Cultural Heritage: World Heritage Sites and Responsible Tourism
    in Argentina**   142
    Albina L. Lara and Alicia Gemelli

12 **Hospitality Enterprise – a Key Influence**   154
    Piotr Zientara

13 **Conclusion**   165
    David Leslie

Index   173

Contributors

————————————

Ralf Buckley, International Centre for Ecotourism Research, Griffith University, Queensland 4222, Australia. E-mail: r.buckley@griffith.edu.au

Alicia Gemelli, Pacheco de Melo 2714 8° (1425), Ciudad de Buenos Aires, Argentina. E-mail: aliciagemelli@gmail.com

C. Michael Hall, Department of Management, College of Business and Economics, University of Canterbury, Private Bag 4800, Christchurch 8140, New Zealand. E-mail: michael.hall@canterbury.ac.nz

Jacqueline Holland, Newcastle Business School, Northumbria University, City Campus East 1, Newcastle upon Tyne, NE1 8ST. United Kingdom. E-mail: jacqueline.holland@northumbria.ac.uk

Albina L. Lara, Guatemala 5963 3ero. A. (1425), Ciudad de Buenos Aires, Argentina. E-mail: albinalara@hotmail.com

David Leslie, 71 Old Mearns Road, Clarkston, Glasgow, G76 7LF, Scotland, UK. E-mail: d.leslie@btinternet.com

Anita Pleumarom, tourism investigation and monitoring team (tim-team), PO Box 51, Chorakhebua, Bangkok 10230, Thailand. E-mail: timteam02@yahoo.com

Andrew Rylance, PO Box 543, Sonpark, Nelspruit, 1206, South Africa. E-mail: andrewrylance@gmail.com

Hugh Somerville, Bridge House, Ferry Lane, Cookham, SL6 9XH, UK. E-mail: somervillehugh@aol.com

Anna Spenceley, University of Johannesburg and Spenceley Tourism and Development (STAND) cc, PO Box 543, Sonpark, Nelspruit, 1206, South Africa. E-mail: annaspenceley@gmail.com

Dallen J. Timothy, School of Community Resources and Development, Senior Sustainability Scientist, Global Institute of Sustainability, Arizona State University, 411 N. Central Avenue, Suite 550, Phoenix, Arizona 85004, USA. E-mail: dtimothy@asu.edu

Piotr Zientara, 177/44 Chylońska St., 81-007 Gdynia, Poland. E-mail: zientara@fest.pl

Preface

_____

The 21st century – at least for the foreseeable future – will see continuing growth in demand and the worldwide expansion of tourism. Awareness and concerns over the importance of the quality of our environment will increase and the shift towards policies and practices intended to reduce negative human impacts and towards more sustainable forms of development will continue. These factors will bring into question the development and progress of tourism and, particularly, put an increased emphasis on the value of tourism to destination localities and more equitable distribution of the related benefits among host communities. It is therefore imperative that the tourism sector takes the necessary steps to address and respond effectively to the twin challenges of worldwide competition and the environmental agenda, including unsustainable patterns of consumption. One such step is encapsulated within the concept of responsible tourism. This text though is NOT about 'responsible tourism' in the sense of being just another form of tourism such as 'sustainable tourism' or 'ecotourism', nor is it a collage of articles each based on some different type of tourism product or form of tourism.

Since the start of this century there has been limited in-depth questioning of the emergent terminology applied to tourism over the last 20 years or so, e.g. 'sustainable … hard … mass … eco … nature … pro-poor …' except in the specific context of a chosen term and then, not necessarily, to any depth nor with a focus on application and practice. Rather, books with titles based on such terms tend to be edited collections of contributions relating to the chosen theme. The scope of this text is broader and with more in-depth discourse.

The text seeks to examine *responsible tourism* per se, to identify and critically discuss it in the context of demand and supply, to analyse and debate its key tenets and explore the application of these tenets in practice in a range of different contexts. A key feature is that while the book is an edited collection of contributions, it is unlike the majority of such publications in that it is not the product of a conference nor a collection of chapters following a call for contributions. In effect, the objective is to present a definitive discourse on just what is meant by *responsible tourism* and what this actually involves in terms of concepts, theory and application in practice. To progress this objective the structure of the text was first conceived, following which authors of international renown were identified and invited to contribute; this proved very successful. Each contribution is thus original, up to date and based on current thinking and, as appropriate, on primary research. Further, each contribution has been reviewed by referees as per best practice.

This text may thus be seen to be at the forefront of identification and analysis of just what *responsible tourism* is 'all about' and a comprehensive discourse in its own right. In total, it provides what we might term, perhaps generously, a 'state of the art' analysis of the current position of tourism and sustainability. The lessons identified should prove invaluable to inform the development of tourism in any location.

David Leslie
Glasgow

Acknowledgements

_____

The undertaking of any book is not without considerable effort, often involving a host of role players without whom there is little chance of a successful outcome. First, I would like to acknowledge the support of Sarah Hulbert of CABI, in particular for her enthusiasm and contributions in the development of this book and remarkable faith in the editor, and Alexandra Lainsbury, also of CABI, for her support, guidance and patience throughout the process. Even with such support, the book would not have come about without the contributors who all readily accepted my invitation and, despite a remarkable range of difficulties and serious misfortunes, still managed to deliver their chapters. Throughout the process they invariably responded readily to my queries and requests and feedback from reviewers with good humour and patience. I would also like to thank Graham Millar, of Surrey University, and particularly Myrene McFee for her invaluable contribution.

Finally, I would like to acknowledge the support and contributions of the ever-present Susan for once again having her time sidetracked by innumerable requests for reviewing work.

1 Introduction

David Leslie
Freelance Researcher and Consultant

This text is not about 'responsible tourism' in the sense that it might be considered as just another form of tourism such as 'sustainable tourism', 'soft tourism' or 'ecotourism'. Neither is it a collage of articles each of which is based on some different type or form of tourism product. Rather, the primary intent is to produce a broad, yet comprehensive, monograph on the concept of responsible tourism (RT), focusing on what is meant by the term and what it encompasses. The text thus presents a critical discourse on what RT is, its key tenets and the extent to which they are applied and realized through illustrations and examples of responsibility (or otherwise) in tourism in practice. In pursuance of this objective, the first consideration is to establish a broad context within which to place the emergence of RT and thereby establish a framework to delineate our discourse and establish both structure and content for the following chapters. The use of the term 'responsible' in this context implies 'responsible for', implying that those involved in tourism are responsible for the consequences of tourism as an activity. For example, responsible providers of tourism products and services may be considered liable for the conduct and outcomes of their operations and trustworthy in their intent. To a greater or lesser extent, this expectation of responsible behaviour is equally applicable to any business activity.

However, raising the expectation in the context of tourism suggests that there are facets of tourism which might not be considered responsible; and hence also in some way not ethical. Further, to be responsible suggests moral accountability for one's actions and the impacts of those actions. So the implication is that it is not just the providers of tourism products and services who have a responsibility but also the purchasers of those products and services, namely the consumers – the tourists. Undoubtedly, such considerations raise many issues not only within the context of the development of tourism but also, significantly, whether tourism itself is being singled out as some form of pariah. That this might be the case demands comparative analyses of tourism with other economic development opportunities and other sectors of the economy which are beyond the scope of this text. Nevertheless, this is a substantive issue: a consideration that should be borne in mind throughout this text and one to which we will return in the concluding pages. Our starting point, however, is how the concept of RT arose.

As a term, RT may be generally attributed to the late 1980s, though certainly more explicitly to the 1990s. The developing environmental agenda of the 1960s/1970s had led to much attention to the impacts of tourism in the 1980s and to the emergence and/or development of terminology to describe various forms of tourism considered in some way(s) different from that which had gone before: for example, from Turner and Ash's (1975) Sunlust/Wanderlust tourists, to concepts such as 'hard' or 'soft' tourism, and to 'green', 'sustainable' or 'eco' tourism. These terms emerged within the context of established concerns arising over the impact of agricultural and industrial practices on the physical environment and the rapid growth of tourism, particularly in the 1970s, with the development of already popular resorts and the establishment of new destinations: in effect, what became known as 'mass tourism'. To varying degrees, such terms arose explicitly or implicitly in response to perceptions of mass tourism – i.e. substantial and sustained influxes of tourists to developed/developing destinations, greatly facilitated by tour operators and the package holidays they offered. But this was not a new phenomenon. A kind of mass tourism, exemplified by the Grand Tour, had already been manifested in the latter part of the 1800s, and the popularity of some tourist resorts of today was well established by the 1800s. The 'elite' in British society were first, and then as trade grew in the 19th century so followed members of the emerging middle class and subsequently of the working class. The societal changes witnessed today in destinations far-flung from the Western world were evident in popular tourist destinations of Europe in the 1700s and 1800s, which experienced early forms of urbanization: witness Bath (UK), Baden-Baden (Germany), Vichy (France), and then the resorts of Nice, Biarritz and Cannes (Hall, 1998). The 1900s saw the expansion of many resorts, and in some cases these experienced a shift in the pattern of demand from winter to summer and the establishment of new seaside resorts. In today's terms, many of these popular destinations experienced 'mass tourism', which was facilitated by the development of infrastructure that enabled thousands of tourist arrivals and then served other development opportunities such as conferences and congresses.

As Briasspoulis (2003) illustrated well, tourism starts incrementally and spreads spatially in the presence of favourable government policies. Once a destination achieves sustainable demand then this attracts inward investment and the location develops into a tourist resort. Whether in the northern European cold-water resorts of the 19th/20th century or in the USA, the entrepreneurs of the day were quick to seize the opportunity to provide for the needs and desires of tourists. As constraints on demand eased, then so tourism developed, often in a rather ad hoc manner, and with a lack of forward planning (Swift, 1972). A key point here is that mass tourism is often seen to exist only in those destinations that have extensively developed over time. Undoubtedly, such development can be achieved in a far shorter time today, given globalization, contemporary building techniques and the involvement of tour operators. But, in the beginning, when a locale is first visited, the early comers – 'wanderlusts' – could well be described in today's terms as tourists or ecotourists.

At what point does a destination begin to be considered as evidencing mass tourism? As Jenkins (1982, p. 247) argued, 'There can be no single determinant of the scale of tourism developments in a country, but rather a consideration of an amalgam of complex and often conflicting criteria. Large-scale tourism projects may not be inevitable, but in many developing countries they will be difficult to avoid without positive government intervention in the formulation of tourism objectives'. Furthermore, as the following pages of this book will attest, such consideration is brought repeatedly into question in terms of efficacy, especially in the absence of regulatory control mechanisms. The earth is not a free good, nor are destinations infinite and, as such, not readily substituted (in the sense of general consumer goods); thus, their value increases over time (Martínez-Alier, 1995). The processes of globalization have accelerated development and also the opportunity for the more affluent in society to visit almost anywhere (Crowley, 1998), followed by the less affluent. Consequently tourism development, in terms of natural capital demand, must be managed appropriately and effectively.

Overall, as means and opportunity increase, so tourism expands temporally and spatially. Just as mass follows class, then so the increasing popularity of one destination leads to development elsewhere. As Graburn (1989) succinctly described: 'Tourism is a service industry whose primary resource is environments and cultures which differ from those where the tourists usually live' (cited in Harrison and Price, 1996, p. 2) As destinations not that distant from home become more visited, so the destination periphery extends as tourists begin to travel further afield (Pattullo and Minelli, 2006). In the 1960s and 1970s, hitherto less popular areas of Europe or eastern destinations in India, Nepal and Thailand became available to package holiday takers, and not necessarily to their benefit (see Noronha, 1999). In the process, as Briasspoulis (2003) argued, tourism often develops in an uncontrolled manner in the absence of an holistic oversight/development plan; witness Blackpool (UK) in the 19th century, the Costa Brava of Spain in the 1970s, and the western Mediterranean area of Turkey in the late 1990s – developments which have had negative impacts on the land and the sea (see Harrison and Price, 1996).

Of significance here is that throughout much of this period of tourism development, certainly in today's terms, there was limited evidence of outcry over the impact of the gradual growth of resorts in the 1800s and 1900s. In contrast, major concerns were raised over the impacts of a mobile populace on the countryside (Pye-Smith and Blackie, 1979; Leslie, 1986). So we identify that the first signs of concern relating to the idea of responsible tourism were manifest in issues raised over access to countryside and the impact of demand on the countryside, but not in the development of tourist resorts. As we move into the 1960s, perceptions of tourism in some quarters changed. This was a time when the main constraints on demand – time, disposable income and transport – eased, thereby enabling substantial increases in demand, which itself brought about reduced prices. This enabled the comparatively less affluent in society to travel to new destinations: notably, in the case of northern and central Europeans, to the northern coast of the Mediterranean Sea, especially Spain. The traditional cold-water resorts of the affluent more northerly countries declined, not only because of the desire for the new, potentially cheaper, package holidays in the rapidly developing warmer resorts of the Mediterranean, but also, for example, as a result of changing tastes and the development of alternative options such as theme parks (see Urry, 1988). Mention of the cost of a holiday here draws attention to a primary influence on destination choice: that of the price. For example, there is little doubt that holidaying in the UK was and still is expensive compared with countries such as France, Italy, Spain and Portugal, where often the cost of accommodation, food and beverage products and services will be lower, and the quality and value better than in the UK.

As these latter-day 'sun, sand and sea' resorts developed in warmer climates, then so too did concerns over the impacts of such developments on the environment gain wider notice. As in the 1960s and 1970s, changes in land use patterns and traditional attitudes came to attention (Swift, 1972) and questions arose over the ongoing development of tourism. As argued by Romeril and Hughes-Evans (1979, p. 1): 'Tourism has now reached that inevitable point where it begins to destroy the beauty it is in search of'. As the 1980s unfolded, commentary on the negative impacts of tourism on the physical environment increased (see UNWTO, 1983; Jafari, 1986), but attention to other key areas such as pollution, water and energy use in areas of very limited supply, for example the Caribbean islands, gained comparatively little attention.

Significantly, such negative impacts, primarily conflicts over tourism and recreation versus conservation and over the use of resources were also noted by international agencies. Recognition of the importance to tourism development of natural resources was highlighted in 1960 by the International Union of Overseas Tour Operators (now the World Tourism Organization, UNWTO), and affirmed in a policy in 1971 which called for new resorts to be carefully planned by a host of experts including ecologists (Jenner and Smith, 1992). Further, the International Union for the Conservation of Nature (IUCN; now known as the World Conservation Union, WCU) staged a conference on ecology, tourism and recreation in 1966 (IUCN/UNESCO, 1967). The first conference on tourism and conservation, hosted by Europa Nostra and the

European Travel Commission, was held in 1973, and the UNEP (United Nations Environment Programme)/UNWTO initiative to promote environmentally sound tourism development was presented in 1982 (Romeril, 1989). The latter had been preceded by the Manila Declaration on World Tourism in 1980; this stressed the quality of environment as a priority, the need to ensure that tourism development is not to the detriment of the (physical) environment, and thus the need for a balance between tourism as an economic activity and the environment. Notably, social considerations were missing at this stage.

In 1983, UNWTO agreed that 'The absence of planning and failure by the public sector to assume responsibilities, leaving the private sector with the task of developing tourism according to the logic of the market-place, which does not always reflect the interests of the community, has been responsible for most of the negative results of tourism development (UNWTO, 1983, para. 48)'. In this, we find the dominance of international hotel chains and tour operators (for example, see NI, 1993). At the supra-national level, and especially notable for its introduction of the term 'responsible tourism', the 1989 European Commission Charter for Cultural Tourism emphasized the need for a responsible tourism policy in the long term (LGA, 2010). The terminology was sub-sequently changed to 'sustainable tourism' and – as with most other international iterations on this theme – the Charter contained explicit, detailed objectives and guidelines for develop-ment. This advocacy of protection of the physical environment and responsibility in the development of tourism appears to be at odds with Jenner and Smith's (1992) perceptions that UNWTO policy was targeted at locations around the world holding potential for development as tourist resorts, and with the intent that such areas should be flagged and reserved for such development! Although perhaps little more than rhetoric, such objections are nevertheless significant in this context given the importance placed on the role of government and related policy in the development of tourism. As Minhinnick (1993, p. 36) somewhat sarcastically commented, where tourism is a key sector of the economy

– as might be argued in the case of Wales (UK) – then the temptation for the country's political leaders would be to maintain and foster further tourism, which could mean 'gradually "liquidating" our greatest asset – the environment – [then] they would not hesitate over it'. Is this not evident in some destinations across the globe? –for example the extensive developments in Bali (see Wall, 1993) or the creation of golf courses in places such as Dubai.

In most of these commentaries on the negative impact of tourism what is inescapable is how invariably they apply to 'new' destination developments – in much the same way that people in post-industrial societies deride the despoliation of what they perceive to be attractive locations elsewhere and support the protection of 'exotic' animals and habitats, yet pay less notice to what is occurring in their homelands. This orientation to developing destinations was noted by Jafari (1986), who observed that while much of the literature is based on receiving countries, and evidences a bias to the less developed countries (and continues to do so), this tends to miss the fact that the majority of international tourism takes place within and between the developed countries of the world. Still, we find com-paratively little written on mass tourism and its impacts in long-established destinations. Are they so different? Cornwall (UK), for example, is a long-established popular tourist destination with a population of approximately a million residents and may receive some 5 million tourists over the summer months. This had led to economic and infrastructural development, but it also gives an obvious boost to energy consumption, pollution and waste-manage-ment costs.

As we move into the 1990s in our review of the development of tourism, we find increasing attention being given to its impact on society, on people and their culture. This concern was heralded predominantly by Young (1973) and was taken up by Sherman (1988) who decried the influx of tourists and attendant problems in the context of government subsidy and promotion. Questioning the costs and benefits of tourism development, his diatribe resonates all too well with popular 'clubbing' resorts of today, such as Faliraki (see Leslie,

Chapter 4). Undoubtedly, tourism is a commonplace vector of social change, a contributory factor in modernization and an influence on host culture (see Harrison, 1992; NI, 1993; Nash, 1996). This is not an unexpected outcome given the intrusiveness of tourism but, to varying degrees, any alien development will have similarly significant impacts: for example, extraction industries can have a substantial impact on the local economy and culture (Anon., 1997).

Overall, the latter part of the 20th century evidenced increasing concern over tourism development, initially orientated to the physical environment and expanding to encompass questions of societal impacts and economic benefits to host communities. Despite this, by the turn of the millennium, little had been achieved in resolving such concerns (Lew, 1999). These concerns have been expanded to encompass the correlating and broader issues within the objectives of sustainable development, the emergent agenda of climate change and the pressing need for responsible tourism. But, let us not lose sight of the fact that tourism does provide a rationale for the preservation of the built environment (see Binney and Hanna, 1978) and the conservation of the 'natural' environment. As such, it has had and continues to have a role in the resurgence of cultural practices in various quarters. Hall (1998), in his informative discourse on conservation and tourism, espouses a principle of balanced development between tourism and conservation, i.e. development based on sustainable resource use and with due consideration for the quality of life of all persons. This accords with 'the public good' (Rowe and Fudge, 2003) and 'weaves together normative ideas such as equity, participation, prudence, welfare and environmental concern' (Lafferty and Meadowcroft, 2000, p. 16; cited in Lightfoot and Burchell, 2004, p. 338).

The attention here to the wider context and the need to address the level and equity of the interrelationships between tourism and the local/regional economy, communities and the environment reflect the objectives of sustainability and what is implied in responsible tourism. To a large extent, the achievement of such objectives (normative ideas) is very much

a matter of individual lifestyle; in effect a shift to sustainable livelihood – a matter of no little complexity. As Tao and Wall (2009, p. 92) confirm: 'A sustainable livelihood approach inherently reveals the multi-sectoral character of real life, integrating environmental, social and economic issues into a holistic framework, which is an opportunity to promote the sort of cross-sectoral and cross-thematic approach that should be the hallmark of sustainability'. This further affirms the need to address tourism not in isolation from but in the context of society and the economy more widely. To a degree, this accounts for the limited progress made in implementing effectively the principles of sustainability into policy documents at local, national and international levels (Koutsouris, 2009).

The UN's clearly enumerated policy is to promote sustainable tourism development and this includes promoting foreign investment and cooperation – in effect supporting tourism development per se (see Holden, 2005). This is also a key message of the EU's latest tourism policy which seeks to promote tourism EU's Objective 2 – development of sustainable, responsible and high quality tourism (EC, 2010 p. 7) – whilst at the same time seeking to make Europe the world's number one tourist destination. But 'The quest for sustainability is already starting to transform the competitive landscape, which will force companies to change the way they think about products, technologies, processes and business models.' (C.K. Prahalad, cited by HRH The Prince of Wales, 2009, para. 15) This echoes the EU's 5th Environment Action Plan (EAP), titled 'Towards Sustainability', which includes the objective: 'working with business and consumers to achieve greener forms of production and consumption and, in general, greening the market' (Connelly and Smith, 2003, p. 284).

The extent to which major stakeholders in tourism (and international agencies such as the UNWTO, UN and OECD – Organisation for Economic Co-operation and Development) are committed to such views is questionable given their recent call for greater 'recognition of the role of Travel and Tourism in key strategic economic areas. It is increasingly seen as part of the solution and a key sector to help the world avoid a jobless recovery' (ICTP, 2011, paras 7–8). This is an agenda that explicitly supports the growth of tourism, open competition, the staging of mega-events and so on, and the continued development and expansion of travel infrastructure. All of this is supported by strong and growing markets for increasing outbound tourism forecasted from Asia, Eastern Europe, Russia and Africa (ICTP, 2011) and from south American countries (WTM, 2008). This reinforces the fact that as economies develop then so too does demand for tourism, a by-product of capitalism and a form of consumption at its most conspicuous. As Crick so neatly encapsulated: 'for all the talk about sacred journeys, cultural under-standing, freedom, play and so on, we must not forget the fundamental truth that international tourism feeds off gross political and economic inequalities' (Crick, 1991, p. 9; cited in Hutnyk, 1993, p. 218). It is not surprising therefore that the countries of Europe and North America, which account for some 75% of global GDP (gross domestic product), also account for the majority of international tourist arrivals and a dis-proportionate share of consumption of the world's resources (Bennett, 2006); for example, the comparatively high living standards experienced in the developed countries account for some 50% of all energy consumption, while the poorest 15% of the population consume the equivalent of 4% (WSCSD, 2004).

We can draw from this discussion that although much consideration is given to the physical environment of the destination, the effects of tourism on communities and culture receive less attention. For many stakeholders, underpinning all this is the fact that tourism means big business for countries and is a valuable export. Thus we have the three pillars of sustainability (environmental, social and economic), and it is an outcome of the emergence of this agenda in the 1980s, and the advocacy of sustainable development and Agenda 21 by the UN, that we find substantial debate arising over tourism development and whether those involved should be responsible for negative impacts and seek to enhance the positive impacts. As the Chairman of the World Travel Market (WTM) is quoted as saying: 'There's a growing realization that

sustainability is absolutely integral to the travel industry's future success. I make no apologies for sounding over-dramatic when I say that the industry will not have a future at all unless it takes responsible tourism as seriously as customer service, value for money and comfy beds' (Anon, 2010). This leads us directly on to establishing the form and structure of this volume, which is as follows.

Part 1

Part 1 aims to develop the major themes encapsulated in the concept of 'responsible tourism', commencing with a broad discussion based on what is encompassed by the term and how it is interpreted. This discussion will give due consideration to related terms used to describe tourism activity, in the process high-lighting and bringing into question substantive facets of practice, and providing a contextual framework for subsequent discussion topics. One point to bear in mind throughout these discussions is the implicit criticism that forms of tourism categorized as nature, eco or adventure tourism (NEAT) have less impact than mass/traditional tourism and that the former are therefore more beneficial. That assumption is certainly questionable. Secondly, we aim to question how we address the considerable dilemma that tourism is an unsustainable pattern of consumption and therefore potentially in conflict with the principles laid down in the Rio Declaration of the Earth Summit of 1992, affirmed in general at the Summit of 2002 and recognized as a need to be addressed within the EU (see Lightfoot and Burchell, 2004, p. 343). The opening chapter of Part 1 (Chapter 2), 'The Responsible Tourism Debate', by David Leslie, explores the background to and emergence of RT. The chapter identifies and discusses related terms and their application in the delivery and development of tourism, with particular emphasis first on enterprises taking responsible action and, secondly, on destination develop-ment with attention to communities. The following chapter brings into focus transport and transportation. Tourists need to get to their destination but transportation is the Achilles heel of tourism in terms of sustainability, given its contribution to greenhouse gases (GHGs). This is particularly so given the not inconsequential shift in environmental politics to an emphasis on climate change. Witness UNWTO's 'Global Code of Ethics for Tourism' (GCET) framework (UNWTO, 1999) which highlights the link between climate change and tourism.

UNEP (2009) stresses the need for greater efficiency in energy use, with the major focus first on air travel and, secondly, on train travel – advocating a shift to trains powered by electricity. The organization notes an 87% increase in the EU's GHG emissions from commercial flights between 1990 and 2007 – evidence of the growth of low-cost carriers. The statistic that 6 tons of transport-related CO_2 are emitted by North Americans compared with 0.1 tons by Tanzanians each year points up the major culprits in this regard. This is an area of major contention despite advances in technology, improved fuel efficiency and the potential for alternative fuels. It still begs the question: is it ever responsible to go on holiday via, for example, a jumbo jet (whether or not the final destination is an acclaimed ecotour)? In recognition of the need to reduce GHGs, the International Civil Aviation Organization (ICAO), the international governing body for air travel, has set a target for carbon-neutral growth by 2020, with a net emissions reduction of 50% by 2050. Notably, British Airways (BA) set such a target in 2008. In support of this objective, there is ongoing research into biofuels (e.g. from waste products) that do not involve taking land over from other uses, use of cleaner fuels, more direct routes, reducing landing delays and establishing a global framework for carbon trading (ICAO, 2010; Counsell, 2010). But how can such goals be achieved given the marked disparities between national carriers and the vested interests of the strongest airline companies? It is not surprising that a vexing issue in the airline sector is that of the possible imposition of regulations by a nation. For example, the UK's air passenger duty (APD), in theory first introduced as a green tax, is described by the International Council of Tourism Partners (ICTP, 2011, para. 11) as 'an unfair anti-trade tax on exports and imports'. ICTP further criticizes green (carbon) taxes on aviation as evidencing

disparities across the globe; its argument amounts to a manifesto for a uniform aviation emissions tax and, not surprisingly, contends that at least some of the proceeds should go to support tourism development. Furthermore, Becken (2004) brings into question who should pay for the emissions arising from travel to/from destinations and the energy consumption while in the destination – the tourists or the destination?

Moreover, we must recognize that although the airline sector plays a major role in tourism it is also a substantial player in the economy of many countries and a contributor in socio-economic terms through employment and the multiplier effect (see Button, 2012). However, given the agendas of sustainability and climate change, there is a clear need for appropriate responsive action, and the air transportation industry must address its responsibilities in these areas. In Chapter 3, 'International Transport and Climate Change: Taking Responsibility Seriously', Hugh Somerville addresses this theme. Rather refreshingly, the discussion opens with a background to the development of the air transport sector, establishing the significance of the sector to tourism and climate change. Key environmental issues are explored and responses considered. In a welcome addition to the debate, valuable attention is given to shipping, which is especially pertinent given the growth of the cruise sector over the last 20 years.

To further debate on RT, it is essential, especially with regard to sustainability, to consider the consumers of tourism, hence tourists and demand. This is the focus of Chapter 4, 'The Consumers of Tourism', by David Leslie, which addresses two primary questions of the RT debate: first that if we have responsible tourism do we have responsible tourists?; secondly, and in the context of consumption more generally, are there responsible consumers who then behave in ways we could consider environmentally friendly (responsible) when being tourists. A key underpinning to this discussion is the question 'Is consumer demand for holidays a necessity, a non-materialistic need, or just a "want", a highly conspicuous form of consumption?'. To a limited extent, an answer lies in what tourists are considered to be purchasing. Britton (1991) says that 'Tourists are purchasing the intangible qualities of restoration, status, life-style signifier, release from the constraints of everyday life, or conveniently packaged novelty' (cited in Hall, 1994). Even so, according to Milne (1998), by the late 1990s we still knew little about tourists and their consumption patterns or indeed about the influences on decision taking about whether or not to choose an alternative holiday product. Certainly, globalization both encourages, and is fuelled by, consumption – thus furthering such notions as 'the consumer [the tourist] is king' that are to be found in the attitudes and behaviours of tourists. This is most notable in the context of being in other places/other cultures that have tended to develop in ways more attuned to the culture of the dominant tourist market segment than that of indigenous communities (see Nash, 1989), a perspective that is not limited to mass tourism. But irrespective of the destination, an inescapable fact is that the impacts of the tourism sector are a function of demand. Hence, while there may be an economic gain, the host is incurring additional costs in providing for tourist needs through imports and increased energy consumption, waste and increased GHG emissions. These latter factors rarely gain attention, despite their significance.

Throughout these opening chapters the recurrent themes of RT, which in application are *the central tenets of responsible tourism*, emerge in any manifestation of tourism. In effect, those involved have a responsibility, further affirmed by the quest for sustainability, to ameliorate the negative and enhance the positive benefits arising from their operations and actions. So in principle the people and community of a destination should gain an equitable share in the development, the businesses involved directly and indirectly should adopt best practices in addressing their environment performance and tourists should explicitly support both. Furthermore, tourism does not develop in a vacuum: the processes of governance need also to adopt this principle. Implicit in these fields is the fundamental tenet of RT – that there is wider respect for the people, the place and the environment. These tenets provide the basis of Part 2.

Part 2

Part 2 commences with the focus on the host community in the tourist destination. This theme, a tenet of RT, is explored in depth in Chapter 5, 'Destination Communities and Responsible Tourism' by Dallen Timothy, who addresses the potential of community empowerment to bring into contention current trends relating to responsible tourism, including heritage, place-based experiences and socio-economic benefits. In the process, he presents an insightful, comprehensive critique, while also establishing a broad context within which to consider the narratives of the other themes presented in Parts 2 and 3.

There is little to gainsay that suppliers should be responsible in their use of a destination's – the community's – resources. For example, water is a remarkably strong and consistent attraction at many destinations, but it is also the essence of life. Its overuse through tourism is an increasing concern, yet this is rarely raised (see Pigram, 1995). Water is also essential to accommodation operations, food preparation and processing, and in maintaining grounds, particularly golf courses. Romeril (1989) notes how much water tourists used compared with locals, particularly citing the water demands of golf courses in Portugal (not to mention the opportunity costs). Fuel is also a requisite, yet again gains little attention, and is evidently often taken for granted and over-consumed, e.g. the use by trekkers in Nepal of scarce wood fuel for cooking fires (see Pobocik and Butalla, 1998). Problematic too is pollution, e.g. by black carbon and nitrogen compounds, arising from the use of poor-quality fuels in vehicles and for farming, and by methane from rubbish tips (Steiner, 2010), to which tourism directly and indirectly contributes.

These indirect and direct negatives arising from tourism need to be addressed and the enterprises involved need to act responsibly and address their environmental performance. In effect, enterprises need to take up 'ecological modernization' (May, 1991), which is production with the accent on reducing waste and energy consumption, and is today encompassed under the umbrella of 'sustainable production and consumption' (see IPPR/Green Alliance,

2006). Of more significance in this context is attention to enterprises: 'Business must operate in a more eco-efficient way, in other words producing the same or more products with less input and less waste, and consumption patterns have to become more sustainable' (EC, 2001, p. 3). This is an agenda which the EU (and the United Nations Conference on Sustainable Development, UNCSD) has been promoting and developing over the last decade and which explicitly includes tourism and tourism enterprises (Leslie, 2012a).

Tourism enterprises are, therefore, challenged to reduce energy consumption, reduce the use of non-renewable resources and waste in buildings, etc., and also to increase the uptake of renewable energy (see LGA, 2010). But the myriad small and micro-enterprises that predominate in supply all too often see insufficient benefit to address such challenges (Leslie, 2009, 2012b). It is clear that the businesses involved in supply do have a responsibility, especially for the impacts on the environment of their operations. Many enterprises already take this up to varying extents, particularly transnational hotel companies (Bohdanowicz and Zientara, 2012), but, beyond first steps, the commitment of many operators has been and continues to be questioned (Milne, 1998; Leslie, 2009). Of note in the case of transnational companies is that they operate their units across the globe in a manner accustomized to in the home base (i.e. where the company initially developed), and generally follow the 'norms' of the business world in their homeland. Thus, where such a company 'goes green', then so too do all their operations, and so a substantial gain is achieved compared with the impact of one independent business.

This tenet of RT is the focus of Chapter 6, 'Environmental Performance' (EP) by Ralf Buckley, who maps out in appropriate detail the impacts arising from inputs (green factors) and outputs (brown factors) due to the processes involved and the consumption of tourism. He cogently addresses, with attention to different environmental contexts, the EP of the tourism sector with attention to aspects of sustainability, establishing clearly that the EP of tourism enterprise depends in the first instance on the location/the resort, and that it is a matter of examining the context as to what is to be deemed best practice rather than of dictating the needs to be considered. Moving on, he discusses the EP of the sector in some depth with reference to the complexities involved in EP measurement and management. The latest morphological development in ecotourism – namely 'ecochic' – is introduced. This is undoubtedly the latest fashion – positional good – in tourism for the affluent few! But who gains? In much the same way as if the local community was producing a product for sale on the market, then so too the economic and social benefits attributed to tourism development should be to the advantage of the local economy and communities.

That tourism does hold economic development opportunities for destinations is beyond doubt. However, in terms of RT, the key question is to what extent does the destination community gain from such development, not only in economic terms but also in respect of its environment and social well-being. This has been the subject of debate for some considerable time, including in expositions on RT and related tourism terms, such as sustainable or ecotourism. It would seem to follow that by today many destinations based on such tourism products should be testament that this progress is actually happening and, most pertinently, in tourist destinations in comparatively less developed economies and locales. But is it? The comparatively recent emergence of 'pro-poor tourism' suggests otherwise; as Saarinen et al.'s (2009) study highlighted, the poorest community members often gain little from tourism development. Furthermore, the point can be made that many of the most undernourished people in the world are in countries popular with tourists (e.g. Gambia, Kenya). So how has tourism development helped them? For example, Holzner's (2007) study of small island economies found that countries with a comparatively high percentage of tourism in GDP terms evidenced higher economic growth, investment and also higher secondary school enrolments. But such successes are often limited by external investment and economic leakages: e.g. in Fiji where, it has been argued, 94% of 32 projects started between 1988 and 2000 were foreign owned, and from such projects 60% of foreign exchange earnings leaked out (Becken, 2004). Particularly important in such projects is that tourism development does 'complement rather than replace existing livelihood sources leading to diversification of livelihood strategies'(Tao and Wall, 2009, p. 98; and see Zientara, 2012). A key in all these cases is the extent to which tourism development is based within and controlled by the local community.

To a major extent, the economic benefits of tourism to a destination are largely a function of the supply and the dominance or otherwise of external stakeholders. The key influential factor in such development, and consequently the scale of tourism in any locality, is superstructure. That is most important in terms of macroeconomics and in the potentially wider distribution of benefits, as, for example, to be found in mass tourism and popular city destinations: the more developed, the greater the volume of tourists. Conversely, small-scale development suggests more local enterprise and local community ownership, thus theoretically more equitable, though not always so, as some ecotourism projects bear witness. This area is explored in Chapter 7, by Anita Pleumarom, who presents a lively, thought-provoking discourse on the theme of 'The Politics of Tourism and Poverty Reduction', bringing into contention such aspects as equity and destination communities. To establish the debate, key questions are raised and explored regarding alternative tourism initiatives – such as their contribution to alleviating poverty, and why there is apparent discontent among some communities. Drawing on a raft of case examples to illustrate, she provides an incisive critique of tourism, drawing attention to many facets and raising many issues as to tourism's actual worth to communities in less developed localities which, paradoxically, are gaining increasing visitation.

As the opening discussion identified, government policy and international iterations of policy by such organizations as the UN and UNWTO, and by professional associations such as the World Travel and Tourism Council (WTTC) and ICTP, in general appear to have little substantive impact on controlling (that is limiting) the scale of tourism development and

operational responsibility. Predominantly, it appears that the expansion of resorts and destinations is more the outcome of the direct involvement of international companies, who may well not consider they have any responsibility for the consequences of their involvement in the destination – especially when such development is favoured by the government. But it is not the government alone to blame: there is a need for a more holistic approach involving all stakeholders. This leads us to the matter of governance: a not inconsiderable focus involving localities, communities, politics and policies, and contingent interrelationships.

Undoubtedly, for governance to be effective and to achieve the best possible outcome, there is a need for alliances with clear leadership, a strong environmental ethic and manifest support from local/regional/national agencies (see Eligh et al., 2002). It is not difficult to identify examples of effective partnerships and collaborations, including the formulation of codes of conduct involving alliances between companies and also involving local community groups (see Bramwell and Lane, 2000). These reinforce the view that 'the environment works better if the people who live, work and play in it are actively involved in its creation and maintenance' (Wates and Krevitt, 1987, p. 18; cited in Urry, 1988, p. 20). Further examples demonstrating responsibility in action by enterprises and through governance are well presented by Herremans (2006). However, and as in the case of the acclaimed 5-star ecotourism resort built in a fragile environment at Kingfisher Bay, Fraser Island (Queensland), which gained many accolades for the way it was developed (WTTC and IHRA, 1999), how many of these developments are maintained as first conceived? For example, ecotourism in Belize started as a low-key and small-scale operation, but by 2000 it was considered more similar to mass tourism (see Holden, 2005). In contrast, ecotourism projects in the Noel Kempff Mercado National Park have been more controlled, notably involving a local supporting network. But that was in 2002 – what is the situation a decade on? Such examples serve to illustrate what can be achieved, but often these are singular cases, not blueprints that can be applied in other contexts. Furthermore, what is the outcome when the government wants to develop tourism and where the communities involved are not so keen (see Pleumarom, Chapter 7; Holden, 2005)? And are the domino effects of development upstream and downstream considered and recognized? Such issues are well illustrated in the global expansion of golf – witness the development of golf courses in India, Vietnam, China, Cuba and Goa (tim-team, 2011). The expansion in China and Vietnam clearly aims to attract international tourists through major developments, but with significant impacts.

Just where and how governance has a role and the ability to effect responsible approaches is the focus of the final chapter of Part 2. Michael Hall's 'Governance and responsible tourism' (Chapter 8) provides essential analysis of how governance is given actual effect, and thereby illuminates the relevance of policy and governance in this context. In developing this theme, four main approaches are discussed, and how these give effect to RT and reflect different modes of governance and their underpinning political philosophies.

Part 3

The final section of the text heralds a shift in focus to the management and operational practices in the delivery and practice of tourism, and thus the dimensions of evidence (or otherwise) of responsible/responsibility in tourism. This takes the form of four chapters, each based on case studies of a specific theme or category of tourism product in which in the principles and practices espoused are manifestly of wider application. All four chapters seek to explore in more detail central tenets of RT and aims to address both 'good' and, as appropriate, 'bad' by way of exemplifying what can be achieved.

Tour operators (TOs) are major stakeholders in many destinations and hold substantial influence in their development and growth (see Briasspoulis, 2003). Carey and Goutas (1997) note the influence of TOs on destinations, and also their ability to influence market trends and the demand for new areas,

and argue that they hold more influence than the marketing efforts of a destination. TOs, more than any other tourism agent, through creating and delivering holiday packages hold substantial potential to influence a responsible approach on the part of the other enterprises involved in their tours; consequently, the importance of supply-chain management is stressed (see TOI, 2011). As Welford et al., (1999) argue, there is a need for closer links between supply and demand and for integration in suppliers. In this, TOs could do more to encourage greater responsibility and thus more attention to sustainability issues, not only in their own business practices but also in informing/educating tourists and in destinations. However, counter to such potential achievements is the growing practice of direct bookings. A second consideration, and one of perhaps of more significance in the short term, is the competition between TOs and hence the greater attention given to cost/price at the expense of responsibility-orientated initiatives. But this need not be the case, as is suggested by the success of TUI Nederland (see Mosselaer et al., 2012). Allowing for scale, the scope of this influence is applicable to all TOs, but may be far more manifest in NEAT niche markets, of which adventure and nature tours are explored in this part of the volume. First, in Chapter 9, Jacqueline Holland takes up the theme of 'Adventure Tours: Responsible Tourism in Practice?'. In developing this theme, she focuses on 'soft' adventure tours; an area of limited research. The chapter explores the extent to which UK-based adventure tour operators have adopted the responsible tourism principles, and the dichotomies that are present while developing, operating and marketing their portfolios of products.

As Sun and Walsh's (1998) review established, and which still largely holds today, there is a lack of quantitative research into differing activities and their impacts on flora and fauna, notably so in forest environments, and with particular regard to scale of use. Approaches to managing visitors and managing the environment to which they are attracted are comprehensively discussed by Pigram and Jenkins (2001), who neatly encapsulate potential effects of tourism and appropriate responsive management strategies. While their context is national parks, the points made are equally applicable to natural environment-based destinations. Again, the need for partnerships between the private and public sectors in environmental management is identified, and the authors also note the need for a balance in education/interpretation/control – too much will be counterproductive in terms of the experience. A major factor in many of these small tours into new areas is that they can involve the development of a locality popular with local people, which is then exploited. This is illustrated by McKercher (2002), who shows how tourism recreation and outdoor activities develop first, then forestry, which opens up new areas further into the hinterland, and in so doing opens up new opportunities for local recreationalists and subsequently tourism; and so the cycle continues. Many of these small tours involve relatively undeveloped locations, which is often the case with nature tours – more specifically in our case, wildlife tours – whether land or sea based. As already noted, this an area of limited research, but has not gone totally unnoticed as evidenced by Holder (1988), who presents comprehensive coverage of the physical impacts of nature tours and notably, in the case of cetaceans, the conflict between their well-being and commercial exploitation. However, this area gained limited attention until the early 2000s (Garrod and Wilson, 2003), evidencing yet again the void between academic comment and research and the actions of tourism enterprises. But practice in this field may well have improved over time. This area is addressed by Anna Spenceley and Andrew Rylance in Chapter 10, 'Responsible Wildlife Tourism in Africa'. They raise fundamental questions of RT in the delivery of wildlife tours by the enterprises involved. After a brief introduction to certification schemes and awards for such operations, they bring into focus the role of policy and the influence of the political environment, subsequently moving on to address a range of impacts and drawing out the significance of the role of government and related agencies in fostering conservation and responsible tourism enterprise.

Moving away from nature, the attention turns to another constant of demand, namely the built heritage. As Urry opined, 'people are,

as we have seen, increasingly "tourists", appropriating places not as centres of production or symbols of power, but as sites of pleasure as visitors' (1988, p. 20) Hence the lure of such icons of tourism as the Pyramids, built structures of the past, and more contemporary renowned structures such as the Taj Mahal; also those of the industrial age, and latterly reconstructed industrial heritage sites which draw visitors through their desire to see buildings and which are distinct to the locality visited (Urry, 1988). With a focus on World Heritage Sites, this is the theme of Chapter 11 by Albina Lara and Alicia Gemelli in 'Cultural Heritage: World Heritage Sites and Responsible Tourism in Argentina'. This chapter also heralds a shift away from the private sector to the more public domain, which is a characteristic of the historic built heritage. The discussion is based on five case studies, including three World Heritage Sites, and draws out substantive issues and responses to the impacts arising from increasing tourist demand which, as the authors note, is a double-edged sword.

The final chapter of Part 3 brings into focus hospitality enterprises. Many countries around the globe are encouraging tourism enterprises to adopt 'responsible behaviour' and address their environmental performance (Leslie, 2009). Steps taken to further this approach include the integration of sustainable development (SD) objectives into policies and into the criteria for funding projects (Leslie, 2012a). In terms of such responsibility, this includes the interrelationships with community – as well as environmental performance – bringing into focus labour issues, employment opportunities and so forth; this is one reason why Milne (1998) raised concerns over the commitment of larger companies to go beyond first steps. As identified, it is the large companies and international operators, particularly in the hospitality sector, that are invariably major role players and stakeholders in most popular tourist destinations and related developments. Thus, their influence is potentially substantial; so too is the impact of their operations, and therefore it is all the more important that they address not only environmental management but their overall environmental performance. After travel costs, the hospitality sector accounts for the largest proportion of tourist spend and employment in tourism. Earlier chapters have drawn attention to this sector and its impacts: however, as a major employer in any destination, this demands further and more specific consideration. This theme is taken up by Piotr Zientara in Chapter 12, 'Hospitality Enterprises: a Key Influence', which explores hospitality-based employment in the context of globalization. The quality of such employment is addressed, bringing into contention corporate social responsibility and related initiatives, as well as expressing the hope that through such processes hospitality enterprises can make a more positive contribution to local communities.

In total, these chapters present a comprehensive discourse on what is meant by 'responsible tourism' and what it involves in terms of concepts, its central tenets and its application in practice. In the process, a contextual framework is established and an in-depth analysis presented. Within this context, scholars could also consider tourism more generally, and especially in relation to developments and initiatives which have appeared in academic discourse and the popular media – predominantly since the rise of and in response to the rhetoric of 'sustainable development'. Certainly readers will find strengths and weaknesses, which will vary for each according to their knowledge and specific interests. This is to be expected given the scope of the text, which itself is essential if we are to achieve to any degree full justice in seeking to address and analyse responsible tourism and the substantive issues that arise around it. In the process, we have sought not only to inform but also to stimulate engagement and promote further debate. To achieve such an outcome undoubtedly makes the contribution of everyone involved all the more worthwhile.

References

Anon. (1997) South Pacific: the last resort. *New Internationalist*, No. 291, Special issue, June 1997.

Anon. (2010) Sustainability – are you meeting visitor's expectations? *Ear to the Ground*, No. 5, p. 3. Tourism Intelligence Scotland, Edinburgh, UK.

Becken, S. (2004) *Climate Change and Tourism in Fiji. Vulnerability, Adaptation and Mitigation, Final Report.* University of South Pacific, Suva, Fiji.

Bennett, L. (2006) Duty Free? *Resource*, No. 20 (July/August 2006), pp. 20–22. Resource Media, Bristol, UK.

Binney, M. and Hanna, M. (1978) *Preservation Pays*. SAVE Britain's Heritage. London.

Bohdanowicz, P. and Zientara, P. (2012) CSR-inspired environmental initiatives in top hotel chains. In: Leslie, D. (ed.) *Tourism Enterprises and the Sustainability Agenda across Europe*. Ashgate, Farnham, UK, pp. 93–120.

Bramwell, B. and Lane, B. (2000) *Tourism Collaboration and Partnerships: Politics, Practice and Sustainability.* Channel View, Clevedon, UK.

Briasspoulis, H. (2003) Crete: endowed by nature, privileged by geography, threatened by tourism? *Journal of Sustainable Tourism* 11, 97–115.

Button, K. (2012) Air transport in Europe and the environmental challenges to the tourist market. In: Leslie, D. (ed.) *Tourism Enterprises and the Sustainability Agenda across Europe*. Ashgate, Farnham, UK, pp. 35–50.

Carey, S. and Goutas, Y. (1997) Tour operators and destination sustainability. *Tourism Management* 18, 425–431.

Connelly, J. and Smith, G. (2003) *Politics and the Environment – from Theory to Practice*. Routledge, London.

Counsell, J. (2010) Flying clean away. In: *Clean Tech: Low Carbon, High Growth. Our Planet*, December 2010, pp. 22–23.

Crowley, K. (1998) 'Glocalisation' and ecological modernity: challenges for local environmental governance in Australia. *Local Environment* 3, 91–97.

EC (2001) *Promoting a European Framework for Corporate Social Responsibility*. Green Paper, Directorate-General for Employment and Social Affairs, European Commission, Luxembourg.

EC (2010) *Europe, the World's No 1 Tourist Destination – A New Political Framework for Tourism in Europe.*

Communication from the Commission to the European Parliament, the Council, the European Economic and Social Committee and the Committee of the Regions, 30 June 2010, Document No. COM (2010) 352 final. European Commission, Brussels. Available at: http://ec.europa.eu/enterprise/sectors/tourism/files/communications2010_en.pdf (accessed 19 April 2012).

Eligh, J., Welford, R. and Ytterhus, B. (2002) The production of sustainable tourism: concepts and examples from Norway. *Sustainable Development* 10, 223–234.

Garrod, B. and Wilson, J.C. (eds) (2003) *Marine Ecotourism – Issues and Experiences.* Channel View, Clevedon, UK.

Hall, C.M. (1994) *Tourism and Politics: Policy, Power and Place.* Wiley, Chichester, UK.

Hall, M. (1998) Historical antecedents of sustainable development and ecotourism: new labels on old bottles? In: Hall, C.M. and Lew, A.A. (eds) *Sustainable Tourism: A Geographical Perspective.* Pearson, Harlow, UK, pp. 13–24.

Harrison, D. (ed.) (1992) *Tourism and the Less Developed Countries.* Wiley, Chichester, UK.

Harrison, D. and Price, M.F. (1996) Fragile environments, fragile communities? An introduction. In: Price, M.F. (ed.) *People and Tourism in Fragile Environments.* Wiley, Chichester, UK, pp. 1–18.

Herremans, I.M. (ed.) (2006) *Cases in Sustainable Tourism: An Experiential Approach to Making Decisions.* Haworth, Binghampton, UK.

Holden, A. (2005) *Tourism Studies and the Social Sciences.* Routledge, Abingdon, UK.

Holder, J.S (1988) Pattern and impact of tourism on the environment of the Caribbean. *Tourism Management* 9, 119–127.

Holzner, M. (2007) Tourism and economic development. The beach disease. *Tourism Management* 32, 922–933.

HRH Prince of Wales (2009) *Opening address at Accounting for Sustainability Project Seminar, St James's Palace, 17th December 2009.* Available at: http://www.princeofwales.gov.uk/speechesandarticles/a_speech_by_hrh_the_prince_of_wales_at_the_accounting_for_su_148511043.html (accessed 2 April 2012).

Hutnyk, J. (1996) *The Rumour of Calcutta: Tourism, Charity and the Poverty of Representation.* Zed, London.

ICAO (2010) ICAO Strategic Objectives 2011–2013: Safety; Security; Environmental Protection and Sustainable Development of Air Transport. International Civil Aviation Organization, Montreal, Canada. Available at: http://www.icao.int/Pages/Strategic-Objectives.aspx (accessed 5 April 2012).

ICTP (2011) Travel and tourism 2011 – a measured analysis and focused response. ICTP News Release, 6 January 2011, International Council of Tourism Partners, Haleiwa, Hawaii.

IPPR and Green Alliance (2006) *A Zero Waste UK.* Institute for Public Policy Research and Green Alliance, London.

IUCN/UNESCO (1967) *Towards a New Relationship of Man and Nature in Temperate Lands. Part 1. Ecological Impact of Recreation and Tourism upon Temperate Environment. Tenth Technical Meeting held at Lucerne, from 26 to 30 June 1966 in conjunction with the Union's 9th General Assembly: Proceedings and Papers.* International Union for Conservation of Nature/UN Educational, Scientific and Cultural Organization, IUCN Publications New Series, No. 007. IUCN, Gland, Switzerland.

Jafari, J. (1986) Tourism for whom? Old questions still echoing. *Annals of Tourism Research* 13, 129–137.

Jenkins, C.L. (1982) The effects of scale in tourism projects in developing countries. *Annals of Tourism* 9, 229–249.

Jenner, P. and Smith, C. (1992) *The Tourism Industry and the Environment.* The Economist Intelligence Unit, London.

Koutsouris, A. (2009) Social learning and sustainable tourism development; local quality conventions in tourism: a Greek case study. *Journal of Sustainable Tourism* 17, 567–581.

Leslie, D. (1986) Tourism and conservation in national parks. *Tourism Management* 7, 52–56.

Leslie, D. (ed.) (2009) *Tourism Enterprises and Sustainable Development: International Perspectives on Responses to the Sustainability Agenda.* Routledge, New York.

Leslie, D. (2012a) Introduction: sustainability, the European Union and tourism. In: Leslie, D. (ed.) *Tourism Enterprises and the Sustainability Agenda across Europe.* Ashgate, Farnham, UK, pp. 1–14.

Leslie, D. (2012b) Key players in the environmental performance of tourism enterprises. In: Reddy, M.V. and Wilkes, K. (eds) *Tourism, Climate Change and Sustainability.* Earthscan, London (in press).

Lew, A.A. (1999) Editorial. *Tourism Geographies* 1(2), 1–2.

LGA (2010) *Knowing Me, Knowing EU: Local Government Association Guide to the Impact of EU Laws on Councils.* Local Government Association, London.

Lightfoot, S. and Burchell, J. (2004) Green hope or greenwash? The actions of the European Union at the World Summit on sustainable development. *Global Environmental Change* 14, 337–344.

Martínez-Alier, J. (1995) The environment as a luxury good or "too poor to be green"? *Ecological Economics* 13, 1–10.

May, V. (1991) Tourism, environment and development – values, sustainability and stewardship. *Tourism Management* 112–118.

McKercher, B. (2002) Tourism as a conflicting land use. *Annals of Tourism Research* 19, 467–481.

Milne, S.S. (1998) Tourism and sustainable development: the global–local nexus. In: Hall, C.M. and Lew, A.A. (eds) *Sustainable Tourism – A Geographical Perspective*. Prentice Hall, Harlow, UK, pp. 35–48.

Minhinnick, R. (1993) *A Postcard Home – Tourism in the Mid-nineties*. Gomer, Llandysul, Wales, UK.

Mosselaer, F. van de, Duim, R. van der and Wijk, J. van (2012) Corporate social responsibility in the tour operating industry: the case of Dutch outbound tour operators. In: Leslie, D. (ed) *Tourism Enterprises and the Sustainability Agenda across Europe* Ashgate, Farnham, UK, pp. 71–92.

Nash, D. (1989) Tourism as a form of imperialism. In: Smith, V. (ed.) *Hosts and Guests: The Anthropology of Tourism*. University of Pennsylvania Press, Philadelphia, Pennsylvania, pp. 37–54.

Nash, D. (1996) *Anthropology of Tourism*. Elsevier, New York.

NI (1993) Tourism – wish you were here. *New Internationalist*, No. 245, July 1993, Special theme issue.

Noronha, F. (1999) Culture shocks for a diatribe on this development. Tourism Concern, London, Spring 1999.

Pattullo, P. and Minelli, O. (2006) *The Ethical Travel Guide: Your Passport to Exciting Alternative Holidays*. Earthscan, London/Sterling, Virginia.

Pigram, J.J. (1995) Resource constraints on tourism: water resources and sustainability. In: Butler, R. and Pearce, D. (eds) *Change in Tourism: People, Places and Processes*. Routledge, New York, pp. 208–228.

Pigram, J.J. and Jenkins, J.M. (2001) *Outdoor Recreation Management*. Routledge, New York.

Pobocik, M and Butalla, C. (1998) Development in Nepal: the Annapurna Conservation Area project. In: Hall, C.M. and Lew, A.A. (eds) *Sustainable Tourism – A Geographical Perspective*. Prentice Hall, Harlow, UK, pp. 159–172.

Pye-Smith, C. and Blackie, J. (1979) The impact of tourism on nature conservation. In: Romeril, M. and Hughes-Evans, D. (eds) *Tourism and the Environment. Proceedings of the First European Conference on Tourism and the Environment, Jersey*. Institute of Environmental Sciences, London, pp. 45–56.

Romeril, M. (1989) Tourism and the environment – accord or discord? *Tourism Management* 10, 204–208.

Romeril, M. and Hughes-Evans, D. (1979) Tourism and the environment – an introduction. In: Romeril, M. and Hughes-Evans, D. (eds) *Tourism and the Environment. Proceedings of the First European Conference on Tourism and the Environment, Jersey*. Institute of Environmental Sciences. London, pp. 1–8.

Rowe, J. and Fudge, C. (2003) Linking national sustainable developing strategy and local implementation: a case study in Sweden. *Local Environment* 8, 125–140.

Saarinen, J., Becker, F., Manwa, H. and Wilson, D. (eds) (2009) *Sustainable Tourism in Southern Africa: Local Communities and Natural Resources in Transition*. Channel View, Clevedon, UK.

Sherman, A. (1988) Falling into a tourist trap. *The Times* (London), Monday 20 June, p. 20.

Steiner, A. (2010) Reflections. In: *Clean Tech: Low Carbon, High Growth. Our Planet*, December 2010, p. 5.

Sun, D. and Walsh, D. (1998) Review of studies on environmental impacts of recreation and tourism in Australia. *Journal of Environmental Management* 53, 323–338.

Swift, J. (1972) What future for African national parks. *New Scientist* 5, 192–194.

Tao, T.C.H. and Wall, G. (2009) Tourism as a sustainable livelihood strategy. *Tourism Management* 30, 90–98.

tim-team (2011) *Global golf course frenzy not over yet*. tourism investigation and monitoring team (tim-team) Clearing House, Bangkok, 21 June 2011.

TOI (2011) *About TOI*. Tour Operators Initiative for Sustainable Development, c/o World Tourism Organization, Madrid. Available at: http://www.toinitiative.org/index.php?id=3 (accessed 16 February 2011).

Travis, A. (1978) *Planning for Tourism Development and Environment Conservation*. Organisation for Economic Co-operation and Development (OECD), Paris.

Turner, L. and Ash, J. (1975) *The Golden Hordes. International Tourism and the Pleasure Periphery*. Constable, London.

UNEP (2009) *Sustainable Transport, on the Right Track. Our Planet*, September 2009. United Nations Environment Programme, Nairobi.

UNWTO (1983) *Study of Tourism's Contribution to Protecting the Environment*. World Tourism Organization, Madrid.

UNWTO (1999) *Global Code of Ethics for Tourism: for Responsible Tourism*. World Tourism Organization,

Madrid. Available at: http://dtxtq4w60xqpw.cloudfront.net/sites/all/files/docpdf/gcetbrochureglobal codeen.pdf (accessed 2 April 2012).

Urry, J. (1988) Post-modernism and the post-tourist. Paper presented at Leisure Studies Annual Conference, University of Sussex, June 1988.

Wall, G. (1993) International collaboration in the search for sustainable tourism in Bali, Indonesia. *Journal of Sustainable Tourism* 1, 38–47.

Welford, R., Ytterhus, B. and Eligh, J. (1999) Tourism and sustainable development: an analysis of policy and guidelines for managing provision and consumption. *Sustainable Development* 7, 165–177.

WSCSD (2004) *Energy and Climate: Facts and Trends to 2050.* World Business Council for Sustainable Development. Geneva, Switzerland.

WTM (2008) *World Travel Market Global Trends Report 2008.* World Travel Market in association with Euromonitor International, London.

WTTC and IHRA (1999) Tourism and sustainable development: the global importance of tourism. Background paper No. 1 prepared by World Travel and Tourism Organization [Council] and International Hotel and Restaurant Association for UN Department of Economic and Social Affairs, Commission on Sustainable Development, Seventh Session, New York, 19–30 April 1999. Available at: http://www.un.org/esa/sustdev/csd/wttc.pdf (accessed 10 April 2012).

Young, G. (1973) *Tourism: Blessing or Blight?* Penguin, Harmondsworth, UK.

Zientara, P. (2012) Sustainable tourism development: a viable development option for Polish rural areas. In: Leslie, D. (ed.) *Tourism Enterprises and the Sustainability Agenda across Europe.* Ashgate, Farnham, UK, pp. 169–196.

2 The Responsible Tourism Debate

David Leslie

Freelance Researcher and Consultant

The 1960s were a time of growing concerns for the protection of the environment (Leslie, Chapter 1; Hardy *et al.*, 2002), a period when we started to see more attention given to tourism development and to the view that it should be considered with some caution as recognition of its impacts arose. This opinion gained momentum in the 1970s and 1980s, leading to alternative forms of tourism (see Scheyvens, 2002), and to the adaptation of tourism development to be more environmentally friendly and community friendly. Butler (1995, p. 5) notes this rise of alternative tourism in the 1980s: 'the industry and tourists individually are being expected and required to shoulder more responsibility for the effects of travel and behaviour on host environments, both physical and human'. In essence, this was a counterpoint to the perceived ills of mass tourism as, for example, represented by the development of major resorts leading in some cases to enclaves. This shift in attention was given impetus by *Our Common Future* (WECD, 1987), with echoes of *The Limits to Growth* (Meadows *et al.*, 1972), and coincides with the emergence of sustainable tourism.

The key element throughout this sequence is the centrality of the importance of the physical environment, which is pervasive in these alternatives to mass tourism, but which has always been a constant of demand for tourism. As Dabrowski (2002) argued, eco-

tourism, for example, could be considered as commencing in the early 19th century as more people began travelling to view landscapes, enjoy the 'natural' environment (with some sense of romanticism) and visit historic monuments (see Ousby, 1990). Over the same period, we identify the emergence of conservation issues and groups. Thus as tourism has increased and expanded so too has the conservation movement. As such, and rather ironically, as Budowskie (1976) argued, tourism has served to bring attention to conservation owing to a large extent as the outcome of its physical impacts, especially in fragile environments. Recognition of the negative impacts of tourism/tourists gained marked attention in the 1980s (see Mathieson and Wall, 1982; Jafari, 1986) and more so in the 1990s. For example, Mason (1990) with his critique of the development of Turkey's Aegean coastline, which was much due to major tour operators, with the Dalyan Delta gaining widespread attention and, subsequently, to an extent, saved by the activist approach of David Bellamy; other particularly notable contributions are those of Price (1996) and of Daneshkhu and Chote (1996), who cite many examples both past and more recent of tourism's invasiveness – be it in mountains, deserts or the Antarctic, or as pollution, as illustrated by the state of the Mediterranean Sea, though this is not solely caused by tourism developments.

It is the conservation versus tourism nexus that lies at the heart of this debate and, as in other cases, the quest for a compromise. However, it is not just conservation of the physical environment but rather the conservation of the natural capital that leads to the greening of tourism. This is essentially a progression from recognition of the physical impacts of people visiting the countryside leading to the introduction of conservation measures and a wider recognition of the outcomes of growing demand, with correlating developments in superstructure and infrastructure, in the absence of which 'tourist use of any area of countryside is essentially superficial' (Robinson, 1980, p. 9) The matter of compromise arises increasingly because tourism is a global system. Its expansion of the 'pleasure peripheries' (see Turner and Ash, 1975) reflects and indeed follows national and international development (Holden, 2005), and its economic activity and potential for foreign exchange and export earnings are reinforced by political perceptions that it can also be a tool for regional development. These two drivers – the environmental agenda of the 1980s, coupled with the rhetoric of sustainable development and economic growth – catalysed the shaping of 'new' forms of tourism, which have certainly gained in pace since the early 1990s. In such terms, it is not just the physical dimensions that are of concern but also social and economic dimensions and related impacts that have been recognized by international agencies and professional organizations for some considerable time (Leslie, Chapter 1). A comparatively recent and particularly notable example in this context, is the Berlin Declaration on Sustainable Development (1997), supported by a host of international agencies including the United Nations Environmental Programme (UNEP), which stated that 'Tourism should be restricted and, where necessary, prevented, in ecologically and culturally sensitive areas' (cited in Johnston, 2003, p. 126). Furthermore, the Tourism Caucus of the United Nations Commission on Sustainable Development (UNCSD) has argued that 'fair and ethical tourism should become the standard, not only focusing on the ecological consequences of tourism, but first and foremost on its social, economic and cultural consequences' (cited in

WTTC, 2002, p. 4) and the World Tourism Organization (UNWTO, 1998), which made reference to 'socially and environmentally responsible travel' (cited in Scheyvens, 2002, p. 6).

But such recognition of the perceived ills of tourism is of little consequence in the absence of appropriate policy and planning at the destination level; that is, government policy which establishes control on tourism development. However, the indications are that where such exists initially it may not be sustained. For example, a weakness of ecotourism is that initially there may be in place clear and strong supportive government policies, but in time this situation can change and once again the economic imperative rises to the top of the agenda (Wight, 2002). In the absence of such control (and the requisite planning policy) on the development of tourism the oft-cited ills of mass tourism can arise, as noted above, and as Cetinel and Yolal (2009) well illustrate in their discussion on tourism development in Turkey, wherein the largely uncontrolled and rapid expansion led to socio-economic and environmental problems in the late 1990s/early 2000s. One response to address these problems, according to Cetinel and Yolal, is for a clearly defined policy and planning regime and a shift to 'environmentally conscious ecotourists' (2009, p. 48); thus quality, i.e. high-spending tourists, but not quantity.

The often found weakness of policy and integrated planning is further affirmed by the study by Yasarata et al. (2010), who note that appropriate policies and planning regulations to ensure that development is commensurate with the needs of local communities are often limited and that tourism is considered more in macroeconomic terms. This encourages rapid growth and development of new resorts, which often leads to disenfranchisement of the local communities involved and a disconnection from the resources on which tourism is built. While such outcomes are not articulated, the basic premise is that tourism is good for the economy and should be encouraged without restricting parity of competition in supply. This is undoubtedly the favoured approach of international stakeholders, a perspective that is well encapsulated in the view of the World Travel and Tourism Council (WTTC) that governments need to recognize not only how big tourism is but also that tourism and travel are 'a vital part of the global economy' (WTTC *et al.*, 2002, p. 7). This is certainly manifest in the approach of the European Union (EU), which while paying lip service to the concept of responsible tourism and the practices encapsulated therein is more orientated to increasing tourism (see Leslie, 2012a).

Hence, international policies such as those of the UNWTO (and indeed within the International Monetary Fund, IMF) are to encourage tourism on the part of the major stakeholders and to discourage the introduction of legislation or regulation that might establish the adoption more widely on the part of all stakeholders of more responsible behaviour in the development, delivery and consumption of tourism. However, the problem with the introduction of national regulation and or taxes (in one form or another) which in some way are designed to control the development of tourism is that internationally, stakeholders will argue that such measures contravene international agreements on fair trade, e.g. the General Agreement on Tariffs and Trade (GATT). An illustration of this is the introduction of an increase in air passenger duty (APD) in the UK, which was criticized by the Secretary-General of UNWTO as not being constructive (Rifai, 2011).

Whether or not the requisite policy and control is present, the facets of tourism development encapsulated in the 'new' terms used for tourism development can, as exemplified by Scheyvens (2002), contribute through appropriate application and practices to a more equitable and responsible tourism sector. The use of these terms in itself begs questions over the alternative – by default – mass tourism. Are these new terms and their related tourist products any better than this alternative or indeed, any better than no tourism? Are they more panacea than nostrum; perhaps an emanation of the 'spirit' of the time? Are they little more than marketing ploys to attract the more discerning tourist – the oft-cited traveller (or replicate of earlier notions of 'the explorer')? Do they fit with responsible tourism (RT)? It is these terms that are the focus of our discussion in this chapter. In the process though bear in mind that apart from

our considerations here, these terms are Western constructs, potentially colonial and, undoubtedly, value laden (see Hummel, 1993). It is thus not solely a matter of terminology and academic debate, nor is it just 'labels' conveniently used to differentiate one tourism product from another and the interpretation of these, but also how they are applied. Therefore, following on from introducing these various terms, the discussion moves on to explore first operational dimensions, followed secondly by attention to the ways through which business can be more responsible. Thirdly, the discussion then moves on to explore, in the context of destinations, ways in which these developments have impacts on local people and their communities. Through this process the objective is to establish both the key tenets of RT and a framework for the following chapters, which explore these areas further.

Terms

As noted, the emergence of terminology to convey conceptual approaches to tourism developments and/or different forms of tourist activity or products is a mix of concepts and applications. The extent to which any of these labels for various modes of the consumption of tourism is actually new is a moot point. However, the appearance of green products in the marketplace became synonymous with consumer goods during the 1980s and so their purchase was something of a fashion statement (see Healy, 1990; Pleumarom, 1990; Rosenthal, 1991). Once this idea was adopted in tourism jargon, then variations, or labels, appeared, e.g. soft (Smith and Eadington, 1992), green, sustainable (Butler, 1991) eco(tourism) (Wood and House, 1991), appropriate (Rosenthal, 1991) and, perhaps more conceptual, responsible (Haywood, 1988) and alternative (Weaver, 1991). The latter term is considered by Scheyvens (2002) as an umbrella encompassing ecotourism, green tourism, cultural tourism, soft tourism, ethical tourism and sustainable tourism. If one accepts such a view then alternative tourism is anything other than mass tourism. Perhaps so, but these labels also in some cases demonstrate product differentiation in the marketplace by tourism enterprises. Furthermore, the tourism products themselves evidence the societal shift in westernized societies to the individual, which is more than just coincidental with the rise in production of small-scale tourism – such as ecotourism. Also, this is an outcome of increasing demand and thus of growing niche market segments, developments in communication and improved marketing effort. The extent to which one may agree with such views may well be influenced by the following discussion on the most regularly used terms.

The aim here is to introduce and, in the process, briefly critique those terms that are used to convey possibly different interpretations of and application of the concept of RT, thereby establishing to what extent they are different and in what ways they are similar. This is by no means exhaustive, nor does it seek to bring in variants on RT which are self-evident, for example, environmentally responsible tourism, as articulated by Green Globe International and for which it offers certification.

Responsible tourism (RT)

RT emerged in the 1980s and in terms of interpretation and application in tourism is well conveyed by the following: 'Responsible tourism is *not* a tourism product or brand. It represents a way of *doing* tourism planning, policy and development to ensure that benefits are optimally distributed among impacted populations, governments, tourists, and investors' (Husbands and Harrison, 1996, p. 1; cited in Scheyvens, 2002, p. 186). Alternatively, it 'simply means treating local people as people – not as beggars, nuisances, servants, con men, thieves or exotic photo opportunities' (Mann 2000, p. 201). This is in the vein of Lea (1993, p. 708) who argued that responsible travel (and therefore, to be a responsible tourist) is based on three key principles: 'to understand the culture that you are visiting; to respect and be sensitive to the people who are hosting your visit; and to tread softly on the environment of your hosts (cited in Scheyvens, 2002, p. 103). So it is a behavioural trait and not a particular type of tourism based on the basic principle of respect

for others and their environment, which many persons would argue should be 'taken as read'. That it is not is an indictment of people generally and of tourism mores specifically.

RT is, therefore, applicable to all tourism contexts and to all stakeholders. To be responsible also implies not only respect for the locality and people but also acting responsibly in terms of one's own actions and, moreover, in the management and operation of business, which is encapsulated in iterations of the terms used in the 2000s, namely environmentally and/or ethically responsible. It should, therefore, be a resource-based, bottom-up approach.

Alternative tourism (AT)

AT is 'broadly defined as forms of tourism that are consistent with natural, social and community values and which allow both hosts and guests to enjoy positive and worthwhile interaction and shared experiences' (Smith and Eadington, 1992, p. 3). On such a basis it is difficult to see how the forms of tourism alluded to are different from that which is already evident in traditional popular tourist resorts. However, an early example of AT (and potentially also of ecotourism – see below) is Tourism for Discovery's trips to Senegal in the 1970s (echoes of early Thomas Cook tours and latterly of 'Tourism with Insight and Understanding'), which to create a meaningful travel experience were small in scale and involved the local community (Mason, 1990).

Essentially, this type of tourism is alternative to what is perceived as mass tourism by default and holds the negative connotations of popular mass tourism. This is supported by non-governmental organizations (NGOs) such as Tourism Concern and Tearfund. But in this, their efforts might be better targeted at aiming to 'transform the mainstream, mass tourism industry, which accounts for the majority of travellers and at whose feet the bulk of responsibility for environmental damage and social decay through tourism, and inequitable benefits for local communities, must rest' (Scheyvens, 2002, p. 231). This is a rather sweeping statement which gives no credence to the actual benefits tourism does hold across a broad spectrum, benefits that are realized in many well-established destinations, particularly in small island economies. This is obviously not to say that improvement, i.e. more responsible behaviour and practice, could not be achieved.

Clearly what is meant by AT is that it is small scale and low impact, but then, as is invariably the case, demand grows and other entrepreneurs and companies enter that marketplace (see Whinney, 1996) in the absence of appropriate and applied policy, planning *and* local control. An example of the presence of such an approach is cited by Weaver (1992), who argues that the Dominican Republic is an AT destination – constrained in its tourist development by government, predominance of locally owned hotels, etc. and as such is not just in a transition stage on the path to mass tourism. But can the same be said today? By way of contrast, O'Grady (1990), in his diatribe on tourism in the Third World, well portrays many of the 'realities of tourism and its effects on people and places' (1990, p. 1), and includes a diverse range of examples to illustrate and challenge the promotion of AT. However, achieving an equitable balance in what is in effect sharing the community's resources is laudable, and as Timothy and Tosun (2003) argue, is more likely to be achieved with community participation and incremental development. Even so, as Crowley (1998) opines, while much is made of community involvement this often does not translate into the level of influence that it infers. Furthermore: 'Alternative tourism may be seen as a means of minimizing physical effects on potentially fragile ecosystems. But as Butler points out, the closer contact between resident and tourist in perhaps the more intimate surroundings of home rather than hotel complex may have a potentially greater impact on host cultures than is the case where tourists are safely isolated in the tourist ghettos' (Ryan, 1991, p. 103). Ioannides and Holcomb (2003, p. 44) continue this vein, noting that '"alternative" tourists are not necessarily high-spending nor environmentally sensitive' and that 'A few tourists in a fragile or pristine environment will have some negative impact on such an environment' while 'a few more bodies on an already crowded beach make little incremental difference'. A more damning critique comes from Hutnyk (1996, p. 215), who makes the telling point that despite the potential advantages of AT: 'Alternative travel, just as much as alternative trade promoted by many organized aid groups, works as a reassuring front for the continued extension of the logistics of the commodity system, even as it masquerades as a (liberal) project of cultural concern, and despite the best intentions of its advocates'.

Perhaps Jones (1987, p. 354), in his critique of AT involving independent travellers, conceptualized this most pertinently in noting that it is not as benign as some commentators evidently think: 'Rather than is there a "real alternative" tourism, perhaps the question we should be asking ourselves is "how can we develop alternative approaches across the whole spectrum of tourism in order to achieve a more real and sustainable industry?"'. In practice, this is the essence of RT.

Ethical tourism (ET)

ET is based on limiting the perceived negative aspects of tourism, while maximizing the positive in destinations. As such, it is essentially 'alternative' and a variant in terminology on the use of responsible. It is seen as holidays that are primarily designed to benefit local people and the community, examples of which may well be limited. It is perhaps not coincidental that *The Ethical Travel Guide* is subtitled *Your Passport to Exciting Alternative Holidays* (Pattullo and Minelli, 2006). In reality, ET is more a case of being responsible and, just as with RT, includes businesses involved in supply thus being ethical in their operations (see Scheyvens, 2002). Furthermore, ET also implies ethics in tourism operations and business practice, a matter of honesty and accuracy in the what and the way of promotion, and also equitable distribution and equitability in the use of resources, e.g. labour, products (see Wheeler, 1994).

So the laudable aims of RT, when applied in practice, are more ethical in the sense that to be responsible in action and deed suggests principled behaviour (see Weeden, 2005).

Green tourism (GT)

GT conjures up images of the countryside and hence is first considered here in the wider context of rural tourism. This, as described by Lane (1988, p. 61), is essentially in features and requisites small in scale, involving 'Closeness to nature, absence of crowds, quietness and a non-mechanized environment', and also personal contact with the local community. But to this we need to add continuity and stability, which leads to thinking of 'green' tourism (also described as soft tourism; see Krippendorf, 1987) and the quality of the environment. This conjures up perceptions of wanderlust as opposed to sunlust (see Turner and Ash, 1975), with its implications of low scale and low key – rather akin to 'softly, softly' tread. That is, before expansion by enterprises seeking to exploit the opportunities as demand is demonstrated to be on the increase. A perspective that rather chimes with Minhinnick's (1993, p. 35) sardonic critique that 'green tourism is a chimera. The idea of making tourism an environmental sustainable activity is at best an exciting dream and at worst a deceit'. But its overall environmental performance can be improved, which underpins Beioley's (1995) argument that GT is interchangeable with sustainable tourism, which in terminology has largely overtaken it.

Irrespective of such argument, of significance here is not GT but rather what it implies, which is also the greening of tourism and thus, among other considerations, the greening of enterprise and of tourism products and services, i.e. the introduction of best environmental management practice and more widely addressing environmental performance on the part of tourism enterprises.

Pro-poor tourism

Another concept applied to tourism is that of 'pro-poor' tourism. This has arisen partly, if not totally, in response to the oft-cited economic benefits to the local community of tourism development which may not be evident. According to some commentators though the outcome may actually be the very opposite: 'We have amassed a great deal of evidence over the years at Tourism Concern that tourism too often maintains people in poverty' (Barnett, 2009, p. 18). This pro-poor stance rather contradicts that of the United Nations Conference on Trade and Development (UNCTAD), which supports tourism, seeing it as a tool in its 'war on poverty', which is manifest in its campaign 'Sustainable Tourism for Elimination of Poverty' (cited in Wijk and Persoon, 2006, p. 381). There is little to doubt that such argument is equally applicable to capitalism in general, so it is difficult to establish in such general terms why tourism should be singled out in such fashion. Not surprisingly 'pro-poor tourism' has 'become increasingly open to contestation and critical debate' (Hall, 2007, p. 2).

Mitchell and Ashley's extensive studies into the impact on poverty of interventions in tourism such as Pro-Poor Tourism, have found that there is 'A serious problem confronting organizations that are either euphoric or despondent about thye destination effects of tourism is that there is the often worryingly weak empirical basis for their assertions. Strong views seem to be strongly held, often without the burden of credible evidence'. (Mitchell and Ashley, 2007, p. 4). Evidence in support of such argument is manifest in a plethora of publications and the promotion of alternative forms of tourism that has been witnessed over the last two decades.

Sustainable tourism (ST)

Thus far, the tourism terms discussed are conceptual, in marked contrast to ST, which basically is tourism development that can be sustained. So development that is appropriate, which invariably means tourism development, is seen in isolation of the wider context – be that economic, social or environmental. It is as if the interrelationships between the production of tourism products and services, and the systems which both generate and support it, are not recognized and that all too little attention is given to social and community aspects (see Hardy et al., 2002; Yasarata et al., 2010). Conceptually, ST is based on best management practice on the part of those organizations, predominantly businesses, that are involved in supply.

In academia, and in professional associations and national tourist organizations, ST was undoubtedly the flavour of the 1990s; first appearing in 1987 (Butler, 1999), coinciding with the Brundtland Report (WECD, 1987). The emergence of ST was led predominantly by major national and international business, and aims to maintain the status quo (see Cronin, 1990; Pleumarom, 1990). This is an argument that is certainly furthered by WTTC *et al.*'s (1995) *Agenda 21 for the Travel and Tourism Industry*. The objective is to manage a destination as far as possible for the continuing enjoyment of tourists rather than for what might be the opportunities for development. In the process, the businesses involved in supply should 'go green' and in this act to the same agenda (see below). Butcher's (1997) critique is that in essence ST has little to offer the tourist. Problems arise due to failure to consider what is in the interests of the local community and is, therefore, desirable, although this may well be the opposite for tourists. Perhaps not surprisingly then, Moscado (2008) identified major weakness with studies into assessing the sustainability of tourism, in that they rarely involve the views of the community or consider how tourism may (or may not be) contributing to the quality of life of the residents: again, a lack of monitoring – or rather evaluation.

By the end of the 1990s, as Butler (1999, p. 20) well argued, ST had essentially become all things to all people: 'At present, there is a disturbing tendency, in the desire to promote sustainable tourism, to claim that any small-scale, environmentally or culturally focused form of tourism is sustainable, particularly where it is development by or for local residents'. To this, Butler added highly pertinent questions such as is tourism the best use of their resources and is the necessary control of any development in place? In effect, from a tourism business perspective, this is the key point: that ST means 'business as usual', albeit that this should involve enterprises addressing resource consumption, with the assumption that everyone else also wants it kept that way too. But what of local business and their potential to expand and/or the

possibilities for alternative economic development rather than further external investment in tourism?

Ecotourism (ET)

In 1991, the International Ecotourism Society defined ET as responsible travel to natural areas that conserves the environment and sustains the well-being of local people – an interpretation which applies to any locality when the first visitor arrives. However, such a definition chimes with RT, on which basis, from a conceptual viewpoint, taking a responsible approach to tourism is encapsulated in those types of tourism package labelled as ET. It is noteworthy that the *Encyclopedia of Ecotourism* (Weaver, 2001) has no index reference to 'responsible' or 'responsibility'. Thus, as the following discussion seeks to highlight, ET, in concept, may be RT, but in practice this is not necessarily so – particularly, and as with any other positional good on the market, other companies will seek to emulate this and produce their own product offerings.

ET was undoubtedly the flavour of the early 2000s, generating many articles and texts (see Weaver, 2001; Buckley *et al.*, 2003, Buckley, 2004; Hall and Boyd, 2005), though this does not mean it is original in concept or design. Tourist offerings such as ecological holidays in natural habitats were on the market pre ET (see Shaw and Williams, 1994), and a probably older form of ET is that of bird watching (Butler, 2001). The American Museum of Natural History started up Discovery Tours in the early 1950s (Blangy and Neilsen, 1993). These tours, exemplars of ET, followed a number of specific strategies (including management education and to increase the benefits to locals), with clear guidelines to keep to help achieve minimum impact of the tourist groups. Another early market leader from the 1980s was Abercrombie and Kent International, e.g. camps in Masai Mara (EIU, 1993). *The Good Alternative Travel Guide* (Mann and Ibrahim, 2002) which aims to identify and thereby promote what the author describes as 'true ecotourism', further illustrates the opportunities for ET. However,

ET has become a label for a differentiated market product and, as the product range expands, so it becomes all the more nebulous.

Thus we identify that ET is both a product and a generic term often encompassing nature and adventure tour packages. This was recognized as an uneasy alliance in the late 1980s (see Ziffer, 1989), given the negative impacts that can arise as a result of development in 'new' locations (Steel, 1995; *Economist*, 1998; Scott, 2001). Even so, such has been the demand for ET that it was acclaimed by 1990 as a 'mini-mass market segment' (Lickorish, 1990; cited in Shaw and Williams, 1994, p. 247) and considered the fastest growing sector in tourism (Cater, 1993); apparently it still is (Leslie, 2009). As Cater (1994) well argued, ET is vague, abused and it is not a given that it is 'good' (see Wight, 1994; Holden, 2005). Certainly, ET in many destinations initially was often small with limited investment, but those packages involving the larger companies (invariably international and based elsewhere) operated in the more popular places (IFC, 2004); to varying degrees, this is a consequence of the activities of the early entrepreneurs. Furthermore, it reflects Wight's (1997) critique that while demand for accommodation for ecotourism packages varies, the indicative evidence is that as demand has increased then so too has the demand for more luxurious accommodation (and, as such, also the involvement of more international companies and the development of resort-style operations in prime settings). As Weaver (2001, p. 3) suggested 'the majority of ecotourism already occurs in the guise of mass tourism, and large scales of operation afford certain advantages in the provision of sustainable outcomes … compared with small scale alternative tourism operations'.

It may well be in response to the foregoing issues that in 1996 the International Union for the Conservation of Nature (IUCN) expressed ET as 'environmentally responsible travel and visitation to relatively undisturbed natural areas, in order to enjoy and appreciate nature (and any accompanying cultural features – both past and present) that promotes conservation, has low negative visitor impact, and provides for beneficially active socio-economic involve-ment of local populations' (Ceballos-Lascuráin, 1996). In the process, indigenous peoples (IPs) become part of the attraction; however, there may be conflict over conservation between these IPs and external organizations seeking to impose their own policy (Survival International, 1995). Conversely, IPs may benefit, e.g. through use of local guides and the revival of culture and support for their heritage, though too often they have little or no control over this; visitors 'see' the culture but not the values and beliefs, and the shift in emphasis towards tourism also changes the socio-economic base, leading to dependency on tourism (Survival International, 1995). Herein lies the funda-mental problem in that these 'relatively undisturbed areas', especially the more attractive ones, are more often than not to be found in lesser developed countries and are therefore all the more susceptible to change.

In such places, ET is seen to be the form for developing tourism, but as Cater argues (1993, p. 86) 'it is not a substantially different hybrid from conventional tourism unless it is carefully planned for and managed'. Hence: 'The overall approach to ecotourism develop-ment must be a holistic one, based on recognition of a complex set of interests, conflicts and trade-offs' (Anon., 1994, p. 10), and this demands cooperation, planning and management to be successful in terms of meeting the multitude of stakeholders and cited benefits (Wild, 1994). But, evidence of such is limited, not least because after some 10 years there was still a lack of standards for what ET actually entails (see Wood, 2002a), not surprising given Weaver's (2001, p. 1) point that 'the knowledge base is incipient, and no consensus currently exists as to the meaning and interpretation of the term itself'. Possibly in recognition of this, and despite the efforts of the Ecotourism Society, UNEP pronounced that ET should address the following: 'Ensures prior informed participation of all stakeholders, Ensures equal, effective and active participation of all stakeholders, Acknowledges Indigenous Peoples communities' rights to say "no" to tourism development – and to be fully informed, effective and active participants in the development of tourism activities within the communities, lands, and territories, and 'Promotes processes for Indigenous Peoples and local communities to control and maintain their resources' (UNEP, 2012). UNEP also says (see Wood, 2002b) that the basic elements of ET include the well-being of local people and responsible action on the part of tourists and tourism businesses, which should be locally owned, small in scale and seek to minimize consumption of non-renewable resources. It is such laudable objectives that account for why Scheyvens (2002, p. 69) argues that there are basically two forms of ET; on the one hand there is the 'genuine, environmentally and socially responsible form of ecotourism', and on the other, there are those packages which are using the label of ET as a marketing tool. In other words, there are hard and soft manifestations of ET. As such, how does the consumer know which one to select – that is, if s/he is primarily interested because of the acclaimed benefits to local people? Further, and as Tsaur et al.'s (2006) studies find, this reinforces the essential prerequisites of control on development, management planning and education for hosts and guests, if equitable access, share in and added value to the community are to be realized. This is well illustrated in the early development of tourism in Bali in the 1980s (Mason, 1990). But, this misses the need for the undertaking of carrying capacity studies, what are all too rarely undertaken, not so much because of what they involve but rather due to the potential costs and implications of the significance of the outcomes (see Romeril, 1989; Butler, 2010). Further, to be realistic, it is not just carrying capacity that needs to be addressed but also ways of measuring whether the designed benefits – economic and social – are actually being met.

Let us not lose sight of the fact that tourism in many localities is promoted with the support of the government, particularly in lesser developed countries wherein the potential foreign exchange earnings are given substantial credence. From the perspective of the latter, a key factor is the level of demand, and as such the higher the numbers of incoming visitors the better and hence their encouragement to increase the availability of ET packages and the consequential expansion of tourism. As Wheat (2003) argued, this is lucrative, with many countries/areas seeking to jump on the ET bandwagon in their quest for the dollar-rich tourist – and in the process in some cases evicting local people, e.g. in Ambulong, Philippines and the Galapagos Islands. But, as Butler (2002, p. 444) argued: 'In terms of fulfilling its role in providing local economic benefits, it is infinitely more successful in a rural setting than in an unpopulated wilderness one'. Hence, not surprisingly, ET is being promoted in the major tourist generating regions. Indeed, Scotland is seeking to be the ET capital of Europe (Leslie, 2010).

ET packages are mostly located in 'less developed' countries (Wight, 2002), but evidently there is a growing number in the Western world, as DMOs (destination marketing organizations) jump on the bandwagon. However, and whether in the Galapagos Islands, the Maldives, Antarctica or Scotland, for the majority of clients this will involve long-haul air travel, flying from the 'west' to exotic locations via jumbo jets and secondary flights: is this responsible? This is a facet of ecotourism that gains so little attention and yet is a contributory factor to climate change and also is hard to reconcile with sustainability. A notable example of such rare attention is in Buckley (2004), wherein the argument propounded is for 'slow travel' – but how is this possible given the typical time constraints on Western tourists if, for example, they are going to an ecolodge in southern Africa?

Overall, these terms implicitly imply that there are alternatives to mass tourism and invariably that the perceived ills of the latter will in some way(s) be avoided through the proposed 'alternative to that of the exploitive industry of times past' (Romeril, 1994, p. 29). But as Hummel (1993) argued, the use of alternative terms is also political in the sense that a government might argue it does not favour tourism per se, but rather supports the development of ET based on the oft-cited localized benefits. This rather serves to illustrate that there is too much preoccupation with terminology and definitions, such that we lose sight of the key point which is that tourism is 'environmentally sensitive and sound' (Romeril, 1994, p. 25).

The fundamental aspect with all these terms is that, implicitly, demand for tourism will continue and that in the process of delivering tourism opportunities there will be negative impacts. In the context of RT, these are well illustrated in a special issue of *Third World Resurgence* on tourism, which presents a range of alternative perspectives on tourism impacts – particularly economic leakages, effects on communities, equity, resources, consumption and IPs (Third World Network, 2007; Timothy, Chapter 5). Many of these impacts are equally applicable to mass tourism, but the key point is that the principal tenet of these alternative forms of tourism is to reduce or even avoid such negative impacts within the destination. However, the fundamental principle of RT is that in every facet of tourism these at least can be ameliorated through the adoption of more responsible practice, be it reducing consumption of non-renewable and limited resources in the destination, increasing local economic and social interrelationships, applying government-led planning controls and, in terms of access, reducing greenhouse gas (GHG) emissions. The common threads here are low impact, community involvement, equity in benefits, quality of the physical environment and respect in all areas, including tourist behaviour (see Leslie, Chapter 4). There are recurrent points of effective government planning and control, management delivery and education, and also that suppliers also have a responsibility for their operations, including their environmental performance and quality of product. In essence, this means that in the delivery of a tour/holiday, all the participants involved should accept responsibility for their actions and that the management of all resources is such as to maintain the integrity of the system – as is encapsulated in responsible tourism.

Thus, we need to attend to tourism supply, the enterprises involved and their management and operations and, in addition, given its reiteration in all forms, the involvement of local communities. These are the three areas that are explored further in the following sections.

Operations

In comparison with small-scale resorts, Wight (1997) argued, quite rightly at the time, and

equally applicable today, that so-called mass tourism is by and large controlled and largely influenced by the tour operators (TOs) and national/multinational companies. Yes, these *are* the dominant providers of products and services, and they may well be adopting best practice in environmental management systems, but they will be performing less well in terms of the broader criteria of sustainability in terms of social/community aspects. For example, a major all-inclusive resort may be a plus for the destination in economic terms but is hardly so when considered on the basis of the overall objectives of sustainable development and, as appropriate, quite probably the principles of ET. Even so, undoubtedly the role of TOs is significant in progressing responsibility (and thus sustainability), as they have influence and power in so many situations. As confirmed by WTTC *et al.* (2002), tourism can be the dominant sector and a transforming sector of an economy, e.g. the Balearic Islands (which changed from a poor region in the 1950s to one of the most affluent in Spain by 2000) or the Maldives. Other examples include Cancún in Mexico, where before tourism the population was approximately 600, but by 2002 it had increased to some 600,000, or Turkey, which gains approximately 30% of its revenues from tourism. In all these cases tourism is predominantly organized by TOs, and in each, tourism developed from a low-impact, low-key activity (AT) and then expanded as demand and supply increased. This scenario is well illustrated by Whinney's (1996) discourse on the Alternative Travel Group (ATG), which was founded in 1979 based on principles now articulated as the basis of RT. Whinney discusses ATG's first experience with two early tours to locations in Turkey that had hardly seen a tourist before. These were very successful and as word spread, so too others followed 'tourism began to grow insidiously' (Whinney, 1996, p. 223), degrading the culture and leading to conflict between locals and tourist companies. The ATG pulled out completely. The outcomes/ lessons for the company were the need for training staff and establishing standards, all with the aim of managing their customers in these 'foreign' environments; lessons that echo the strategies of Discovery Tours of the 1950s.

In 2002, it was advocated that TOs 'need to develop a responsible tourism policy' (WTTC et al., 2002, p. 27). How extensively this has been taken up is debatable (see Holland, Chapter 9; Spenceley and Rylance, Chapter 10; Mosselaer et al., 2012). The take-up is certainly limited, as Frey and George's research in southern Africa of some 7 years later suggests: 'Only 2% of tourism businesses globally are participating in responsible tourism or CAR [Central African Republic] initiatives such as the Global Compact, and South African studies into the hotel and tour operator sub-sectors show low levels of transformation' (Frey and George, 2009, p. 621) This finding is not dissimilar to that from the Fair Trade in the Tourism South Africa (FTTSA) programme, established in 2001 – another certification scheme which includes attention to fair wages, ethical business practices, support for local culture and the environment (WTM, 2008). In 2008, there were 30 FTTSA-registered companies, with a growing number who were niche operators in the UK (e.g. Tribes) and the USA (e.g. Hills of Africa).

If best practices, as advocated in the Tour Operators Initiative (TOI) (introduced in 2001), were adopted then the indications are that the overall benefits would increase and also there would be a more equitable sharing in such by the local community. However, some 5 years later there are but limited signs of real impact as regards the latter (see Wijk and Persoon, 2006). On a more positive note, more recently there have been clear indicators of better progress (see Holland, Chapter 9; Spenceley and Rylance, Chapter 10; Mosselaer et al., 2012). Particularly pertinent to best practice by TOs is supply chain management. Comprehensive guidelines on this have been promoted since the early 2000s, including not only on whom to choose but also how to develop better linkages with the local/regional economy and the community (Anon., 2006). The 'Pro-Poor Tourism partnerships' affirm the importance of attention to sustainable supply chain management, claiming this to have played a key role in their efforts in the Gambia to alleviate poverty in tourism destinations (see Goodwin and Bah, 2004). This is a counterpoint success to the all-inclusive resorts which developed, largely as a result of the influence of European operators, which rather demonstrate the very opposite. As Action for Southern Africa (ACTSA, 2002, p. 2) so well sums up here 'One British tour operator offers an all inclusive beach holiday to the Seychelles. You fly with a British airline and stay in a British owned hotel. Within the hotel resort there is a range of restaurants, bars and leisure facilities, so you may not spend any money outside the resort. People on this kind of holiday contribute virtually nothing to the local economy. The only local people who benefit are those directly employed in the resort'.

It is clear is that it is often smaller enterprises that adopt the practices invariably encompassed in these supply chain guidelines and, in so doing, adopt a far more comprehensive approach (see Holland, Chapter 9; Spenceley and Rylance, Chapter 10). In contrast, as Ryan (1991) argued in the context of small or niche tourism enterprises, much tourism is about numbers – quantity – and far less about the environment or social/community dimensions; hence we find the development of all-inclusive resorts, mega-resorts and purpose-built theme parks and attractions such as Disney World. As such, the small-scale products do little to address issues arising in more mainstream tourism packages, as epitomized by the cruise market (see Bennett, 2006). Scott (2001) in particular highlights the major influence that cruise ship companies have on the development and maintenance of the popularity of destinations, and the cruise sector is important given its access to many fragile environments which might otherwise be untouched directly by tourism. So while it is known that statistically small enterprises dominate supply, this fails to reflect the commanding role of multinational corporations in supply. As illustrated by Scott (2001), tourism in Alaska is dominated by the cruise sector, which in turn is dominated by three companies; this is similar to the situation in the Caribbean and the Bahamas. She notes instances of conflict between IPs and their activities, and the demands of the cruise companies – invariably the latter win to the loss of the locals. For instance, inroads are made to open up 'wilderness', e.g. to facilitate fishing, but often at the expense not only of the physical environment but also of the needs of the locals and their communities.

As some commentators argue, the cruise sector is the epitome of globalization: 'Cruise ships represent the ultimate in globalization: physically mobile; massive chunks of multinational capital; capable of being "repositioned" anywhere in the world at any time; crewed with labour migrants from up to 50 countries on a single ship; essentially unfettered by national or international regulations' (Wood, 2000, p. 369) Furthermore, Johnson (2002) notes the lack of infrastructure to cope with cruise ship waste in many popular destination ports and the lack of enforcement of protocols. But it is not just major players who may be seen to act irresponsibly. The field of wildlife or nature tourism also evidences problems, often arising from small enterprise operations seeking to gain from evident opportunity. Blane and Jaakson (1995) cite examples of over-commercialization, notably in Canadian waters, and the related avoidance behaviour of whales, while whales around Washington State have been found to have increased the duration of their calls since the number of whale-watching boats increased dramatically in the 1990s (Highfield, 2004). The demand for such activities can also lead to overdependence on tourism; for example, the town of Denham, Australia, is very dependent on tourists visiting mainly for sole purpose of seeing and possibly feeding the dolphins at the shoreline, despite other attractions, e.g. Woomarel Banks, a World Heritage Site (Raffaele, 2003). In summation, and as Scherrer et al. (2010, p. 1218) established, visitor management practices vary strongly between operators with 'vast room for improvement by some operations', although this is not to say that all such enterprises operate with limited regard for protocols (see Spenceley and Rylance, Chapter 10).

As the foregoing discussion highlights, it is not just some nature tourism operators and cruise lines but many operations across the whole spectrum of tourism that do not operate responsibly. The common factor to all is the business enterprise itself. Thus, irrespective of the type of product or destination there is little to excuse a business from not acting responsibly in terms of its management; in other words tourism enterprises have also a responsibility for their own operations. It is to this area that our attention now turns.

Responsibility in Business

Calls for greater responsibility in business practice have abounded for well over a century. It is but comparatively recently that this has been applied to tourism, which has long been considered a smokeless sector. A recent iteration of such promotion is as follows. 'As a global industry dependent on high quality natural environments for its attractiveness, tourism cannot hide from its responsibility to promote more sustainable tourism practices' (Williams and Ponsford, 2009, p. 403). As Walle (1995) argued some 15 years earlier, socially responsible behaviour on the part of a business ultimately benefits the organization and can help to prevent government interference, and such behaviour can enhance the standing of the firm. Recognition of this is manifest in myriad codes of practice, protocols on conduct and guidelines, albeit they invariably have weaknesses, particularly on social aspects (see Font and Buckley, 2001; Rosselson, 2001; Scheyvens, 2002; Leslie, 2009). One reason for such proliferation is that almost every agency and professional association appears to want its own 'label' scheme. Even so, such schemes are indications of a more responsible approach in management practice and, as such, a progressive step. True, the WTTC (2002) presents numerous examples of best practices drawn from a range of companies, which are all international. But such progress is slow, and all the more so in retrospect. For example, 20 years ago, Wheatcroft (1991, p. 119) identified that the 'BA [British Airways] corporate plan explicitly recognized that no business would prosper (or even survive) in future unless it persuaded a growing public opinion that its production/operational activities met acceptable environmental standards'.

One practice that has been promoted for over two decades is the adoption of an environmental management system (EMS), which is primarily about eco-efficiency in managing operational resources more effectively; in effect 'ecological modernization'. These systems invariably lead to ongoing cost savings through, for example, reducing energy consumption. The promotion of EMS by government and professional associations has led to a plethora of EMS ecolabelled certification schemes, but to limited effect (Leslie, 2009, 2012b,c). EMS practices are a step forward, but enterprises also need to address their overall environmental performance (EP), which brings into contention corporate social responsibility (CSR). This has been gaining increased attention and responsive action since the 1990s; as the WTTC (2002, p. 2) notes: '68 per cent of CEOs agree that the proper exercise of corporate social responsibility is vital to companies' profitability'. This is an attitude which is undoubtedly more prevalent today (see Bohdanowicz and Zientara, 2012; Mosselaer et al., 2012). It is not only profitability that counts, it has been argued, but also the more that a firm entrenches CSR and is sustainability focused the more likely it will be survive economic downturns (Anon., 2009).

A key driver in business today is that CSR activity will make for a competitive advantage; this is increasingly recognized by larger firms (see Lee and Park, 2009; Williams and Ponsford, 2009; Leslie, 2012b; Bohdanowicz and Zientara, 2012). However, of particular significance in terms of adopting CSR best practices is the attitude of the company and thus the leadership and the need for a champion of sustainability to be at the helm (Huimin and Ryan, 2011). The absence of such largely explains Starmer-Smith's (2008) findings that many companies are promoting green credentials but not performing that well across a range of criteria, including contributing to conservation schemes, buying local produce and services, employing local staff and adopting carbon reduction and carbon offsetting schemes. The luxury category has also been identified as performing comparatively poorly, while best performances are found among the smaller operators in the adventure sector (see Holland, Chapter 9; Spenceley and Rylance, Chapter 10); but the poorest

performance overall by far was that of the cruise sector (except for the Royal Caribbean). On the more positive side, Nicholas (2011) argues that CSR is beneficial to local communities and affirms that it is to the financial benefit of the company. He cites a number of examples of start-up enterprises, including The Eden Project, a substantial development and major tourist attraction in Cornwall, UK, which is involved in many local projects, and extensively buys local produce and products. The benefits of being a responsible business are neatly summed up as 'brand value and reputation; employees and future workforce; operational effectiveness; risk reduction and management; direct financial benefit; organizational growth; business opportunity' (Nicholas, 2011, p. 46).

In comparison with (primarily) hotels, the extent of research in the tourism field on EMS and EP is limited, and notably so with regard to tour operators. However, it appears that there is not such a bias to adoption by large companies, as Wijk and Persoon (2006) established in their research into the environmental performance of TOs. These authors found that compared with other categories of tourism supply, TOs performed generally weakly, including the top companies (based on turnover) but that there were marked variances between them. TUI Travel was identified as achieving the highest performance but even then this was little above average. However, in contrast to other categories of supply, TOs do perform slightly better when it comes to supply chain management issues. Interestingly, Germany- and UK-based firms were very similar in performance, while Dutch firms were considered laggards. Since Wijk and Persoon's (2006), study there has been substantial progress in the Netherlands-based companies (Mosselaer et al., 2012). Still, the latter are comparatively significantly smaller companies, and whereas the smaller operators may well perform better based on sustainability criteria, it is the big firms that have the substantial influence on development and supply issues; without them on board little wider effect can be achieved. While Mosselaer et al.'s (2012) study affirms that the larger companies are more likely to be more attentive to social responsibility, this is partly if not wholly attributable to the fact that firms remain tuned to their home country in terms of business and social norms. A second factor is that if a multinational hotel company decides to adopt an EMS system, then this applies to all their operations, which, in many cases, is a substantial number across the globe in contrast to such adoption by one of the myriad small/ micro enterprises that dominate supply in terms of actual numbers of enterprises. A third factor is that actual and potential shareholders are becoming more concerned over the environmental performance of the companies in which they invest.

Finally, with regard to responsible management, there is the contentious issue of carbon offsetting (for a comprehensive discussion of carbon offsetting, see EC, 2007). This is a consequence of climate change debate and outcomes. Rather ironically, the climate change issue inverts the tourism/environment construct as companies begin to realize the possible impacts of the environment on tourism and respond accordingly; for example, increasing costs of air travel promote tele-conferencing (GreenBiz, 2007). This has also led to the establishment of carbon offsetting schemes within the tourism sector (e.g. planting trees). However, where such schemes are voluntary, the take-up is at best limited (see Leslie, Chapter 4). Moreover, questions as to the real value of these schemes have been raised. Offsetting is generally based on 'savings' elsewhere, e.g. renewable energy, planting trees, so if the offset is not immediate then what happens when someone flies twice in one year? A further and substantive issue raised by the spectre of climate warming is that of water consumption by tourism-related activities, and especially consumption by those tourists who consume disproportionate quantities of water; such consumption is already a case of conflict in some destinations and, according to commentators on climate change, will become increasingly a problem which needs to be addressed sooner rather than later, particularly by accommodation operations. Reference to water consumption draws our attention to the wider context of the destination and this, therefore, is the focus of the following section.

Destination Perspectives on Community Involvement

Irrespective of the steps taken by businesses in the promotion and delivery of tourism products and services to be more responsible through the adoption of EMS and CSR, it is inescapable that once a destination starts developing other businesses will seek to capitalize on the potential demand and exploit evident opportunities. Witness Kenya, Belize and the Maldives, whose tourist numbers doubled between 1981 and 1989 (Cater, 1993) – what has happened since? The Maldives, for example, is almost wholly dependent on tourism and seeks to be a totally sustainable tourism destination, yet external investment is increasing and it has major problems with waste – hardly a sustainable approach! In the case of Belize, an oft-cited example of ecotourism, questions arise over the extent of tourism development, how much is managed by external investment interests and, among other considerations, what has been the impact on land prices? Furthermore, Belize is notable for the popularity of scuba diving, and this has led to an increased number of operators – the latter arguably more interested in making money than in concern for the reefs. Coral reefs around the globe are under threat, with major problems in Caribbean and South-east Asia due to various reasons, such as climate change, overfishing, and some methods of fishing; given their attractiveness, this is of significance to tourism (WRI, 2012). How much of this damage arises directly – and also indirectly – as a result of tourism development and related activities? As these cases well illustrate, destination localities expand. Apart from environmental damage, secondly, and a another key tenet of RT, is that the potential benefits should be to the advantage of the local community. It is these two areas on which we now focus. Many of the examples cited are drawn from the literature of the late 1980s/ early 1990s and serve to illustrate early development of variously termed small-scale/ low-key tourist destinations/products. In general terms, the lessons to be learnt are equally applicable to 'new' destinations i.e. what happened in these cases will just as likely occur there today – only more quickly. The key determinant is that of achieving a balance between tourism growth and small-scale development, which is a primary principle of ET, but such a balance has been found to be difficult as in the destinations cited above, to which we could add Costa Rica and the Yucatán Peninsula (see Albuquerque and McElroy, 1995). Hummel's (1993) study based on Costa Rica and its Tortuguero National Park exemplifies how a bespoke trip arranged for a less able couple involving a tour by water led to a major (and unintended) tourist development within the Park. Costa Rica also serves to exemplify that ecotourism, given the principle that it should contribute to conservation, also has a potential role in contributing to the effective management of natural resources (see IRG, 1992), but as O'Brien (1997, p. 21) postulated with reference to the country: 'in general there is still an unwillingness by the Government and the tourist industry to adequately reinvest in parks, conservation and training'. This not only implies a lack of government policy and planning but also a lack of control, in the absence of which it is not surprising that these initially niche touristic developments expand. The key factor with all these niche market products as regards economic benefits for the local community is a need for the development of hospitality services. This is epitomized by Moore and Carter (1993), both working in the private sector at the time, who advocated that as demand increases, prompted by promotion (and, ironically, controversy, e.g. see it before it is too late; see Jones and Phillips, 2010), not only should potential expansion be considered before any development takes place but also appropriate policy and plans should be formulated. Otherwise, the situation is as Tsaur et al.'s research found, which is that 'Many destinations are suffering from the phenomenon of "… honoring the name of ecotourism on the surface but destroying the environment in reality"'. (Tsaur et al., 2006, p. 648).

Overall, the low volume of these comparatively high-cost packages comes into question when all the tourists involved in any one area are collated, as Lickorish (1990; cited in Shaw and Williams, 1994, p. 247) so aptly expressed: it is a 'mini-mass market' indeed. However, as the number of opportunities increase, then so do tourist revenues regionally, although in the process, so will the leakages. Often such ET products are for comparatively affluent tourists and developed by companies in the USA or Europe, and so a high percentage of the total price of the package leaks out of the destination locality (see Asher, 1985; Sinclair, 1991; Gabriel, 2006). These tourists have expectations of the accommodation provided, and albeit it may be a nature tour with an option for tented accommodation (see Honey, 2008), this does not necessarily mean they wish it to be very basic – and even then, tented accommodation gives rise to potential negative impacts (see Holland, Chapter 9). In addition, tourist satisfaction with the provided accommodation is very influential on their attitudes towards the success of the tour (see Nepal, 2007; Torres-Sovero et al., 2011), and thus on repeat business. As hospitality operations increase, then potentially so too does demand, and then the infrastructure develops to facilitate access, which encourages more expansion. Rodenberg (1980) and Mason (1990) discuss how expansion of Bali's airport in the 1960s led to increased tourist numbers and the enclave of Nusa Dua, a totally integrated resort, with a consequent loss of benefit to the local community (see Nash, 1996); this is also illustrated by Long's (1991) case study of Las Bahias de Huatulco in Mexico. The same concerns have recently emerged in the context of tourism develop-ments in India, and this reinforces arguments against enclaves when they are designated, designed and developed for 'others' at a cost to local communities (Equations, 2007); similarly, today's all-inclusive resorts, which are hardly representative of an equitable partner-ship. Further manifestations of expansion, and, at best, of limited controls, are to be found in the relatively rapid development of ET in southern Africa in the 1990s. This was greatly aided by improvements to local airports which also facilitated 'fly-in' safaris and '4 × 4' vehicular routes; one critique of this was the impact of 'uncontrolled development around Victoria Falls' (Grundy, 1998). More recently, Gabriel (2006) notes, with reference to Thailand, that the concentration of tourism in mountainous areas to the north and in the coastal beaches of the south has generated many issues for the local people owing to land prices increasing, unequal access to benefits arising from tourism, environmental degradation and increased energy usage and waste management problems.

Such uncontrolled expansion brings into question whether this is RT in any guise. Furthermore, when the economy is heavily based on tourism what happens when demand declines, to which many destinations of the past bear witness. As Bachvarov (1999), writing on Bulgarian seaside resorts, notes, the impacts of decline in demand for the large resort complexes of the 1980s/early 1990s led to major issues of saturation and overcapacity. He argues that while a number of these areas developed as specialized (sustainable) resort communities, among these, the high-quality, ecologically designed resort complexes presented a major problem – suggesting that best practice of the time can no longer be viewed as models of sustainable tourism! One other factor that merits recognition is that of the availability of staff in the destination area, and that in many cases they may not be readily available and thus need to be drawn in from outside; their presence also introduces change (May, 1991). However, when such expansion arises there is no one set of criteria for the planning, management and indeed control of any destination that fits all localities (see Buckley, Chapter 6). One key element applicable to all situations is that of community involvement in the process and community development (see Scheyvens, 2002; Singh et al., 2003). This is a central tenet of RT and sustainability; as Pepper (1998) opined, sustainable development is anthropocentric, i.e. equitable balance of humankind and nature, not a predominance of either. To be achievable, this requires the local community to take control, to decide on its needs, how to satisfy them and, as far as possible, to do this within its own locality/region. This demands that communities are empowered and brings into contention the rights of IPs, which are not always recognized (see Johnson, 2002; Pleumarom, 2007, and Chapter 7). As a reviewer of Johnston's (2005) book on tourism and IPs commented, based on the text 'Ecotourism is basically a promotional gimmick, and indigenous peoples

have been badly treated by everyone involved in the tourism industry ... [and] ... the direction currently taken by tourism (especially ecotourism) is wrong' (Anon., 2008). But how much of this is based on Western values and rather echoes the *Myth of the Noble Savage* (see Whelan, 1999)? Yet, engagement with local communities is possible, albeit time-consuming and time demanding, as Hall et al.'s (1993) case study of the New Zealand heritage trails programme run by the Nature of New Zealand Programme attests. This illustrates the requisite to success of involving local people and, given the importance of nature and the land and culture to the Maori, the need to build up trust and consensus with them, which takes time; in this case, it took 4 years for the heritage trail to be established.

As the United Nations (UN) has stated, community development is 'economic and social progress for the whole community with its active participation and the fullest possible reliance on the community's initiative' (UN, 1955, p. 6; cited in Telfer, 2003, p. 163); Telfer illustrates that this can be successful, but he also highlights problems such as gaining full representation of all members of the community (see also Bramwell and Lane, 2000). This is well illustrated in the Annapurna area of Nepal, which suffered from a major rise in visitor numbers throughout the 1980s, with subsequent impacts on comparatively scarce resources, e.g. timber and the disposal of waste. To an extent, this and related problems were addressed through community involvement in the Annapurna Conservation Area Project; as Tuting (1989) noted, in formulating solutions, a key point is the need for agreement, cooperation and control by the primary stakeholders (in this case the community) to their benefit and that of tourists and the environment. But, and particularly pertinent to the pro-poor tourism lobby, it is after the initial changes were achieved that an increasing gap emerged between those involved in supply and those that were not, i.e. the poor in the area were getting poorer (Hummel, 1993). Hummel's study is also notable for identification of the 'power plays' taking place between the various stakeholders and how alliances may form to gain support for particular matters. This aspect is also exemplified by Plfanz

(2007), who discusses proposed development at the Smaburu National Reserve, and also in the Buffalo Springs Reserve, in Kenya. The plans included almost doubling capacity of the lodges, and were also for new hotels (including a swimming pool); these were approved, as well as the granting of licences for new temporary camps (though the latter evidenced more substantial foundations), despite local community opposition. In contrast, a proposed large hotel development planned within a designated park area in the Masuria Lakes region of eastern Poland was stopped. The municipal authorities supported it for economic reasons, but the local community was opposed (Dabrowski, 2002). Another example of community success comes from the island of Moorea in French Polynesia, where the local community took successful action against the development of a luxury resort (Hauteserre, 2003).

While there is recognition that community involvement is complex, there is also a concern that such an approach is seen to be the answer to the perceived ills of tourism, and one that is easily achieved. First, the community is, in effect, taken as homogenous and as sharing similar values and views, which is clearly not the case (Leslie, 2005). Secondly, it is assumed that people of the community will make the decision that commentators (often from a distance) would like them to make and not what major stakeholders in a development may want. Crowley (1998, p. 91) provides an interesting spin on this: that 'entrusting green decisions to local communities which may lack the appropriate ecological consciousness and expertise' is not necessarily going to lead to the desired outcomes. A case in point is that of St Lucia in Natal, where the locals supported a proposal for mining rather than for conservation of the sand dunes, which would be affected by mining activity. Similarly, the proposed funicular railway in the Cairngorms (now a National Park) in Scotland, UK, was opposed by many environmental organizations and environmentalists, but evidently the local community supported its development. A final point on communities, given our context here, is that, interestingly, throughout the world they respond in similar ways and demonstrate similar attitudes according to their differing

values, interests and activities. Trier and Maiborada's (2009) study, based on a project to involve a whole community in adopting more sustainable practices, found that the responses could be categorized into three groupings: those who associate with the objectives and those who disassociate – in this case with preconceptions as to what 'green' means; and those who have no association because they felt they were already doing something.

There is an unsaid element in much of this discussion and in the commentaries on destination development – the majority of these are on destinations that are comparatively underdeveloped and found in attractive, 'unspoilt' environments, which are far removed from the desks of the writers. Many of the writers are in the post-industrial societies of the world, and this is a major influence on their values, views and attitudes. The unsaid comment is that these destinations should be maintained as they are – conservation at a distance (!), and that this is the way IPs want it to be, so giving rise to romantic notions such as the *Myth of the Noble [Eco-]Savage* (see Whelan, 1999). This attitude is also often implicit in the expectations placed on local people and the local community: that not only do they want tourism but they should seek to maintain it at a level of demand which does not lead to environmental degradation. Thus, the economic benefits will be constrained as development is restricted – by their choice; as if not to do so is acting irresponsibly. However, this is hardly the stance taken by any aspiring business, nor is it the economic model of the Western world. To advocate that the former should be the case is to imply that the local community should not develop. This situation is well captured by Colvin (1994) in commenting on Capirona and Quichua Indian families who initially found that ET was insufficient in economic terms to meet their needs and also that it was generating problems with food supplies (which were insufficient for visitor numbers) and waste disposal. To capitalize more on the visitors, they diversified activities into the production of local crafts. However, given the need to buy in additional supplies, they considered expanding the area given over to crops, which might also lead to a surplus that could then be sold, leading to some forest clearance. What this case illustrates particularly well is that as the Capirona gained financially from ET they could then buy in goods and materials, for example to convert from candlelight to generators for light, etc. They therefore began to slowly develop and become more like their visitors than as the Indians the visitors expected to find. If the community enjoy the gains then the negative impact on their environment is accepted in the process. Conversely, for the visitor, the original attractiveness of the small-scale ecotours and their expectations of the 'primitive savage' are lost. But then that is their choice and they are but following the development path their visitors have travelled over time. This scenario is further explored by Stronza and Gordillo (2008), who argue that ecotourism develop-ment is a double-edged sword which while holding benefits also brings disbenefits, especially social changes, such as time pressures, decline in traditional relationships, social conflict, introduction of working practices and dislocation from previous activities, e.g. working the land. Is this to the detriment of the people involved? Tourism is undoubtedly a vector of social change, as also demonstrated by Mbaiwa's (2011) study into tourism development in Botswana; this identified that local people, where opportunity arises, will change from traditional to 'modern' jobs in tourism, which bring income and lead to increased demand for improvement in housing, consumer goods and foreign foods. Would not the same findings have arisen in almost all populated destinations in the early years of tourism development? Is this not a basis of capitalism?

Conclusion

This chapter has sought to introduce and analyse responsible tourism (RT), placing it in context through the due consideration of other popular terms applied to variously conceived forms of touristic activity. In contrast to the latter, RT is seen to be the most conceptual approach, encompassing all elements of the tourism system. Thus, in application, tourists, the enterprises that directly and indirectly

respond to their needs and wants, and government and related agencies, all have a responsibility to seek to reduce the negative and enhance the positive impacts associated with tourism. As such, RT is equally as applicable to traditional (mass) tourism as it is to small-scale tourism developments. In all cases, there is a requisite need for community involvement and equitable shares and, on the part of all participants, respect and responsibility for their actions and the impacts of those actions. To explore these areas and further debate, in the process establishing the central tenets of RT, the discussion has sought to embrace the broad spectrum of tourism and in so doing purposely draw to attention early commentary and research. The objective of this was twofold. First, to convey a temporal perspective to the debate and, secondly, to provide a basis for consideration of the extent to which progress towards more responsible tourism has been achieved since its early inception in the 1980s. An outcome of this has been to show how little attention is given throughout to mass tourist market develop-ments and sustainability, yet much more could be given (see Butler, 1998).

To develop this theme, the chapter first established the background context to the emergence of RT, bringing into contention international policy initiatives which, while laudable conceptually, are of questionable effect. Subsequently, those terms most associated with RT were identified and analysed, leading to perceptions that they are amorphous and have evident overlap, causing some degree of terminological confusion. Compared with mass tourism, these alternative forms of tourism are more upmarket, limited in supply and higher in cost. So they have a limited overall market and, arguably, a lower propensity for repeat custom, which brings into question their sustainability. Furthermore, with the exception of RT, these terms to varying degrees are limited in scope and invariably considered as involving small-scale tourism developments. This encourages a destination-centred focus with the emphasis on the locality, which is a fundamental problem that distracts from the need for a more holistic approach. In contrast, RT, in its fullest sense, is more conceptual and encompasses all facets of tourism – thus transportation, supply and the enterprises involved, the destination environment and communities; it therefore implicitly involves governance (see Lara and Gemelli, Chapter 11). This analysis brought to attention a number of other substantive issues meriting further discussion. While these gain consideration in different contexts in the following chapters, they have been given more consideration here in furtherance of the debate; all the more so as they are germane to the central tenets of RT.

The first area so considered was operational issues, which drew attention to major facets of tourism supply. This established the substantial influence of tour operators (TOs, large and small) and brought into focus responsible practices in business, as well as drawing attention, by way of contrast, to the major growth markets of all-inclusive resorts and cruises. The adoption of the tenets of RT by tour operators is all the more important given their influence (see Holland, Chapter 9; Spenceley and Rylance, Chapter 10). However, and irrespective of size and scale, all enterprises need to accept that they have a responsibility for the impacts of their operations and the management of their businesses. As such, they need to address their environmental performance (EP) and corporate social responsibility (CSR), topics that are addressed in the second area to be considered: responsibility in business (see also Buckley, Chapter 6; Zientara, Chapter 12). In this context, it was additionally noted that tourist enterprises hold the potential to extend their influence through adopting and promoting sustainability in supply chain management (see Holland, Chapter 9). In concluding the discussion on responsibility, the vexing issue of carbon offsetting, most often associated with the greenhouse gas (GHG) emissions of transport, was brought to attention, and raised a number of issues, including its value and voluntary take-up by tourists (see also Somerville, Chapter 3).

The attention then turned, in the last section of the chapter, to discuss a variety of perspectives on destinations, with an emphasis on expansion aligned with consideration of governance. As identified, not only are some of the perceived ills of tourism development the result of a lack of clear government policies but also a lack of appropriate planning guidelines and a lack of control (see Hall, Chapter 8; Lara and Gemelli, Chapter 11). The alternatives to mass tourism may be small in scale to start with, but this does mean that their impacts, particularly on the physical environment, are of little significance. Moreover, the subsequent expansion of these small-scale developments brought into question just who does such expansion serve? Also, what we find with these alternative forms of tourism is not new. Access has, and will continue to be, the key factor in expansion, which with increasing perceptions of market opportunity will lead to greater commercialization such that, to paraphrase William Wordsworth, no corner of the world will be secure from the rash assault of tourism. Basically, there is invariably little to discourage this and much facilitating it, not the least of which is short-term economic imperatives underpinning the promotion of tourism with often, at best, social and environment dimensions, which are longer term objectives, taking second place (see Pleumarom, Chapter 7; Hall, Chapter 8). In the short term, the promotion of tourism arguably is the easy option but there may well be potential for alternative developments (see Moscado, 2008). Other economic activity might be possible that is more resource based, more in tune with sustainability.

Furthermore, it is inescapable that marketing and product diversification/differentiation is more responsible for the growth of these alternative forms of tourism, especially ecotourism (ET), than demand solely based on consumers motivated by a desire to study the flora and fauna or culture of the people in any particular destination. Also, it is evident that many of these products are market led rather than resource based. Even so, to confine development to low-key, small tourism products logically increases their attraction and status as a positional good. The associated comparatively high prices further arguments of commodification and barriers to access due to cost. As such, a destination where tourism is *the* economic activity then becomes dependent on predominantly the major developed nations of the world – a precarious situation given the fickle nature of tourists, and the fact that today 'new' destinations can be established very quickly so that the life of the latest 'must go' resort is all the shorter.

This final section of the chapter also brought into context varied perspectives on destinations and community involvement, highlighting actual and potential domino effects of tourism development on the communities and also from employment opportunities (see Timothy, Chapter 5; Zientara, Chapter 12). In this area, perhaps more especially, there is sense gained from some commentaries that such outcomes are in some way less desirable. Yet 'Wherever resorts are found, in no matter what remote area, they are assembled from the same social establishments' (MacCannell, 1976, p. 184), and therefore they are just as likely to develop in ways similar to their Western counterparts. Moreover, while tourism is often berated for its influence on a destination community and culture there is a failing to recognize, especially today, that societies are not insular. They are not isolated from external affairs or immune to them (see Harrison and Price, 1996). Thus, any analysis and evaluation of tourism development must include the

'political and social structure, economic relations and the role and activities of the state' (Kirby, 1985, p. 80). All too often this is not the case, and tourism is treated rather in isolation of these other dimensions of society (see Pleumarom, Chapter 7; Hall, Chapter 8).

In concluding, a number of emergent issues demand consideration. First, there is a need for research into the effectiveness of management strategies and, particularly, with regard to alternative tourism (AT) projects: where are the objective, verifiable analyses of whether these projects meet the rhetoric of those promoting them? Also on this theme, where is the research into the influence of power in shaping tourism development? The second emerging issue is that while much discourse is on alternative forms of tourism, there is comparatively very little on mass tourism: where is the debate that mass tourism is deliberately developed, that countries and business expressly seek to maximize incoming visitor numbers and in the process maximize economic leakage and minimize benefits for local persons? In addressing these factors and the overarching issues of sustainability, RT certainly has a major role to play.

References

ACTSA (2002) *People-first Tourism*. Action for Southern Africa, London.

Albuquerque, K. de and McElroy, J.L. (1995) Alternative tourism and sustainability. In: Conlin, M.V. and Baum, T. (eds) *Island Tourism: Management Principles and Practice*. Wiley, Chichester, UK, pp. 23–32.

Anon. (1994) Editorial. *The Rural Extension Bulletin*, 5 August 2004, pp. 2–10. Agricultural Extension and Rural Development Department, University of Reading, UK.

Anon. (2006) The know-how section. *Green Hotelier* (London), 11 January 2006.

Anon. (2008) Book review: Johnston, A.M. (2005) *Is the Sacred for Sale? Tourism and Indigenous Peoples*. Earthscan/Routledge, London. Available at: http://www.earthscan.co.uk/?tabid=263 (accessed 22 September 2008).

Anon. (2009) Green companies do better during downturn: study. *Greenbiz*, 10 February 2009. Available at: http://www.greenbiz.com/news/2009/02/10/green-companies-do-better-during-downturn-study (accessed 4 April 2012).

Asher, F. (1985) *Tourism: Transnational Corporations and Cultural Identities*. United Nations Educational, Scientific and Cultural Organization, Paris.

Bachvarov, M. (1999) Troubled sustainability: Bulgarian seaside resorts. *Tourism Geographies* 1, 192–203.

Barnett, T. (2009) The green future of travel: accepting the responsibility and spreading the benefits. *Tourism*, No. 142, p. 18. The Tourism Society, Sutton, UK.

Beioley, S. (1995) Green tourism – soft or sustainable? *INsights*, May 1995, pp. B75–B89. English Tourist Board, London.

Bennett, L. (2006) Duty free? *Resource*, No. 29 (July/August), pp. 20–22. Resource Media, Bristol, UK.

Blane, J.M. and Jaakson, R. (1995) The impact of ecotourism boats on the St Lawrence Beluga whales. *Environmental Conservation* 27, 267–269.

Blangy, S. and Neilsen, T. (1993) Ecotourism and minimum impact policy. *Annals of Tourism Research* 20, 357–360.

Bohdanowicz, P. and Zientara, P. (2012) CSR inspired initiatives in top hotel chains. In: Leslie, D. (ed.) *Tourism Enterprises and the Sustainability Agenda across Europe*, Ashgate, Farnham, UK, pp. 93–120.

Bramwell, B. and Lane, B. (2000) *Tourism Collaboration and Partnerships: Politics, Practice and Sustainability.* Channel View, Clevedon, UK.

Buckley, R. (ed.) (2004) *Environmental Impacts of Ecotourism.* Ecotourism Series 2, CAB International, Wallingford, UK.

Buckley, R., Weaver, D.B. and Pickering, C. (eds) (2003) *Nature-based Tourism, Environment and Land Management.* Ecotourism Series 1, CAB International, Wallingford, UK.

Budowskie, G. (1976) Tourism and conservation: conflict, coexistence, or symbiosis? *Environmental Conservation* 3, 5–9.

Butcher, J. (1997) Sustainable development or development? In: Stabler, M.J. (ed.) *Tourism and Sustainability: Principles to Practice.* CAB International, Wallingford, UK, pp. 27–39.

Butler, R. (1991) Tourism, environment, and sustainable development. *Environmental Conservation* 18, 201–209.

Butler, R. (1995) Introduction. In: Butler, R. and Pearce, D. (eds) *Change in Tourism: People, Places and Processes.* Routledge, New York, pp. 1–11.

Butler, R. (1998) Sustainable tourism – looking backwards in order to progress? In: Hall, C.M. and Lew, A.A. (eds) *Sustainable Tourism – A Geographical Perspective.* Prentice Hall, Harlow, UK, pp. 35–48.

Butler, R. (1999) Sustainable tourism: a state-of-the-art review. *Tourism Geographies* 1, 7–25.

Butler, R. (2001) Rural development. In: Weaver, D.B. (ed.) *The Encyclopedia of Ecotourism.* CAB International, Wallingford, UK, pp. 433–446.

Butler, R. (2010) Carrying capacity in tourism – paradox and hypocrisy. In: Pearce, D.G. and Butler, R.W. (eds) *Tourism Research: A 20-20 Vision.* Goodfellow, Oxford, UK, p. 53–64.

Cater, E. (1993) Ecotourism in the third world: problems for sustainable tourism development. *Tourism Management* 14, 85–90.

Cater, E. (1994) Introduction. In: Cater, E. and Lowman, G. (eds) *Ecotourism – a Sustainable Option.* Wiley, Chichester, UK, pp. 3–17.

Ceballos-Lascuráin, H. (1996) [Section] 2. Tourism and the environment. In: Ceballos-Lascuráin, H. *Tourism, Ecotourism, and Protected Areas. IUCN Protected Areas Programme, IV World Congress on National Parks and Protected Areas.* International Union for Conservation of Nature (IUCN), Gland, Switzerland. Available at: http://data.iucn.org/dbtw-wpd/html/Tourism/section5.html (accessed 2 April 2012).

Cetinel, F. and Yolal, M. (2009) Public policy and sustainable tourism in Turkey. *Tourismos* 4(3), 35–50.

Colvin, J.G. (1994) Capirona: a model of indigenous ecotourism. *Journal of Sustainable Tourism* 2, 174–177.

Cronin, L. (1990) A strategy for tourism and sustainable developments. *World Leisure and Recreation*, 32, 12–18.

Crowley, K. (1998) 'Glocalisation' and ecological modernity: challenges for local environmental governance in Australia. *Local Environment* 3, 91–97.

Dabrowski, P. (2002) Tourism for conservation, conservation for tourism. *Unasylva*, No.176, pp. 1–5.

Daneshkhu, S. and Chote, R. (1996) Wish you weren't here: even the most remote places on the planet have felt the effects of mass tourism. *Financial Times* (London), 3 August 1996, p. 10.

EC (2007) Carbon offsets products report. *Ethical Consumer*, No. 106, pp. 12–20.

Economist (1998) A survey of travel and tourism: [1] How green can you get? 8 January 1998; [2] Handle with care (environmental damage caused by tourism and measures the industry is taking to prevent such harm), 10 January 1998. *The Economist*, Haywards Heath, UK/St Louis, Missouri.

EIU (1993) *Travel and Tourism Analyst*, No. 1. Economic Intelligence Unit, London.

Equations (Equitable Tourism Options) (2007) Enclavisation of tourism: Special Tourism Zones in India. *Third World Resurgence*, No. 207/208, pp. 19–24. Third World Network, Penang, Malaysia/Geneva, Switzerland. Available at: http://www.twnside.org.sg/title2/resurgence/207-208/cover4.doc (accessed 19 April 2012).

Font, X. and Buckley, R.C. (eds) (2001) *Tourism Ecolabelling: Certification and Promotion of Sustainable Management.* CAB International, Wallingford, UK.

Frey, N. and George, R. (2009) Responsible tourism management: the missing link between business owners' attitudes and behaviour in the Cape Town tourism industry. *Tourism Management* 31, 621–628.

Gabriel, N. (2006) Environmental and social change in Thailand. *CSR Asia Weekly* 3(9), 3–7.

Goodwin, H. and Bah, A. (2004) The Gambia: paradise or purgatory? *Developments: The International*

Development Magazine, No. 27, pp. 4–7. Available at: http://webarchive.nationalarchives.gov.
uk/20100823124637/http://www.developments.org.uk/articles/the-gambia-paradise-or-purgatory/
(accessed 3 April 2012).

GreenBiz (2007) Businesses want green IT, but aren't taking action. Available at: http://www.greenbiz.com/
news/2007/06/25/study-businesses-want-green-it-arent-taking-action (accessed 4 April 2012).

Grundy, T. (1998) Tourist hoards threat to falls. *Scotland on Sunday*, Edinburgh, UK, 28 June 1998, p. 20.

Hall, C.M. (ed.) (2007) *Pro-poor Tourism: Who Benefits? Perspectives on Tourism and Poverty Reduction.*
Channel View, Clevedon, UK.

Hall, C.M. and Boyd, S. (eds) (2005) *Nature-based Tourism in Peripheral Areas: Development or Disaster?*
Channel View, Clevedon, UK.

Hall, C.M., Springett, D.V. and Springett, B.P. (1993) The development of an environmental education tourist
product: a case study of the New Zealand Natural Heritage Foundation's Nature of New Zealand
Programme. *Journal of Sustainable Tourism* 1, 130–136.

Hardy, A., Beeton, R.J.S. and Pearson, L. (2002) Sustainable tourism: an overview of the concepts and its
position in relation to conceptualisations of tourism. *Journal of Sustainable Tourism* 10, 475–496.

Harrison, D. and Price, M.F. (1996) Fragile environments, fragile communities? An introduction. In: Price,
M.F. (ed.) *People and Tourism in Fragile Environments*. Wiley, Chichester, UK, pp. 1–18.

Hauteserre de, A.-M. (2003) A response to 'Misguided policy initiatives in small island destinations: why
up-market tourism policies fail'. *Tourism Geographies* 5, 49–53.

Haywood, K.M. (1988) Responsible and responsive tourism planning in the community. *Tourism Management*
19, 105–118.

Healy, M. (1990) *Consumers and the Environment*, Summer 1990. National Consumer Council, London, p.
6.

Highfield, R. (2004) Killer whales drowned out by noise of tourists/boats. *The Daily Telegraph* (London), 29
April 2004, p. 4.

Holden, A. (2005) *Environment and Tourism*. Routledge, London.

Honey, M. (2008) *Ecotourism and Sustainable Development: Who Owns Paradise?* 2nd edn. Island Press,
Washington, DC.

Huimin, G. and Ryan, C. (2011) Ethics and corporate social responsibility – an analysis of the views of
Chinese hotel managers. *International Journal of Hospitality Management* 30, 875–885.

Hummel, J. (1993) Ecotourism development in protected areas of developing countries: changing
perspectives, a discussion paper illustrated with examples from case-studies in Nepal and Costa Rica.
Paper presented at World Leisure and Recreation Congress, Jaipur, 5–10 December 1993.

Hutnyk, J. (1996) *The Rumour of Calcutta: Tourism, Charity and the Poverty of Representation*. Zed, London.

IFC (2004) *Ecolodges: Exploring Opportunities for Sustainable Business*. International Finance Corporation,
Washington, DC. Available at: http://www.ifc.org/ifcext/enviro.nsf/AttachmentsByTitle/p_EBFP_
ecolodge/$FILE/Ecolodge_Publication.pdf (accessed 4 April 2012).

Ioannides, D. and Holcomb, B. (2003) Misguided policy initiatives in small island destinations: why
up-market tourism policies fail. *Tourism Geographies* 5, 39–48.

IRG (International Resources Group) (1992) *Ecotourism: A Viable Alternative for Sustainable Management of
Natural Resources in Africa*. US Agency for International Development, Bureau of Africa, Washington,
DC.

Jafari, J. (1986) Tourism for whom? Old questions still echoing. *Annals of Tourism Research* 13, 129–137.

Johnson, D. (2002) Environmentally sustainable cruise tourism: a reality check. *Marine Policy* 26, 261–2007.

Johnston, A.M. (2003) Self-determination: exercising indigenous rights in Tourism. In: Timothy, D.J. and
Dowling, R.K. *Tourism in Destination Communities*. CAB International, Wallingford, UK, pp. 115–134.

Johnston, A.M. (2005) *Is the Sacred for Sale? Tourism and Indigenous Peoples*. Earthscan/Routledge, London.

Jones, A. (1987) Green tourism. *Tourism Management* 18, 354–356.

Jones, A.L. and Phillips, M. (2010) *Disappearing Destinations: Climate Change and the Future Challenges for
Coastal Tourism*. CAB International, Wallingford, UK.

Kirby, A. (1985) Leisure as commodity – the role of the state in leisure provision. *Progress in Human
Geography* 9, 64–84.

Krippendorf, J. (1987) *The Holidaymakers*. Butterworth-Heinemann, Oxford, UK.

Lane, B. (1988) What is rural tourism? In: Talbot-Ponsonby, H. (ed.) *Changing Land Use and Recreation*.
Countryside Recreation Research Advisory Group, Bristol, UK, pp. 60–63.

Lee, S. and Park, S.-Y. (2009) Do socially responsible activities help hotels and casinos achieve their financial
goals? *Journal of Hospitality Management* 28, 105–112.

Leslie, D. (2005) Effective involvement in the development and sustainability of cultural tourism: an exploration in the case of New Lanark. In: Sigala, M. and Leslie, D. (eds) *International Cultural Tourism: Management, Implications and Cases*. Elsevier Butterworth-Heinemann, Oxford, UK, pp. 122–136.

Leslie, D. (2009) *Tourism Enterprises and Sustainable Development – International Perspectives on Responses to the Sustainability Agenda*. Advances in Tourism Series, Routledge, New York.

Leslie, D. (2010) *Tourism Bute and Inchmarnock Fish Farm Proposal. Precognition. Interim Scheme for the Authorisation of Fish Farms Application by Offshore Farm Development Ltd. Fish Farm North of Inchmarnock, Isle of Bute*. Public Enquiry. Directorate for Planning and Environmental Appeals, Scottish Government (DPEA), Reference IQC/35/24 March 2010.

Leslie, D. (2012a) Introduction: sustainability, the European Union and tourism. In: Leslie, D. (ed.) *Tourism Enterprises and the Sustainability Agenda across Europe*. Ashgate, Farnham, UK, pp. 1–14.

Leslie, D. (ed.) (2012b) *Tourism Enterprises and the Sustainability Agenda across Europe*. Ashgate, Farnham, UK.

Leslie, D. (2012c) Key players in the environmental performance of tourism enterprises. In: Reddy, M.V. and Wilkes, K. (eds) *Tourism, Climate Change and Sustainability*. Earthscan, London (in press).

Long, V.H. (1991) Government–industry–community interaction in tourism development in Mexico. In: Sinclair, M.T. and Stabler, M.J. (eds) *The Tourism Industry: An International Analysis*. CAB International, Wallingford, UK, pp. 205–222.

MacCannell, D. (1976) *The Tourist – a New Theory of the Leisure Class*. Schocken, New York.

Mann, M. (2000) *The Community Tourism Guide: Exciting Holidays for Responsible Travellers*. Earthscan, London/Sterling, Virginia.

Mann, M. and Ibrahim, Z. (2002) *The Good Alternative Travel Guide: Exciting Holidays for Responsible Travellers*, 2nd edn. Earthscan, London/Sterling, Virginia.

Mason, P. (1990) *Tourism: Environment and Development Perspectives*. World Wide Fund for Nature, Godalming, UK.

Mathieson, A.R. and Wall, G. (1982) *Tourism: Economic, Physical and Social Impacts*. Longman, Harlow, UK.

May, V. (1991) Tourism, environment and development – values, sustainability and stewardship. *Tourism Management* 12. 112–118.

Mbaiwa, J. (2011) Changes on traditional livelihood activities and lifestyles caused by tourism development in the Okavango Delta, Botswana. *Tourism Management* 32, 1050–1060.

Meadows, D.H., Meadows, D.L., Randers, J. and Behrens, W.W. III (1972) *The Limits to Growth: A Report for the Club of Rome's Project on the Predicament of Mankind* [1st edn]. Universe Books/Potomac Associates, New York.

Minhinnick, R. (1993) *A Postcard Home – Tourism in the Mid-nineties*. Gomer, Llandysul, Wales, UK.

Mitchell, J. and Ashley, C. (2007) *Tourism and Poverty Reduction: Pathways to Prosperity*. Earthscan, London/Sterling, Virginia.

Moore, S. and Carter, B. (1993) Ecotourism in the 21st century. *Tourism Management* 14, 123–130.

Moscardo, G. (2008) Sustainable tourism innovation: challenging basic assumptions. *Tourism and Hospitality Research* 8, 4–13.

Mosselaer, F. van de, Duim, R. van der and Wijk, J. van (2012) Corporate social responsibility in the tour operating industry: the case of Dutch outbound tour operators. In: Leslie, D. (ed.) *Tourism Enterprises and the Sustainability Agenda across Europe*. Ashgate, Farnham, UK, pp. 71–92.

Nepal, S.K. (2007) Ecotourists' importance and satisfaction ratings of accommodation-related amenities. *Anatolia* 18, 255–276.

Nicholas, S. (2011) Neighbourhood watch. *Director*, September 2011, pp. 42–46. Institute of Directors, London. Available at: http://www.director.co.uk/MAGAZINE/2011/8_September/regenerating-communities_65_01.html (accessed 6 April 2012).

O'Brien, P. (1997) Can eco-tourism save Costa Rica, 'the jewel of nature'? *EG: Local Environment News* 3(10), 20–21.

O'Grady, A. (ed.) (1990) *The Challenge of Tourism: Learning Resources for Study and Action*. Ecumenical Coalition on Third World Tourism, Bangkok.

Ousby, I. (1990) *The Englishman's England: Taste, Travel and the Rise of Tourism*. Cambridge University Press, Cambridge, UK.

Pattullo, P. and Minelli, O. (2006) *The Ethical Travel Guide: Your Passport to Exciting Alternative Holidays*. Earthscan, London/Sterling, Virginia.

Pepper, D. (1998) Sustainable development and ecological modernization: a radical homocentric perspective. *Sustainable Development* 6, 1–7.

Pleumarom, A. (1990) Alternative tourism – a viable solution. *Contours* 4(8), 12–15.

Pleumarom, A. (2007) Does tourism benefit the third world? *Third World Resurgence*, No. 207/208, pp. 10–12. Third World Network, Penang, Malaysia/Geneva, Switzerland. Available at: http://www. twnside.org.sg/title2/resurgence/207-208/cover1.doc (accessed 19 April 2012).

Plfanz, M. (2007) Hotels threaten herds of roaming elephants. *The Daily Telegraph* (London), 28 April 2007, p. 14.

Price, M.F. (ed.) (1996) *People and Tourism in Fragile Environments.* Wiley, Chichester, UK.

Raffaele, P. (2003) Feeding frenzy at Shark Bay. *The Daily Telegraph Saturday Magazine* (London) [date unknown], pp. 42–47.

Rifai, T. (2011) Making the case for tourism. *Hospitality*, No. 21, p. 19. Institute of Hospitality, Sutton, UK.

Robinson, K. (1980) Tourism and conservation – friends or foes? In: Anderson, P. (ed.) *Tourism and Countryside Conservation. A Joint Seminar [Held by the Peak National Park Study Centre] with the Countryside Recreation Management Association: A Conference Held at Losehill Hall, Castleton, Derbyshire, 31 October–2 November 1980.* Peak National Park Study Centre, Losehill Hall, Castleton, UK, pp. 9–10.

Rodenberg, E. (1980) The effects of scale in economic development: tourism in Bali. *Annals of Tourism Research* 7, 177–196.

Romeril, M. (1989) Tourism and the environment – accord or discord? *Tourism Management* 10, 204–208.

Romeril, M. (1994) Alternative tourism: the real tourism alternative? In: Copper, C. and Lockwood, A. (eds) *Progress in Tourism, Recreation and Hospitality Management* 6, 22–29.

Rosenthal, R. (1991) Sustainable tourism – optimism or pessimism? *In Focus*, No. 1, Summer 1991, pp. 2–3.

Rosselson, R. (2001) Ethical tourism. *Ethical Consumer*, No. 69, pp. 28–29.

Ryan, C. (1991) Tourism and marketing – a symbiotic relationship? *Tourism Management* 12, 101–110.

Scherrer, P., Smith, A.J. and Dowling, R.K. (2010) Visitor management practices and operational sustainability: expedition cruising in the Kimberley, Australia. *Tourism Management* 32, 1218–1222.

Scheyvens, R. (2002) *Tourism for Development: Empowering Communities.* Prentice Hall, Harlow, UK.

Scott, G. (2001) Ecotourism discovers the last frontier: the Cascadia Wildlands Project, Alaska. ClearingHouse for Reviewing Ecotourism, No. 8. tourism investigation and monitoring team (tim-team), Bangkok. Available at: http://www.twnside.org.sg/title/eco8.htm (accessed 19 April 2012).

Shaw, G. and Williams, A.M. (1994) *Critical Issues in Tourism: A Geographical Perspective.* Blackwell, Oxford, UK.

Sinclair, T. (1991) The tourism industry and foreign exchange leakages in a developing country: the distribution of earnings from safari and beach tourism in Kenya. In: Sinclair, M.T. and Stabler, M.J. (eds) *The Tourism Industry: An International Analysis.* CAB International, Wallingford, UK, pp. 185–204.

Singh, S., Timothy, D.J. and Dowling, R.K. (eds) (2003) *Tourism and Destination Communities.* CAB International, Wallingford, UK.

Smith, V.L. and Eadington, W.R. (eds) (1992) *Tourism Alternatives: Potentials and Problems in the Development of Tourism.* Wiley, Chichester, UK.

Starmer-Smith, C. (2008) How green is your travel company? *The Daily Telegraph* (London), 12 January 2008. Available at: http://www.telegraph.co.uk/travel/hubs/greentravel/739212/How-green-is-your-travel-company.html (accessed 4 April 2012).

Steel, P. (1995) Ecotourism: an economic analysis. *Journal of Sustainable Tourism* 3, 29–31.

Stronza, A. and Gordillo, J. (2008) Community views on ecotourism. *Annals of Tourism Research* 35, 448–468.

Survival International (1995) *Parks and People – Tribal Peoples and Conservation.* Survival International, London.

Telfer, D.J. (2003) Development issues in destination communities. In: Singh, S., Timothy, D.J. and Dowling, R.K. (eds) *Tourism and Destination Communities.* CAB International, Wallingford, UK, pp. 155–180.

Third World Network (2007) *Rethinking Tourism: An Engine for Third World Development? Third World Resurgence*, No. 207/208. Third World Network, Penang, Malaysia/Geneva, Switzerland. Available at: http://www.twnside.org.sg/title2/resurgence/twr207-208.htm (accessed 19 April 2012).

Timothy, D.J. and Tosun, C. (2003) Appropriate planning for tourism in destination communities: participation, incremental growth and collaboration. In: Singh, S., Timothy, D.J. and Dowling, R.K. (eds) *Tourism and Destination Communities.* CAB International, Wallingford, pp. 181–204.

Torres-Sovero, C., Gonzalez, J.A., Martin-Lopez, B. and Kirkby, C.A. (2011) Social-ecological factors influencing tourism satisfaction in three ecotourism lodges in the southeastern Peruvian Amazon. *Tourism Management* 33, 545–552.

Trier, C. and Maiborada, O. (2009) The Green Village project: a rural community's journey towards sustainability. *Local Environment* 14, 819–831.

Tsaur, S.-H., Lin, Y.-C. and Lin, J.-H. (2006) Evaluating ecotourism sustainability from the integrated perspective of resource, community and tourism. *Tourism Management* 27, 640–653.

Turner, L. and Ash, J. (1975) *The Golden Hordes. International Tourism and the Pleasure Periphery*. Constable, London.

Tuting, L. (1989) Trekking in Nepal: Western achievement attitudes vs ecological renewal: a promising approach: the Annapurna Conservation Area Project. In: Euler, C. (ed.) *Tourismus und Ökologie*. Focus Verlag, Giessen, Germany, pp. 11–19.

UNEP (2012) Ecotourism: What is Ecotourism? Available at: http://www.unep.fr/scp/tourism/topics/ecotourism/ (accessed 2 April 2012).

Walle, A.H. (1995) Business ethics and tourism: from micro to macro perspectives. *Tourism Management* 16, 263–268.

Weaver, D.B. (1991) Alternatives to mass tourism in Dominica. *Annals of Tourism Research* 19, 414–431.

Weaver, D.B (1992) Contention for deliberate alternative tourism. *Annals of Tourism Research* 19, 788–791.

Weaver, D.B. (2001) Introduction to ecotourism. In: Weaver, D.B. (ed.) *The Encyclopedia of Ecotourism*. CAB International, Wallingford, UK, pp. 1–3.

WECD (1987) *Our Common Future*. [Report of the] World Commission on Environment and Development [The Brundtland Commission]. Oxford University Press, Oxford, UK/New York.

Weeden, C. (2005) Ethical tourism – is its future in niche tourism? In: Novelli, M. (ed.) *Niche Tourism – Contemporary Issues, Trends and Cases*. Elsevier, Oxford, UK, pp. 233–246.

Wheat, S. (2003) Eco or ego? *Green Futures*, January/February 2003, pp. 44–45.

Wheatcroft, S. (1991) Airlines, tourism and the environment. *Tourism Management* 12, 119–124.

Wheeler, M. (1994) The emergence of ethics in tourism and hospitality. In: Cooper, C.P. and Lockwood, A. (eds) *Progress in Tourism, Recreation and Hospitality Management* 6, 46–56.

Whelan, R. (1999) *Wild in Woods: The Myth of the Noble Eco-savage*. Studies on the Environment No. 14, Institute for Economic Affairs, London.

Whinney, C. (1996) Good intentions in a competitive market: training for people and tourism in fragile environments. In: Price, M.F. (ed.) *People and Tourism in Fragile Environments*. Wiley, Chichester, UK, pp. 221–230.

Wight, P. (1994) Environmentally responsible marketing of tourism. In: Cater, E. and Lowman, G. (eds) *Ecotourism – A Sustainable Option*. Wiley, Chichester, UK, pp. 39–56.

Wight, P. (1997) Ecotourism accommodation spectrum: does supply match demand. *Tourism Management* 18, 209–220.

Wight, P.A. (1998) Tools for sustainability analysis in planning and managing tourism and recreation in the destination. In: Hall, C.M. and Lew, A.A. (eds) *Sustainable Tourism – A Geographical Perspective*. Prentice Hall, Harlow, pp. 75–91.

Wight, P.A. (2002) *Supporting the Principles of Sustainable Development in Tourism and Ecotourism. Government's Potential Role*. Pam Wight Associates, Edmonton, Alberta, Canada.

Wijk, J.V. and Persoon, W. (2006) A long-haul destination: sustainability reporting among tour operators. *European Management Journal* 24, 381–396.

Wild, C. (1994) Issues in ecotourism. In: Copper, C. and Lockwood, A. (eds) *Progress in Tourism, Recreation and Hospitality Management* 6, 21–31.

Williams, P.W. and Ponsford, I.F. (2009) Confronting tourism's environmental paradox: transitioning for sustainable tourism. *Futures* 41, 396–404.

Wood, K. and House, S. (1991) *The Good Tourism*. Mandarin, London.

Wood, M.E. (2002a) Developing a framework to evaluate ecotourism as a conservation and sustainable development tool. Paper presented at the Conference on Ecotourism and Conservation in the Americas at Stanford University, May 2002.

Wood, M.E. (2002b) *Ecotourism: Principles, Practices and Policies for Sustainability*. United Nations Environment Programme (UNEP), Paris. Available at: http://www.pnuma.org/industria/documentos/Ecotourism1.pdf (accessed 4 April 2012).

Wood, R. (2000) Caribbean cruise tourism: globalisation at sea. *Annals of Tourism Research* 27, 345–370.

WRI (2012) Reefs at Risk. World Resources Institute, Washington, DC. Available at: www.wri.org/reefs (accessed 4 April 2012).

WTM (2008) Global Trends Report 2008. World Travel Market and Euromonitor International, London. Available at: http://en.kongres-magazine.eu/data/upload/World_Travel_Market___Global_Trends_Report_2008.pdf (Accessed 8 April 2012).

WTTC (2002) Corporate Social Leadership in Travel & Tourism. World Travel and Tourism Council, London. Available at: http://info.worldbank.org/etools/antic/docs/Resources/Sectors/Retail%20Leisure/WTC%20corporatesocialleadership.pdf (accessed 4 April 2012).

WTTC, UNWTO and Earth Council (1995) Agenda 21 for the Travel and Tourism Industry: Towards Environmentally Sustainable Development. World Travel and Tourism Council, London, with World Tourism Organization, Madrid and Earth Council, Costa Rica.

WTTC, IFTO, IHRA and ICCL (2002) Industry as a Partner for Sustainable Development. World Travel and Tourism Council, International Federation of Tour Operators, International Hotel and Restaurant Association, International Council of Cruise Lines, London.

Yasarata, M., Altinay, L., Burns, P. and Okumus, F. (2010) Politics and sustainable tourism development – can they co-exist? Voices from North Cyprus. Tourism Management 31, 345–356.

Ziffer, K.A. (1989) Ecotourism: The Uneasy Alliance. Conservation International/Ernst andYoung, London.

3 International Transport and Climate Change: Taking Responsibility Seriously

Hugh Somerville
University of Surrey, UK

Introduction

The primary aim of this chapter is to provide the reader with a view of the development of the air transport industry and of how, over the last two decades, the current and potential contribution from aviation to man's impact on the climate has become of vital importance to the future of the aviation and tourism industries, which are inextricably linked. The responsible tourism movement has developed largely around issues at destinations and has, until recently, steered clear of the issue of transport used by tourists to and from tourism destinations. None the less, if tourism is to be responsible, transport must be considered as an integral part. With the rising relevance of climate change, it is vital that due attention is paid to the contribution of transport to tourism's long-term sustainability. The thrust of this chapter is to demonstrate that the aviation sector has become well aware of its role in responsibility and sustainability and has programmes in place that are relevant to the tourism sector. It is not in the scope of the chapter to carry out a similar review of the development of global shipping, which, of course, has a far longer history, that largely predates the modern interpretation of tourism. However, the emergence and huge growth of the cruise industry has taken place largely over the last two decades. Thus, tourism related to both aviation and shipping is growing globally and both face difficult challenges in managing their climate impact, particularly from international operations. Part of this chapter, therefore, is directed at placing the climate impact of shipping in context with that of aviation.

Flying – the Early Days

There are libraries filled with details of the history of aviation and the valiant efforts, often heroic, that have led to the development of this industry at the heart of our ever-expanding global communications network. As the technology developed from kite flying and the use of hot air military balloons in China in the 3rd century AD, through the designs of Leonardo Da Vinci, to balloons used in the 19th century, for example in the American Civil War, it is unlikely that any of these pioneers foresaw the current scale of global activity. At the time of the first powered flights of airships towards the end of the 19th century it was not clear whether the major route of development would be through powered airships or by heavier-than-air machines. It was probably the dramatic impact of the disasters that befell hydrogen airships that determined their virtual elimination from long-term development, although there are those that still see an important role for them in the future.

It is doubtful whether early pioneers foresaw the huge social and economic impact that would result from bringing global horizons within reach through air transport. From the very earliest stages of aviation, there was enormous determination to push back geographical boundaries, prompted by the legendary efforts of the Wright Brothers and others around the early 1900s, with international flight pioneered by Bleriot in 1909 across the English Channel. The New Year's Day flight by Tony Jannus on 1 January 1914 was the first scheduled airline flight with a passenger, and used a Benoist seaplane in the flight from St Petersburg to Tampa in Florida, reportedly at a height of 15 feet. Deutsche Luftschiffahrts-Aktiengesellschaft was the world's first airline, founded in November 1909, with government assistance, and operated airships manufactured by the Zeppelin company. It is highly unlikely that even the visionaries involved in early commercial aviation foresaw that by the turn of the century, there would be some 3000 billion passenger kilometres being flown by scheduled flights (ICAO, 2000) with 31 million tonnes of freight being transported on such flights.

It is just as unlikely that those pioneers predicted the environmental challenges that the use of aircraft would have to address. Early aviation was a spectacle to be admired and the noise of low flying aircraft was a thrill, whether at air circuses or in races such as the Schneider Trophy, a prize competition for seaplanes which until the early 1930s helped to develop sleeker, faster aircraft (the race was revived in 1981 by the Royal Aero Club of the UK). Yes, there was noise, but it was more a contribution to the excitement than a nuisance. As commercial aviation grew, it was the public reaction to the noise generated by aircraft at airports that became the first great environmental challenge. This became even more of an issue with the advent of commercial jet aircraft. While the noise performance of aircraft on an individual basis has improved enormously over the years, the increasing numbers of flights at most airports has ensured that noise has remained a major issue for communities close to most of these. The fuel burned was only part of the burgeoning exploitation of oil for transport and other purposes and, at that time, there seemed to be a limitless supply which could be used with little impact on the environment.

Commercial Aviation Services Develop

The First World War stimulated rapid development of flying technology. The postwar period saw a golden age of flying, with air shows touring cities and towns across the USA and other countries, and air races driving forward airframe design and engine performance. The first airmail flights in the USA, between New York and Washington, with a stopover in Philadelphia, took place in 1918. The requirements for such services contributed directly towards developing larger aircraft with longer ranges (see, for example, US Centennial of Flight Commission, 2012).

The flights of Alcock and Brown in 1919 and of Lindbergh in 1927, and the trans-Pacific crossing by Kingsford Smith in 1928, signalled the potential for commercial passenger and freight traffic. Early commercial flights between Florida and Cuba were offered in 1920 using flying boats. This was also the great age of dreamers, with many enterprises failing but, after Lindbergh's flight, commercial aviation became a much more serious business with large-scale investment. It was a period of rapid growth – for example, in the USA, there were less than 10,000 commercial travellers in 1926 but this grew to around 170,000 a year by the end of that decade. At this time, most of the traffic was business, with leisure air travel confined to the well-off.

Development in the USA was paralleled elsewhere. By August 1919, a daily service operated between Paris and London for as many as 14 passengers. This proved not to be financially viable because of high operating costs, high fares and low passenger turnout. One of the early international collaborations was Franco-Roumaine in 1920, a joint project between Romania and France. Worldwide, individual nations rushed to establish their own flag carriers. In the Netherlands, KLM was formed on 7 October 1919. Aeroflot was founded as Droboflovlot in 1928. Air France was formed in 1933 through the merger of several smaller companies with extensive routes across Europe, the French colonies in northern Africa and elsewhere. In Britain, European and intercontinental flights remained largely separate until 1974.

During the early 1920s, development was sporadic, and most airlines at the time were focused on mail. The all-metal 12 passenger Ford Trimotor became the first successful American airliner. Around that time, Pan American World Airways (Pan Am, founded as Pan American Airways) began to create a network with flying boats that linked Los Angeles to Shanghai and Boston to London. Pan Am and Northwest Airways were the leading US airlines to go international before the 1940s. Around the early 1930s, aircraft such as the Ford Trimotor and the Boeing Model 80 still could not avoid turbulence and air travel was almost inevitably accompanied by air sickness. Pan Am introduced male stewards and Boeing Air Transport was the first to introduce stewardesses. The Douglas Aircraft Company (founded in 1921) entered the fray, notably with the DC-3 in 1936; over 17,000 of these were built, and some are still flying today. The DC-3s carried around 75% of internal US traffic by the beginning of the Second World War, and eliminated much of the passenger discomfort by flying at around 20,000 ft.

Countries rushed to protect their airline's rights; an aspect that has continued to plague attempts to rationalize the global aviation industry in recent years. In November 1944, at an international conference in Chicago, 32 US states signed the Chicago Convention which led to the establishment of ICAO (International Civil Aviation Organization) in 1947. The Convention laid the foundation for a set of regulations which has made safety a paramount consideration and paved the way for the application of a common air navigation system throughout the world.

Aviation after the Second World War

Traditional piston-engine, propeller-driven aircraft technology reached its height during the Second World War. More revolutionary was the turbojet engine, which opened the way to much higher speeds through jet engines, and was co-invented by Dr Hans von Ohain in Germany and Sir Frank Whittle in Britain. After the war, tension between the USA and the Soviet Union led to a drive for supremacy in aerospace technology, including the first faster-than-sound flight by the Bell X-1 in 1947.

The next impact of the aeroplane came in commercial transportation (Heppenheimer, 1995). By 1950, the airliner was well on the way to replacing the train and the ocean liner as the primary means of long-distance travel. The entry of the first turbojet airliners into scheduled service in 1952 accelerated the pace of this revolution. These three decades after the Second World War were good years for the American airframe and engine industry, with the jet-engined products of Boeing, McDonnell-Douglas, Lockheed and other US firms dominating the international air routes. Most of these new aircraft were based on American bombers, which had spearheaded new technologies such as pressurization. In Europe, the 1950s saw the De Havilland Comet emerge as the forerunner of the jet age, with other leaders including the Sud Aviation Caravelle and the Soviet Tupolev Tu-104 and Tu-124. Concorde first flew in 1969 and operated until 2003. The Boeing 727 and, subsequently the Boeing 737, were leaders in the narrow-bodied jet category, with over 6000 of the various marques of the 737 having been produced to date.

The wide-body age began in 1970 with the entry into service of the four-engined, double-deck Boeing 747 (Sutter and Spenser, 2006). Three-engined aircraft followed, including the McDonnell Douglas DC-10 and the Lockheed Tristar. The first wide-body twin jet, the Airbus 300, entered service in 1974. Several successors have arrived since, including the Airbus A330–A340 series and the Boeing 767 and 777, with the 'Superjumbo' Airbus A380 starting commercial services in 2007.

For US carriers, however, the era of growth and optimism stuttered in the 1970s as the industry became plagued by a stream of problems, including labour unrest, congestion, increased fuel costs, and public concern over issues ranging from safety and service to air and noise pollution. The Airline Deregulation

Act of 1978 did initially attract new competitors into the field and led to lower ticket prices. But deregulation brought with it difficulties, such as opaque fare structures. Then there was the rise of the fringe 'no-frills' carriers led by Southwest Airlines in the USA (Calder, 2002; Gitell, 2003). The challenge to established airlines by low-cost carriers such as South-West was to be repeated in Europe, initially through airlines such as Laker Airways, and subsequently through others such as easyJet and Ryanair.

The postwar air transport boom was nothing short of a social revolution. With regional and local airlines and airfreight operations linking to international air carriers, aviation became the key communication system for globalization of economies, communication, migration and tourism. The economic, social and political consequences included the creation of global markets, opportunities for global travel undreamed of a generation before, the opening up of a global tourism industry and increased cultural interchange. While in-depth analysis of the benefits and costs of globalization does not belong here, it is pointed out that aviation-based tourism is one of the few sources of wealth for many developing countries.

The Modern Industry

There are four key components of the aviation industry: manufacturing; airports; airlines and air navigation service providers (ANSPs). The public generally sees airlines as the face of the industry as they are the consumer-facing element. Competition between airlines is a mixture of fierce commercial pricing and subsidies from governments, often simultaneous and leading to calls from some airlines for a 'level playing field'. It is not difficult to start an airline but just as easy to go bust (Button, 2012). The famous financier, Warren Buffet, is often quoted as saying that 'If a farsighted capitalist had been present at Kitty Hawk, he would have done his successors a huge favour by shooting Orville down'.

Manufacturers have consolidated globally to a handful of airframe and engine companies that face considerable challenges in bringing new products to the market. As environmental pressures increase, manufacturers, airlines and aviation regulators are faced with addressing the interdependencies, often conflicting, between noise and emissions. One dilemma currently facing the industry is the replacement for the narrow-bodied Boeing 737 and similar types: will it be a similar looking aircraft or a more radical 'open rotor' type – introduced to reduce fuel burn and CO_2 emissions?

Airlines interface with the consumer and have to provide a safe and reliable service that meets the expectation of the customer in terms of schedule, comfort and price. Also, we should not forget airfreight, some carried by dedicated aircraft and some in the holds of passenger airliners. For example, British Airways cargo accounted for some 25% of total revenue tonne kilometres (the product of payload weight and distance) in 2008. With a typical working life of 30 years, it is not surprising that the airline fleet replacement rate varies, depending on the business model and the regulatory environment. Some observers have suggested that scrapping schemes, such as those used recently in Europe and the USA for cars, could be used to provide incentives for the introduction of more modern aircraft.

Airports, often locally owned and managed, have to serve the interests of the communities they serve. They are in the front line over environmental issues such as noise and ground traffic congestion. Capacity is limited in some areas, leading to high landing charges and contributing to the use of airports that are further 'out of town', and less expensive, by some no-frills airlines such as Ryanair. Examples of major current capacity issues include London's Heathrow airport, where there was much debate over a third runway before the UK government decided against this expansion.

The ANSPs manage the challenge of routing the aircraft safely and efficiently, sometimes through skies that carry a huge amount of air traffic, particularly in Europe, the Eastern seaboard of the USA and over the North Atlantic. Globally, there are moves to improve routing and to fly direct routes; however, many routes are still typically 3–10% longer than the 'great circle' direct line.

Environmental Issues

This section will concentrate on the noise and climate impacts of aviation. There are other environmental impacts, including effects on land use and on local air quality – the latter an issue at some major airports where road traffic is generally the major contributor. Consideration is also given here to shipping to place climate impacts in context.

Noise

Historically noise has been more of an issue for departing aircraft than for arrivals, although in recent years arrivals have also become important. At most airports, attempts to minimize noise impact have led to more or less defined departure routes (sometimes referred to as noise 'sewers') which concentrate the impact on the houses underneath the departing flight path. These defined routes are sometimes accompanied by requirements to fly particular vertical profiles to minimize noise at certain distances along the preferred track. Arrival noise is also an issue; one example of measures to improve this is the wider application of continuous descent approaches, which bring both noise and fuel burn benefits, with engines at a consistent thrust level.

Thus, noise is subject to local controls such as flight paths, night-time restrictions and curfews, and control over types of aircraft using individual airports. This is accompanied by regulatory control through noise standards set through ICAO, which define noise performance standards measuring noise generated by aircraft under standard conditions (ICAO, 2012). One of the main problems with noise is that individual responses vary widely and it is difficult to measure the impact on individuals in a wholly objective manner. Apart from pressure to reduce the noise at source and to limit the number of flights, measures that have been introduced include (though not all at any one airport) clauses in property purchase agreements making individual house purchasers aware of the noise impact of nearby airports at the time of purchase: these could be coupled to control over integrated noise as

expressed at some airports through noise contours, and/or through limits on maximum noise from individual movements or the number of movements. The improvements in noise performance of aircraft over the last few decades have been substantial, yet this has done nothing to assuage the complaints from householders, many of whom have only occupied their homes during a period of overall noise decline.

The climate challenge – carbon dioxide (CO_2)

While a small minority of climate scientists still believe that the man-made greenhouse effect is not a problem, there is general scientific and political consensus that the greatest problem facing the aviation industry today is the growing contribution to the impact on the climate. Globally, aviation accounts for some 2–3% of the total man-made emissions of CO_2, with some states contributing disproportionately; for example, internal flights in the USA account for some 25% of the total, and all flights departing from UK airports for about 6% of the total. Aircraft are also known to have other impacts on the climate, mainly associated with the formation of cirrus cloud and condensation trails, and through emissions of nitrogen oxides (NO_x). These are not as well understood (see below) and, for the time being, the attention of the industry is focused on reducing CO_2. The general view of the industry and of some regulators is that there is a clear need to gain a better understanding of the other climate impacts before regulating to control them.

Advances in engine and airframe technology alone are unlikely to be sufficient to allow aviation to achieve broad targets, such as the European Union (EU) objective to reduce CO_2 emissions by 80–95% by 2050, compared with 1990. A key area for the future growth of flying could be access to sustainably produced biofuel for aircraft, and the extent to which biofuel can be produced. Long-term CO_2 targets will probably only be achieved by a combination of technological development, operational improvements, the introduction of sustainable alternative fuels and the use of market mechanisms such as emissions trading, in which aviation buys CO_2 reductions from sectors where the cost of reducing CO_2 emissions is lower than it is for aviation. If emissions of greenhouse gases (GHGs) are to be reduced to levels deemed acceptable by organizations such as the Intergovernmental Panel on Climate Change (IPCC) then aviation faces a particularly tough challenge; failure to reach targets through technology, trading, etc., could result in demand control, with access to flying rationed in some as yet undetermined way. Of course, one consequence is that the real cost of flying is likely to increase. Sustainable Aviation in the UK has published a road map of how the UK aviation industry perceives the future trend in CO_2 emissions (Sustainable Aviation, 2008, 2012 see also references). Road maps with similar overall features but different conclusions have been published by other organizations, including the UK's Committee on Climate Change (2009) and, on a global basis, the International Air Transport Association (IATA, 2008).

Aviation's non-CO_2 emissions and trade-offs

The climate impact of aviation is complicated by other impacts at cruise altitude that are unique to aviation. These have been reviewed by the IPCC (Penner *et al.*, 1999). Unfortunately, although there has been some improvement in understanding since publication of this IPCC report, a clear picture has not yet emerged. The main non-CO_2 impacts associated with aviation are related to NO_x (produced by the interaction of nitrogen and oxygen in the air passing through the engine), condensation trails (contrails) and cirrus cloud formation (related to water vapour emissions). There is a lower level of understanding of the chemical and physical processes involved in these non-CO_2 impacts than there is of CO_2 impacts, and there is currently no consensus on a metric that accounts for their very different lifetimes and which would allow the impacts of each to be expressed on an 'apples to apples' basis. As a result, there is still

considerable uncertainty on how to account for their effects on climate change.

The effect on climate of aircraft emissions of NO_x at cruise altitudes is linked to chemical changes resulting in increases in ozone concentration, which at cruise altitudes leads to a warming effect. Ozone also leads to the destruction of methane, a GHG gas, which reaches cruise altitudes by diffusion from ground sources such as agriculture. Methane is a very potent GHG and thus there are opposing warming and cooling effects of NO_x emissions from aircraft. Current opinion tends to favour a net warming effect. As ozone has a shorter life than methane, the warming effect of increased ozone is concentrated around the areas of high aviation activity – northern mid latitudes with concentrations over North America, Europe and Japan and China, whereas cooling from the destruction of methane is more widely spread around the global atmosphere.

Many of the measures being developed to reduce CO_2 emissions will also lead to reductions in other emissions. Progress is being made in the design of engines that emit less NO_x, in parallel with improvements in fuel efficiency. Contrail formation could be reduced or avoided by adopting different flight patterns, in particular lower cruise altitudes. However, this could have the perverse effect of increasing CO_2 emissions. Because of the different nature of non-CO_2 emissions and their impacts, these emissions should probably be addressed separately from CO_2 emissions and on an individual basis, rather than be expressed and treated as CO_2-equivalent emissions. Local and global regulators face a challenge to give clear guidance on whether to optimize gains in fuel efficiency and CO_2 emissions, or to concentrate on noise, which continues to be a major nuisance to communities living under airport flight paths, or, indeed, to focus on emissions of NO_x, which has impacts on both climate and local air quality.

Shipping – CO_2 and sulfur dioxide (SO_2) emissions

According to the second greenhouse gas study by the International Maritime Organization

(IMO, 2009), shipping is estimated to have emitted in total 1046 million tonnes of CO_2 in 2007, of which 870 million tonnes originated from international shipping. These figures are similar to the global emissions from aviation, at around 3% of total global emissions from all sources. As an illustration, the CO_2 emissions attributable to a week's cruise holiday for an individual are similar to those of a return long-haul flight.

However, the picture for shipping is complicated by the relatively high level of sulfur emissions. It has been estimated that toxic SO_2 emitted by burning bunker fuel accounted for the deaths of an estimated 60,000 people worldwide in 2001 through cancer and heart and lung disease (Isomaki and Pettay, 2011). A clean-up, which is in hand, would thus indirectly save many lives. From 1 January 2012, and as a result of mandatory measures approved by the IMO, the global limit on marine fuel sulfur content has been reduced from 4.5 to 3.5%, a limit that a good proportion of bunker fuel supplies have difficulty in meeting. Sometime between 2020 and 2025 the limit is to come down to just 0.5%. Already, in the designated emission control areas (ECAs) of the Baltic Sea, North Sea and along the North American coastline, the sulfur limit has dropped to 1% and, by 2015, it is due to be cut to just 0.1%. By comparison with the current amount of sulfur in shipping fuel, there is little sulfur in aviation fuel and this is limited to 0.3% by weight, with most airline fuel having around 0.05% (Penner et al., 1999).

Sulfur pollution from the fast-growing cruise industry also helps create clouds by providing tiny seeds around which droplets form. Clouds have a cooling effect because sunlight 'bounces' off their tops. Enforcement of the IMO measures might not only make it more difficult to reduce the CO_2 emissions from the shipping sector, it might also indirectly increase the net global warming effect from shipping – by almost 50% according to some estimates (for example Fuglestevdt et al., 2009; Isomaki and Pettay, 2010). Indirectly, it could also increase CO_2 emissions because of the increased energy consumption required to remove the sulfur at refineries.

While aviation and shipping both face challenges to reduce their CO_2 emissions, one major difference is that while shipping could turn, for example, to liquefied natural gas as a fuel (Fuglestevdt et al., 2011) in order to reduce sulfur emissions and introduce opportunities for more energy-efficient technology, aviation is bound to the use of kerosene for the foreseeable future. Although hydrogen is an alternative for aviation, its use is predicated by uncertainty over the climate impact of cirrus clouds generated by aircraft and not least by the infrastructure requirements. This is largely because of energy density – aircraft could fly on hydrogen but the volumetric requirement for liquid hydrogen is about four times that for kerosene; although demonstration flights have taken place, the use of hydrogen as an aircraft fuel is not foreseen at this time.

Emissions trading

While emissions of CO_2 from developed countries belonging to national inventories are covered by the Kyoto Protocol of 1997, those from developing countries are subject to less control. International emissions arising from shipping and air travel between nations are not included under Kyoto. ICAO and IMO are facing the challenge of controlling and reducing such emissions. These are probably the only two major sectors of commercial activity where CO_2 emissions are growing, and both face the challenge of trade-offs with other emissions that have climate impacts. The general political consensus is that some form of global trading scheme offers the best option for long-term management. This would involve a 'cap and trade' system in which emissions from aviation (and shipping, probably through a separate system) are capped and allocated to registered carriers (aviation and shipping companies), and any emissions above individual company caps could be offset by purchase of reductions in emissions from other sectors, where emission reductions can be achieved at lower cost than in aviation or shipping. The European Emissions Trading Scheme (EU ETS) provides the best-developed example of such a scheme and it has been planned to include aviation – all carriers flying to and from EU airports – in it from 1 January 2012. However, this has led to challenges from non-European aviation bodies, including those in the USA and China. In the face of a threatened international withdrawal, the European airline associations have said the scheme must apply to all airlines, regardless of origin, or to none. European airlines have demanded that auction revenues be used by states to fund clean technology investment, particularly in developing alternative sustainable fuels. Thus, as this chapter is written, there is considerable uncertainty as to the long-term inclusion of aviation in the EU ETS. Over the last few years, emissions trading has also been advocated as a mechanism for allowing the access of shipping to CO_2 reductions (Faber *et al.*, 2010) and, while trading is considered the most likely option, various market approaches for shipping have been discussed (Kågeson, 2011).

Regulation and reduction of the climate impact from aviation and shipping

Both shipping and aviation are global industries involving the transport of goods and people between nations. As indicated above, CO_2 emissions from domestic shipping and aviation are both accounted for through national CO_2 inventories, but both industries face similar problems in coming to terms with international emissions. The chance to overcome the resistance among leading developing nations such as China and India to the idea of worldwide market-based schemes for shipping and aviation is crucially dependent on the ability to agree on such measures. Those who drafted the Kyoto Protocol clearly failed to foresee the complexity of implementing the CBDR principle (Common but Differentiated Responsibility, a constitutive principle in the United Nations Framework Convention on Climate Change).[1] What has happened since the Rio Declaration of 1992 and the Kyoto Protocol shows that the legal interpretation of CBDR is subject to dispute. In 1997, the USA had already refused to take on binding obligations unless key developing nations also took similar steps. Conversely, states such as China, Brazil, India and Saudi Arabia maintain that the Protocol restricts the enforcement of binding obligations to developed countries.

The more recent Copenhagen Accord of 2009 does not deal specifically with emissions from the aviation and maritime sectors. However, one objective of the Accord is to raise 100 billion US dollars a year by 2020 to address the needs of developing countries. Potentially, this could partially be achieved by contributions from market-based mechanisms in the maritime and aviation sectors (Faber *et al.*, 2010; Kågeson, 2011). However, this issue is not yet anywhere near a final decision. The task of introducing a market-based instrument in the shipping sector remains primarily a matter for IMO, and in the aviation sector for ICAO. Industry groups such as IATA and SEAaT (Shipping Emissions Abatement and Trading) will also play an important role.

Trade-offs

The environmental impacts of aviation through noise and emissions with GHG effects provide a vivid illustration of the challenges faced by regulators. The noise impact is local and is immediately felt by those close to airports who, as a result, encourage their political representatives to bring in stringent noise controls. These noise controls lead to manufacturers developing further noise-control engineering which, in turn, is often achieved at the expense of weight on the aircraft and of options that could improve fuel efficiency and lead to reduced climate impact. While those living around airports may have a general interest in climate impact, the CO_2 impact is global and is not as immediately apparent to residents around airports. There is an argument that reducing aircraft movements will reduce both of these impacts, but the overall demand for aviation continues to rise and, thus, regulators are faced with the trade-off dilemma and the knowledge that different political constituencies will express different demands.

Shipping is faced with a different trade-off between the climate impact of the CO_2 emissions and the 'masking' effect of the sulfur emissions. Some might argue that it makes sense from the climate aspect to retain a high level of sulfur in marine fuel but, clearly, the health effects and the potential of sulfur emissions to lead to other effects such as acid rain confirm that partially neutralizing one impact with another is not really feasible.

Looking ahead

The subsectors of the aviation industry in the UK have suggested that the UK industry is capable of reducing its CO_2 emissions to 2005 levels by 2050 (Sustainable Aviation, 2008, 2012). This has been challenged by the UK Committee on Climate Change (2009), but is supported by the position of IATA which has indicated that global aircraft emissions of CO_2 can be halved by 2050 (IATA, 2008) – including trading – compared with 2005. The UK is, however, a relatively mature market for aviation compared with countries such as India and China where more rapid growth could continue for a number of years.

While the pattern of change in the aviation industry varies from country to country, aviation continues to grow globally. In 2004, the total scheduled traffic carried by the airlines of the 188 contracting states of ICAO amounted to almost 1890 million passengers and some 38 million tonnes of freight. The overall passenger/freight/mail tonne-kilometres performed showed an increase of some 13% over 2003.

All this while, the aerospace industry has been driving technological advance in a wide variety of fields. The great breakthroughs in materials science and technology, electronics and computer sciences are inextricably reflected in the possibilities of air travel. No one can accurately predict the future, but it does seem that air travel will be around for a long time, even if the cost goes up significantly and the aircraft we fly look different. In Europe and North America, aviation is approaching maturity as an industry, and predictions of growth are much lower than for other parts of the world, such as India and China. It is these areas that will have the major input into aviation's worldwide impact on the climate. No doubt, as airport numbers and other infra-structure grow, these areas will also experience local issues such as noise. They will also play a vital role in the development of an international framework of regulation through ICAO, the UN body that picks up responsibility for aviation, in particular noise standards and the

impact on climate change of international flights (as already noted, CO_2 emissions from domestic flights are included in national inventories, under the Kyoto Agreement). Progress in ICAO has historically been slow, but there are signs that the key nations are engaged in finding appropriate ways to address the problem, including emissions trading.

Conclusion

The development of commercial shipping and aviation has made the world a smaller place. After the Second World War, the development of international air networks brought access to world travel within the grasp of a wider range of people. But it was deregulation and the rapid development of low-cost carriers in the last decades of the 20th century, coupled with growing prosperity, that really made a difference to access, such that today it is estimated that some 50% of people in the UK fly at least once a year and that a growing proportion are leisure travellers. One reputable estimate for March 2009 was a global total of 2.38 million flights for the month, offering 289.8 million seats. This, of course, still means that a significant proportion of people in developed countries, and the vast majority in less developed economies, do not have access to aviation.

Aviation has promoted international trade through bringing producers and purchasers together across the globe. Video conferencing and better telecommunications may substitute for a lot of air travel, but there is a strong conviction that if you wish to 'cut a deal', politically or in business, then eye-to-eye contact is necessary. Indeed, it may be that there is a rebound effect from communication technology that sparks the need for direct contact. It can be argued that better face-to-face communication between government representatives has brought benefits in political understanding. One undoubted benefit to people has been the opening up of the world of tourism and the possibility of visiting friends and relatives. Many of these visits have resulted from the migration of individuals and families to take up new opportunities; a process which will continue, and create ongoing demand for air transport. This opening up of the world has led to an ever-growing list of tourism destinations and, from the UK, remarkable growth in 'long-haul' tourism.

Tourism and aviation are likely to continue to grow globally for the foreseeable future, and the challenge is to continue to develop in a responsible and sustainable way, in which the benefits to tourists and local communities are balanced against any undesirable impacts. As identified above, the main environmental issue for transport in general is the climate impact. Programmes are underway in the UK (Sustainable Aviation, 2008, 2012) and by IATA (2009) which have set out relevant and ambitious climate goals, along with ways in which these can be reached. Responsibility in this area could be identified as a reduction in the net impact on the climate. This is likely to be achieved through a combination of aircraft and operational improvements, and emissions trading and sustainable alternatives to fossil-derived kerosene as fuel.

The climate problem is clearly shared by the shipping sector (see, for example, Gilbert et al., 2010) but this has different critical aspects. There is the potential to improve technology and to use alternative fuels such as liquefied natural gas, and also the potential for new technology. The shipping sector has been much slower than the aviation sector to begin to seek long-term solutions which, as with aviation, will have to be largely global in nature. This slow awakening may have resulted from lack of public pressure on the sector, in contrast with the widespread comments from some sections of the media and not-for-profit organizations over the last 1–15 years on the impact of aviation.

We can all predict the future based on our own current knowledge, but it is highly likely that any prediction that is correct is at least partly fortuitous. One thing is sure, that the next decade will not see a decline in public, scientific and regulatory interest in the climate impact of shipping and aviation.

Note

1 In view of the different contributions to global environmental degradation, states have common but differentiated responsibilities. The developed countries acknowledge the responsibility that they bear in the international pursuit of sustainable development in view of the pressures their societies place on the global environment and of the technologies and financial resources they command.

References

Button, K. (2012) Air transport in Europe and the environmental challenges of the transport market. In: Leslie, D. (ed.) *Tourism Enterprises and the Sustainability Agenda across Europe.* Ashgate, Farnham, UK, pp. 35–50.

Calder, S. (2002) *No Frills: The Truth behind the Low-cost Revolution in the Skies.* Virgin Books, London.

Committee on Climate Change (2009) *Meeting the UK Aviation Target – Options for Reducing Emissions to 2050.* Committee on Climate Change, London.

Faber, J., Markowska, A., Eyring, V., Cionni, I. and Solstad, E. (2010) *A Global Maritime Emissions Trading System: Design and Impacts on the Shipping Sector, Countries and Regions.* CE Delft, The Netherlands.

Fuglestevdt, J., Bernsten, T., Eyring, V., Isaksen, I., Lee, D.S. and Sausen, R. (2009) Shipping emissions: from cooling to warming of climate – and reducing impacts on health. *Environmental Science and Technology* 43, 9057–9062.

Gilbert, P., Bows, A. and Starkey, R. (2010) *Shipping and Climate Change: Scope for Unilateral Action.* Sustainable Consumption Unit, University of Manchester, UK.

Gittell, J.H. (2003) *The Southwest Airlines Way.* McGraw-Hill, New York.

Heppenheimer, T.A. (1995) *Turbulent Skies: The History of Commercial Aviation.* John Wiley, New York.

IATA (2008) *IATA Technology Road Map Summary.* International Air Transport Association, Geneva, Switzerland/Montreal, Canada. Available at: http://www.iata.org/SiteCollectionDocuments/Documents/IATATechnologyRoadmapsummary.pdf (accessed 5 April 2012).

IATA (2009) *Aviation and Climate Change: Pathway to Carbon-neutral Growth in 2020.* International Air

Transport Association, Geneva, Switzerland/Montreal, Canada. Available at: http://www.iata.org/SiteCollectionDocuments/AviationClimateChange_PathwayTo2020_email.pdf (accessed 5 April 2012).

ICAO (2000) *Airline Traffic and Load Factors Highest Ever in 2000*. ICAO Press release PIO 14/2000. International Civil Aviation Organization, Montreal, Canada. Available at: http://legacy.icao.int/icao/en/nr/2000/pio200014_e.pdf (accessed 5 April 2012).

ICAO (2012) Aircraft Noise, Environment Branch, Air Transport Bureau, International Civil Aviation Organization, Montreal, Canada. Available at: http://legacy.icao.int/env/noise.htm (accessed 5 April 2012).

IMO (2009) *The Second IMO Greenhouse Gas Study*. International Maritime Organization, London.

Isomaki, R. and Pettay, E. (2011) *Ships, Sulphur and Climate*. Into Publishing, Helsinki.

Kågeson, P. (2011) *Applying the Principle of Common but Differentiated Responsibility to the Mitigation of Greenhouse Gases from International Shipping*. CTS Working Paper 2011:5, Centre for Transport Studies, Stockholm.

Penner, J.E., Lister, D.H., Griggs, D.J., Dokken, D.J. and McFarland, M. (eds) (1999) *Aviation and the Global Atmosphere: A Special Report of IPCC Working Groups I and III in Collaboration with the Scientific Assessment Panel to the Montreal Protocol on Substances that Deplete the Ozone Layer*. Published for the Intergovernmental Panel on Climate Change by Cambridge University Press, Cambridge, UK.

Sustainable Aviation (2008) *Sustainable Aviation CO$_2$ Road Map*. Available at: http://www.sustainableaviation.co.uk/wp-content/uploads/sa-road-map-final-dec-08.pdf (accessed 5 April 2012).

Sustainable Aviation (2012) *Sustainable Aviation CO$_2$ Road Map*. Available at: http://www.sustainableaviation.co.uk (accessed 23 August 2012).

Sutter, J. and Spenser, J. (2006) *Creating the World's First Jumbo Jet and Other Adventures from a Life in Aviation*. Smithsonian Books, Washington, DC.

US Centennial of Flight Commission (2012) History of Flight. Available at: http://www.centennialofflight.gov/essay_cat/8.htm (accessed 5 April 2012).

4 The Consumers of Tourism

David Leslie
Freelance Researcher and Consultant

Introduction

A key question in any discourse on responsible tourism (RT) is what do we mean by responsible? – and who exactly is responsible? Are tourists responsible for the choices they make, or (and) for the impacts/consequences of those choices? In what sense are/can tourists be responsible?

Addressing these questions brings to the fore ethical and moral considerations, and raises substantive issues – not least because discussion would ultimately lead us to ask whether tourist consumption is in itself 'wrong'. If it is, then much tourism and tourism-related consumption would be unsupportable. To take two simple though perhaps not obvious examples: the purchase of cosmetics for the holiday (e.g. sunblock or waterproof make-up) which have involved animal testing might be considered unethical; or visiting a destination in anticipation of opportunities for sexual engagements may well be considered immoral. These are areas that have been the focus of some debate: for example, on ethical tourism (see Jenkins, 2002) and on themes of the moralization of tourism (see Butcher, 2003). The goal of 'ethical' or 'principled' behaviour by tourists would seem to create limitations or pressures on their behaviour in some form: for example, supporting local community involvement, equitable sharing of economic benefits,

purchasing local products, not taking advantage and so forth. Based on such criteria, we can say that there are ethical tourists who take pains to display 'more responsible behaviour' (Scheyvens, 2002, p. 244).

In effect, to be responsible as a tourist suggests, first, some consideration for the destination locality, including the local community, which in the first instance invariably means concern for the physical environment. As is clear on the web site of responsibletravel. com, this simply means holidays that care about the local community, their culture and their environment. Why has such concern over tourism destinations arisen? A particularly germane perspective is that:

> The everyday environment needed for subsistence presents no problems; it is only the environment for Sundays or holidays which becomes problematical. The environment becomes a luxury good; its value increases (to use Inglehart's terminology) because of 'post materialist' concerns. (Martínez-Alier, 1995, p. 4)

Secondly, to have concern over what one is purchasing, for example – as in fair-trade goods or recycled products – is considered environmentally friendly behaviour. Practitioners of such behaviours are seen to be responsible consumers; this leads us to green consumerism. As Bergin-Seers and Mair

(2009) suggest, a greater focus on green consumerism could lead to greater interest in being green tourists, i.e. responsible tourists.

To explore such issues further is the focus of the following discussion. However, we will begin by considering briefly the rise of green consumerism, which is particularly pertinent in that if there are green consumers, then logically, there are green tourists; as such, the greening of consumer purchasing lays a potential foundation, and target markets, for RT and related initiatives. Following on from this we then bring into contention the question of whether consumers are actually interested in and concerned over such (responsible) environmental matters as the impact of tourism on destination environments and on local communities and, more generally, in the negative impacts associated with overseas holidays. This is addressed primarily through discussion of the outcome of surveys, but also with reference to supplier views of tourists' interest in what we can call 'responsible practices'. Next, we ask whether tourists are interested in 'responsible' opportunities in the marketplace and what might be the level of demand for such options? Then, having found that such demand is limited, we question why that is the case, including a consideration of the opportunity for RT. Finally, given that demand for RT is limited and that there is little evident interest in responsible behaviour, we ask what could be done to influence behaviour. This brings us to consider the questions of why people go on holiday in the first place, and how less responsible tourists might be influenced to behave more responsibly.

Green Consumerism

Green consumerism arose in the 1980s (Elkington, 1987), a time of sustained economic growth in postindustrial countries which witnessed substantial development of green organizations such as WWF and Greenpeace (Millman, 1989; Leslie, 1991). This is a logical progress following on from the rise in attention to and concerns over environmental matters in Western societies in the 1960s and 1970s (Krippendorf, 1987). The increase in green consumers in the 1980s affirms that in the

'good times' there is a shift towards quality-of-life issues and attractive environments; such concerns arise in times of prosperity once material needs are met (Martínez-Alier, 1995). The 1980s also witnessed the development by travel organizations of more 'sensitive forms of tourism' (Millman, 1989, p. 277). Conversely, some commentators argue that the growth in interest in the environment in the late 1980s was a fad; evidence supporting that stance is the drop by 11% of people saying that environmental issues would influence their purchase patterns (Beioley, 1995). However, such a decline is more likely attributable to the weaker UK economy (and across Europe) of the mid 1990s compared with the late 1980s (thus affirming the Martínez-Alier point above). Even so, there has been sustained growth in demand for green products and produce until recently, with the late 2000s showing a slight decline as recessionary times have returned. But, as KeyNote's report (2008) on 'ethical consumerism' suggests, this will pick up again in the 2010s as economic conditions become more favourable. Conversely, a prevailing economic downturn can actually encourage businesses to take actions that can be interpreted as 'going green or greener' (Masero, 2009; WWF, 2011).

By the late 1980s, the environmental agenda expanded to encompass the objectives of sustainable development. As the 1990s unfolded, the political bias shifted to climate change (Leslie, 2009). This bias then developed, with an accent on fossil fuels, energy consumption and greenhouse gases (GHGs) and a correlating increase in attention to sustainable consumption. The objective was to encourage consuming *differently* – i.e. more sustainable products – rather than consuming *less* (Jackson and Michaelis, 2003), a distinctly market/capitalist approach. When one considers that home, travel (including holidays) and food account for 80% of GHG emissions, then the focus on consumption is understandable (SCRT, 2006). But, and given the GHG emissions associated with travel, the raised profile of alternatives to so-called mass tourism is strange to say the least; that is, with the exception of the alternative 'slow tourism'. However, while the green agenda may have expanded, and the emphasis shifted, evidently the profile of green consumers – comparatively older, more affluent and middle class with a bias to women (Mintel, 2007; Han et al., 2009) – has changed little since the 1980s.

As we have green consumers, so we may also have 'green tourists' who display responsible concerns and behaviours. The response in the tourism market to this green agenda has led to the appearance of a range of terms evidencing some degree of product differentiation – alternative, green, sustainable, nature and eco-tourism. These reflect environmental and societal trends of the 1980s and have gained substantial attention in marketing terminology. To an extent, the emergence of these ostensibly responsible forms of tourism appears to be in line with Krutilla's point, made over 40 years ago, that 'the central issue seems to be the problem of providing for the present and future generation the amenities associated with unspoiled natural environments, for which the market fails to make adequate provision' (Krutilla, 1967, p. 778; cited in Martínez-Alier, 1995, p. 3). To this we should add – with due regard to sustainability and climate change – the caveat of being responsible in the process.

Are Tourists/consumers Interested in 'Responsibility'?

Throughout the 1970s and 1980s, and indeed since then, surveys in postindustrial societies which have in part or in whole addressed environmental matters have consistently found that people generally express concern and support for all manner of environmental initiatives: from conservation measures and protection of endangered species to organic food and, most recently, carbon offsetting. Furthermore, since the early 1980s, concern has grown over the quality of food and animal husbandry. To varying degrees, such environmental concerns are to be found in studies into the attitudes of consumers of tourism, as the following discussion identifies: in *attitude* these are responsible tourists. In fact, surveys of consumers consistently find respondents willing to pay more for what they perceive as more environmentally considerate tourism packages (Wight, 1994; Weiss et al., 1998),

and this has continued over the past decade (Hudson and Ritchie, 2001; Dodds, 2008; Leslie, 2012a).

But in the late 1990s, a downward trend became evident in people's willingness to pay extra for environmental protection and environmentally friendly products, while awareness of companies showing commitment to the environment had only marginally increased. Furthermore 'public sensitivity to environmental problems on holiday/business trips has not increased and is no more of a deterrent to repeat travel than it was previously' (WTTC and IHRA, 1999, p. 7). This trend is noted by Welford et al. (1999, p. 175), who saw 'no great demand from the tourists themselves for the greening of the supply function' (see also Williams and Ponsford, 2009). Also, a major stakeholder in the travel sector asserted: 'Ethics don't interest clients' (Josephides, 2001, p. 3). The same perception was evident in the actions of the Dutch tour operator (TO) TUI Nederland, which 'stopped offering sustainable tourism packages because of a lack of demand' (Wijk and Persoon, 2006, p. 383; see also Holland, Chapter 9). However, while there is now growing demand for green consumer goods and growing interest in the greener alternatives to sunlust-style holidays, the problem, still, is the limited extent of such demand. Goodwin and Francis' (2003) study found that tourists expressed concern over the loss of local culture and affirmed the importance of the quality of the environment. They found that the proportion of guests prepared to pay extra for conserving the destination environment was nearly 50%. Thus, with all other things being equal, TOs with clearly RT practices would gain business over those without. That TOs are perceived to have a responsibility for the local environment and culture is an outcome of many studies (see Lim, 1996; Woolford, 2001; Choat, 2004), and evidences continuity (e.g. see Mintel, 2005, 2007).

Attributing responsibility to other agencies is also commonly found in consumer surveys (see Defra, 2007, 2009). Often it is the government that is considered to be responsible for destination localities, maintaining their attractiveness and ensuring that they do not become overcrowded with tourists (Ryerson

University, 2010). However, in the same study two-thirds of the tourists surveyed also considered that tourists should pay towards protecting sites such as the coral reefs. Many consumers also say that they are more likely to book a holiday with a company that promotes a responsible policy that is seen to be beneficial to the environment and the communities therein (Mintel, 2007); such responses, including demand for environmentally friendly products, are also manifest in international surveys (Davies, 2007). Operators with such a policy include MyTravel, Thomson, Thomas Cook and First Choice. Another such TO is the Travel Foundation, which introduced carbon offsetting schemes and promotes sustainable tourism initiatives. The Travel Foundation encourages its customers to donate to the Foundation – but their efforts have been criticized as little more than tokenism (see responsibleTravel.com). Such perceptions of tokenism are supported by other studies: for example, while a majority of those surveyed in one study indicate awareness of what carbon offsetting is (Webb, 2010) and a willingness to pay for it (Bremner, 2009), very few actually do so (CAA, 2010). As Sagoff (1988) noted:

> As citizens, individuals may support or vote in favour of environmental initiatives, but in the role of consumer, they may not give much thought to such factors. (Cited in Blamey, 1997)

A further complication arises from the assumption that participants in these surveys share the same understanding of terms such as 'responsible' or 'sustainable' (Williams and Ponsford, 2009; Miller et al., 2010). An ABTA (Association of British Travel Agents) Convention Special Report conducted in November 2005 to explore tourists' opinions on travel and the environment found that there is little evidence of interest in the idea of RT, and that it is unlikely to be a concern when choosing a holiday. Similarly, research done in 2007 found that 67% of British holidaymakers do not think about the impact their trips could have on the environment – whether they are in the Maldives or Caribbean or on the Mediterranean coast – sunlust still holds sway. Thus, the onus is very much on the TO to produce attractive options based on concerns

such as RT, although not necessarily marketed as such (see Mintel, 2005). But there is evidence of some interest: for example Sustainable Travel International (STI) in 2010 had over 230,000 visits to its web site every month (Dolnicar et al., 2010). Even so, as Mintel (2005) found, while surveys suggest that there is growing interest in the tourism market for RT this is very much passive, and consumers still view cost, weather and quality of facilities as the paramount considerations in their destination choice.

Demand for 'Responsible Holidays'

That some consumers are taking interest in 'responsible' holidays is evident from Mintel's (2007) research which suggests that 'green' travellers are something of a rapidly expanding minority. According to this study, in 2006 there were over 1 million responsible or ecotourism holidays, which accounts for approximately 1.2% of the total travel market. Mintel predicted that growth would increase by 25% per year, attaining approximately 3.4% of the total travel market by 2011 (see also Deloitte, 2007). A subsequent study by SNV (2009) found that demand for RT has increased as a result of consumers seeking more authentic experiences as well as being influenced by green issues. But due to the recession, these responsible tourists, while still travelling, were also seeking lower cost trips (Kuoni, 2011), possibly therefore going to long-established resorts, and thereby – perhaps ironically – being effectively more responsible for that reason. In contrast, the take-up of ecotourism packages demonstrates that the comparatively affluent in society are still prepared to meet the price. But a note of caution is that such holiday packages may also be attractive to a variety of other consumers and thus their take-up is not necessarily a signifier of the environmental values and attitudes of the purchasers.

There also are, and will continue to be, tourists seeking a holiday on the basis that they wish to have a learning experience. Further, the global trend is reported to be towards 'social and environmental responsibility, social interaction, authentic travel experiences and fair trade practice' and 'trade up for sustainability' (WTM, 2008, p. 5; Kuoni, 2011). This is indeed a trend, but one limited in demand and likely to materialize in a commodified form at comparatively high cost – e.g. ecochic (see Buckley, Chapter 6). It is also potentially at odds with KeyNote's (2008) study into the 'Green and Ethical Consumer' which found that over 50% of participants did not consider the carbon footprint of a company, or whether it was eco-friendly, to be an influential factor in their holiday choice, and found some degree of ambivalence overall regarding ethical matters. These outcomes are also evident in Mintel's (2010) study involving air travellers, which found little interest in what the airline companies are doing about their GHGs and also about schemes to offset carbon emissions; TravelMole's (2007) survey of international tourists gave similar results. The decisive factor for most tourists as to who to fly with is price. Further, there is little evidence that people are flying less or are inclined to do so (see Defra, 2009), in spite of the efforts of organizations to encourage people to take holidays that do not include air travel (for example, Defra, 2006) and the promotion of 'slow tourism' (Leslie, 2012a).

Tourist surveys into environmental concerns show similar results to those which are to be found in any general survey into popular consumer goods, and also in the growing demand for environmentally friendly products. For example, Defra's (2009) survey into attitudes and environmental behaviour found that 58% of respondents agreed that if the government did more they would do more. This evidences little significant change to outcomes of their earlier surveys and affirms the 'I will if you will' syndrome (see SCRT, 2006). What is considered ethical consumption – fair trade, organic, freedom foods, sustainable fish – and within that context the use of energy efficient lighting and appliances – increased above general household expenditure over the period 1999–2005, but even then accounts for only a small percentage of general household spend. Interestingly, consumers selecting purchases on the basis of company reputation showed little increase over the same period (Anon., 2007). Perhaps a false dawn given the ongoing recession, but the Green Brands Survey 2010 (Romero and Percifield, 2010)

found that the majority of consumers are willing to spend more on green products in the coming year and that this trend is being driven by consumer perception and purchasing behaviour. Again, we identify a gap between what consumers say they will or are likely to do and what they actually do. This is particularly clear in the case of surveys, which find that respondents support buying local and/or organic foods, but when sales forecasts are based on such responses they are found to be woefully high when compared with actual sales. As England (2010) opines, people seek to respond in terms of what they think they ought to do, not what they actually do.

Overall, we find that just as there are varying shades of green consumer, equally we have varying degrees of responsible tourists. Recent research (SNV, 2009) into responsible behaviour and tourists identified four categories. There are 'unethical tourists', who just wish to relax on their holiday and not be concerned with ethical issues; 'apathetic tourists', who do not have any particular response to ethical holidays; 'conscientious tourists', who try to learn about the local cultures they visit; and 'ethical tourists', who are highly concerned about ethical issues while holidaying. This brings to our attention to what the opportunities are for those seeking more RT. Although discussed in a variety of contexts in Part 3 of this book, some consideration to the supply is pertinent here.

Opportunity for Responsible Tourism

Ecotourism offers such as nature or soft adventure tours may (should) include attention to conservation and respect for local people and customs (see Leslie, Chapter 2). Offers that do this potentially influence the tourist's environmental behaviour directly, as well as socially demonstrating RT on the part of the provider. Indeed, Orams (1968, p. 48) argues that in the mix of management strategies involved in ecotourism, particular emphasis should be placed on education to 'encourage a transition from a passive to an active role on the part of the ecotourist', and that 'ecotourism has a further role in encouraging a transition from more visitor enjoyment to more environmentally sound human behaviour' – that is, *responsible* behaviour.

There are also opportunities for tourists themselves to develop their understanding of and participate in what can be considered RT holidays. Perhaps the most obvious example of this is the British Trust for Conservation Volunteers, which offers opportunities to combine a holiday with working on conservation projects. More explicit in terms of RT are Voluntary Service Overseas (VSO) and GAP Adventures, initiatives which serve to illustrate how organizations can help to reduce economic leakages and promote community benefits by informing and educating tourists on local customs, and providing packages which do not exploit the environment or local economy (see TOI, 2011). The VSO organization has introduced the 'WorldWise' campaign, which promotes the message that there is more to a holiday than can be gained from staying within the confines of a hotel, and urges tourists to explore local markets, crafts and produce to benefit local people. The second initiative, GAP Adventures, which gained 85,000 customers in 2008 (Tip, 2009), promotes trips designed to benefit the local community. For example, home stays are available for tourists in the Amazon through cooperation with the local community, and this initiative has benefited local economies, including the building of a new school (Tip, 2009). Another 'greening' initiative is 'Leave No Trace' (LNT), a global programme which aims to persuade 'outdoors tourists' to reduce their environmental impacts (Dolnicar *et al.*, 2010).

This theme of providers seeking to influence customers to be more responsible consumers/tourists through promoting environmentally friendly behaviour has been recognized as another dimension of the environmental performance of tourism enterprises (see Leslie, 2009). The idea is that visitors are encouraged to adopt responsible behaviour by increasing their awareness of local environment initiatives – for example by saving water, or contributing to a local conservation project. However, while the majority of tourism enterprises consider environmental issues important, comparatively few consider them a priority. It has been argued that instituting accreditation for the introduction

of environmental management systems could influence responsible demand, and that there is some evidence of willingness on the part of tourists to pay a premium for such accredited operations (Leslie, 2012a). But as Leidner (2004) and Leslie (2012b) note, many enterprises do not consider there to be demand for 'going green', which obviously influences the availability of opportunities for tourists to select what might be termed 'responsible operations' (see Buckley, Chapter 6; Holland, Chapter 9; Spenceley and Rylance, Chapter 10; Zientara, Chapter 12; also Leslie, 2009).

Nevertheless there are opportunities, and increasingly so, for example: the company Travelroots seeks to create packages that are based on locally owned accommodation and use local guides – 'Organic places to stay' (Moss, 2008); and the promotion of guest house style accommodation operations across the UK and mainland Europe – such as Eco. Retreats, 'eco' places to stay and 'biohotels' (see Winkler, 2008). The latter is a good example of social marketing (see Dinan and Sargeant, 2000), which equally applies to destination areas such as wildlife parks which are marketed to 'green' consumers/responsible tourists. However, as identified by Frame and Newton (2007), in many circumstances the extent to which social marketing campaigns are effective and successful is unclear. This is equally applicable to ecolabels, whether attached to a holiday package or to specific enterprise (see Font and Buckley, 2001; Leslie, 2012c). Social marketing can be taken a step further, as Hwang *et al.* (2005) show, by involving visitors more in the destination environment (in this case, a national park) through interpretation and education, which increases visitor satisfaction and can significantly increase their attachment to the locality, thereby engendering a sense of 'place'. These authors argue that the aim should be to develop appropriately scaled tourism supply rather than to focus on the infrastructure and access routes. This approach also emerges in the Ryerson University study (2010; see also Tubb, 2003). Thus, the argument goes, responsible behaviour on the part of tourists can be influenced through education and codes of conduct (see Genot, 1995; Bramwell and Lane, 2000).

But how sustained is the effect and to what extent is it restricted to the chosen destination locale? What is inescapable here is that such social marketing is targeting in one way or another those tourists who are 'ecocentric' (Uysal *et al.*, 1994; Wurzinger and Johansson, 2006; Ballantyne *et al.*, 2010). This does not mean though that they are prepared to 'rough it' by using limited serviced accommodation, showering less' and so forth. Also, though the target market empathizes with the message, are ecotourists really any more responsible than 'other' tourists? For example, ecotourists predominantly fly from the 'west' to exotic locations via jumbo jets and secondary flights. Is this responsible?

Promotion of ecotourism also addresses potential tourists who might not necessarily be responsible in their general lifestyle behaviours. However, as Uysal *et al.* (1994) argued, the least ecocentric are most likely to be on a cruise ship, leading to speculation that the substantial growth in demand for cruise holidays is a counterpoint to the argument that there is a disproportional increase in the number of ecocentric tourists. As Hemmel-skamp and Brockman (1997) identified, attitudes towards environmental aspects and ecolabels are influenced by different factors: for example, consumer satisfaction is driven by personal needs and desires, and by identification with a particular lifestyle. Not surprisingly, therefore, some customers/tourists expect tourism enterprises (including TOs) to be responsible for their own environments. There are also doubts regarding the value of ecolabels. As Sasidharan *et al.* argued (2002, p. 171) 'no conclusive evidence exists to support [the ecolabelling agencies'] assertive claims that ecolabels improve the environment'. This is an argument that is furthered by claims of 'greenwashing' (Greenpeace, 2011), as Honey (2002) remarked with reference to tourism companies in Costa Rica, which are greenwashing by offering the same (unaltered) product but adding the 'eco' prefix: 'The only thing green about these places is the dollars they are earning' (A. Becher, a developer of an early certification programme in Costa Rica; cited by Honey, 2002, p. 7). These issues, coupled with the increasing array of such schemes, have led to the abuse of ecolabels

(Budeanu, 2007) and to further questioning of their value, and correlates with research into other areas of ecolabel use: for example, the use of healthy option labels on designated foods has been found to be of little effect in influencing consumer choice or behaviours (University of Hertfordshire *et al.*, 2010). So the promotion value (not to mention the veracity!) of such labelling may be open to question. But, in the context of the enterprise, the adoption of environmentally friendly management and operational practices to reduce environmental impacts and provide opportunities for tourists to opt for more RT enterprises and services must rightly be expected.

Variously labelled opportunities for the tourist seeking a more responsible holiday appear plentiful: alternative, ethical, re-sponsible, nature, eco-; for example, oppor-tunities 'for alternative holidays' are listed in Mann's (2000) *The Community Tourism Guide: Exciting Holidays for Responsible Travellers*, and in the follow-up publication by Pattullo and Minelli (2006), *The Ethical Travel Guide: Your Passport to Exciting Alternative Holidays*. Further expanding the range is a plethora of NEAT (nature-based, ecotourism, adventure tourism) opportunities. As with food labelling, it seems that any company offering an experience in the great outdoors can simply add the word 'ecotourism' to its advert or brochure; whether the holidays live up to the prescribed principles is another matter (Baker, 2005). How many companies really attend to these principles and how much of the ecolabelling is little more than greenwashing (Powell and Ham, 2008)? Also, from the consumer side, there is no definite indicator that a person who opts for an ecotour that has been acclaimed for its manifest practice of the principles of 'ecotourism' is any more of a 'green consumer' than another person booking the same trip. But what does emerge from these so-called niche markets is, as Thake (2009) noted, a shift to the individual – and this generates additional consumption, which is counter to the tenets of sustainability. The Future Laboratory (2010), in a study for Thomson Holidays, argues that by 2030 all holidays will have to take into account sustainability issues and, notably, that it will be the mass market that is key to sustainable travel. The organization's view of 'tomorrow's holidays' appears to be very much based on assumptions that high-tech (computerized) advances in hospitality operations will drive down energy consumption. A downside, of course, is that computer-based systems are not all that green (Greenbiz, 2007). Luckily, according to Lindholdt (1986, p. 6), 'More and more students of literature and culture are coming to acknowledge the negative consequences of technology on people and the environment'.

In effect, dependence on technology is literally a technical fix, and more suited to major stakeholders, and national and international chains with the requisite capital for investment. This is a forecast that holds far more meaning in terms of responsible tourists, as it is a clear steer to promote environmentally friendly holidays in much the same way as other green consumer products. The need for this is additionally manifest in KeyNote's (2010) finding that, of the nearly 90% of people who regularly recycle waste materials, fewer than 50% will do so while away from home. But given that they are in someone else's establishment, they might rightly argue that the onus is on the owners of the enterprise to ensure that the waste arising from guests is recycled, and so forth. KeyNote also found that for approximately one in five persons, the environment gains little if any consideration while away from home. This outcome evidences limited progress in responsibility. Witness Weaver (2005), who argued that for many people the holiday is a temporary escape from the trials and tribulations at home and as such little thought is likely to be given to its impact otherwise. This is perhaps most manifest in the increasing demand for cruise holidays and all-inclusive resorts where customers have little awareness of the impacts (positive or negative) of their holiday choice (see Williams and Ponsford, 2009). One might expect that skiers, given the importance of the environmental conditions to their chosen activity, might be more concerned over such matters, but apparently this is not the case (see Weiss et al., 1998; Hudson and Ritchie, 2001).

The expectation implicit in RT is that reducing energy consumption, waste and pollution, and promoting local community involvement and development is the right way forward – and a way that is supported by tourists who indicate they would like to behave responsibly (as surveys invariably attest). However, this is not the case in practice. In the light of sustainability, climate change and unsustainable consumption, we must ask what can be done to generate more environmentally responsible behaviour. Thus our focus now turns to how to influence consumers who are not otherwise ecocentric to accept some degree of responsibility for the impacts arising from their holiday taking. This leads us, first, to consider why people go on holiday today, and what the key factors are that have a bearing on whether they opt for a responsible holiday.

The Holiday and Factors of Influence

The motivations and determinants of why people go on holiday are well covered in general tourism texts which list, for example, to take a break, to escape for pleasure or thrills, to do something different, or to do something familiar but for an extended period (see Krippendorf, 1987). But what are the underlying drivers of tourism demand? To conform to societal norms is certainly a factor, so too is fashion, so perhaps is to experience something different and, depending on disposable income, the holiday may be seen as a positional good (see Holden, 2005). Fundamentally, though, holiday taking is an outcome of capitalism, a by-product of affluent society; a form of consumption at its most conspicuous. Tourism is an add-on to materialism, and a function of being able to save now in order to spend later. Just as with many other products, consumers want nice places to visit and, for the majority, not too different from home. The holiday is still an essentially short-term experience involving a change of physical environment. In general, tourists do not seek the solitude of landscape and wilderness with little evident presence of others. As the poet Wordsworth aptly captured: 'cataracts and mountains are good occasional society, but they will not do for constant companions' (quoted in Kane, 1999, p. 9). Neither do tourists want to continuously revisit places where 'Everything has been visited, everything [is] known, everything exploited. Beaches are plowed, mountains smoothed and swamps cleaned … . Everywhere there are buildings, everywhere people, everywhere communities, everywhere life' (Tertullian; cited in Kane, 1999). So the desire to move on to a 'new' destination arises – albeit one often very similar in character to the previous one.

What then is the consumer – the tourist – purchasing? Says Britton (1991, p. 465; cited in Hall, 1994, p. 194): '"Tourists" are purchasing the intangible qualities of restoration, status, life-style signifier, release from the constraints of everyday life, or conveniently packaged novelty'. In so doing, many people on holiday will do 'the same type of things as they could do at home' (Holder, 1988, p. 120; see also Shaw et al., 1999); in the process they will often consume more, for example, more food and beverage, water and energy than when at home (see Williams and Ponsford, 2009). But, holidays are also about enjoyment, in part a trade-off against 'good behaviour' at home and in more 'exotic' locations. We can also identify segmentation based on age groupings, as illustrated in the success of packaged hedonistic holidays for the 18–30 bracket (though often more the 18–22 bracket). This reflects wider changes in society over the last two decades, but resonates remarkably with Krippendorf's (1987, p. 33) observation of tourists:

> they 'have a good time' ideology and the 'tomorrow we shall be gone again' attitude set the tone. Responsibility is rejected, egoism rules. And when entire groups of people behave this way the result is bewildering.

Young people in the West have more time and money, and holiday packages are relatively cheaper providing more 'freedom' than that at home. This is well exemplified by the popularity of packages with youngsters from the UK to destinations such as Faliraki, Greece or Malia in Crete – another clubbing resort which witnessed substantial increase in demand after well-publicized sexual activities (Anon., 2003). But their behaviour is not so markedly different from similar gatherings in July in Torquay in the UK. In contrast, for older age groups, 'The all-inclusive resort and cruise has become the

perfect product for the cash-rich and time-poor who, above all else, want to minimise risk' (Tibbott, 2001, p. 15).

In the choice of holiday, price is a major determinant of demand (SNV, 2009). The long-standing practice of many tourists is to save-up for the 'annual holiday' so that, in general, they seek to maximize their spending by opting for comparatively cheaper destinations. As Clobourne (2008) expressed it, this saving of money (rather than of fuel or food) in industrial/postindustrial societies is a precautionary approach to enhance resilience to loss of spending power. As Wright argues, the point of the surplus, i.e. money beyond primary needs, is 'To trade with, show off with, buy power and favours, give ourselves meaning and, yes, a place to stand' (2002, p. 23). But much of what is seen as desirable involves expense (and not necessarily satisfaction) in today's consumer based economies. As Wright (2002: 24) puts it:

> Once basic material needs are met, what really makes people happy are decent relationships: an interesting job. Financial security is important, so that they don't have to worry. But having more stuff isn't.

But just as consumer products are increasingly not made for repair, and while marketers promote 'every home should have one' and 'have it now', so too tourist places are consumed – as so well represented in the slogan 'Been there, done that, got the T-Shirt'. Thus, just as price has an impact on engaging in environmental concerns, as Pearce (2005) argues, so destination choice also ultimately depends on pricing and current exchange rates, and generally is not influenced by green initiatives or promotion of the tenets of RT. Nor are tourists anthropologists or philanthropists: 'few tourists are really interested in anything other than a superficial interpretation of the "the local"', and 'few companies practice an ethic of reciprocity' (Johnston, 2003, p. 117; see also Krippendorf, 1987). Furthermore, Atkins (2010), drawing on his study in popular tourist destinations, reported that he 'met a lot of holiday-makers who scoffed at the idea that they should feel obliged to pay attention to the people and places around them. If tourists are spending their money, that's enough, several people told me', he said (see also Baobab, 2012). Another factor to consider is that holidaying is not only perceived as a 'right' by Western tourists (see Veal 2002; Johnson and Turner, 2003), but also as part of the general pattern of life for the majority in postindustrial societies: not a luxury for the few, but a necessity for all. To this demand we should add the many already travelling, and the many more to follow, as the economies of developing and lesser developed countries continue to grow.

Will these travellers be any more or less responsible in their environmental behaviour and in their choice of holiday opportunity? As the European Union (EU) has stated, there is a need to: 'encourage changes in the behaviour of consumers' (EU, 2004, p. 12), and therefore tourists too. But, as Seabrook notes, 'Purpose-less mobility has now become a basic need for well-to-do people: a busy hither and thither which distracts from the most disagreeable question of all – what is wrong with home, that it can no longer furnish us with delight and satisfaction? (2007, p. 14).

In the light of such a critique, how can the modern day 'golden hordes' be influenced towards engaging in responsible behaviour?

How to Influence Behaviour?

To influence change in the behaviour of people is generally difficult and complex. How individuals or groups respond to any given stimulus is varied, unpredictable and possibly of only short-term duration. What behaviours and attitudes are thought of as the social norms reflect very much the spirit of the times. Even what questions are asked about responsible behaviour reflect the values and attitudes of those who seek to comment and influence that behaviour. In the context of the present discussion, if the reason for urging change is based on reducing cost (i.e. avoiding penalty) then this is a rational decision, but not one that changes behaviour in the sense of persons being 'converted' (i.e. extrinsic versus intrinsic) to what some agency or other may desire. Not surprisingly, and as already noted, we find consumers recycling materials at home, but often making little effort while away from

home; or, perhaps more accurately, they make the effort at home when this is explicitly encouraged and facilitated.

Arguably, therefore, the most effective way to bring about responsible behaviour, certainly in the short term, is through government policy and direct action; for example, the EU has been: 'increasingly seeking to use policy instruments that tap into market dynamics such as taxation, eco-labeling' (Johnson and Turner, 2003, p. 289; Leslie, 2012d). First, a government can legislate – for example, ban an activity (e.g. smoking in public buildings) – but if the ban is lifted the practice will return. The list of such bans over time in many countries is a long one, yet many of the activities banned may well have been the social norm at the time. Secondly, government can regulate, for example regarding pollution, and institute penalties for failure to comply. Thirdly, governments can tax, for example, energy/fuel sources, to discourage consumption. But such a cost increase will often be gradually assimilated and the original intent becomes ineffective. An alternative tax strategy is the 'carrot and stick' approach: higher taxes are placed on what is seen as the least desirable products, behaviours or outcomes, and the lowest taxes on the most desirable – e.g. high petrol consumption cars and hybrid cars; this can work with varying degrees of success (see GFC, 2008). But where a tax is introduced as a penalty to discourage use, then questions arise as to how such tax revenues are used, especially when such a tax is presented as being a positive step for the environment. For example, an environmental tax introduced in the UK realized an estimated revenue of £29 billion, but the £607 million apparent spend on green projects was only a tiny fraction of that revenue (Russell-Walling, 2008). Hence, it is not surprising to find that commentators consider such taxes as the government merely gaining revenue in a different guise – somewhat counterproductive to 'the message' being promoted. Such approaches may work in the home environment where people respond because they have to, but remove that incentive and/or supporting facility and they will more than likely revert to the earlier behaviour pattern. Thus, it is unlikely that responsible practices at home will translate into responsible behaviour while away. More specific to tourism, taxes could be levied to raise funds for conservation, as in the case of the Balearic Islands, where such a tax quickly became known as the 'Balearic ecotax' (Palmer and Riera, 2003). However, the stakeholders on the islands strongly objected to the ecotax, arguing that it would lead to a decline in demand; and ultimately it was dropped. Local governments could also introduce a tourist tax (as did Rome in 2011) applicable to hotels, museums and galleries and put to use for supporting preservation efforts and developing infrastructure. Local governments might introduce campaigns such as the one in Cinque Terra, Venice, to address the problem of the ubiquitous plastic bottles left by tourists. That campaign – promoting branded reusable bottles and branding fountains – successfully reduced the quantity of discarded plastic bottles (Venice Tourist and Information Centre, 2010).

Another approach would be to encourage initiatives such as the voluntary donation scheme of the Tourism and Conservation Partnership in the Lake District National Park of England, which involves the voluntary addition of a nominal sum to a customer's account. Although this has been acclaimed as one of the most successful of such schemes, many enterprises do not participate and many, many tourists decline to have the nominal donation added to their bills (Leslie, 2001). That the majority of visitors do not contribute in this instance reinforces again that while visitors may say in surveys that they are supportive of conservation efforts and willing to pay, the truth is often very different. As the scheme in the Lake District exemplifies, the 'message' needs to be positive, locally relevant, personal and show how taking action is beneficial within the local context. Hence the view that information campaigns need to think more in terms of 'concepts of immediacy, transience and wider societal concerns' (England, 2010, p. 13) if they are to achieve more participation and, further, for such behaviour to become the norm (see Souterton et al., 2011).

Even then, wrapping the message in such terms will not necessarily work, as Jackson et al. (2008) argue. To effect change beyond simple first steps is difficult – for example, eating red meat and consuming dairy products are considered potentially detrimental to one's health, and their production is a contributory factor to climate warming. However, a survey by Downing and Ballantyne (2007) found that, of 12 options relating to beneficial environmental behaviours, the least likely to be adopted was a low-climate impact diet that would substantially reduce red meat and dairy consumption. This is, in itself, perhaps surprising given that factors affecting health are a major influence on behavioural change. But then, 'only 9% of UK population believe climate change will have a significant impact upon them personally' (Downing and Ballantyne, 2007, p. 4). Perhaps this reflects that reiterations of the 'message' can also be counterproductive; as England notes, 'people are becoming resilient to environmental warnings' (2010, p. 12). Even so, Holden (2009, p. 385) says, knowledge of the harmful effects will eventually lead to 'incremental and progressive rather than sudden changes' in tourist behaviours.

As has been well argued, information, while useful, is in itself hardly influential on behavioural change; as Sasidharan et al. commented, 'environmental education of consumers and increasing environmental awareness does not stimulate environmentally responsible behaviour' (2002, p. 172). Cultural/social factors, and indeed habit, as well as opportunity to do a desired action, are all more significant (see Lindholdt, 1998; Levett, 2001; Fedrigo-Fazio et al., 2011; Souterton et al., 2011). Basically, what is required is a shift from extrinsic to intrinsic values: for example switching to low-energy lighting. Other particularly influential factors on behaviour are (older) age, and the presence of young children in the family: both factors are consistently reflected in greater concern over environmental matters (Defra, 2009). However, it is the knowledge that we have, and the beliefs, values and attitudes that we hold, that are most influential in terms of perceptions of responsibility – whether for other members of society, or for environmental matters such as one's personal contribution to climate change, or the inequities in resource usage evident in comparisons of postindustrial societies and lesser developed economies. To effect long-term change towards more responsible behaviours in tourism, it is clear that the approach adopted must be a combination of strategies. Furthermore, it is also clear that the effects of an approach in one context or case will not automatically be replicated in other applications (Souterton et al., 2011). In this, there is a need for champions, people held in high esteem nationally and internationally. But a problem here for RT is that the media have a heavily influential role in promoting destinations, for example through films or reports on where major celebrities go for their holidays, which can be counterproductive to such aims. Irrespective of approach, the strategies adopted must recognise and address barriers such as those most often cited – namely cost, time, convenience and access. There is also the element of mistrust; for example, inaccurate or misleading use of green messages in marketing, commonly termed greenwash, as discussed earlier. This has increased substantially in recent years and, at the same time, so has the number of companies found to be presenting misleading 'green messages' (Dahl, 2010). Similarly, there is the increasing array of ecolabels, which has led to the Global Ecolabel Monitor that has found substantial variance between such ecolabels, and a lack of consistency and criteria (see Ecolabel Index at www.ecolableindex.com).

Conclusion

At the outset of this chapter two questions were raised. First, are there responsible tourists who seek out what they perceive as responsible holidays on the basis of the associated principles, be it an acclaimed ecotour, a stay in an accredited green hotel, or opting for slow travel? Second, are there are tourists who, irrespective of how and where they go, seek to practise environmentally friendly behaviour and thus exhibit responsible behaviour? As established, there is no doubt that consumers of tourism are generally supportive of any RT initiatives, including more responsible operational practices and more equitable participation by local communities. Supportive and willing they may be, but this does not translate into actual practice – as increasing demand bears witness. Further, where do we identify demand for explicitly responsible operations and products? We do not know the make-up of such demand in terms of green consumers (or green tourists, as in the spectrum of unethical to ethical) and those others who see the products as just a particularly attractive opportunity. Equally in the context of traditional (mass) tourism, we know little about the environmental behaviour and associated attitudes of tourists. Indeed, there is little evidence to confirm that they are any less responsible in their behaviour, in their expenditure patterns or in the way that they treat local people. Irrespective of tourist demand, then it is all the more important that those involved in seeking to meet the needs and wants of tourists should be more environmentally conscious and more responsible (see Buckley, Chapter 6). The onus is, therefore, clearly on supply rather than on the consumer.

However, the primary concern of the enterprises involved in tourism is sustaining the company concerned. So in an increasingly competitive marketplace, coupled with the ongoing recession in northern hemisphere countries and the potentially small profit margins, any perception that being more responsible will increase costs for a company is likely to negatively influence the expansion of RT opportunities. Despite this, we have established that there are RT products currently available on the market (see Holland, Chapter 9; Spenceley and Rylance, Chapter 10), although these are predominantly niche market opportunities and, if demand increases (as so often it does), then suppliers may not be able to continue to deliver with the same degree of responsibility. Furthermore, as is all too evident with ecotourism, increased demand encourages new entrants into the marketplace who may be far less responsible in their management and operations. This is the crux of the problem with those alternative forms of tourism considered to be small scale and low key; success encourages growth and expansion, which is not necessarily to the benefit of local communities (see Leslie, Chapter 2).

A major factor in consumer choice of the type of holiday is that of price, which also reflects the scarcity and/or exclusiveness of the product. This is prevalent in tourism: witness the growth of ecotourism and now 'ecochic' (see Buckley, Chapter 6) and 'ultratourism' – lavish luxury accommodation operations, visits to Antarctica, and – today's most recent and undoubtedly most elitist package – trips into space developed by Virgin plc. These products with their fashionable labels and connotations of luxury must be regarded as the least responsible. Conversely, mass tourism is the opposite when one considers that much of it is well integrated in established resorts in which there will also be more environmentally friendly options and facilitating measures. These mainstream markets hold the benefit of generally long-standing, fairly sustainable, demand, in comparatively built-up destinations with a developed infrastructure. In such destinations, the adoption of the central tenets and related practices of RT in combination can have a far more substantial impact, both in addressing the consumption of non-renewable resources and related waste, and in terms of local community benefit (see Zientara, Chapter 12). Certainly, suppliers could do more and gradually will, if for no other reason than as a result of policy initiatives designed to address climate change and the promotion of alternative energy sources. However, there is still a need for the consumers of tourism to address their consumption patterns, and in the process to be more responsible. How this is to be achieved is undoubtedly a complex issue which brings into question why people go on holiday. Of all the reasons to be considered, not one relates to being more responsible in the way(s) of consumption, while some suggest the very opposite to be more likely. Fundamentally, there is a need for tourists to be more responsible in choice and deed – whether on the grounds of sustainability, climate change or in reducing consumption per se. In this, it is clear that it is not the tourist – who is but the manifestation of consumption in this context – but the consumer who needs to be persuaded.

References

Anon. (2003) New rules for Faliraki revellers, 9 September 2003. Available at: http://news.bbc.co.uk/1/hi/world/europe/3302911.stm (accessed 6 April 2012).

Anon. (2007) Ethical consumerism on the up and up. *Ethical Consumer* (Manchester, UK), No. 101 (March/April) p. 9.

Atkins, R. (2010) What's it like to live with tourists? Available at: http://www.guardian.co.uk/travel/blog/2010/apr/07/living-with-tourists-tourism (accessed 6 April 2012).

Baker, N. (2005) Know your greens. *The Guardian* (London), 10 December 2005, p. 7. Available at: http://www.guardian.co.uk/travel/2005/dec/10/ecotourism.guardiansaturdaytravelsection2?INTCMP=ILCNET TXT3487 (accessed 10 April 2012).

Ballantyne, R., Packer, J. and Falk, J. (2010) Visitor's learning for environmental sustainability: testing short- and long-term impacts of wildlife tourism experiences using structural equation modelling. *Tourism Management* 32, 1243–1252.

Baobab (2012) Carbon Offsetting – Responsible Flying. Available at: http://www.baobabtravel.com/carbon_offsetting (accessed 10 April 2012).

Beioley, S. (1995) Green Tourism – soft or sustainable? *INsights*, May 1995, pp. B75–B89. English Tourist Board, London.

Bergin-Seers, S. and Mair, J. (2009) Emerging green tourists in Australia: their behaviors and attitudes. *Tourism and Hospitality Research* 9, 109–119.

Blamey, R.K. (1997) Ecotourism: the search for an operational definition. *Journal of Sustainable Tourism* 5, 109–130.

Bramwell, B. and Lane, B. (2000) *Tourism Collaboration and Partnerships: Politics, Practice and Sustainability.* Channel View, Clevedon, UK.

Bremner, C. (2009) Sustainable Tourism Moves Slowly in the Right Direction: Analyst Insight. EuroMonitor, London, 29 June 2009. Available at: http://www.euromonitor.com/Sustainable_Tourism_Moves_Slowly_in_the_Right_Direction (accessed 6 April 2012).

Budeanu, A. (2007) Sustainable tourist behaviour: a discussion of opportunities for change. *International Journal of Consumer Studies* 31, 499–508.

Butcher, J. (2003) *The Moralisation of Tourism: Sun, Sand ... and Saving the World?* Routledge, London/New York.

CAA (2010) CAA publishes 2009 air passenger survey. Available at: http://www.caa.co.uk/application.aspx?c atid=14&pagetype=65&appid=7&mode=detail&nid=1928 (accessed 6 April 2012).

Choat, I. (2004) Package firms urged to be responsible. *The Guardian* (London), 13 March 2004, p. 16. Available at: http://www.guardian.co.uk/travel/2004/mar/13/travelnews.guardiansaturdaytravelsection (accessed 6 April 2012).

Clobourne, L. (2008) *Sustainable Development and Resilience: Think Piece for Sustainable Development Commission.* Sustainable Development Commission, London.

Dahl, R. (2010) Greenwashing: do you know you're buying? *Environmental Health Perspectives* 118(6) A246–A252.

Davies, P. (2007) Travellers back radical moves to protect environment. Press Release, 8 August 2007, TravelMole, London/Hong Kong/Sydney/New York/Delhi. Available at: http://www.travelmole.com/ stories/1121133.php (accessed 8 April 2012).

Defra (2006) Go green: travellers urged to consider the environment. Press Release, 3 April 2006, Department of Environment, Food and Rural Affairs, London. Available at: http://www.newmaterials.com/ Customisation/News/General/Government_Departments/Go_green_travellers_urged_to_consider_the_ environment.asp (accessed 6 April 2012).

Defra (2007) Parents and retired more likely to adopt pro-environmental behaviours. Press Release, 23 November 2007, Department of Environment, Food and Rural Affairs, London. Available at: http://www. whitehallpages.net/news/archive/51473 (accessed 6 April 2012).

Defra (2009) *Public Attitudes and Behaviours towards the Environment Tracker Survey.* Department of Environment, Food and Rural Affairs, London.

Deloitte Development (2007) *Deloitte 2007 Annual Holiday Survey.* New York.

Dinan, D. and Sargeant, A. (2000) Social marketing and sustainable tourism – is there a match? *International Journal of Tourism Research* 2, 1–14.

Dodds, R. (2008) Assessing the demand for sustainable tourism. The Quebec source for information on global trends in international tourism, Montreal, Canada. Available at: http://tourismintelligence.ca/2008/04/04/ assessing-the-demand-for-sustainable-tourism/ (accessed 6 April 2012).

Dolnicar, S., Crouch, G.I. and Long, P. (2010) Environment-friendly tourists: what do we really know about them? *Journal of Sustainable Tourism* 16, 197–210.

Downing, P. and Ballantyne, J. (2007) *Turning Point or Tipping Point? Social Marketing and Climate Change.* Ipsos MORI Social Research Institute, London. Available at: http://www.lowcvp.org.uk/assets/reports/ ipsos_mori_turning-point-or-tipping-point.pdf (accessed 6 April 2012).

Elkington, J. (1987) *The Green Capitalists: Industry's Search for Environmental Excellence.* Victor Gollanz, London.

England, R. (2010) Unravelling the psychology of recycling. *Resource*, No. 56 (November/December 2010), pp. 11–13. Resource Media, Bristol, UK. Available at: http://www.resource.uk.com/article/Futurevision/ Unravelling_psychology_recycling (accessed 6 April 2012).

EU (2004) *The European Union 6th Environmental Action Programme – Towards a Thematic Strategy on the Sustainable Use of Natural Resources. 'Pathways through Society'.* Working Group 2, Use of Natural Resources, Final Report COM (2003) 572. Commission of the European Communities, Brussels.

Fedrigo-Fazio, D., Baldock, D., Farmer, A. and Gantioler, S. (2011) *EU Natural Resources Policy: Signposts on the Roadmap to Sustainability.* Directions in European Environmental Policy (DEEP) Policy Papers, 2 May 2011, Institute for European Environmental Policy (IEEP), London. Available at: http://ec.europa.eu/ environment/resource_efficiency/pdf/IEEP.pdf (accessed 8 April 2012).

Font, X. and Buckley, R.C. (eds) (2001) *Tourism Ecolabelling: Certification and Promotion of Sustainable Management.* CAB International, Wallingford, UK.

Frame, B. and Newton, B. (2007) Promoting sustainability through social marketing: examples from New Zealand. *International Journal of Consumer Studies* 31, 571–581.

Genot, H. (1995) Voluntary environmental codes of conduct. *Journal of Sustainable Tourism* 3, 166–172.

GFC (2008) *The Case for Green Fiscal Reform: Final Report.* Green Fiscal Commission, London.

Goodwin, H. and Francis, J. (2003) Ethical and responsible tourism – consumer trends in the U.K. *Journal of Vacation Marketing* 9, 271–284.

GreenBiz (2007) Consumers only partially embrace green products, CEOs say. Available at: http://www.

greenbiz.com/news/2007/06/24/consumers-only-partially-embrace-green-products-ceos-say (accessed 6 July, 2012).

Greenpeace (2011) Greenwashing. Available at: http://stopgreenwash.org/ (accessed 6 April 2012).

Hall, C.M. (1994) *Tourism and Politics: Policy, Power and Place*. Wiley, Chichester, UK.

Han, H. and Hsu, L.-T. and Lee, J.-L. (2009) Empirical investigation of the roles of attitudes toward green behaviours, overall image, gender, and age in hotel customers' eco-friendly decision-making process. *International Journal of Hospitality Management* 28, 519–528.

Hemmelskamp, J. and Brockmann, K. (1997) Environmental labels: the German 'Blue Angel'. *Futures* 29 (1) 67–76.

Holden, A. (2005) *Tourism Studies and the Social Sciences*. Routledge, Abingdon, UK/New York.

Holden, A. (2009) The environment–tourism nexus. *Annals of Tourism Research* 36, 373–389.

Holder, J.S. (1988) Patterns and impact of tourism on the environment of the Caribbean. *Tourism Management* 9, 119–127.

Honey, M. (ed.) (2002) *Eco-Tourism and Certification: Setting Standards in Practice*. Island Press, Washington, DC.

Hudson, S. and Ritchie, B. (2001) Tourist attitudes towards the environment: a critique of the contingent valuation method as a research tool for measuring willingness to pay. *Journal of Teaching in Travel and Tourism* 1(4) 1–18.

Hwang, S.-N., Lee, C. and Chen, H.-J. (2005) The relationship among tourists' involvement, place attachment and interpretation satisfaction in Taiwan's national parks. *Tourism Management* 26, 143–156.

Jackson, B., Lee-Wolf, C., Higginson, F., Wallace, J. and Agathou, N. (2008) *Strategies for Reducing the Climate Impacts of Red Meat/Dairy Consumption in the UK*. Report for World Wide Fund for Nature. Imperial College. London.

Jackson, T. and Michaelis, L. (2003) *Policies for Sustainable Consumption*. Sustainable Development Commission. London.

Jenkins, T. (2002) *Ethical Tourism: Who Benefits? Debating Matters*. Institute of Ideas/Hodder and Stoughton, London.

Johnson, D. and Turner, C. (2003) *International Business – Themes and Issues in the Modern Global Economy*. Routledge, London.

Johnston, A.M. (2003) Self-determination: exercising indigenous rights in tourism. In: Singh, S., Timothy, D.J. and Dowling, R.K. (eds) *Tourism in Destination Communities*. CAB International, Wallingford, UK, pp. 115–134.

Josephides, N. (2001) Ethics don't interest clients. *Travel Trade Gazette* (London), 4 February, pp. 3–4.

Kane, P. (1999) So what does come naturally. *The Herald* (Glasgow), 7 February, p. 9.

KeyNote (2008) *Green and Ethical Consumer: Market Assessment Report*. KeyNote, London.

KeyNote (2010) *Travel Agents and Overseas Tour Operators: Market Report*. KeyNote, London.

Krippendorf, J. (1987) *The Holiday Makers: Understanding the Impact of Leisure and Travel*. Butterworth-Heinemann, Oxford, UK.

Kuoni (2011) *Kuoni Holiday Report 2011: Are Britons Different People on Holiday?* Kuoni Travel, Dorking, UK. Available at http://www.kuoni.co.uk/en/services/about_kuoni/news/press_releases/holiday-report-2011/pages/holidayreport2011.aspx (accessed 8 April 2012).

Leidner, R. (2004) *The European Tourism Industry: A Multi-Sector with Dynamic Markets. Structures, Developments and Importance for Europe's Economy*. Report prepared for Enterprise DG (Unit D.3) of the European Commission. Europa, Publications Office of the European Union. Available at: http://ec.europa.eu/enterprise/sectors/tourism/files/studies/european_tourism_industry_2004/european_tourism_industry_2004_en.pdf (accessed 8 April 2012).

Leslie, D. (1991) Leisure policy and practice revisited: how green is your party? In: Botterill, D. and Tomlinson, A. (eds) *Ideology, Leisure Policy and Practice*. Leisure Studies Association, University of Brighton, UK, pp. 155/162.

Leslie, D. (2001) *An Environmental Audit of the Tourism Industry in the Lake District National Park*. Report for Friends of the Lake District/Council for the Protection of Rural England, Kendal, UK.

Leslie, D. (ed.) (2009) *Tourism Enterprises and Sustainable Development: International Perspectives on Responses to the Sustainability Agenda*. Routledge, New York.

Leslie, D. (2012a) Tourism, tourists and sustainability. In: Leslie, D. (ed.) *Tourism Enterprises and the Sustainability Agenda across Europe*. Ashgate, Farnham, UK, pp. 15–34.

Leslie, D. (2012b) Key players in the environmental performance of tourism enterprises. In: Reddy, M.V. and Wilkes, K. (eds) *Tourism, Climate Change and Sustainability*. Earthscan, London (in press).

Leslie, D. (ed.) (2012c) *Tourism Enterprises and the Sustainability Agenda across Europe*. Ashgate, Farnham, UK.

Leslie, D. (2012d) Introduction: sustainability, the European Union and tourism. In: Leslie, D. (ed.) *Tourism Enterprises and the Sustainability Agenda across Europe*. Ashgate, Farnham, pp. 1–14.

Levett, R. (2001) Sustainable development and capitalism. *Renewal* 9(2/3), 1–9.

Lim, N. (1996) To take a stand: the greening of tourism. *BusinessWorld* (Philippines), p. 4.

Lindholdt, L. (1998) Writing from a sense of place. *Journal of Environmental Education* 30(4), 4–10.

Mann, M. (2000) *The Community Tourism Guide: Exciting Holidays for Responsible Travellers*. Earthscan, London/Sterling, Virginia.

Martínez-Alier, J. (1995) The environment as a luxury good or 'too poor to be green'? *Ecological Economics* 13, 1–10.

Masero, S. (2009) Why it pays to act now. *Sustainable Business* 155, 18–19.

Miller, G., Holmes, K., Rathouse, K., Scarles, C. and Tribe, J. (2010) Public understanding of sustainable tourism. *Annals of Tourism Research* 37, 627–645.

Millman, R. (1989) Pleasure seeking v the 'greening' of world tourism. *Tourism Management* 10, 275–277.

Mintel (2005) *Sustainable Tourism in the Travel Industry – International – February 2005*. Reports, Travel and Tourism Analyst, Mintel, London, Chicago, New York, Sydney, Tokyo and Shanghai. Details and summary available at: http://oxygen.mintel.com/sinatra/oxygen/display/id=148248 (accessed 8 April 2012).

Mintel (2007) *Holiday Lifestyles – Responsible Tourism – UK – January 2007*. Reports, Travel and Tourism Analyst, Mintel, London, Chicago, New York, Sydney, Tokyo and Shanghai. Details and summary available at http://oxygen.mintel.com/sinatra/oxygen/display/id=221204 (accessed 8 April 2012).

Mintel (2010) Holidays – Attitudes and the Impact of Recession – UK – January 2010. News Stories: Travellers green habits are forgotten once they are on holiday, 28 June 2010. Details and summary available at: http://oxygen.mintel.com/sinatra/oxygen/display/id=173590/display/id=479788/list/id=479788&type=NSItem&class=NewsAndMgr&context=vanilla_search&sort=z2a&display=header&page=1 (accessed 6 April 2012).

Moss, L. (2008) *Organic Places to Stay in the UK*. Green Books, Dartington, Totnes, UK.

Orams, M.B. (1996) A conceptual model of tourist–wildlife interaction: the case for education as a management strategy. *Australian Geographer* 27, 39–51.

Palmer, T. and Riera, A. (2003) Tourism and environmental taxes. With special reference to the 'Balearic ecotax'. *Tourism Management* 24, 665–674.

Pattullo, P. and Minelli, O. (2006) *The Ethical Travel Guide: Your Passport to Exciting Alternative Holidays*. Earthscan, London/Sterling, Virginia.

Pearce, P.L. (2005) *Tourist Behaviour: Themes and Conceptual Schemes*. Channel View, Clevedon, UK.

Powell, R.B. and Ham, S.H. (2008) Can ecotourism interpretation really lead to pro-conservation knowledge, attitudes and behaviour? Evidence from the Galapagos Islands. *Journal of Sustainable Tourism* 16, 467–489.

Romero, M. and Percifield, D. (2010) Press Release: [Green Brands] Survey identifies varied green beliefs and behaviours among global consumers. Available at: http://www.wpp.com/wpp/press/press/default.htm?guid=%7B7d135945-e34d-456b-a209-b27156624ce7%7D (accessed 6 March 2012).

Russell-Walling, E. (2008) Blue chips turn green. *Director*, November 2008, pp. 39–40. Institute of Directors, London. Available at: http://www.director.co.uk/magazine/2008/11%20November/climate_change_62_4.html (accessed 6 April 2012).

Ryerson University (2010) *Sun, Surf and Sustainability? Tourists Divided on Who Should Pay to Keep Vacation Spots Eco-friendly*. Newswise, 24 November 2010. Available at: http://newswise.com/articles/sun-surf-and-sustainability (accessed 6 April 2012).

Sasidharan, V., Sirakaya, E. and Kerstetter, D. (2002) Developing countries and tourism ecolabels. *Tourism Management* 23, 161–174.

Scheyvens, R. (2002) *Tourism for Development: Empowering Communities*. Prentice Hall, Harlow, UK.

SCRT (2006) *I Will if You Will: Towards Sustainable Consumption*. Sustainable Consumption Roundtable, London. Available at: http://www.sd-commission.org.uk/data/files/publications/I_Will_If_You_Will.pdf (accessed 19 April 2012).

Seabrook, J. (2007) Tourism, predatory and omnivorous? *Third World Resurgence*, No. 207/208, pp. 13–14. TWN: Third World Network, Penang, Malaysia/Geneva, Switzerland. Available at: http://www.twnside.org.sg/title2/resurgence/207-208/cover2.doc (accessed 8 April 2012).

Shaw, G., Agarwal, S. and Bull, P. (1999) Tourism consumption and tourist behaviour: a British perspective. Paper presented at the conference on British Tourism, University of Exeter, 21–23 September 1999.

SNV (2009) *The Market for Responsible Tourism Products: With a Special Focus on Latin America and Nepal.* SNV Netherlands Development Organisation, The Hague, The Netherlands. Available at: at http://www.responsibletravel.org/resources/documents/reports/The%20Market%20for%20Responsible%20Tourism%20Products.pdf (accessed 8 April 2012).

Souterton, D., McMeekin, A. and Evans, S.D. (2011) *International Review of Behaviourism Change Initiating Climate Change Behaviours.* Research Programme, Scottish Government Social Research, Edinburgh, UK.

Thake, S. (2009) *Individualism and Consumerism: Reframing the Debate.* Joseph Rowntree Foundation, York, UK.

The Future Laboratory (2010) *Thomson Holidays: Sustainable Holiday Futures.* The Future Laboratory. London. Available at: http://www.e-tid.com/getdoc/b7e621f9-96db-4e45-9f69-a989ca162676/SustainableHolidayFuturesReport.aspx (accessed 8 April 2012).

Tibbott, R. (2001) New lives, new leisure. *Locum Destination Review,* No. 5 (Summer 2001), pp. 14–16. Colliers International Destination Consulting, London. Available at: http://www.locumconsulting.com/pdf/LDR5NewLives.pdf (accessed 8 April 2012).

Tip, B.P. (2009) Sustainable tourism. *International Trade Forum* 1, 21–23.

TOI (2011) About TOI. Tour Operators' Initiative for Sustainable Tourism Development, Switzerland. Available: http://www.toinitiative.org/index.php?id=3 (accessed 8 April 2012).

Tubb, N. (2003) An evaluation of the effectiveness of interpretation within Dartmoor National Park in reaching the goals of sustainable tourism development. *Journal of Sustainable Tourism* 11, 476–498.

University of Hertfordshire *et al.* (2010) *Effective Approaches to Environmental Labelling of Food Products. Appendix C: Consumer and Industry Costs, Benefits and Behaviour.* Final Report for Defra Project FO0419, Department of Environment, Food and Rural Affairs, London, 15 November 2010. Coordinated by Agriculture and Environment Research Unit, Science and Technology Research Institute, University of Hertfordshire with Food Ethics Council, Brighton, UK and Policy Studies Institute, London. Available at: http://randd.defra.gov.uk/Document.aspx?Document=FO0419_9999_FRP.pdf (accessed 8 April 2012).

Uysal, M., Jurowski, C., Noe, F.P. and McDonald, C.D. (1994) Environmental attitude by trip and visitor characteristics. *Tourism Management* 15, 284–294.

Veal, A.J. (2002) *Leisure and Tourism Policy and Planning,* 2nd edn. CAB International, Wallingford, UK.

Venice Tourist and Visitor Information Site (2010) Venice sinking under 13 million plastic bottles per year. News Release, 3 November 2010. Available at: http://www.veniceinfosite.com/2010/11/help-rid-venice-of-13-million-plastic (accessed 8 April 2012).

Weaver, A. (2005) Representation and obfuscation: cruise travel and the mystification of production. *Tourism, Culture and Communication* 5, 165–176.

Webb, T. (2010) Few air travellers offset carbon emissions, study finds. *The Guardian* (London), 30 August 2010. Available online at http://www.guardian.co.uk/business/2010/aug/30/carbon-emissions-offset-civil-aviation-authority (accessed 6 April 2012).

Weiss, O., Norden, G., Hilscher, P. and Vanreusel, B. (1998) Ski tourism and environmental problems: ecological awareness among different groups. *International Review for the Sociology of Sport* 33, 367–379.

Welford, R., Ytterhus, B. and Eiligh, J. (1999) Tourism and sustainable development: an analysis of policy and guidelines for managing provision and consumption. *Sustainable Development* 7, 165–177.

Wight, P. (1994) Environmentally responsible marketing of tourism. In: Cater, E. and Lowman, G. (eds) *Ecotourism – A Sustainable Option.* Wiley, Chichester, UK, pp. 39–56.

Wijk, J. van and Persoon, W. (2006) A long haul destination: sustainability reporting among tour operators. *European Management Journal* 24, 381–395.

Williams, P.W. and Ponsford, I.F. (2009) Confronting tourism's environmental paradox: transitioning for sustainable tourism. *Futures* 41, 396–404.

Winkler, E. (2008) Wish you were here. *Living Earth,* Spring 2008, pp. 22–24. Soil Association, Bristol/Edinburgh, UK.

Woolford, J. (2001) Rights of package. *Green Futures* (London), No. 28 (May/June 2001), p. 45.

Wright, M. (2002) Sustainable stufflust? *Green Futures* (London), No. 35 (July/August), pp. 22–26.

WTM (2008) *Global Trends Report 2008.* World Travel Market and Euromonitor International, London.

Available   at: http://en.kongres-magazine.eu/data/upload/World_Travel_Market___Global_Trends_
    Report_2008.pdf (Accessed 8 April 2012).
WTTC and IHRA (1999) *Tourism and Sustainable Development: The Global Importance of Tourism.*
    Background paper No. 1 prepared by World Travel and Tourism Organization [Council] and International
    Hotel and Restaurant Association for UN Department of Economic and Social Affairs, Commission on
    Sustainable Development, Seventh Session, New York, 19–30 April 1999. Available at: http://www.un.
    org/esa/sustdev/csd/wttc.pdf (accessed 10 April 2012).
Wurzinger, S. and Johansson, M. (2006) Environmental concern and knowledge of ecotourism among three
    groups of Swedish tourists. *Journal of Travel Research* 45, 217–226.
WWF (2011) *WWF Report UK 2011. Moving On: Why Flying Less Means More for Business.* WWF-UK
    Godalming, UK. Available at: http://assets.wwf.org.uk/downloads/moving_on_report.pdf (accessed 8
    April 2012).

5 Destination Communities and Responsible Tourism

Dallen J. Timothy
Arizona State University, USA

Introduction

The growth of modern-day tourism in the late 19th century, and its rapid popularization after the Second World War, effected many changes to the sociocultural, economic and ecological environments of tourist destinations (Wall and Mathieson, 2007). One of the oft-cited problems associated with mass tourism is its near-synonymous correspondence to booster-ism, or a lack of planning and imposed development at all costs for the sake of monetary gain. Mass tourism grew especially fast during the second half of the 20th century via boosterist marketing efforts by destinations and subsequent organic growth as word spread of enticing touristic opportunities. Much of this growth took place in the less-developed regions of the world, including the Caribbean, Latin America, South-east Asia, South Asia, the Pacific Islands and parts of Africa, where export earnings were in critical short supply and tourist spending was urgently needed (Apostolopoulos *et al.*, 2001; Mowforth *et al.*, 2008).

In the wake of tourism's rapid growth, many important stakeholders were left out of development programmes (Wall, 1995), some of which were imposed upon destination communities by national decision makers and foreign investors. This typically resulted in people in positions of power at national or regional levels, as well as foreign conglomerates and financiers, becoming wealthier through economic leakage and corruption, while destination residents often became poorer and were left to bear the burden of the social, cultural, economic and environmental costs of tourism. This led many critics to liken tourism to the exploitative hallmark of colonialism (Hall and Tucker, 2004; Wall and Mathieson, 2007; Gibson, 2010; Snyder and Sulle, 2011).

Fortunately, late 20th century observers and scholars of tourism, as well as many visionary service providers, have realized the unsustainable imbalances of mass tourism and offered alternatives that seem to provide more feasible, long-term options for destination communities. Responsible tourism is one such alternative; this is not itself a type of tourism, but rather an approach to a variety of types of tourism (e.g. heritage, sport, nature-based, religious) development that is guided by principles of sustainability, such as equity, holism, balance, harmony, cultural and ecological integrity, and the economic and social good of the destination. Its goal is to create high-quality destinations and ex-periences both for visitors and residents of the places tourists visit by supporting accountability among all users of tourism spaces and providers of tourism services (Spenceley, 2008). In accordance with the spirit of responsible tourism and sustainable development, this chapter examines one facet of responsible tourism: the destination community. It explores how communities can be empowered through tourism, which leads into an examination of some current trends that touch upon responsible and sustainable forms of tourism development for destination communities, including heritage, place-based experiences and the potential socio-economic benefits of tourism in empowered communities.

Destination Communities, Empowerment and Sustainable Tourism Development

As noted above, the most common beneficiaries of tourism's wealth and those with the loudest voice in its development have been outsiders. It is now recognized, however, that the people most affected by the industry's impacts – residents and other stakeholders in the destination – must be included in the planning and decision-making process. While this seems like common sense from a Western perspective, participatory development is a relatively new concept in the less-developed portions of the globe, and is still severely lacking in many parts of the world for a variety of sociocultural and political reasons (Timothy, 1999; Tosun, 2000).

The notion of empowerment entails many elements of sustainable tourism and responsible tourism in that it involves destination residents in life-changing decision making, can contribute to more economic opportunities, and can build solidarity in disparate communities. This helps to assure more equitable relationships between stakeholders and tourism, creates more harmony and cooperation at the local level, and helps to assure that cultural and ecological integrity are upheld as residents work together to achieve common goals and objectives.

Development specialists often speak of empowerment as the epitome of good practice, suggesting that those most affected by development should be the most involved in its planning and execution (Gow and Vansant, 1983; Campbell and Marshall, 2000; Lyons *et al.*, 2001). It could be argued, therefore, that the most responsible destinations are the most empowered destinations. Empowerment entails a dynamic process by which people and

places can acquire higher levels of agency. This can happen either as those with authority devolve some of that power intentionally or when the masses wrest power from those who possess it. The dynamism associated with empowerment can also go in opposite directions, whereby communities lose agency through the reverse process of disempowerment. In the context of tourism development, Timothy (2007) has identified four degrees of empowerment, namely imposed development, tokenistic involvement, meaningful participation and true empowerment. These also represent stages, or a continuum, along which destination communities may progress through the process of empowerment.

Imposed development is not empowerment at all. In this instance, tourism is compelled upon destinations because outsiders see the economic potential of their resources. Tokenistic involvement occurs when people in power seek nominal input from community members, sometimes only local elites, to fulfil participatory policies. The input received may or may not be regarded in final decision making. Meaningful participation occurs when resident opinions and concerns are sought by outsiders. In this case, destination community issues are more likely to be addressed in the final analysis and can truly help to inform policy formulation and decision making. Finally, empowerment is achieved when the ideas derive from the grassroots level in the destination. Local stakeholders, such as business people, politicians and other leaders work closely with residents to find solutions to problems or to devise ways of creating tourism opportunities. Empowerment happens only when development ceases to be a top-down process and becomes a bottom-up process that benefits everyone who wishes to benefit.

Besides these scales of empowerment, several types of empowerment have been identified in the research literature (Scheyvens, 1999, 2002, 2003; Brown, 2002; O'Neal and O'Neal, 2003; Timothy, 2007). Social empowerment occurs when community members cooperate for the betterment of the whole community. Social unity prevails, and community services are enriched because of tourism (Scheyvens, 1999). Indigenous knowledge is a salient part of this line of thinking, because it is now recognized as a crucial part of the development process for its problem-solving abilities and harmony with nature and culture. Grassroots knowledge is credible knowledge because it is more context specific. The powerful elites in faraway capital cities are often unaware of local conditions, so native and immigrant familiarity with place is a critical element of tourism's success. Socially empowered tourist destinations have a higher quality of life, with strengths such as leadership, social capital, cultural integrity and solidarity of purpose.

Individual sense of value and collective self-esteem are a requisite part of psychological empowerment. Communities thus empowered take pride in their traditions and are willing to share them with tourists (Scheyvens, 1999). This is very helpful in preserving elements of native culture that were in danger of disappearing and encourages communities to have an interest in their heritage.

Economic empowerment is achieved as tourism results in true monetary benefits for the destination community. Much of this fiscal element plays out as money is earned in the community and shared through community-wide networks (Scheyvens, 2002; Sofield, 2003). Of chief importance is that the disadvantaged population cohorts are enabled and encouraged to participate in the economic advantages provided by tourism. This makes obvious sense to most outsiders, but in the developing world there have long been many barriers to residents of tourist destinations genuinely benefiting economically by tourism (Timothy, 1999, 2002). Responsible and sustainable forms of 'pro-poor' tourism aim to alleviate poverty by assuring, inasmuch as possible, that the less affluent of society are empowered with opportunities to partake of tourism's fiscal rewards through employment, entrepreneurialism, grants for small business creation and basic public services (e.g. education, health care, clean water) (Torres and Momsen, 2004; Chok et al., 2007; Hall, 2007; Harrison, 2008; Scheyvens, 2011).

The final type of empowerment, political empowerment, is realized when communities and their individual stakeholders, including residents, have a voice in planning and decision making. Without a mechanism to voice their

concerns and received answers to their questions, they are much less likely to support development initiatives (Timothy, 1999). This might take the form of tokenistic involvement or meaningful involvement, as noted earlier, but true political empowerment only exists when ownership of development benefits and problems lies with the people most affected by tourism. Communities who have the power and authority to initiate tourism development or reject it are the most empowered of all (Timothy, 2007).

With increased empowerment, however, comes increased responsibility. Participatory ability and empowerment include rights and responsibilities, not simply a voice or a source of income (Timothy and White, 1999; Cornwall, 2003). Responsibilities include the right to decide whether to conserve or to utilize, as well as ownership of failures and successes. This rationale extends far beyond normative notions of empowerment to incorporate obligations of citizenship to become involved in development and to be liable for development successes and failures (Osborne, 1994; Timothy, 2007).

The importance of social, political, economic and psychological empowerment lies in its ability to give a voice to the people whose views have long been muted. The voiceless in most of the world include ethnic or racial minorities (or majorities subjugated by powerful minorities), women, the poor, undocumented immigrants and people with disabilities. These people truly have existed 'outside the plans' (Wall, 1995) as tourism has been a significant development focus in much of the world during the past half century. Rarely have these population segments had the prospect of deciding their own personal futures, 'let alone initiat[ing] development programs or participat[ing] in a meaningful way in the development of tourism' (Timothy, 2007, p. 206).

Trends in Responsible Tourism and Destination Communities

There are numerous engaging and interrelated discussions going on in the field of sustainable tourism that highlight new ways of thinking about the destination community's role in responsible travel (Beeton, 2006). Only a few of these will be examined in the sections that follow. One such set of discussions focuses on cultural heritage and its use and exploitation in the empowerment or disempowerment of host communities. Another is how new views of tourism development and sense of place are enveloping existing frameworks for community-based development. Finally, how residents should benefit socio-economically from tourism development is examined.

Cultural heritage empowers destinations

One contemporary issue is indigenous rights in tourism. Living native cultures and their material manifestations are among the most valued heritage resources for tourism. For centuries, 'tourists' and other travellers of white, European descent have gazed upon the cultural heritage of indigenous peoples in Africa, Asia, Latin America and Native North America. In neocolonialist fashion, however, the natives being viewed have had little voice in how their cultural expressions have been depicted, mass produced or fabricated for tourist consumption.

Outsiders have long profited by selling native cultures, both as a tourist spectacle and as commodified souvenirs made in faraway lands with little connection to the people whose culture is for sale (Aldred, 2000; Simons, 2000; Johnston, 2003, 2006). This raises many questions about intellectual property rights for native peoples, including those pertaining to music, dance, beliefs, architecture, cultural symbols, folklore, historical artefacts, and handicrafts. International treaties have been signed (e.g. the Berne Convention and the UN Declaration on the Rights of Indigenous Peoples) to help protect the world's aboriginal cultures, but relatively few signatory states have made progress in enforcing the agreed upon policies and practices. The publicity is there, but the political will is lacking.

Unfortunately, this lack of enforcement has led to the exploitation of the cultural heritage of many indigenous groups for tourism. As noted above, it is common for souvenirs to be patterned after some semblance of native cultural features, but in most cases they are mass produced, inauthentic and sold by non-natives without permission from the people whose heritage it is (Johnston, 2006; Timothy, 2011). This is insulting for many groups, because not only do these outsiders produce cultural emblems, many of which are felt to be sacred and deeply meaningful, for large profits without permission, they also perpetuate non-native stereotypical and untruthful images of indigenous cultures.

One of the timeliest debates in this regard deals with the spiritualist New Age movement, which began in the mid-20th century. Numbering in the millions, New Agers adhere to a wide range of spiritual philosophies, much of them animistic in origin. These spiritualists are well known for their propensity to travel to powerful natural areas and to sites that indigenes around the globe hold sacred. The New Age crusade has adopted many aboriginal rites and rituals, including many Native American practices. Several American Indian tribes have complained of New Age pilgrims desecrating their sacred sites with fires, ritual litter, and disturbed stones and vegetation, but perhaps even more crucial is the spiritualists' adoption of Native American customs such as sweat lodges, certain herbal treatments, dances and medicine man ceremonies. Many self-proclaimed New Age shamans have amassed considerable wealth by pilfering the religious and cultural traditions of America's aboriginals, while many of the indigenes still live in poverty (Timothy, 2011).

For decades, national tourism organizations and other service providers have adopted native symbols and images as part of their marketing efforts. These representations are commonly seen by the world at large as symbolic of certain countries' tourist appeal. Images of New Zealand's Maori, the Andean peoples of Peru, the Maasai of East Africa, the Navajo of the US South-west, the Lapps of Sweden and Finland, and the Hill Tribes of Thailand are all featured prominently in those destinations' promotional literature and depict so much of what the world associates with the images of those regions. Several indigenous groups have begun suing for intellectual rights over their cultural traditions being depicted in such a way. Other groups have become empowered in recent years to such an extent that they themselves now determine what elements of their cultures can and will be shared with tourists. The Maori of New Zealand, the Kuna of Panama and the Hopi of the USA are good examples (Breslin and Chapin, 1984; Lew, 1996; Scheyvens, 2002). The Hopis, for instance, are able to determine what areas of their lands outsiders can access and what elements of their cultural traditions can be preserved outside the tourist gaze. By extension, some indigenous peoples are benefiting from fair trade shops, which sell handicrafts from the less-developed world that are produced by local artisans and guaranteed to be locally designed and crafted in ecologically sensitive ways by people who are sufficiently compensated for their work.

A unique perspective related to this is the idea of technology and its interface with native culture. It is now not requisite for 'visitors' to visit the sites of indigenous culture to be able to acquire cultural artefacts and handicrafts. Many native tribes in the USA and Canada, for example, sell 'authentic' arts and crafts through the Internet as souvenirs of places people no longer have to visit. Such items range from inexpensive replicas to high-priced, one-of-a-kind pieces of artwork. While some observers see this as a form of displaced authenticity and further marginalization of native peoples (Scrase, 2003), in some ways it is more beneficial than on-site tourism because it eliminates the physical presence of tourists while remaining under the control of the indigenes themselves at the point of production. This approach is, however, still subject to the whims and desires of the digital market.

An additional heritage-related view is the development of cultural routes for tourism. While cultural routes have been around for millennia, especially for pilgrims and traders, the modern-day development of heritage trails and routes is becoming a more popular endeavour. Heritage routes have the potential to empower communities and improve the quality of life for residents by developing rural economies and linking places together to share what they have in common rather than to compete against one another. Cultural routes help stimulate cooperation and partnership between local areas and require more meaning-

ful community participation than many other forms of tourism development (Means, 1999; Briedenhann and Wickens, 2004; Meyer-Cech, 2005).

Another heritage concept is the notion of designating places for one purpose by outsiders, while destination stakeholders desire another. The Caribbean region provides some of the best examples of this. For many decades, the Caribbean has been the focus of mass tourism growth based upon the region's sun, sea and sand (3S) product. Demand for warm weather, white sandy beaches, and azure water has driven cruise and resort tourism on most of the islands. Today, however, there is a strong grassroots movement to reduce the region's dependence on these unsustainable forms of mass tourism in favour of more local, place-based tourism, including cultural heritage. The Caribbean islands are under-represented on UNESCO's World Heritage List, although recent years have seen the inscription of cultural heritage sites in Barbados, Curaçao and St Kitts and Nevis. None the less, there is a rich living and historic culture associated with the region. Many island populations desire to depict their history and living cultures to outsiders and see this as a less damaging expression than the resource-intensive 3S tourism. The Caribbean islands, with their mix of native past, African slavery and plantation agriculture, and colonial cultural imprints now desire to reposition themselves as viable heritage destinations (Pattullo, 1997; Cameron and Gatewood, 2008).

Pattullo (1997, p. 136) noted that the Caribbean in general has suffered from an inferiority complex owing to its troubled colonial past. The 3S tourism that dominates the Caribbean Basin has tended to accentuate the inequalities of the region, reconfirm dependency and neocolonialist relationships, and repress the potential value of the cultural heritage product. However, cultural heritage is increasingly being viewed as a tool for empowering communities psychologically, socially and politically in the Caribbean and elsewhere through critical partnerships between the general public, government agencies and the private sector (Boyd and Timothy, 2001; Aas et al., 2005; Girard and Nijkamp, 2009).

Place-based tourism development

While all tourism forms are place based, there is a new discussion emerging that examines the special qualities of place in relation to the people who live there. Cultural heritage is an important part of this re-emerging discussion and model that many places are beginning to emulate. There are two ways of understanding the relatively new term 'geotourism'. The first refers to tourism based on geological and landscape features, where people go to natural areas for their geological significance and beauty (Newsome and Dowling, 2010). The second use of 'geotourism', more popular in North America than in other parts of the world, is a situation where tourism grows because of a destination's unique geographical characteristics, including the natural environment, history and living culture (Boley et al., 2011). This second definition, which closely resembles and encapsulates many other best practices approaches to tourism, such as community-based tourism, sustainable tourism and responsible tourism, seems to take the concept a step further by suggesting that it can, if done properly, sustain and enhance the unique characteristics of place and build upon the features than define a sense of place. It also overlaps with responsible tourism in that it aims to contribute to the well-being of destination communities. While the National Geographic Society originated the term to be more encompassing than ecotourism or sustainable tourism, there is very little that is actually different from the principles of sustainable tourism or ecotourism. Critics have argued that such a separate definition is unnecessary (e.g. Buckley, 2003), because ecotourism, sustainable tourism, community-based tourism and responsible tourism all have both natural and cultural environments as their focus and all have as their ideal the betterment of the destination community through job creation, conservation of nature and culture, and the advancement of human empowerment.

Socio-economic community benefits

Besides the psychological and political empowerment engendered by appropriate uses of heritage and as exemplified in the identification of new approaches to tourism, there are many economically and socially empowering elements of tourism that can be highlighted as well. Although it is easy to say that tourism creates jobs, regional income, tax funds and foreign exchange earnings, it is also easy to see how little of total tourist spending remains in the destination economy to benefit residents.

According to the principles of sustainability and responsibility, tourism should provide socio-economic benefits that improve the lives and communities of tourism stakeholders. However, in most of the developing world, this has not been the case until very recently. Many destinations are beginning to understand better the notion of community-based development, and as noted before, scholars are now studying the benefits and challenges associated with 'pro-poor' tourism – an approach to tourism that improves the quality of life of the people who have traditionally been on the margins of economic growth (Chok et al., 2007; Scheyvens, 2011). Pro-poor tourism is not without critics, however, who argue that it is akin to any other form of tourism in that those who are in the most desperate circumstances remain there regardless of what labels are placed on tourism, and that it continues to be an exploitative effort imposed upon many communities who might have other desires for earning a living (Hall, 2007). Scepticism also abounds; in the words of Snyder and Sulle (2011, p. 947), 'Many questions remain about whether tourism will alleviate poverty among Maasai communities or simply entrench them in it by threatening their pastoralist livelihoods further, with greater loss to land and other vital natural resources'.

Besides upfront job creation, there are other socio-economic gains that are also important from tourism. The first is a balanced spread of employment to all parts of a country or region for all who desire to work. There has been a long tradition of the best-funded development projects and the highest paying jobs to be located in urban areas and in places that are well represented in government circles. There is a need for tourism to be decentralized from capital cities and regional centres so that more people can be gainfully employed (Timothy, 1999). While tourism depends on accessibility, there are certain types of tourism that thrive on remoteness. Some of the poorest people are those who live in the remotest areas of a country. Product diversification is a potential means of achieving this goal, as is improving access, as long as it is done in harmony with the local people's desires for development.

A second socio-economic boost is the encouragement and facilitation of small-scale business ventures. In Indonesia, the government has recognized the important role that street vendors, guest house owners and other resident entrepreneurs play in tourism's success and has granted permits and other forms of official recognition, rather than closing down the unlicensed grassroots operations that are often disallowed in other developing regions (Timothy and Wall, 1997; Ashley et al., 2000; Dahles, 2000).

One way that governments and non-profit organizations (NGOs) have recently helped to empower residents is by providing small grants and microfinancing for small business entrepreneurs in tourism (Ashley et al., 2000; Rogerson, 2005). These monetary gifts and loans help destination residents purchase start-up equipment and merchandise, and provide some forms of advertising. Similarly, some communities have found success because of educational and training programmes offered by ministries of tourism or the private sector. In Yogyakarta, Indonesia, during the 1990s, the provincial government provided entrepreneurial training for taxi drivers, street vendors, guest house owners and small restaurateurs in the areas of hygiene, accounting, foreign languages and general hospitality. The local government also tried to provide a more hospitable environment for foreign visitors via public-awareness campaigns (Timothy, 2000).

Besides education and small-scale financial assistance for people directly involved in tourism, the community at large should also benefit as they are the ones to live with its consequences. Responsible tourism should consider the needs of the broader community and ensure that at least some of the income derived from the industry goes to help finance public schools, health care, environmental cleaning and public services (Chakravarty and

Irazábal, 2011). Unfortunately, these additional benefits are not frequently factored into the costs and benefits of tourism development from the viewpoint of the public sector. Widespread corruption often leads to the misappropriation of tourism earnings from public services to line the pockets of politicians and other elites in positions of power – at the expense of providing for the community (Albuquerque and McElroy, 1995; Wanhill, 2004).

Conclusion

Responsible forms of tourism are those that adhere to the principles of sustainable development, including economic and social benefits for destination communities and improved well-being for hosts and their environment. By looking at several trends in community-based tourism development, this chapter has illustrated the commonalities and linkages between psychological, political, social and economic empowerment of destination communities and responsible tourism.

Communities that are empowered politically and psychologically have a voice in tourism development efforts, and in fact are usually the drivers of development initiatives. However, it is worth noting that not all forms of development from 'above' or programmes initiated at other scales beyond the very local are harmful or disempowering (Zientara, 2009, 2011). It has not been the intention of this chapter to suggest otherwise. In some cases, more top-down development has seen considerable success, while at the same time, bottom-up approaches are not immune to failure. Nevertheless, this chapter does advocate the importance of grassroots control over a community's future as an important element of responsible tourism.

Many examples of community empowerment can be seen in the context of heritage, where indigenous communities are beginning to take back their exploited cultures, where cultural routes are being developed to provide more holistic products and opportunities for communities to work together for the common good, and are increasing self-determination regarding what elements of culture a nation is eager to share with visitors. Likewise, new trends in identifying novel forms of tourism (e.g. geotourism) are focusing on the unique characteristics of place that make each destination special and aim to uphold and enhance a sense of place. Even though the principles of responsible tourism of the National Geographic Society's geotourism are already embraced by other development tactics related to sustainable tourism, it is remarkable how destination well-being and responsibility are becoming the focus of so much debate today. Finally, beyond the rhetorical description of job provision, several benefits of tourism have been examined to illustrate ways in which destinations can be socially and economically empowered as employment is generated, jobs are spread to marginal areas, small enterprises are encouraged and supported, and training and education for community members are provided.

Situations where the destination population is empowered to benefit from tourism, and not just to bear the burden of its costs, are obviously more sustainable than situations where these conditions do not exist. In the process of empowerment, community members, especially those who have been excluded from development and planning in the past, can realize more of the rewards of tourism and gain a voice in decision making. In so doing, they become co-owners of the successes and failures of tourism and have more control over how it develops to suit local conditions, for they are the purveyors of what is distinct and special about their home regions. While it is not a perfect system, grassroots empowerment brings an improved quality of life into the destination, not just for the elite and powerful, but for all stakeholders, and has the potential to bring with it forms and methods for tourism development that minimize the negative impacts of tourism, generate economic benefits for residents, enhance other aspects of quality of life, provide better experiences for tourists through their interactions with destination populations, and build local pride, solidarity and confidence.

References

Aas, C., Ladkin, A. and Fletcher, J. (2005) Stakeholder collaboration and heritage management. *Annals of Tourism Research* 32, 28–48.

Albuquerque, K. de and McElroy, J.L. (1995) Tourism development in small islands: St Maarten/St Martin and Bermuda. In: Barker, D. and McGregor, D.F.M. (eds) *Environment and Development in the Caribbean: Geographical Perspectives.* University of the West Indies Press, Kingston, pp. 70–89.

Aldred, L. (2000) Plastic shamans and astroturf sun dances: New Age commercialization of Native American spirituality. *American Indian Quarterly* 24, 329–352.

Apostolopoulos, Y., Sönmez, S. and Timothy, D.J. (eds) (2001) *Women as Producers and Consumers of Tourism in Developing Regions.* Praeger, Westport, Connecticut.

Ashley, C., Boyd, C. and Goodwin, H. (2000) *Pro-poor Tourism: Putting Poverty at the Heart of the Tourism Agenda.* Natural Resource Perspectives No. 51, March 2000, Overseas Development Institute, London.

Beeton, S. (2006) *Community Development through Tourism.* Landlinks Press, Collingwood, Victoria, Australia.

Boley, B.B., Nickerson, N.P. and Bosak, K. (2011) Measuring geotourism: developing and testing the geotraveler tendency scale (GTS). *Journal of Travel Research* 50, 567–578.

Boyd, S.W. and Timothy, D.J. (2001) Developing partnerships: tools for interpretation and management of World Heritage Sites. *Tourism Recreation Research* 26(1), 47–53.

Breslin, P. and Chapin, M. (1984) Conservation Kuna style. *Grassroots Development* 8(2), 26–35.

Briedenhann, J. and Wickens, E. (2004) Tourism routes as a tool for the economic development of rural areas – vibrant hope or impossible dream? *Tourism Management* 25, 71–79.

Brown, K. (2002) Innovations for conservation and development. *Geographical Journal* 168, 6–17.

Buckley, R. (2003) Ecotourism: geotourism with a positive triple bottom line? *Journal of Ecotourism* 2, 76–82.

Cameron, C.M. and Gatewood, J.B. (2008) Beyond sun, sand and sea: the emergent tourism programme in the Turks and Caicos Islands. *Journal of Heritage Tourism* 3, 55–73.

Campbell, H. and Marshall, R. (2000) Public involvement and planning: looking beyond the one to the many. *International Planning Studies* 5, 321–344.

Chakravarty, S. and Irazábal, C. (2011) Golden geese or white elephants? The paradoxes of world heritage sites and community-based tourism development in Agra, India. *Community Development* 42, 359–376.

Chok, S., Macbeth, J. and Warren, C. (2007) Tourism as a tool for poverty alleviation: a critical analysis of 'pro-poor tourism' and implications for sustainability. *Current Issues in Tourism* 10, 144–165.

Cornwall, A. (2003) Whose voices? Whose choices? Reflections on gender and participatory development. *World Development* 31, 1325–1342.

Dahles, H. (2000) Tourism, small enterprises and community development. In: Hall, D. and Richards, G. (eds) *Tourism and Sustainable Community Development.* Routledge, London, pp. 154–169.

Gibson, C. (2010) Geographies of tourism: (un)ethical encounters. *Progress in Human Geography* 34, 521–527.

Girard, L.F. and Nijkamp, P. (eds) (2009) *Cultural Tourism and Sustainable Local Development.* Ashgate, Farnham, UK.

Gow, D. and Vansant, J. (1983) Beyond the rhetoric of rural development participation: how can it be done? *World Development* 11, 427–446.

Hall, C.M. (2007) Pro-poor tourism: do 'tourist exchanges benefit primarily the countries of the South'? *Current Issues in Tourism* 10, 111–118.

Hall, C.M. and Tucker, H. (eds) (2004) *Tourism and Postcolonialism: Contested Discourses, Identities and Representations.* Routledge, London.

Harrison, D. (2008) Pro-poor tourism: a critique. *Third World Quarterly* 29, 851–868.

Johnston, A.M. (2003) Self-determination: exercising indigenous rights in tourism. In: Singh, S., Timothy, D.J. and Dowling, R.K. (eds) *Tourism in Destination Communities.* CAB International, Wallingford, UK, pp. 115–134.

Johnston, A.M. (2006) *Is the Sacred for Sale? Tourism and Indigenous Peoples.* Earthscan, London/Sterling, Virginia.

Lew, A.A. (1996) Tourism management on American Indian lands in the USA. *Tourism Management* 17, 355–365.

Lyons, M., Smuts, C. and Stephens, A. (2001) Participation, empowerment and sustainability: (how) do the links work? *Urban Studies* 38, 1233–1251.

Means, M. (1999) Happy trails: regional cooperation is alive and well in heritage corridors. *Planning* 65(8), 4–9.

Meyer-Cech, K. (2005) Regional cooperation in rural theme trails. In: Hall, D., Kirkpatrick, I. and Mitchell, M. (eds) *Rural Tourism and Sustainable Business.* Channel View, Clevedon, UK, pp. 137–148.

Mowforth, M., Charlton, C. and Munt, I. (2008) *Tourism and Responsibility: Perspectives from Latin America and the Caribbean.* Routledge, London.

Newsome, D. and Dowling, R.K. (eds) (2010) *Geotourism: The Tourism of Geology and Landscape.* Goodfellow, Oxford, UK.

O'Neal, G.S. and O'Neal, R.A. (2003) Community development in the USA: an empowerment zone example. *Community Development Journal* 38, 120–129.

Osborne, S.P. (1994) The language of empowerment. *International Journal of Public Sector Management* 7(3), 56–62.

Pattullo, P. (1997) Reclaiming the heritage trail: culture and identity. In: France, L. (ed.) *The Earthscan Reader in Sustainable Tourism.* Earthscan, London, pp. 135–148.

Rogerson, C.M. (2005) Unpacking tourism SMMEs in South Africa: structure, support needs and policy response. *Development Southern Africa* 22, 623–642.

Scheyvens, R. (1999) Ecotourism and the empowerment of local communities. *Tourism Management* 20, 245–249.

Scheyvens, R. (2002) *Tourism for Development: Empowering Communities.* Prentice Hall, Harlow, UK.

Scheyvens, R. (2003) Local involvement in managing tourism. In: Singh, S., Timothy, D.J. and Dowling, R.K. (eds) *Tourism in Destination Communities.* CAB International, Wallingford, UK, pp. 229–252.

Scheyvens, R. (2011) *Tourism and Poverty.* Routledge, London.

Scrase, T.J. (2003) Precarious production: globalisation and artisan labour in the Third World. *Third World Quarterly* 24, 449–461.

Simons, M.S. (2000) Aboriginal heritage art and moral rights. *Annals of Tourism Research* 27, 412–431.

Snyder, K.A. and Sulle, E.B. (2011) Tourism in Maasai communities: a chance to improve livelihoods? *Journal of Sustainable Tourism* 19, 935–952.

Sofield, T.H.B. (2003) *Empowerment for Sustainable Tourism Development.* Elsevier, Oxford, UK.

Spenceley, A. (ed.) (2008) *Responsible Tourism: Critical Issues for Conservation and Development.* Earthscan, London/Sterling, Virginia.

Timothy, D.J. (1999) Participatory planning: a view of tourism in Indonesia. *Annals of Tourism Research* 26, 371–391.

Timothy, D.J. (2000) Building community awareness of tourism in a developing country destination. *Tourism Recreation Research* 25, 111–116.

Timothy, D.J. (2002) Tourism and community development issues. In: Sharpley, R. and Telfer, D.J. (eds) *Tourism and Development: Concepts and Issues.* Channel View, Clevedon, UK, pp. 149–164.

Timothy, D.J. (2007) Empowerment and stakeholder participation in tourism destination communities. In: Church, A. and Coles, T. (eds) *Tourism, Power and Space.* Routledge, London, pp. 199–216.

Timothy, D.J. (2011) *Cultural Heritage and Tourism: An Introduction.* Channel View, Bristol, UK.

Timothy, D.J. and Wall, G. (1997) Selling to tourists: Indonesian street vendors. *Annals of Tourism Research* 24, 322–340.

Timothy, D.J. and White, K. (1999) Community-based ecotourism development on the periphery of Belize. *Current Issues in Tourism* 2, 226–242.

Torres, R. and Momsen, J.H. (2004) Challenges and potential for linking tourism and agriculture to achieve pro-poor tourism objectives. *Progress in Development Studies* 4, 294–318.

Tosun, C. (2000) Limits to community participation in the tourism development process in developing countries. *Tourism Management* 21, 613–633.

Wall, G. (1995) People outside the plans. In: Nuryanti, W. (ed.) *Tourism and Culture: Global Civilization in Change,* Gadjah Mada University Press, Yogyakarta, Indonesia, pp. 130–137.

Wall, G. and Mathieson, A. (2007) *Tourism: Changes, Impacts and Opportunities.* Prentice Hall, London.

Wanhill, S. (2004) Government assistance for tourism SMEs: from theory to practice. In: Thomas, R. (ed.) *Small Firms in Tourism: International Perspectives.* Elsevier, Oxford, UK, pp. 53–70.

Zientara, P. (2009) A few remarks on globalisation, democracy and spatiality. *Economic Affairs* 29(2), 56–61.

Zientara, P. (2011) When environmental protection collides with economic development: scalar interpretation of conflicts in Polish localities. *Eastern European Economics* 49(2), 65–83.

6 Environmental Performance

Ralf Buckley
Griffith University, Australia

Introduction

In corporate as in individual human terms, responsibility is seen more as an attitude than an outcome; but in those same terms, actions speak louder than words, and performance means more than pretences. Corporate responsibility includes environmental as well as social components, and for both components, companies are judged less on their statements of intent and internal processes, and more on their actual achievements. Environmental performance is thus a key component of corporate responsibility, in tourism as in any other industry sector.

Measures of corporate environmental performance may include any parameter or activity where the company's operations create environmental impacts, and any actions that the company may take to limit or offset those impacts (see Zientara, Chapter 12). In the same way that there is no single parameter for use in environmental accounting (Buckley, 2003, 2009), there is no single aggregate measure of environmental performance. In addition, some environmental performance parameters are correlated with each other positively, and others negatively, either because of physical mechanisms which produce or reduce impacts, or because of financial trade-off factors.

Environmental impacts, and associated management measures and performance parameters, are commonly divided broadly into two major groups, known as green and brown (or grey) factors, respectively. Green factors are those related broadly to inputs from the natural environment into the human economy through the consumption of natural resources, and through associated impacts on biodiversity, species habitats and food chains, ecological communities and ecosystem functions. Brown impacts are those associated with the discharge of wastes from the human economy into the natural environment, which create air and water pollution, noise and radiation, and associated effects.

Different components of the tourism industry produce different sets of environmental impacts; and the types, intensities and significance of these impacts commonly depend on the ecosystem where they occur. Hence there are different impacts, and different environmental management approaches, for the accommodation, transport and activity components of tourism. In addition, impacts and management differ with scale and type of accommodation, from temporary tents to tourist towns. They also differ with scale and type of transport, from kayaks to cruise ships, hot-air balloons to jumbo jets, or hiking boots to off-road vehicles and tour buses. Similarly, activities range from minimal impact leave-no-trace wilderness travel, to high-impact activities such as competitive motorized sports; the accompanying recreational infrastructure includes ski resorts, marinas, golf courses and the associated residential development.

For each of these components, impacts also depend on location. The impacts and management of any tourism development or activity generally differ between, e.g., tropical rainforest, oceanic coral cay, hyper-arid desert, alpine mountain top or temperate grassland. The same component or activity is usually more significant ecologically in less modified natural environments than in towns or farmland, for two reasons. First, national parks and other relatively unmodified areas support a wider range of plant and animal species, some of them rare and endangered, which can be affected by tourism and related activities. Secondly, because urban and agricultural areas have already experienced major human impacts, the relative change as a result of tourism is generally less than that caused by primary industries or by residential or industrial development.

The measurement and management of environmental performance is thus an enormously complicated process. Each component of any given tourism operation in any given location is likely to produce a large suite of different impacts, each with different ecological significance, different potential management approaches, and different possible performance benchmarks. Impacts, ecological significance and management have been examined quite extensively, as outlined in the next section. Environmental performance benchmarks, however, are more contentious.

Benchmarks and best practices

In general, there are two main types of environmental performance benchmark, each of them as diverse as the impacts and management measures to which they apply. The first is legal. Many countries and jurisdictions maintain a range of environmental laws, regulations and standards, and compliance with these is the most basic measure of environmental performance. Only some are specific to tourism. Most refer more broadly either to planning processes or pollution control or environmental quality.

These environmental laws and standards can differ greatly between countries and jurisdictions. One oft-debated issue is whether performance should be judged only against local legislation, no matter how lax; or whether it should be judged against more stringent standards which may apply in other countries, such as those where the company is based or where its clients originate. If local standards are adopted, difficulties arise in comparing environmental performance between tourism operations in different countries. Suppose, for example, that one company meets relatively lax standards for a particular parameter in one country, whereas a second company fails to meet much more stringent standards in a second country, but that the second company actually generates a lower impact, for the parameter concerned, than the first. In a global sense, the second company has better environmental performance than the first, but if local regulatory standards are used a basis for comparison, the reverse would be reported.

Rather than using regulatory standards as a benchmark of environmental performance, an alternative approach is to identify 'best practice' for a particular environmental management issue, a particular subsector of the tourism industry and a particular geographical region, and to use that as a benchmark of performance. This approach has advantages, but is also fraught with certain difficulties. The same difficulties apply in legal instruments that incorporate concepts of best practice or analogous terms.

Complexities arise for three main reasons. The first is that best practice can be defined in different ways: for example, by means of technologies, management processes or final results. The second is that technologies and practices to minimize impacts may indeed differ between different types of environment and different types and scales of tourism activity: that is, different approaches may constitute best practice under different circumstances. The third reason is that industry interests sometimes take advantage of the first two issues to generate uncertainty about what constitutes best practice. That is, while there are indeed differences in what might be considered reasonable or appropriate in any particular circumstances, some enterprises may take advantage of this uncertainty to avoid adopting particular practices even when very similar enterprises in the same area have indeed already done so.

The whole point of environmental best practice, however, is that it is defined by the lowest impact approaches which comparable operators have actually taken. From an environmental perspective, therefore, the distinction between best and second best is commonly rather clear. If any one enterprise adopts or adapts new environmental management approaches that produce better results in reducing environmental impacts than those of any similar enterprise, then that new approach defines best practice until it, in turn, is superseded. There are caveats, but these are minor. There is no need, for example, to define 'similarity' between enterprises, because the functional test is simple. If any enterprise could reduce its own environmental impacts by adopting environmental management practices which are already used by any other enterprise, then until it does so, it will only be operating at second best.

There are then two further considerations. The first is the test of overkill: that is, improvements which would involve large investment for a small reduction in impacts. For example, technologies or practices designed for large-scale enterprises may represent overkill for small-scale analogues; and approaches which are appropriate in wilderness areas may represent overkill in areas which have already suffered severe impacts from other sources or sectors. The key test for potential overkill is the ecological significance of the expected reductions in environmental impact.

The second consideration is the question of retrofitting. Some environmental management practices, notably those that depend heavily on technologies or building design, are much easier and cheaper to adopt for new enterprises than for existing ones. Once again, the question is how to determine when retrofitting is justified in order to reach best practice, and when it is more reasonable to remain at second best for the life of the facility concerned. Clearly, many factors may be considered, including expected longevity, other refits and refurbishments, and the environ-mental impacts of the retrofitting itself, as well as financial costs and environmental improvements.

As a notional test, one may apply the same efficiency principle that underlies the pollution-control concepts of offsets and bubbles. Under this test, the expected environmental improvement from any particular retrofitting operation can be compared against the expected environmental improvement if the same investment were made in environmental improvements elsewhere in the enterprise's operations. This is only a partial test, as there may be the option to make both investments and improvements simultaneously; but it is at least one useful measure which can be applied.

Environmental Impacts and Management

The environmental impacts of tourism have been described in detail elsewhere (Warnken and Buckley, 1998; Gossling, 2002; Buckley, 2004, 2011). Tables 6.1 and 6.2, reproduced from Buckley (1991, 2009), summarize the major types of impact for some of the major components of the industry. From the perspective of corporate responsibility, the key issue is what measures have been taken, by corporations at all scales, to minimize these impacts.

Auditor, shareholder, customer perspectives

Given the enormous range and breadth of environmental impacts produced by different subsectors of the tourism industry, it is beyond the scope of this contribution to list impacts, management measures and performance criteria individually. Instead, I will consider here the different perspectives of an auditor, a shareholder and a customer in assessing environmental performance as a component of corporate responsibility; and also the depth, accuracy and reliability of the various information sources they may have at their disposal.

There are critical differences in access, transparency and comprehensibility of the relevant data both for individual corporations

Table 6.1. Environmental impacts of accommodation and shelter (Buckley, 1991, 2009).[a]

A

Type of accom-modation or shelter	Vegetation clearance or damage	Soil erosion and/or compaction	Wildlife disturbance or habitat destruction	Firewood collec-tion and campfires
Resorts, hotels: construction	Site clearance	Short term, during construction	Habitat cleared, noise	
Continuing	Tracks, etc.	Unsealed tracks, etc.	Shyer species leave area	Collected elsewhere, if used
Fixed car or caravan camps	Site clearance initially and continuing, tracks, etc.	If ungrassed and increasing with use	Habitat clearance, shyer species leave area	Large area often denuded
Overnight car/four-wheel drive camps	Increasing with use	Increasing with use	Depends on frequency of use	Large campfires common
Horse/hiker huts	Local site clearance, trampling	Localized, depends on soil type, etc.	Minor, localized	Large area often affected, regular large campfires
Boat-access shore sites	Increasing with use	Bank erosion	Minor, localized	Large area often affected, regular large campfires
Often-used bush camps	Localized, new tent sites	Localized, depends on soil type, etc.	Minor, localized	Depends on vegetation type, large area may be affected
Single-use camps and bivouacs	Minimal or none	Generally none	Temporary or none	Minimal or none

B

Solid wastes	Water pollution	Noise	Visual
Construction rubbish, builders' rubble	Sediments	Construction plant	Construction site and plant
Garbage, treated sewage	Sullage, increased nutrients	Machinery and motors	Conspicuous buildings and infrastructure, large vehicles
Garbage, litter, toilets	Sullage, increased nutrients, bacterial	Generators, car engines, chainsaws, radios, voices	Vehicles, caravans, large tents, equipment, campfires
Litter, human wastes	Bacterial, soap	Car engines, chainsaws, radios, voices	Cars, large tents, campfires
Litter, horse dung, human wastes	Bacterial	Saws, voices	Huts, cleared paddocks, campfires
Litter, fish guts, human wastes	Petroleum residues	Outboard motors, voices	Boats, large tents, fires, clearance
Some paper, human wastes	Bacterial, soap	Voices	Small tents, fires
Generally none	Generally none	Minimal or none	Minimal and temporary

[a] The 4 columns in Part B follow on from the 5 columns in part A.

and comparative benchmarks. As a result, raw information on the various aspects of environmental performance passes through a number of filters and smoothing steps before it becomes accessible to retail clients and the general public. Only in the extreme case of major environmental disasters does raw information sometimes become available in real time via the mass media.

Ideally, an environmental auditor has access to every aspect of a corporation's operations. In reality, however, this is far from

Table 6.2. Environmental impacts of transport and travel (Buckley, 1991, 2009). [a]

A

Means of transport or travel	Vegetation clearance or damage	Soil erosion or compaction	Wildlife disturbance, shooting or habitat destruction	Solid wastes
Light planes, helicopters	Airstrips only	Airstrips only	Depends on speed, altitude, frequency of flights	Empty fuel drums at remote strips
Bus or car on road	Roads and verges cleared	Compaction and erosion on unsealed roads	Noise depends on traffic density; roads can act as barriers; road kills	Litter
Car or four-wheel drive on tracks	Tracks cleared; tend to be widened and new tracks cut	Dust, gully erosion and compaction widespread	Road kills, noise, shooting	Litter
Off-road vehicles (ORVs) off track	Severe and extensive vegetation damage	Erosion widespread, depends on terrain and soil type	Widespread noise disturbance; ORVs used for shooting	Litter, human wastes
Mountain bikes	Less severe than ORVs	Localized in heavily used areas	Disturbance in heavily used areas	Litter, human wastes
Horses	Trampling on horse trails	Localized, trails and holding paddocks	Minimal, unless riders rowdy or shooters	Horse manure
Hiking	Trampling on heavily used trails	Localized on heavily used areas	Generally minimal	Human wastes
Power boats	Campsites, shoreline and aquatic vegetation	Not applicable	Noise, fishing and shooting	Garbage at campsites, jetsam
Unpowered water-craft	Generally none	Not applicable	Fishing only	Garbage and jetsam

B

Water pollution	Air pollution	Noise	Increased fire risk	Weed and pathogens
Refuelling spills	Greenhouse gases	Loud, but intermittent	Little or none	Airstrips only
Petroleum residues in runoff from roads	Exhaust fumes	Line source, volume depends on traffic density	Sparks, cigarette butts	Along road verges
Turbid runoff	Exhaust fumes	As above	Sparks, cigarette butts	Along track verges
Campsites, etc: bacteria, soap	Exhaust fumes	Major impact as ORVs can enter otherwise quiet areas	Sparks, butts, campfires	Spread on tyres
Campsites, etc: bacteria, soap	None	Voices only	Butts, campfires	Spread on tyres
Nutrients, bacteria, downstream of holding paddocks	None unless very crowded	Voices only	Butts, campfires	Spread in fodder if carried
Campsites etc: bacteria, soap	None	Voices only	Butts, campfires	Minimal, on boots and socks
Fuel residues, nutrients, bacteria, antifouling paints	Exhaust fumes	Engine noise	Campsites only	Campsites only
Bacteria, soap	None	Voices only	Campsites only	Campsites only

[a] The 5 columns in Part B follow on from the 5 columns in part A

the case. Only if a swarm of auditors equipped with every relevant measuring device were to monitor every aspect of the corporation's activities moment by moment might this ideal possibly occur. Much more typically, an auditor makes a short site visit and carries out limited visual inspections in person. For quantitative data on parameters which are not immediately detectable to the naked eye, auditors must rely on the company's own monitoring data. This would include, e.g. water quality parameters, rare species populations, or even the smooth operations of fundamental facilities such as sewage treatment plants.

Most monitoring costs money, and environmental monitoring is rarely at the top of a private corporation's priorities. It is commonplace that the parameters monitored are chosen for convenience rather than ecological significance (Warnken and Buckley, 1998). Records are rarely complete, if they are kept at all. Even in a developed country where planning or pollution control law require regular and specified environmental monitoring, a company may make just enough measurements to prevent prosecution in case a government inspector might show up on site. Tourism corporations involved in eco-certification programmes intended to demonstrate high environmental performance may still provide incomplete data despite several years in the programme (K. Forche, personal communication).

Even luxury lodges running their own private game reserves, which may track the exact daily locations of each individual for their rarer wildlife species, may not retain any written records. From an auditor's perspective, therefore, there is only a single person's verbal assurances to rely on; and if such a company, or indeed a public national park, relies on icon species to attract tourists, they may be reluctant to report publicly if all individuals of that species have vanished from the premises. There seem to be examples of this both for the giant panda in China and the tiger in India (Buckley, 2010).

There are even examples where large-scale conspiracies to conceal environmental data have been alleged. The best-known example is that of air quality in aircraft cabins. For decades, passengers and aircrew have

complained about this issue, and airlines have denied that there is any problem. Long-haul aircraft have a plentiful supply of clean air immediately outside the fuselage, but it consumes fuel to compress and heat that air for use in the cabin. Therefore, it is cheaper simply to bleed in a small proportion of new air which has already been heated and compressed by the jet engines, and to recycle the rest repeatedly. Claims have surfaced recently, on the web sites of public health advocacy groups, that the airline industry has systematically concealed evidence on the adverse health and safety effects of polluted cabin air.

For a corporation's owners or share/stockholders, access to environmental performance data depends both on company structure and individual technical expertise. For a sole proprietor or a partnership, all of the organization's data are open to scrutiny, but data will only exist if the owners have decided to collect them. For individual stockholders in a large publicly listed corporation, environmental data may be filtered through several layers of management and a board of directors before being summarized for annual reports. Even if a company carries out its own internal environmental audits, or commissions external auditors, audit reports will not necessarily be available in full to stockholders; and even if detailed data are indeed provided, stockholders may not necessarily be in a position to interpret them independently.

For clients, potential clients and the general public, access to environmental performance data is generally restricted to what a company chooses to make public, unless an environmental crisis triggers an independent investigation. In releasing such data, corporations generally intend to convey one of only three possible messages. In the event of a disaster, the company will generally aim to convey that things are now under control. For most companies, routine annual reports aim only to convey that the company complies with applicable legislation. For companies seeking to claim green credentials so as to gain political or market advantages, the main message is that they are better than their competitors.

In making such assertions there are two

main approaches. The first is simply to illustrate a series of environmental actions or achievements, commonly with rather limited quantitative data or comparative benchmarks, so as to create an impression. The second is to rely on some form of third-party endorsement, either from a certification agency, an award scheme or an individual celebrity. In technical terms, these approaches have significant shortcomings in demonstrating actual environmental performance. Awards are commonly made purely on the basis of comparison between applicants, without reference to any baseline standards. Eco-certification programmes differ greatly in structure and reliability. Some rely only on process-based checklists. Some claim to maintain confidential comparative databases, but refuse to open these to public scrutiny. Very few publish the actual technical environmental performance criteria which they use to determine whether or not to certify individual tourism corporations (Font and Buckley, 2001; Black and Crabtree, 2007).

Overall, therefore, it is remarkably difficult for members of the general public, or actual or potential customers of any tourism corporation, to obtain access to reliable and ecologically meaningful raw data on its environmental performance; and most of the various secondary methods which companies use to report or promote their own environmental performance are of very dubious validity.

Conclusions

Perhaps the principal conclusion to be drawn is that environmental performance data for tourism corporations are rather hard to come by. For most companies, environmental data are not collected or reported at anything close to the level of detail that is routinely required for financial performance. For the latter, there are legislated standards and professional codes and protocols for tracking every single unit of currency through every corporation, and for accounting, auditing and archiving information on assets, income and expenditure. Corresponding rules for environmental accounting, audit and reporting are far weaker, and in most countries they are voluntary.

In addition, the tourism industry is not generally a leader in this field, because it prefers to promote an erroneous image of itself as an industry without significant environmental impacts. In recent years, however, attention to the greenhouse gas emissions associated with tourism has focused more attention on the industry's environmental impacts in general. The low-impact image is therefore no longer tenable or convincing to customers, stockholders and the general public in most countries. As a result, more attention has been focused on a range of different environmental impacts caused by tourism corporations, and hence also on their measurement and management.

Over the past one to two decades, three parallel and perhaps converging trends in the tourism industry have indeed yielded some improvements in environmental management, though these are by no means universal. The first of these is a trend, in some countries at least, to the broader adoption of basic environmental management technologies such as effective sewage treatment systems. This was most probably triggered by a number of well-publicized instances where large-scale development of oceanfront tourism accommodation led to severe pollution of waters used for beach bathing, and in some cases also to algal degradation of coral reefs, with consequent reductions in visitor numbers or yield. On purely commercial grounds, this led local government agencies, or individual resort corporations, to halt previous practices of pumping sewage directly into the ocean.

The second trend is the widespread adoption, in the transport and accommodation sectors, of energy-saving and sometimes water-saving measures which seem to be driven principally by a concern to cut costs, but which do also yield some environmental gains. These range from the widespread – and often ridiculed – invitations, in urban hotel rooms, to save the planet by hanging up your towel; to large-scale and continuing attempts to improve fuel economy in aircraft.

The third trend is the continuing growth in so-called 'ecochic', the gradual intrusion of ecotourism approaches into mainstream and indeed luxury tourism. This is an interesting phenomenon, rather different from the so-called mainstreaming of ecotourism principles that was hypothesized and hoped for at the World Ecotourism Summit a decade or so ago. What seems to have happened is that the large-scale urban and resort tourism subsectors have adopted only the most minor and basic of environmental management measures and technologies, as outlined in preceding paragraphs. This is perhaps better considered as veneer environmentalism or, at best, very shallow mainstreaming.

Instead, ecotourism approaches have made their way into the mainstream travel media and markets only as luxury boutique products: hence the term ecochic. The marketing approach is very much luxury first, environment as bonus; rather than environment first, luxury as bonus. From an environmental performance perspective, of course, the way in which products are marketed is largely irrelevant to what they may or may not achieve. The critical issues are thus first, whether the ecochic approach can expand to occupy a significant proportion of the luxury market; and secondly, having made the bold leap from backpacker to luxury level, whether it can now penetrate back down through the much larger mid-tier family market.

At present, ecochic is very small in scale. There are indeed individual commercial tourism enterprises with very high environmental performance (Buckley, 2010), but as yet they remain very much the minority. Luxury travel magazines may run eco-awards, but they still devote only one or two pages to promoting or reporting them. Similarly, the destination sustainability surveys carried out annually by *National Geographic Traveller* make up only a tiny proportion of the organization's total publications. The travel sections in general-circulation newspapers, magazines and television programmes make an obligatory nod to environmental issues and options on occasion, but this is by no means a key focus.

Overall, therefore, it seems likely that if there is any general improvement in the environmental performance components of corporate responsibility in the mainstream tourism industry, it is more likely to be driven by possible broad-scale changes in social attitudes and values, than by initiatives originating within the tourism industry itself.

References

Black, R. and Crabtree, A. (eds) (2007) *Quality Assurance and Certification in Ecotourism.* CAB International, Wallingford, UK.

Buckley, R.C. (1991) Environmental planning and policy for green tourism. In: Buckley, R.C. *Perspectives in Environmental Management.* Springer, Heidelberg, Germany, pp. 226–242.

Buckley, R.C. (2003) Environmental inputs and outputs in ecotourism geotourism with a positive triple bottom line? *Journal of Ecotourism* 2, 76–82.

Buckley, R.C. (ed.) (2004) *Environmental Impacts of Ecotourism.* CAB International, Wallingford, UK.

Buckley, R.C. (2009) *Ecotourism: Principles and Practices.* CAB International, Wallingford, UK.

Buckley, R.C. (2010) *Conservation Tourism.* CAB International, Wallingford, UK.

Buckley, R.C. (2011) Tourism and environment. *Annual Review of Environment and Resources* 36, 397–416.

Font, X. and Buckley, R.C. (eds) (2001) *Tourism Ecolabelling: Certification and Promotion of Sustainable Management.* CAB International, Wallingford, UK.

Gossling, S. (2002) Global environmental consequences of tourism. *Global Environmental Change* 12, 283–302.

Warnken, J. and Buckley, R.C. (1998) Scientific quality of tourism environmental impact assessment. *Journal of Applied Ecology* 35, 1–8.

7 The Politics of Tourism and Poverty Reduction

Anita Pleumarom

Tourism investigation and monitoring team (tim-team), Bangkok, Thailand

Introduction

An uprising of the poor against responsible tourism is hard to imagine. But this is exactly what happened in Kochi in the southern Indian State of Kerala. On 22 March 2008, people from poor communities – fisher-folk, tribals, Dalits, women and youth – and their supporters from civil society organizations, academia and intellectual circles held a street protest and then gathered for an '"Irresponsible Tourism Convention" [in] Kerala' (KTW, 2008b). These actions were the response to the non-participatory nature of the International Conference on Responsible Tourism, held at the same time under the banner of Kerala's and India's tourism departments and the Indian section of the International Centre for Responsible Tourism (ICRT) (Goodwin and Venu, 2008).

The public outcry against Kerala's 'responsible tourism' initiative stunned many observers. The controversy had actually begun 2 years earlier, when the World Travel and Tourism Council (WTTC) announced the finalists for the 2006 Tourism for Tomorrow Awards, and Kerala was selected as one of the three finalists in the 'Destination' category. This attracted widespread civil society criticism, maintaining that Kerala was not a model of 'sustainable' or 'responsible tourism' by any international standard. It was argued that

tourism had in fact contributed little, if anything, to ensure 'maximum positive benefit' to and 'minimum negative impact' on local communities, which were mentioned as key criteria for the award. The WTTC eventually dropped the nomination, dealing a temporary setback to the overzealous ambitions of the state-sanctioned Kerala 'responsible tourism' drive (KTW, 2006).

Following the announcement of the prestigious ICRT conference in 2008, contentious tourism issues flared up again in Kerala and deepened the divide between local communities affected by tourism and the state's tourism authorities. Disadvantaged and poor sections of society had lost confidence in the government's policies and practices as burning problems such as tourism's encroachment on shorelines and forests, displacement of poor villagers, environmental degradation and commercialization of culture remained unsolved. The failure to address 'irresponsible tourism' issues appeared to prove right the critics' argument that the Kerala 'responsible tourism' initiative represented little more than a public relations exercise. Kerala Tourism Watch (KTW, 2008a), a coalition of local grassroots activists and organizations, stated: 'There is no paradigm shift in the way Kerala is developing its tourism sector. The current discussions are just a hype to change the fading images of Kerala tourism and portray it as a

© CAB International 2012. *Responsible Tourism: Concepts, Theory and Practice* (ed. D. Leslie)

responsible destination in the international market'.

KTW decided to organize an alternative event after repeated requests to the Indian conference organizers and to Harold Goodwin, the ICRT founder, to give local people the opportunity to air their views in the official event were turned down (tim-team, 2008). Participants in the 'Irresponsible Tourism' Convention claimed that the discussions in the official conference were superficial and only served big tourism players. Their final statement said: 'The conference in its very structures and deliberations was non-inclusive and remained inaccessible to [the] majority of the real stakeholders and civil society organizations in Kerala. ... We ask: "To who are the Government responsible and whose interests does the Government protect?"' (KTW, 2008c).

The angry protest was certainly an embarrassment for the 503 delegates from 29 countries who attended the official conference. After all, many of them professed to work for a benign form of tourism aimed to 'create better places for people to live in and for people to visit' and to 'involve local people in decisions that affect their lives and life chances' (Kerala Tourism, 2008). There was evidently a great contradiction in the way the conference was organized and what it promised.

If the conference organizers had provided an open forum for the 'expert' conference delegates and people from the grassroots to meet and exchange information and views, it would have been a unique opportunity not only to gain new knowledge but also to demonstrate that the 'responsible tourism' advocates actually meant what they said about participation and partnership building. But by excluding very important local actors from the discussions, the conference lost much credibility, and an important chance to put democratic principles into practice was missed. The debate on tourism in general and on tourism as a strategy for poverty reduction in particular is fraught with ideology owing to the diverging backgrounds, values, perceptions and interests of tourism players. As Hall pointed out, there is no objective or value-free approach to tourism (see Hall, 1996, Chapter 8).

Based on a political economy approach, a number of tourism researchers in the 1970s questioned that tourism is a 'passport to development' (Kadt, 1978). Many attempts have been made since then to improve the socio-economic and environmental performance of this sector through 'responsible', 'eco', 'sustainable', 'community-based' and 'pro-poor' tourism. Key questions that will be explored in this chapter are: How useful have these initiatives been, particularly in terms of poverty reduction? Have they helped to change the economic fundamentals to transform international tourism into a 'passport' to poverty alleviation and sustainable development? If responsible poor-friendly tourism is underway and progressing, why is there still so much discontent among people in Kerala and other tourist destinations?

The following section will give an overview of the work that has been done in the field of tourism and poverty reduction and the major policy statements of the 'pro-poor tourism' proponents. Then there will be a brief outline of the historical controversy of tourism as development before a critical look is taken at various aspects that play a crucial role in the tourism debate, with a focus on poverty. The aspects discussed here include: economic performance, livelihoods, land and natural resources, food security, environmental sustainability, climate change, the role of women, etc.

The key message of this chapter is that all discourses and initiatives on pro-poor tourism are of little value unless the realities on the ground and the voices of the poor are fully taken into account. It is also vital to make tourism part of a wider political debate on how to effectively tackle the root causes of poverty and inequality in the context of globalization.

Global Army of 'Pro-poor Tourism' Promoters

International, government, non-governmental and private sector organizations have given considerable attention to the argument that tourism can be made a viable tool to alleviate poverty. It is generally assumed that the international tourism sector can generate economic and other benefits for poor people and communities in the context of responsible and sustainable tourism development and can thus serve as an instrument to help achieve the Millennium Development Goals (MDGs) that aim to tackle the world's major development challenges (e.g. poverty, gender equality, environmental sustainability) by 2015 (UNDP, 2011a). The United Nations Economic and Social Commission for Asia and the Pacific (UN-ESCAP, 2007) and the World Tourism Organization (UNWTO) consider that tourism will contribute to achieving these goals. Indeed, UNWTO (2010, p. 4) has stated that 'Responsible and sustainable tourism allows destinations and companies to minimize the negative impacts of tourism on the environment and on cultural heritage while maximizing its economic and social benefits'. Further, UNWTO suggests that investing in 'sustainable tourism' can play a key role in creating a global green economy, reducing poverty, boosting job creation and addressing major environmental challenges (UNEP, 2011). The linking of tourism to poverty reduction and the MDG agenda have led to the emergence of the 'pro-poor tourism' concept (Ashley *et al.*, 2001), which is 'an overall approach *designed to unlock opportunities for the poor*' (Jamieson *et al.*, 2004, p. 3) and is particularly spear-headed by the UK-based Pro-Poor Tourism (PPT) Partnership. Meanwhile, there is a long list of organizations, including United Nations (UN) agencies such as UNWTO, the UN Development Programme (UNDP), the UN Conference on Trade and Development (UNCTAD) and the UN Environment Programme (UNEP), as well as the European Union (EU) and a number of bilateral development agencies that actively support poverty-focused tourism projects. Private sector organizations such as WTTC have adjusted their strategic frameworks to fit into the 'new tourism'paradigm. Albeit reflecting the typical growth-oriented approach, WTTC (2003) emphasizes its commitment to 'building New Tourism, helping to bring new benefits to a wider world' (p. 2) and calls on all tourism players to 'Cooperate in identifying opportunities for growth; focus on building Travel & Tourism that opens prospects for people – from employment to development; work together to remove impediments to growth – from infrastructure to pollution, and from

outdated legislation to unmet health and security concerns' (p. 11).

A plethora of pro-poor programmes and projects have been designed and implemented by individual organizations or in partnerships (see Equations, 2008a,b; ITC, 2009; UNWTO ST-EP, 2012). It is assumed that poverty can be reduced when tourism creates employment and diversified livelihood opportunities, which provide additional income. Moreover, it is argued that tourism can contribute to direct taxation by generating taxable economic growth, so more funds will be available to alleviate poverty through education, health and infrastructure development (UN-ESCAP, 2007, p. 74).

Special attention has been paid to tourism's extensive links with other sectors. For instance, the tourism sector requires support to build and operate tourism facilities through backwards linkages with basic infrastructure services such as energy, telecommunications and environmental services, as well as with agricultural, manufacturing and construction services. Moreover, it has forward linkages with sectors supplying services to tourists, including financial, retail, recreational, cultural, hospitality and health services. 'Strong linkages catalyze a multiplier effect that generates broad-based economic benefits at the national level as well as *in situ* employment opportunities and poverty reduction at the local level. Without strong tourism linkages, such benefits do not materialize' (UNCTAD, 2010, p. 7). Therefore, one of the main objectives of poverty-focused projects is to enhance the linkages between tourism businesses and poor people at the community level. 'Links with many different types of "the poor" need to be considered: staff, neighbouring communities, land-holders, producers of food, fuel and other suppliers, operators of micro tourism businesses, craft-makers, other users of tourism infrastructure (roads) and resources (water) etc.' (PPT Partnership, 2011).

As there have been serious concerns over poor employment conditions for workers in the tourism sector, the International Labour Organization (ILO) emphasizes the importance of 'decent work' in the context of poverty alleviation strategies (Bolwell and Weinz, 2008, p. 2). It has also stressed the need to transform pro-poor tourism from a niche market into mainstream tourism for development: 'PPT should be on a big scale rather than a piecemeal micro-enterprise approach. All forms of decent work should be considered in assessing value chain benefits to the poor' (Bolwell and Weinz, 2008, p. 19). As regards the role of poor women in tourism it was recently stated that in global terms 'tourism in developing regions ... presents a wide range of income-generation opportunities for women' (UNWTO and UN Women, 2011, p. i).

During the 4th UN Conference on Least Developed Countries (LDC-IV) in Turkey in 2011, a Tourism Special Event for sustainable development and poverty reduction was organized by the UN Steering Committee on Tourism for Development (SCTD). This meeting was an important milestone as the UN system for the first time expressed a clear commitment to making tourism work as a tool for poverty reduction and development, and outlined that their support services 'are built around four pillars: building good governance and sustainability in tourism development; promoting investment in the tourism economy; fostering the poverty reduction impact of tourism; and encouraging human resources development, and will contribute to the preservation and safeguarding of natural and cultural assets that form the basis of tourism in LDCs' (UNCTAD, 2011). Meanwhile, UNEP has coordinated a major initiative for the establishment of a Global Partnership for Sustainable Tourism (GPST), a main objective of which is promoting tourism as a way of alleviating poverty. UNEP puts much hope in the GPST saying that it 'has the potential to transform the way tourism is done worldwide, at all scales, by consumers, by enterprises, and by the governments that plan and regulate destination' (UNEP, 2010, p. 3).

Despite all the efforts over the last decade to boost tourism's image as a key driver for development, some trade experts and tourism leaders believe that the tourism sector is still lacking due political and economic recognition in developing countries; for example, questions have been raised as to why tourism has been 'neglected' in the Doha Development Agenda of the World Trade Organization (WTO) (Honeck, 2008). Noting that very few develop-

ing countries and none of the LDCs have made commitments under the General Agreement on Trade in Services (GATS) (a multilateral agreement under the General Agreement on Tariffs and Trade (GATT) and WTO), it recommends, among other things, that the service negotiations should highlight the linkages between GATS infrastructure commitments and poverty alleviation as well as the role of GATS commitments in promoting sustainable tourism development to ensure that the importance of tourism for LDCs is acknowledged and acted upon (Honeck, 2008, p. 29).

In another offensive to make tourism a priority on the global agenda, UNWTO and WTTC jointly launched a 'Global Leaders for Tourism Campaign' in early 2011 (UNWTO, 2011a) which was aimed to persuade governments around the world that tourism is 'one of the most effective solutions to today's global challenges' (UNWTO, 2011b) and should therefore be given especially high priority in national policies. An Open Letter to political leaders states: 'Through the creation of sustainable enterprises and decent jobs, Travel & Tourism provides the necessary security and stability for millions of people worldwide to build better lives. As a fast entry point into the workforce for young people and women, it provides crucial opportunities for fair income, social protection, gender equality, personal development and social inclusion' (UNWTO, 2011c).

'Dismal Science' Reviewed

The pro-poor argument in tourism is by no means new. While international agencies and major stakeholders have touted tourism as a panacea for poor nations and people, critics have rebutted their glaringly positive descriptions and assumptions, pointing out the adverse effects and raising challenging questions, such as: Who actually benefits from tourism? (Equations et al., 2004; Hall, 2007; Pleumarom, 2007).

As early as 1970, a group of Tanzanian students presented a groundbreaking study that exploded major myths about the socio-economic benefits of Third World tourism

(Lea 1988; Crick 1989). First, in contrast with the argument that tourism boosts revenue for the public sector through taxes and duties, the figures for Tanzania showed that for each tourist dollar, 40 cents went on imports, 40 cents went to private hotels and businesses, and merely 20 cents were collected by the government in taxes. There was little evidence that this public money was spent to improve social services for the poor. Secondly, the value of tourism as a job generator was brought into question. Comparing an investment in tourism with an equivalent in a labour intensive textile factory, it was found that around 20 times the number of new jobs would be created by investment in textiles rather than in tourism (Lea, 1988, p. 39). Shivji, one of the leading Tanzanian academics involved in the debate at that time, concluded: 'The justification for tourism in terms of it being "economically good", ... completely fails to appreciate the integrated nature of the system of under-development' (Lea, 1988, p. 36).

Turner and Ash (1975) called tourism a 'dismal science', arguing that 'the economics of tourism are totally deceptive' (Turner and Ash, 1975, p. 113). They warned that tourism could harm traditional economies and ways of life: 'The locals build the resorts and serve in them which, if fully controlled by foreigners, will contain few really worthwhile jobs. In the meantime, the fields return to weeds; the locals lose their traditional skills; they lose their ability to produce anything of direct practical use to themselves. While they've been building the resorts, they haven't been building the schools, the irrigation systems or the textile factories which would educate, feed or clothe them... . For the sake of this industry, they can lose their land, their jobs and their way of life – for what? (Turner and Ash, 1975, p. 123).

One of the main reasons why tourism was objected to was because of the uneven and unjust relations that it creates: the 'rich' tourists who are served and the 'poor' locals who serve. It was also denounced as wrong and unethical that tourism in poor countries 'inject the behaviour of a wasteful society into the midst of a society of want, but the profits go to the elites – those already wealthy, and those with political influence' (Crick 1989, p. 317).

In 1976, after more than a decade of financing large-scale tourism projects, the World Bank, in cooperation with UNESCO, funded an epoch-making international seminar on tourism and development. Researchers raised serious questions about international tourism as 'a passport to development', arguing that this was perpetuating the structures of domination inherited from colonialism and adding to already apparent asymmetries and inequalities between developed and developing nations. There was also the concern that tourism was creating a new kind of dependency for poor nations, as international debt politics and tourism development were tightly knotted together. Moreover, tourism's fickle nature was highlighted because of uncontrolled growth and overexploitation of natural and cultural resources (Kadt, 1979; Hawkins and Mann, 2007). In the wake of these criticisms, the World Bank closed down its tourism projects department. This is remarkable because tourism, along with nuclear energy, belongs to the few industries that the World Bank decided not to support, although the International Finance Corporation (IFC) – a sister unit of the World Bank – as well as regional development banks – including the African, Asian and Inter-American Development Banks – continued to engage in tourism-related development activities.

Under the pressure to address the problems of conventional tourism, a great number of 'new tourisms' were introduced in the 1980s and 1990s (see Leslie, Chapter 2). The concept of an environmentally and socially acceptable tourism provided an opportunity for a comeback of the World Bank. The Global Environment Facility (GEF) – a partnership between the Bank and the UNDP formed in 1991 – funded many conservation projects that included tourism as a major component (Hawkins and Mann, 2007). In 2007, the World Bank addressed a tourism strategy paper for Latin America and the Caribbean (LCR), which included the rationale that the Bank should take advantage of the growing country demand for innovative approaches to the tourism sector to develop 'a new line of business – a *non-traditional tourism* that reduces poverty by combining infrastructure, environmental and cultural sustainability, and local economic development' (Chavez, 2007,

p. 4) The new term, 'non-traditional tourism', was probably chosen to clearly distinguish it from the 'traditional tourism' that the World Bank had dropped from its agenda.

Many projects developed as alternatives to the much-criticized conventional tourism focused on environmental and social sustainability, and stressed the need to improve people's participation. The new, ostensibly benign, forms of tourism often owed more to labelling and marketing than to any profound change in the organization, basic values or power patterns of tourism (Pleumarom, 1990, 1994; Mowforth and Munt, 2003).

Importantly, the strong global forces for economic deregulation and privatization in fact increased the global reach of international tourism corporations (TNCs), thus undermining efforts to transform tourism into being more responsible and sustainable. Under new bilateral and multilateral free trade agreements such as GATS, governments were called upon to liberalize trade and investment in services so there was actually little space left for industry regulation or the implementation of measures aimed at environmental improvement and more benefit sharing of tourism income (Pleumarom, 1999, 2003).

As the prevailing structures of power and increasing inequalities resulting from globalization and liberalization remained unchallenged, it is not surprising that the new emphasis on poverty reduction was met with great scepticism. As Mowforth et al. (2008, p. 94) noted, the new strategy 'ran aground on the spin of the politicians who described it as the way forward for their national industries but who at the same time gave incentives only to the large-scale, transnational tourism enterprises. The activities of the latter were aimed at reducing to the minimum the economic benefits that might be left within the local community in order, of course, to maximize the profits to be repatriated to head offices and shareholders in the rich countries'.

Alleviating or Aggravating Poverty?

Viable poverty-focused policies and programmes would require a thorough and holistic understanding of poverty. But in the pro-poor tourism debate, very important questions remain unexplored; for example: How is 'poverty' to be defined? People living in tourism destinations are 'poor' in what sense? Which are the root causes of poverty? What tourism impacts can aggravate poverty? Are there other options than tourism to confront the problem of poverty?

While tourism's negative impacts are undeniable, there is still the tendency to hide the inconvenient truth about tourism as an industry and to emphatically point out the positive impacts. The euphemistic rhetoric prevails, and the emphasis is on what pro-poor tourism 'can' do, what its 'potential' is and what 'opportunities' it provides so as to conclude that tourism is definitely the right answer. This kind of discourse can be confusing because instead of talking about what *is*, the focus is on what *should be*. This is a method to gloss over the harsh realities and to give the impression that pro-poor tourism is in practice and doing well.

Economic progress?

What is the reason for this unbridled optimism that poor countries and people will economically progress through tourism development? Hawaii, for example, was paraded as a tourism success story for decades, but has been facing bankruptcy for several years. The islands' two economic pillars – tourism and the military industry – have almost crashed with little hope for a recovery in the foreseeable future (Kalani, 2011).

Apparently, tourism has also not resulted in economic prosperity and stability in Greece, Portugal, Spain and Italy; these countries now belong to the most debt-stricken eurozone states and have subsequently been forced into drastic austerity programmes that will further depress their economies and severely affect the majority of the population. Tunisia and Egypt which were, until recently, hailed as Africa's most successful tourist destinations, were shaken by mass uprisings in the beginning of 2011 because of economic impoverishment – including high unemployment, declining wages and skyrocketing costs of living, which led to an overthrow of governments in both countries. Discussions about the role of tourism in all these economic and political woes are generally avoided.

A major weakness in the economics of tourism is the lack of systematic studies on where the tourists' expenditure actually ends up, how much 'leaks' away, how much remains in the national economy, and how much 'trickles down' to ordinary citizens. Although the relevance of leakages, occurring as a result of the repatriation of profits by foreign-owned companies, expatriate salaries and imports, has been repeatedly stressed by economists and agencies including UNCTAD, it is conspicuous as to how little research is available on this important issue. For most countries, there are no data on leakages available at all. The World Bank estimates an average leakage level of 55% for developing countries. According to reports from UNCTAD and UNEP, leakages in some LDCs and remote small island states can amount to more than 80% (Pleumarom, 2009b, p. 4). In the world of business, an enterprise that only calculates profits and ignores the direct and indirect costs would hardly be called viable. So it appears unreasonable that governments responsible for economic development and stability in their countries are not producing proper balance sheets for tourism. While income and jobs created by tourism are counted, the losses that occur in other economic sectors or in public services as a result of tourism development never appear in the calculations. An appropriate cost–benefit analysis would, among other things, include the opportunity costs. For example, it would state how many farmers, fisher folk, and non-tourism workers and entrepreneurs would have to give up their economic activities as a result of tourism development, and how much income would be lost from non-tourism activities. As such surveys are virtually non-existent, we can only speculate about figures. Given the sheer scale of tourism, the economic losses in other sectors are likely to be huge. The costs that governments usually have to bear to back up the tourism sector – e.g. for the development of infrastructure, the maintenance of tourist sites and promotional campaigns, as well as for security, disaster preparedness and environmental services – also need to be included in the calculations. It is assumed that continued development of tourism plus targeted interventions – such as boosting the linkages between tourism and the rest of the economy – will lead to the generation of more net benefits for the poor. According to Jamieson et al. (2004, p. 2), however, the methodological shortcomings to measure tourism development impacts on poverty are hard to come by as there are no means 'of determining the scale of the impact on the poor or even the trends which result from overall growth or decline on the poor'.

Recent experiences suggest that while local communities have lost their existing income sources, very little has been achieved to bring about more balanced development and equitable distribution of income secured from tourism. A very clear example is Cambodia, where IFC and German Technical Cooperation (GTZ, now GIZ), in cooperation with the Cambodian Ministry of Tourism, launched the 'Stay Another Day' campaign in 2007 to promote tourism that benefits poor Cambodian communities, protects the environment and safeguards Cambodian culture (Kim and Campbell, 2009). Siem Reap, where the Angkor temples are located and which is designated as a World Heritage Site, has been a major focus of the initiative. But after running the IFC/GTZ campaign for 3 years, Siem Reap is still one of the poorest parts of Cambodia, despite the annual flood of international tourists and the millions of dollars they bring each year (Doherty, 2010). More than half of all families in Siem Reap district live below the poverty line, surviving on less than US$1.25 a day. Four villages in ten have no access to safe drinking water and 53% of all children are malnourished. Literacy rates are some of the lowest in the country, at 64%, and only 10% of children finish high school (Doherty, 2010). The case of Siem Reap confirms that most tourist dollars are being spent on foreign-owned hotels, tour companies and restaurants. The anomaly of such out-of-town wealth surrounded by so much local poverty even seems to grow starker every tourist season. Local residents reported that package tourists spend a week in Siem Reap without even once visiting a local business or using public transport as their tours are managed by tour operators who control every minute of their itinerary and herd them to particular spots for dining and shopping (Doherty, 2010). One of the significant obstacles in Siem Reap relates to the way the entry to the Angkor temples is managed by the government and local authorities. The temple complex is operated by a large petroleum company called Sokimex, which has close links to high-ranked government officials. The company controls the ticket sales from the temple complex, which are worth about US$30 million a year, and the revenue is split between government coffers in Phnom Penh and Sokimex. Nothing of the money is spent on community projects (Doherty, 2010). Economic experts have confirmed that owing to the dominance of foreign ownership in Cambodia's tourism sector, the inflow of tourist dollars into the national economy is very limited (Peou and Lipes, 2010); and it is exacerbated by the lack of linkages between tourism and the agricultural and food sector (UNDP, 2011b, p. 32).

Apparently, the IFC/GTZ initiative ignored taking into account some of the key issues, e.g. the prevailing structures of ownership and power, and thus failed to bring about positive change. Without drawing lessons from such experiences, one should not be surprised when expanding portfolios for planning and implementing pro-poor projects are wasted for nothing.

Loss of resources and traditional livelihoods

Poverty is not just a factor of jobs and wages. It is necessary to note that while many rural and indigenous communities appear to live in poor economic and social conditions, they do not consider themselves as poor if they can preserve their culture, living close to the natural environment and utilizing land, water and biological resources for their livelihood. According to Johnston (2006, p. 37): 'The "pro-poor" argument is particularly disturbing in light of [the tourism] industry's penchant for Indigenous territories. Indigenous Peoples who exercise their ancestral title are not poor. It is only when they are stripped of their lands, relocated and/or corralled into a colonial reserve that they live in the severest of poverty. Even then, they are not "poor", if poverty is understood spiritually'.

Undoubtedly, rapid and uncontrolled tourism development across the world is still aggravating poverty on a massive scale. Available documentation shows that, in many parts of the world, small-scale farmers continue to be driven from their land and fisher folk are denied access to beaches, mangrove forests and marine resources because of tourism. In tourism areas, frequent land conflicts constitute a fundamental issue, as developers use all legal and not-so-legal methods to appropriate land for tourism purposes. The property market becomes a highly volatile affair owing to speculation and rocketing prices, and then has seriously impacts on traditional livelihoods. For the ordinary people, there is not much point in continuing careful productive cultivation because land as a commodity divorced from production has unprecedented monetary value.

If pro-poor tourism advocates believe that tourism can easily be linked to the agricultural sector so that poor farming communities can capture a share from the tourism income by providing their products to hotels and restaurants, experiences indicate the contrary. The significant land use changes, increasing land alienation and landlessness among farmers has rendered many new tourism areas dependent on the import of food from other places. For example, 'Kerala has now become a net importer of its staple food rice and depends heavily on neighboring states for the everyday supplies of vegetables, meat, egg and milk' (KTW, 2008c). While the communities confront food shortage, one cannot expect them to provide locally produced food to tourists and earn an income.

The subject of 'land grabs' by large corporations for mega-tourism projects is a particular issue of concern. Are these land acquisitions likely to provide a reasonable substitute and socio-economic opportunities to local communities who are displaced from the land? Community representatives participating in a the global tourism forum during the 2009 World Social Forum in Belém, Pará, in the Brazilian Amazon region, denounced the rapidly increasing land grabs for mega-tourism complexes that include hotels, residential housing, golf courses, marinas, shopping centres and other facilities as a reflection of predatory and hegemonic tourism policies. They pointed out that efforts to battle hunger and poverty in poor and developing countries are being undermined by the massive land use change from food-producing land and marine areas to tourism zones (tim-team, 2009).

Sustainable development or environmental impoverishment?

A Statement of civil society organizations presented to the 7th Conference of Parties of the Convention on Biological Diversity (CBD) in Kuala Lumpur in 2004 said: 'Most tourism as practiced today is a pronounced form of consumerism which knows no limits and gets by on the fantasy of doing good…. Ecotourism and new programs linking tourism and poverty … are actually promoting industrial tourism models oriented to economic growth. These forms of so called "sustainable" tourism are known to be exploitative of both people and land. They dangerously distort the relationship between tourism and biological diversity' (ISCST, 2004). The lack of safeguards for environmental and cultural sustainability in tourism policies and programmes poses threats particularly to areas inhabited indigenous peoples, whose cultural landscapes and even their traditional knowledge, ceremonies and sacred sites are being exploited for tourism purposes, often without their consent. At the UN Permanent Forum on Indigenous Issues and at many other UN events, indigenous leaders stressed that all processes on sustainable tourism under the CBD, UN Conference on Sustainable Development (UNCSD) and International Year of Ecotourism (IYE) were not representative of indigenous peoples (McLaren, 2003; Johnston, 2007; tim-team, 2002).

A particularly serious problem is the degradation and depletion of scarce freshwater resources in major tourist destinations. According to the Human Development Report 2006 (UNDP, 2006), the aggravating global water crisis is closely related to poverty. For instance, there are 'Some 1.8 million child deaths [in the developing world] each year as a result of diarrhea', and 'Millions of women [are] spending several hours a day fetching water' (UNDP, 2006, p. 6). Considering these alarming facts, the excessive use of water in tourism facilities – luxury hotels, golf courses, pool villas, spa businesses, etc. – is certainly highly irresponsible. The US-based action-research group Worldwatch Institute presented some mind-boggling data on water consumption in golf courses: It would take 2.5 billion gallons of water a day to support 4.7 billion people at the UN daily minimum; the same amount of water – 2.5 billion gallons – is used, daily, to irrigate the world's golf courses (Worldwatch Institute, 2004).

Threats related to climate change

The increasingly felt climate change and extreme weather events around the world just add to the burden of communities, with the poor being most severely affected. Despite grave concerns about unsustainable tourism development aggravating the climate crisis, the tourism sector has not moved to change anything fundamental. Leading representative organizations have not yet made any clear quantifiable commitments to reduce greenhouse gas emissions in the UN climate change negotiations, holding to the mantra that unrestricted tourism growth is necessary to meet pro-poor targets. UNWTO insists that its climate change policy is consistent with its poverty elimination initiative and the MDGs (Pleumarom, 2009b, p. 2). However, such 'unrestricted growth' and 'business as usual' leads to the conclusion that tourism activity in total will become the most pernicious contributor to climate change. 'Green economy' is another buzzword now being widely used in the world of tourism to give the impression that efforts are being made at all levels to transform tourism into an environmentally and climate-friendly activity while enhancing the socio-economic well-being of local people. But serious concerns have been raised on what 'green economy' actually means and what it implies for less developed countries (Khor, 2011).

Whereas climate change has become one of the most pressing issues for tourism, decision makers appear to mainly engage in bragging and surface manoeuvring to hide the basic emptiness of their activities. In the meantime, the world's most disadvantaged and vulnerable social groups are facing immeasurable and ongoing adverse threats on their human and environmental health, including food and water security and livelihoods (see Pleumarom, 2009a; Jones and Phillips, 2011).

Unlocking opportunities for women?

When UNWTO chose for World Tourism Day 2007 the theme 'Tourism opens doors for women' in appraisal of the second MDG on gender equality, UNWTO's then Secretary General Francesco Frangialli asserted that: 'Tourism is a sector of the economy that not only employs significant numbers of women, but provides enormous opportunities for their advancement'. Whereas the decision to pay attention to the issues of tourism and women was welcomed, Frangialli's statement in its almost comical simplicity was rebuked by civil society organizations and networks. Their criticism was that UNWTO's optimism was unreasonable, given the well-documented sexual exploitation of both women and children and the deplorable working conditions for women in the tourism sector (tim-team, 2007). The Ecumenical Coalition on Tourism (ECOT) countered with the slogan 'tourism closes doors for women' and stated: 'A tourism that is propped up by images of women and the lure of sexual pleasures is not one that liberates women' (tim-team, 2007, p. 3). The Philippine Tourism Action Group expressed the view that the unprecedented growth of the tourism-related sex industry is the result of a failed development model that has deepened the poverty of the rural population, and of women in particular, thus forcing girls and women to enter the sex trade (tim-team, 2007, p. 3).

The *Global Report on Women in Tourism 2010* (UNWTO and UN Women, 2011, p. vii) states that: 'The capacity of tourism to empower women socially, politically and economically is particularly relevant in developing regions where women may face the greatest hardships and inequalities'. Without an examination of the underlying structural problems, however, UNWTO feeds delusions of easy solutions. Promises are made without any elaboration on how these will be accomplished. For instance, the report mentions the most contentious and troublesome issue of sex tourism, but does not provide any ideas or a path on how to curb the still growing multibillion dollar sex industry that enslaves women and children.

Medical tourism versus health care for locals

The privatization and commercialization of health care has created this new brand of tourism where people from rich countries travel to poor countries such as India, Thailand and the Philippines to obtain medical care and at the same time enjoy a tour programme, all at a relatively cheap price. It is a strange logic indeed when cash-strapped governments subsidize or help finance the corporate medical tourism sector on the basis that such efforts will generate revenue that can be used for eradicating poverty. It is not the rich medical tourists that contribute to poverty alleviation, but quite the contrary; poor tax payers in developing countries subsidize the rich foreign patients (Vijay, 2007, p. 39). In 2010, the Department of Medical Services Support in Thailand presented a 5-year strategic plan which would spend US$100 million of taxpayer money to promote the 'medical hub' initiative, and it was estimated that once it was implemented medical tourism could earn the country about US$13 billion annually. But Ammar Siamwalla, a highly respected Thai economist, warned that the national health system could go bankrupt if the plan goes ahead. 'The medical hub project is the worst policy the government is going to implement. It draws doctors out of the system and sabotages public healthcare services struggling to make ends meet for the sake of paying medical professionals' (Treerutkuarkul, 2010). As so often in the world of tourism, the potential tourist dollars are being counted, while the losses are not.

Lessons learned from 'pro-poor' ventures

Evaluations of pro-poor tourism projects that take a holistic and grassroots-oriented approach are very rare. One such review was conducted by Equations in 2008 on the Endogenous Tourism Project–Rural Tourism Scheme (ETP-RTS). In a way, this shows a radical shift from conventional governmental tourism schemes because it extends beyond the fulfilment of mere economic objectives and focuses on sustainable livelihoods and community involvement (Equations, 2008b). Even though the sites reviewed by Equations were found to have a potential of increased economic opportunities for locals as a result of the initiation of the project, concrete conclusions on an increase of employment and income could not be provided at the time of the evaluation. Equations pointed out that in the ETP programme, community development is not a side agenda but a co-agenda in order to 'add value' to the tourism process. Nevertheless, Equations found that a wide range of issues needed to be addressed and tackled. It was doubted, for example, whether the beneficiaries of the projects were really the poorest and most marginalized people: 'It is not uncommon in rural tourism projects to see funds and institutional arrangements, designed to benefit the poor[,] being passed on to the not so poor' (Equations, 2008a, p. 5). A major problem mentioned was that poor communities are usually regarded as homogenous, which patently they are not. The review team concluded that 'tourism cannot and will not be the solution to the rural crisis – and the introduction of tourism must not be seen as a substitute for more stable and sustainable livelihood action' (Equations, 2008a, p. 6).

In the meantime, the UNDP team made a first attempt to assess tourism and poverty reduction strategies in LDCs by analysing 30 Diagnostic Trade Integration Studies (DTIS) (UNDP, 2011b). The DTIS represent an innovative approach to provide information on LDCs, combining macroeconomic and sectoral analysis with 'stakeholder' consultations and a participatory validation process. The results left much to be desired however. In conclusion, most of the examined DTIS with tourism sections showed major shortcomings, and it was suggested that governments' tourism-related work has so far not really been satisfactory in terms of addressing pro-poor concerns, gender issues, sustainability considerations and community participation (UNDP, 2011b, p. 35). The report ended with the advice that in the preparation for the next round of DTIS under the Enhanced Integrated Framework (EIF), 'it will be important to highlight pro-poor measures that have a positive impact on human development' (UNDP, 2011b, p. 37).

'Regulation bad – growth good'

Many pro-poor tourism advocates agree that coherent policy frameworks and efficient institutions must be in place to ensure that policies translate into action – e.g. in terms of reducing leakages, redistributing tourism income in favour of the poor, and fostering meaningful participation of communities (UNDP, 2011b). That means that government regulation and policies are indispensable to achieve social, developmental and environmental objectives. This, however, is in stark contradiction to the neoliberal agenda of the tourism sector that operates along the lines of 'regulation is always bad – growth is good'. Thus, the predominance of voluntary industry initiatives such as 'best practices', codes of ethics and corporate social responsibility to ensure unrestricted tourism growth. Therefore, even when well-organized pro-poor micro-projects may be beneficial in local terms, it is highly questionable whether poverty reduction programmes can be mainstreamed in a way that they challenge the dominant global tourism system.

In a study that integrates tourism in a continuum of poverty alleviation strategies within the antipodes of neoliberalism and protectionism, Schilcher (2007, p. 56) observed that 'the most influential international organisations, as well as governments worldwide, follow a largely neoliberal laissez-faire approach to poverty alleviation coupled with market-friendly "pro-poor" supplements'. Given the political economic realities, she argued, only tourism strategies that are largely in line with the prevalent neoliberal ideology will have a chance to be implemented on a large-scale basis. More progressive approaches such as poverty-focused regulation and distribution – the equity side of the continuum – 'are bound to remain predominantly rhetoric of some United Nations organisations' (2007, p. 56).

Exposing the poor to a high-risk sector?

Tourism is well known to be highly vulnerable to unpredictable events, including economic downturns, social and political turmoil, extreme weather events and natural disasters and health threats. Dangerous crises abound: 2010 was one of the most disastrous and costliest years for tourism ever, with earthquakes, volcano eruptions, floods, super-typhoons, heat waves, droughts, landslides and blizzards wreaking havoc and causing unprecedented business interruptions around the world. Experts also warned that the global economic crisis that began in 2008 is far from over. More tumultuous events in 2011 and beyond are likely to go well beyond monetary problems, increasingly involving rising wealth disparities, exploding food prices, geopolitical volatility and other factors (Pesek, 2011).

The corporate industry has responded by establishing 'risk management' committees and plans. For tourism operators, risks are primarily undesirable economic setbacks, loss of revenue and loss of consumer confidence. But for the poor eking out a living from tourism, the risks are much more existential as their livelihoods are at stake temporarily or even permanently. One lesson learned from the increasing waves of natural and human-made disasters is that if tourism-related risk management plans exist, they have so far done little to help the poor and weaker sections involved in tourism. Given its unstable and volatile nature, policies that try to involve the poor and disadvantaged in the 'tourism value chain' and make them dependent on this high-risk sector can be hardly called sound and responsible.

Conclusion – a 'Barefoot' Approach is Needed

To reiterate, the Kerala Declaration, the outcome of the ill-fated ICRT conference in Kochi, stated: 'Patience and persistence are required, proceed with wisdom and hope' (Goodwin and Venu, 2008). But why should the poor, who have been marginalized by tourism development for so long, still have trust in tourism experts and politicians and patiently and persistently wait for 'responsible tourism' that is unlikely to ever arrive? Despite all the promising discourses of tourism as a strategy for poverty alleviation and sustainable development, local communities in many parts of the world have given lukewarm or negative responses to tourism development. The high outmigration of locals from tourist centres is also an indication that ordinary people are not experiencing an improvement of their lives and livelihoods through tourism. Everywhere, locals are being replaced in tourism by migrant workers who provide the cheapest labour and endure the harshest working and living conditions (Pleumarom, 2007, p. 12). Furthermore, many communities, and particularly indigenous peoples, are speaking out against tourism, irrespective of the label attached, that they consider harmful and is beyond their control; witness Kerala's people's organization, while some communities have resisted tourism altogether, from the Maasai in Africa and the aborigines in Australia and the USA to the Mayans in Chiapas, Mexico (McLaren 2003; Johnston, 2006). Most recently, Nazareth, a small community in the Colombian Amazon region, gained international news as village elders had decided to say 'No' to tourism that is not beneficial to the community and threatens their culture (Muse, 2011).

Whether or not tourism benefits the majority of people or leads to impoverishment and disruption of communities is a question that ultimately needs to be settled by actual, concrete investigation of people's lived experiences. Unfortunately, however, rarely are the voices of the poor and underprivileged really being heard in the world of tourism and development, despite the rhetoric of 'inclusiveness', 'participation' and 'empower-ment'. The tourism critique that has been spearheaded by progressive civic groups, scholars and media people has been pushed into the domain of the 'underdogs' and is often rejected as unqualified, unscholarly, polemic or 'anti-development'. A debate on the political economy of tourism that would contextualize local people's struggles for equality and social justice is almost non-existent. Tourism is all about politics, but as Hall (1996, p. 7) aptly observed: 'If one agrees with [Max] Weber's dictum that "the essence of politics is struggle", then it can be safely stated that the vast majority of researchers in tourism have failed to detect it or have deliberately chosen to ignore it'. At the grassroots level, people have experienced the ignorance and arrogance of power in abundance; as illustrated by the following example. At the Southeast Asia UN conference to mark the 'International Year of Ecotourism 2002', a young woman from the indigenous community of Banaue in the Philippines read a statement on behalf of participating local community representatives. Among other things, she said: 'We were invited to participate. You told us we are equal partners and that you encourage community participation, and so we travelled from far away places to talk with you, only to find out that conclusions ready to be imposed upon us have already been ironed out even before we arrived to this conference' (cited in tim-team, 2008, p. 3).

There should be something learned from Chilean economist, Manfred Max-Neef, the founder of 'Barefoot Economics', who shared his experience on poverty-related work: 'Economists study and analyze poverty in their nice offices, have all the statistics, make all the models, and are convinced that they know everything that you can know about poverty. But they don't understand poverty. And that's the big problem. And that's why poverty is still there' (Democracy Now! 2010). As an economist, and teaching in Berkeley University (California), Max-Neef realized when he was facing extreme poverty in Latin America that he had nothing coherent to say to the poor which would be both meaningful and helpful. He concluded that a completely new concept of economics was needed. This was the origin of 'barefoot economics', which Max-Neef defines as 'the economics that an economist who dares to step into the mud must practice', an economics that is not just about free markets, capitalist growth and profitability, but also entails the notions of compassion and solidarity of people (Democracy Now! 2010), human qualities that are hardly found in the upper echelons of the tourism and development community.

Politicians and development experts, including those at the UN and the World Bank, know well that tourism – both conventional and new forms of tourism – is not a 'passport to development' and poverty alleviation. Yet, no serious efforts are made to conduct a fundamental and systematic review of tourism development and in-depth studies on the critical issues, which is needed to develop credible, savvy and forward-looking poverty-focused policies. Instead, the movement advocating 'new tourism' – responsible, sustainable, pro-poor – creates a speculative reality that distracts and diverts attention from the real issues, and initiate a great number of programmes and projects based on illusions. Though it seems to be quite an impossible undertaking, the tourism debate must first be freed from speculative reality, duplicity and falsehood, and brought down to the realities on the ground – the realities of the majority of people who live with and are affected by the tourism – before it can deliver something reasonable and responsible. That is, away from the status quo and policies that can only bring about tourism forms that perpetuate the prevalent structures of injustice and inequality, and which are not acting responsibly to the social whole. What is needed is not cosmetic change, but profound change.

Given the wide range of problems that need to be confronted in the context of globalization, tourism policies must be made part of a wider political debate on how to reform and improve the global economic frameworks and processes in a way that developing countries can effectively tackle their problems and bring about socially and environmentally sustainable development. A 'barefoot' and rights-based approach to development is particularly important; whether this will include tourism development or not needs to be decided according to local conditions and aspirations. In view of the many looming social and environmental crises, governments need to prioritize people's basic needs while ensuring their rights to work, to food, to clean water, to health and to sanitation, and they need to respect the UN Declaration on the Rights of Indigenous Peoples, rather than spending scarce financial and human resources on an unstable and volatile sector such as tourism.

References

Ashley, C., Roe, D. and Goodwin, H. (2001) *Pro-poor Tourism Strategies: Making Tourism Work for the Poor. A Review of Experience.* Pro-Poor Tourism Report No.1, Overseas Development Institute (ODI), International Institute for Environment and Development (IIED) and Centre for Responsible Tourism (CRT). Available at: http://www.propoortourism.org.uk/ppt_report.pdf (accessed 15 May 2011).

Bolwell, D. and Weinz, W. (2008) *Reducing Poverty through Tourism.* Working Paper No. WP.266, International Labour Organization, Sectoral Activities Programme, Geneva, Switzerland. Available at: http://www.ilo.org/wcmsp5/groups/public/---ed_dialogue/---sector/documents/publication/wcms_162268.pdf (accessed 10 April 2012).

Chavez, R. (2007) *Non-traditional Sustainable Tourism and Poverty Reduction: Toward a Development Strategy for a New Business Line.* World Bank Discussion Paper, 19 March 2007. World Bank, Washington, DC. Available at: http://siteresources.worldbank.org/INTLACREGTOPSUSTOU/Resources/StrategyPaperSustainabletourism507.pdf (accessed 1 July 2011).

Crick, M. (1989) Representations of international tourism in the social sciences: sun, sex, sights, savings, and servility. *Annual Review* of *Anthropology* 18, 307–344.

Democracy Now! (2010) Chilean Economist Manfred Max-Neef on Barefoot Economics, Poverty and Why the U.S. is Becoming an 'Underdeveloping Nation'. Transcript of an interview with Manfred Max-Neef on 26 November 2010. Available at: http://www.democracynow.org/2010/11/26/chilean_economist_manfred_max_neef_on (accessed 1 July 2011).

Doherty, B. (2010) Angkor butterfly hunters tell of poverty amid tourist wealth. *The Guardian* (London), 27 September, 2010, p. 4. Available at: http://www.guardian.co.uk/world/2010/sep/27/ankor-butterfly-hunters-cambodia-poverty (accessed 10 April 2012).

Equations (Equitable Tourism Options), Ecumenical Coalition on Tourism, EED-Tourism Watch and Arbeitskreis Tourismus und Entwicklung (2004) Who really benefits from tourism? Statement of Concern of the Tourism Interventions Group at the 4th World Social Forum in Mumbai, India, 16–21 January 2004.

Equations (2008a) Community-based rural tourism in developing countries: insights and lessons from the Endogenous Tourism Project in India. In: MoT-GoI and UNDP India, *Redefining Tourism: Experiences and Insights from Rural Tourism Projects in India. A Dossier Accompanying the Film* Redefining Tourism: Voices from Rural India. Ministry of Tourism, Government of India (MoT-GoI) and UN Development Programme (UNDP) India, New Delhi, India, pp. 2–15. Available at: http://www.equitabletourism.org/files/fileDocuments838_uid13.pdf (accessed 10 April 2012).

Equations (2008b) *Sustainability in Tourism – A Rural Tourism Model. A Review Report.* MoT-GoI and UNDP India, New Delhi, India. Available at: http://www.equitabletourism.org/stage/files/fileDocuments913_uid15.pdf (accessed 20 June 2011).

Goodwin, H. and Venu, V. (2008) Kerala Declaration on Responsible Tourism, 24 March. Kerala Tourism, Department of Tourism, Government of Kerala, Thiruvananthapuram, Kerala. Available at: http://www.responsibletourism2008.org/keraladeclaration.php (accessed 10 April 2012).

Hall, C.M. (1996) *Tourism and Politics: Policy, Power and Place,* 2nd edn. John Wiley, Chichester, UK.

Hall, C.M. (ed.) (2007) *Pro-poor Tourism: Who Benefits? Perspectives on Tourism and Poverty Reduction.* Channel View, Clevedon, UK.

Hawkins, D.E. and Mann, S. (2007) The World Bank's role in tourism development. *Annals of Tourism Research* 34, 348–363.

Honeck, D. (2008) *LDC Poverty Alleviation Agenda and the Doha Development Agenda: Is Tourism Being Neglected?* World Trade Organization (WTO) Staff Working Paper No. ERSD-2008-03, Geneva, Switzerland. Available at: http://www.mdg-trade.org/ersd200803_e.pdf (accessed 1 July 2011).

ISCST (2004) International Indigenous Forum on Biodiversity [Joint NGOs] Statement on Tourism [to the Convention on Biological Diversity], Working Group 1, Agenda Item 19.7, COP7 [7th Conference of Parties], Kuala Lumpur, Malaysia, 17 February 2004. International Support Centre for Sustainable Tourism, Leeds, UK. Available at: http://www.twnside.org.sg/title2/ttcd/TA-05.doc (pp. 3–5; accessed 10 April 2012).

ITC (2009) Tourism-Led Poverty Reduction Programme (TPRP). International Trade Centre, Geneva, Switzerland. Available at: http://www.intracen.org/exporters/tourism/ (accessed 10 April 2012).

Jamieson, W., Goodwin, H. and Edmunds, C. (2004) *Contribution of Tourism to Poverty Alleviation – Pro-poor Tourism and the Challenge of Measuring Impacts.* Prepared for the Transport Policy and Tourism Section of UN-ESCAP, November 2004. Available at: http://haroldgoodwin.info/resources/povertyalleviation.pdf (accessed 15 May 2011).

Johnston, A.M. (2007) Tourism, biodiversity and indigenous peoples: new invitations for social change. *Third World Resurgence* 207/208, 34–36. Third World Network, Penang, Malaysia. Available at: http://www.twnside.org.sg/title2/resurgence/207-208/cover7.doc (accessed 19 April 2012).

Jones, A. and Philipps, M. (eds) (2011) *Disappearing Destinations: Climate Change and Future Challenges for Coastal Tourism.* CAB International, Wallingford, UK.

Kadt, E. de (ed.) (1978) *Tourism: Passport to Development? Perspectives on the Social and Cultural Effects of Tourism in Developing Countries.* Published for the World Bank and UNESCO, Oxford University Press, New York.

Kalani, N. (2011) Hawaii house speaker tired of 'band-aid approach' to fixing deficit. *Honolulu Civil Beat,* 15 March 2011.

Khor, M. (2011) Challenges of the green economy concept and policies in the context of sustainable development, poverty and equity. In: UN-DESA (Division for Sustainable Development, UNEP and UNCTAD). *Report by Panel of Experts on the Transition to a Green Economy: Benefits, Challenges and Risks from a Sustainable Development Perspective. Report by a Panel of Experts to Second Preparatory Committee Meeting for United Nations Conference on Sustainable Development,* pp. 69–97. Available at: http://www.uncsd2012.org/rio20/content/documents/Green%20Economy_full%20report%20final%20for%20posting%20clean.pdf (accessed 15 May 2011).

Kim, N. and Campbell, S. (eds) (2009) *Stay Another Day: Cambodia 2009–2010: Promoting Sustainable Tourism.* Cambodian Ministry of Tourism and *Economics Today* (Cambodia) in cooperation with the German Technical Cooperation (GTZ), Phnom Penh, Cambodia. Available at: http://www.stayanotherdaycambodia.com/download/Stay-Another-Day-Cambodia-2009-2010.pdf (accessed 19 April 2012).

KTW (2006) Against WTTC Destination Award: Equations' Open Letter to WTTC opposing Kerala's nomination for Destination Award. Kerala Tourism Watch, Kokkalai, Thrissur, Kerala, India. Available at: http://www.keralatourismwatch.org/taxonomy/term/4 (accessed 1 July 2011).

KTW (2008a) Conference on Responsible Tourism: Pushing Irresponsible Agendas, Alienating Stakeholders. Available at: http://www.keralatourismwatch.org/node/37 (accessed 10 April 2012).

KTW (2008b) Media Release on 'Irresponsible Tourism Convention', Kochi, India, 22 March 2008. Available at: http://www.keralatourismwatch.org/node/45 (accessed 1 July 2011).

KTW (2008c) Kerala Declaration on Irresponsible Tourism, Kochi, India, 22 March. Available at: http://www.keralatourismwatch.org/node/51 (accessed 1 July 2011).

Lea, J. (1988) *Tourism and Development in the Third World.* Routledge, London

McLaren, D. (2003) *Rethinking Tourism and Ecotravel,* 2nd edn. Kumarin Press, Bloomfield, Connecticut.

Mowforth, M. and Munt, I. (2003) *Tourism and Sustainability: Development and New Tourism in the Third World,* 2nd edn. Routledge, London.

Mowforth, M., Charlton, C. and Munt, I. (2008) *Tourism and Responsibility: Perspectives from Latin America and the Caribbean.* Routledge, London.

Muse, T. (2011) Amazon town bans tourists. *The Guardian* (London), 25 March 2011, p. 7. Available at: http://www.guardian.co.uk/world/2011/mar/25/indigenous-peoples-amazon-tourism-pressures (accessed 10 April 2012).

Peou, K. and Lipes, J. (2010) Little profit despite tourism growth. *Radio Free Asia,* 14 November 2010.

Pesek, W. (2011) Bubbles galore will make 2011 year to remember. *Bloomberg News,* 5 January 2011, p. 5. Available at: http://www.bloomberg.com/news/2011-01-05/bubbles-galore-to-make-2011-year-to-remember-commentary-by-william-pesek.html (accessed 10 April 2012).

Pleumarom, A. (1990) Alternative tourism: a viable solution? *Contours* 4(8), 12–15.

Pleumarom, A. (1994) The political economy of tourism. *Ecologist* 24, 142–148.

Pleumarom, A. (1999) Tourism, globalization and sustainable development. *Third World Resurgence*, No. 103, pp. 4–7. Third World Network, Penang, Malaysia.

Pleumarom, A. (2003) Our world is not for sale! The disturbing implications of privatization in the tourism trade. Paper presented at the International Seminar on 'Tourism: Unfair Practices – Equitable Options', 8th–9th December 2003, Hannover, Germany, hosted by DANTE/ the Network for Sustainable Tourism Development.

Pleumarom, A. (2007) Does tourism benefit the Third World? *Third World Resurgence*, No. 207/208, pp. 10–12. Third World Network, Penang, Malaysia. Available at: http://www.twnside.org.sg/title2/resurgence/207-208/cover1.doc (accessed 19 April 2012).

Pleumarom, A. (2009a) Asian tourism: green and responsible? In: Leslie, D. (ed.) *Tourism Enterprises and Sustainable Development – International Perspectives on Responses to the Sustainability Agenda*. Routledge, New York, pp. 36–54.

Pleumarom, A. (2009b) *Change Tourism, Not Climate!* TWN Climate Change Series No.3, Third World Network, Penang, Malaysia.

PPT Partnership (2004) *Tourism and Poverty Reduction – Making the Links*. Pro-Poor Tourism Partnership Info-Sheets, Sheet No. 3. Available at: http://www.propoortourism.org.uk/info_sheets/3%20info%20sheet.pdf (accessed 15 May 2011).

PPT Partnership (2011) What is pro-poor tourism? Available at: http://www.propoortourism.org.uk/what_is_ppt.html (accessed 10 April 2012).

Schilcher, D. (2007) Growth versus equity: the continuum of pro-poor tourism and neoliberal governance. In: Hall, C.M. (ed.) *Pro-poor Tourism: Who Benefits? Perspectives on Tourism and Poverty Reduction*. Channel View, Clevedon, UK, pp. 56–83.

tim-team (2002) 2002: International Year of Reviewing Ecotourism. tourism investigation and monitoring team, Bangkok, Thailand. Available at: http://www.twnside.org.sg/title/iye.htm (accessed 15 July 2011).

tim-team (2007) 2007 World Tourism Day theme under debate, tim-team Clearinghouse, 27 September 2007, pp. 2–3. tourism investigation and monitoring team, Bangkok, Thailand.

tim-team (2008) Convention on 'Irresponsible Tourism' in Kerala. tim-team Clearinghouse, 22 March 2008. tourism investigation and monitoring team, Bangkok, Thailand.

tim-team (2009) Change is Needed in Tourism! tim-team Clearinghouse, 16 February 2009. tourism investigation and monitoring team, Bangkok, Thailand.

Treerutkuarkul, A. (2010) Medical hub strategy 'will hurt hospitals'. *Bangkok Post*, 31 October 2010. Available at: http://www.bangkokpost.com/news/local/204063/medical-hub-strategy-will-hurt-hospitals (accessed 10 April 2012).

Turner, L. and Ash, J. (1975) *The Golden Hordes: International Tourism and the Pleasure Periphery*. Constable, London.

UNCTAD (2010) *Contribution of Tourism to Trade and Development*. Note by the UNCTAD Secretariat. Trade and Development Board, Trade and Development Commission, Second Session, Geneva, 3–7 May 2010, Item 5 of the Provisional Agenda. Publication No. TD/B/C.I/8, United Nations Conference on Trade and Development, Geneva, Switzerland. Available at: http://www.unctad.org/en/docs/cid8_en.pdf (accessed 1 July 2011).

UNCTAD (2011) UN Agencies commit to make tourism work for development. Press Release UNCTAD/Press/PR/2011/019, Istanbul, 12 May. Available at: http://www.unctad.org/templates/webflyer.asp?docid=14945&intItemID=1634&lang=1 (accessed 1 July 2011).

UNDP (2006) *Human Development Report 2006. Beyond Scarcity: Power, Poverty and the Global Water Crisis*. United Nations Development Programme, New York. Available at: http://hdr.undp.org/hdr2006/pdfs/report/HDR06-complete.pdf (accessed 10 April 2012).

UNDP (2011a) The Millennium Development Goals: Eight Goals for 2015. Available at: http://www.beta.undp.org/undp/en/home/mdgoverview.html (accessed 15 May 2011).

UNDP (2011b) *Tourism and Poverty Reduction Strategies in the Integrated Framework for Least Developed Countries*. Discussion paper, Geneva, April 2011. Available at: http://portal.unesco.org/en/files/48503/13045122901Tourism_Poverty_Reduction_LDCs_web.pdf/Tourism_Poverty_Reduction_LDCs_web.pdf (accessed 10 April 2012).

UNEP (2010) *Project Concept: The Global Partnership for Sustainable Tourism – 'Transforming Tourism Worldwide'*. United Nations Environment Programme, Division of Technology, Industry and Economics (DTIE), Paris. Available at: http://www.unep.fr/scp/tourism/activities/partnership/Documents/2010mrc19-UN-partnership-on-sustainable%20tourism_concept-paper.pdf (accessed 10 June 2011).

UNEP (2011) Tourism: investing in energy and resource efficiency. Prepared in partnership with UNWTO (World Tourism Organization). In: *Towards a Green Economy: Pathways to Sustainable Development and Poverty Eradication. A Synthesis for Policy Makers*. UNEP, Geneva, Switzerland, pp. 410–447. Available at: http://www.unep.org/greeneconomy/Portals/88/documents/ger/GER_synthesis_en.pdf (accessed 19 April 2012).

UN-ESCAP (2007) Tourism and the Millennium Development Goals. In: UN-ESCAP, *Study on the Role of Tourism in Socio-economic Development*. Publication No. ST/ESCAP/2478, United Nations Economic and Social Commission for Asia and the Pacific, Bangkok, Thailand, pp. 74–83. Available at: http://www.unescap.org/ttdw/Publications/TPTS_pubs/pub_2478/pub_2478_ch6.pdf (accessed 15 May 2011).

UNWTO (2010) *Tourism and the Millennium Development Goals*. World Tourism Organization, Madrid. Available at: http://www.unwto.org/tourism&mdgsezine/ (accessed 1 July 2011).

UNWTO (2011a) UNWTO/WTTC [World Tourism Organization/World Travel and Tourism Council] Leaders for Tourism Campaign. Available at: http://leadersfortourism.unwto.org/en (accessed 1 July 2011).

UNWTO (2011b) Tourism a poverty reduction tool says President Guebuza of Mozambique – joins UNWTO/WTTC global campaign. Press Release No. PR11061, Madrid, London, 8 July 2011. Available at: http://www2.unwto.org/en/press-release/2011-07-08/tourism-poverty-reduction-tool-says-president-guebuza-mozambique-joins-unwt (accessed 10 April 2012).

UNWTO (2011c) *Open Letter to Heads of State and Government*. UNWTO/WTTC Leaders for Tourism Campaign. Available at: http://www2.unwto.org/sites/all/files/pdf/final_golden_book_open_letter_text_0.pdf (accessed 19 April 2012).

UNWTO ST-EP Foundation (2011) UNWTO Sustainable Tourism for Eliminating Poverty Foundation. Seoul, South Korea. Details available at: http://unwtostep.org/ (accessed 10 April 2012).

UNWTO and UN Women (2011) *Global Report on Women in Tourism 2010. Preliminary Findings*. UNWTO, Madrid/United Nations Entity for Gender Equality and the Empowerment of Women, New York. Available at: http://www2.unwto.org/sites/all/files/pdf/folleto_global_report_on_women_in_tourism-corregido.pdf (accessed 10 July 2011).

Vijay, N.M. (2007) Medical tourism – subsidizing health care for developed countries. *Third World Resurgence* 207/208, 39–40. Third World Network, Penang, Malaysia/Geneva, Switzerland. Available at: http://www.twnside.org.sg/title2/resurgence/207-208/cover9.doc (accessed 19 April 2012).

Worldwatch Institute (2004) Matters of scale – planet golf. *World Watch Magazine* 17(2). Available at: http://www.worldwatch.org/node/797 (accessed 10 April 2012).

WTTC (2003) *Blueprint for New Tourism*. World Travel and Tourism Council, London. Available at: http://www.tourismfortomorrow.com/bin/pdf/original_pdf_file/wttc_blueprint_final.pdf (accessed 10 April 2012).

8 Governance and Responsible Tourism

C. Michael Hall
University of Canterbury, New Zealand

The role of government in tourism has changed markedly over the past 50 years, an era which could well be described as the hypermobile age of modern tourism. Over this period of growing individual mobility for leisure, recognition of the effects of tourism has changed substantially at the level of national governments and international institutions. Initially regarded as relatively benign in its impacts, social externalities began to be recognized in the 1970s, while the 1980s was the period in which attention began to be drawn to the growing effects of tourism on the natural environment. In the late 1980s, the desire to 'balance' the social, environmental and economic goals of tourism was put centre stage in policy terms in the concepts of sustainable tourism development and responsible tourism. Indeed, in many ways the terms were, and in some cases are, used almost interchangeably. More recently, the focus on the effects of tourism has expanded to include specific attention to concerns such the use of tourism as a means of poverty reduction, the contribution of tourism to global climate and environmental change, and the relationship of tourism to development goals.

Movements in the international policy focus of tourism should not be understood as initiatives which replace more traditional policy concerns that focus on economic development. Instead, they are best regarded as additional concerns or variations on long-standing policy themes such as the potential of tourism as a mechanism for modernization and economic growth in less developed countries. Such shifts in the policy agenda are also important because they go hand in hand with the changing sets of institutional arrangements that surround tourism policy making. Certainly, the two are arguably inseparable as, for example, the emergence of interest in sustainable tourism cannot be understood unless one is also aware of the institutional architecture of soft and hard international law, policy making and knowledge transfer that led to the emergence of sustainable development as a concept in the first place. Such a situation means that to understand responsible tourism there is, therefore, a necessity to gain insights into its governance and into how the concept is transformed from being a term used in policy documents (a policy output) to having an actual effect in terms of decision making, the allocation of resources and the actions and behaviours of individuals and organizations (a policy impact) (Hall, 2009).

This chapter therefore seeks to outline the relevance of policy and governance for responsible tourism. It first outlines the nature of the governance before detailing the four main approaches to governance: via hierarchies, the market, networks and communities. A main theme of the chapter will be the range of approaches that are utilized to give effect to responsible tourism and how they are reflective of different modes of governance and the political philosophies that underlie them.

Why Governance?

The role of government in tourism and the influence of state policy on tourism development have long been of interest to scholars (Hall, 1994; Hall and Jenkins, 1995; Bramwell and Lane, 2000). Since the 1990s though, there has been a gradual shift in approach in the tourism policy literature from the notion of government to that of governance (Hall, 1999; Yüksel et al., 2005; Beaumont and Dredge, 2010; Bramwell and Lane, 2011, 2012). This change in terminology is not just a reflection of new theories of the role and nature of the state and policy effectiveness, it is also indicative of new sets of local and supranational institutional arrangements that emerged to give the state the tools it needed to deal with new policy fields such as the environment, human rights and increased international mobility of capital, firms and people. This shift in the terrain of thinking on government has had profound implications for responsible tourism given that it influences such factors as the relationships between policy actors, the capacity of the state to act, the selection of policy instruments and indicators and, potentially, even the definition of policy problems (Tyler and Dinan, 2001; Bramwell, 2005; Pforr, 2005; Hall, 2008a, b; Dinica, 2009; Ruhanen et al., 2010; Wesley and Pforr, 2010).

Governance is the act of governing. It is what governments do with respect to their management of the affairs of a state. However, the growing use of governance rather than government in tourism policy reflects the changed political nature of the state within current set of globalized relations. Although there is no single accepted definition of governance, as reflected in Kooiman's (2003, p. 4) concept of governance as 'the totality of theoretical conceptions on governing', definitions tend to suggest a recognition of a change in political practices involving such things as increasing globalization, the emerg-

ence and growth of policy networks that cross the public–private divide, the marketization of the state and increasing institutional fragmentation (Pierre and Peters, 2000, 2005).

Despite the absence of an accepted definition, Hall (2011a) suggested that there are two broad meanings of governance. First, it is used to describe contemporary state adaptation to its economic and political environment with respect to how it operates. This is sometimes referred to as 'new governance' and refers to 'new governing activities that do not occur solely through governments' (Yee, 2004, p. 487). The second broad meaning of governance is that it is used to denote a conceptual and theoretical representation of the role of the state in the coordination of socio-economic systems. Still, as Hall (2011a) suggests, the two approaches are not mutually exclusive as the use of the term 'governance' as a form of shorthand for new forms of governance in Western societies is itself influenced by particular concepts of what the role of the state should be in contemporary society and the desirability and nature of state intervention. Indeed, this second meaning can itself be divided into two further categories (Peters, 2000). The first focuses on state capacity to 'steer' the socio-economic system and therefore the relationships between the state and other policy actors (Pierre and Peters, 2000). The second focuses on coordination and self-government, especially with respect to network relationships and public–private partnerships (Rhodes, 1997b).

Governance, broadly understood, is therefore of great significance for responsible tourism. Most importantly, understanding the different ways in which the state undertakes governance with respect to trying to achieve or encourage responsible tourism may help to shed light over why some forms of policy instruments are selected and others not. Furthermore, Hall (2008a, 2011a) has argued that the focus of most discussions on policy instruments in tourism is on their utilization or their effects rather than on the understandings of governance that led to the identification and selection of such instruments in the first place. Several studies have put forward different typologies of policy instruments. For example,

Beaumont and Dredge (2010) examined the advantages and disadvantages of three different local tourism governance approaches: a council-led network governance structure; a participant-led community network governance structure; and a local tourism organization-led industry network governance structure. Hall (2009) identified three approaches to implementation and the policy–action relationship and discussed their implications for state intervention in tourism planning and policy: 'top-down rational', 'bottom-up' and 'interactional network'. However, neither of these studies fully related back their typologies to different conceptualizations of governance. The next section utilizes a typology of different approaches to governance in tourism to identify different approaches by the state with respect to responsible tourism.

A Typology of Governance

Typologies have long been recognized as an important tool in policy studies in helping to categorize policies 'in such a way that the relationship between substance and process can be more clearly understood' (Steinberger, 1980, p. 185). Hall (2011a) utilized an analysis of the core concepts of governance to develop a typology with application to tourism. According to Hall (2011a), the most common focus of contributions to the governance debate in public policy terms is 'the role of the state in society' (Pierre, 2000, p. 4). Therefore, the core concept in governance in public policy terms is the relationship between state intervention (also referred to as public authority) and societal autonomy (self-regulation).

In order to clarify the semantic field of governance for developing a typology, categorical variables were identified by Hall (2011a) that referred to the relative use of hierarchical forms of regulation, i.e. legislation, and the relative power balance in the relationship between the state and other policy actors. Drawing on the work of Frances et al. (1991), three different models of coordination, also referred to as meso-theoretical or intermediate theoretical categories, were recognized in Western liberal democratic countries: hierarchies, markets and networks. These categories were found to be useful not only in national political life but also in analysing the external relationships between states. Therefore, as Frances et al. (1991, p. 1) observed, 'the three forms of social organization have a general applicability that transcends any particular geographical space or temporal order. They exemplify genuine "models" of coordination that can be characterized abstractly and then deployed in an analytical framework'. To these categories, Pierre and Peters (2000) added a fourth common governance type that they termed 'community', which was also incorporated by Hall (2011a) into his typology (Fig. 8.1). Each of the modes of governance within the typology is then connected with different policy instruments that are used to achieve policy goals. The core elements are outlined in Table 8.1, and are discussed in more detail below.

Hierarchical Governance Approaches

'Governance conducted by and through vertically integrated state structures is an idealized model of democratic government and the public bureaucracy' (Pierre and Peters, 2000, p. 15), and provides the 'traditional' hierarchical model of state governance. Although this approach, in which power is located in central state authorities, has been challenged by the growth of supranational institutions and the local state, by the emergence of trans-border problems such as pollution control and by contemporary globalization, the state still holds enormous authority and remains the basis of international relations as well as contemporary politics. The legislative and regulatory role of the state therefore remains highly significant for responsible tourism, particularly with respect to wildlife and natural heritage conservation (Hall and Jenkins, 1995; Litchfield, 2001; Bramwell, 2005; Duffy and Moore, 2011) as well as in the conservation of cultural heritage. The regulatory role of the state is also fundamental in allowing international tourists access to a country and also in subjecting them

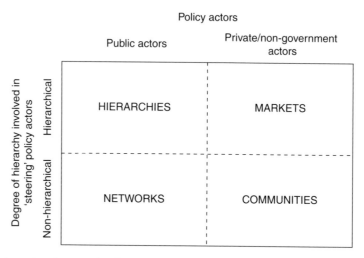

Fig. 8.1. A typology of the frameworks of governance (after Hall, 2011a).

to the laws of the destination and is, therefore, arguably the most basic means of controlling tourists and hence tourism (Coles and Hall, 2011). Furthermore, state law in areas such as human and labour rights may also prove extremely important in ensuring that undesirable social impacts of tourism development do not occur (Hemingway, 2004).

Despite the significance of the central state authority in regulating tourism and tourist behaviour, there is a surprising lack of direct analysis of hierarchical governance in tourism (Hall, 2011b). Instead, the supposed failure of regulation as a means to ensure more sustainable and responsible forms of tourism has almost been accepted as a given, even though other forms of governance, such as collaborative networks, have also been demonstrated to have significant shortcomings (Hall, 1999). Nevertheless, the reality behind the failure of regulatory governance is highly debatable and reflects issues of political philosophy and the interests that benefit from such changes as much as it might the failure of the state. According to Davis et al. (1993, p. 24) three principal economic reasons can be identified for dismantling of regulatory approaches and the privatization or corporatization of state assets and functions: 'governments are interested in reducing the dependency of public enterprises on public budgets, in reducing public debt by selling state assets, and in raising technical

efficiencies by commercialisation'. However, the economic reasons are themselves shrouded in political rationales that relate to broader philosophical perspectives which have most often been associated with a 'New Right', corporatist or neoconservative political economic agenda. Indeed, Hall (2011c) goes so far as to suggest that such is the dominance of neoliberal thinking in tourism policy and research that it is increasingly hard to see or think any other.

In such a political economic climate, the role of government in tourism has undergone a dramatic shift from a traditional public administration model that sought to implement government policy for a perceived public good, to a corporatist model that emphasizes efficiency, investment returns, the role of the market and relations with stakeholders, usually defined as industry (Hall, 1999). Corporatism is used here in the sense of a dominant ideology that claims rationality as its central quality and which emphasizes a notion of individualism in terms of self-interest rather than the legitimacy of the individual citizen acting in the democratic interest of the public good (Saul, 1995). Nonetheless, in tourism, the changed role of the state and the individual's relation to the state provides a major policy challenge. On the one hand there is the demand for less government interference in the market and for allowing industries to develop and trade

Table 8.1. Frameworks of governance and their characteristics in relation to responsible tourism (Source: after Hall 2009, 2011a).

	Hierarchies	Communities	Networks	Markets
Characteristics of mode of governance	• Idealized model of democratic government and public administration • Distinguishes between public and private policy space • Focus on public or common good • Command and control (i.e. 'top-down' decision making) with respect to responsible tourism • Hierarchical relations between different levels of the state and private policy actors	• Notion that communities should resolve their common problems with respect to tourism with minimum of state involvement • Builds on a consensual image of community and the positive involvement of its members in collective concerns • Governance without government • Fostering of civic and community spirit	• Facilitate coordination of public and private interests and resource allocation and therefore enhance efficiency of policy implementation • Range from coherent policy communities/policy triangles through to single issue coalitions • Regulate and coordinate policy areas with respect to responsible tourism according to the preferences of network actors • Mutual dependence between network and state(s)	• Belief in the market as the most efficient and just resource allocative mechanism • Belief in the empowerment of citizens via their role as consumers • Employment of monetary criteria to measure efficiency of mechanisms designed to achieve more responsible tourism • Policy arena for economic actors where they cooperate to resolve common problems
Governance/ policy themes	• Hierarchy, control, compliance	• Complexity, local autonomy, devolved power, decentralized problem solving	• Networks, multi-level governance, steering, bargaining, exchange and negotiation	• Markets, bargaining, exchange and negotiation
Policy standpoint	• Top: policy makers; legislators; central government	• Bottom: implementers; 'street level bureaucrats' and local officials	• Where negotiation and bargaining take place	• Where bargaining takes place between consumers and producers
Underlying model of democracy	• Elitist (often emphasizes role of internal and external experts)	• Participatory	• Hybrid/stakeholder; significant role given to interest groups	• Consumer determined; citizen empowerment
Primary focus with respect to responsible tourism policies and actions	• Effectiveness: to what extent are responsible tourism policy goals actually met?	• What influences action with respect to responsible tourism as an issue area?	• Bargained interplay between goals set centrally and actor (often local) innovations and constraints with respect to responsible tourism	• Efficiency: markets will provide the most efficient outcome for responsible tourism

Continued

Table 8.1. Continued

	Hierarchies	Communities	Networks	Markets
View of non-central (initiating) actors	• Passive agents or potential impediments	• Potentially policy innovators or problem shooters	• Tries to account for the behaviour of all those who interact in the development and implementation of policy	• Market participants are best suited to 'solve' policy problems
Criterion of success	• When outputs/outcomes are consistent with a priori objectives	• Achievement of actor (often local) goal	• Difficult to assess objectively, success depends on actor perspectives	• Market efficiency
Reason for gaps between policies and actions	• Good ideas poorly executed	• Bad ideas faithfully executed	• 'Deficits' are inevitable as abstract policy ideas are made more concrete	• Market failure; inappropriate indicator selection
Primary policy instruments with respect to achieving responsible tourism	• Laws • Regulation • Clear allocation and transfers of power between different levels of the state • Development of clear set of institutional arrangements • Licensing, permits, consents and standards • Removal of property rights • Development guidelines and strategies that reinforce planning law	• Self-regulation • Public/community meetings • Public/community participation • Non-intervention • Voluntary instruments • Information and education • Volunteer associations • Direct democracy • Community opinion polling • Capacity building of social capital	• Self-regulation and coordination • Accreditation schemes • Codes of practice • Industry associations • Utilization of non-governmental organizations (NGOs)	• Corporatization and/or privatization of state bodies in order to bring them closer to the market • Use of pricing, subsidies and tax incentives to encourage desired behaviours • Use of regulatory and legal instruments to encourage market efficiencies • Voluntary instruments • Non-intervention • Education and training to influence behaviour

without government subsidy or assistance, while on the other, industry interest groups seek to have government policy developed in their favour, including the maintenance of government funding for promotion as in the case of the tourism sector (Hall, 1999, 2008a). Similarly, non-governmental organizations (NGOs) and some advocates of responsible tourism continue to demand government action with respect to minimizing the costs of tourism. This policy conundrum has generally been resolved through the restructuring of national and regional tourist organizations to: (i) reduce their planning, policy and development roles (which could be interpreted as state regulation of tourism) and increase their marketing and promotion functions (which is presented as state support of the market); and (ii) engage in a greater range of partnerships, network and collaborative relationships with stakeholders. Such a situation was described by Milward (1996) as the 'hollowing out' of the state, in which the role of the state has been transformed from one of hierarchical control to one in which governing is dispersed among a number of separate, non-government entities – what, as noted above, has been referred to as 'new governance' (Yee, 2004). This has therefore led to increased emphasis on governance through network structures as a 'new process of governing; or a changed condition of ordered rule; or the new method by which society is governed' (Rhodes 1997a, p. 43), as well as on the role of the market as an allocative mechanism for resources.

Governance via the Market

The contemporary emphasis on the role of the market as a governance mechanism is very much associated with the influence of neo-liberal political philosophy on considerations of the appropriate level of state intervention in socio-economic systems (Harvey, 2005). From this perspective, 'The market has come to be seen as everything Big Government is not; it is believed to be the most efficient and just allocative mechanism available since it does not allow for politics to allocate resources where they are not employed in the most

efficient way' (Pierre and Peters, 2000, pp. 18–19). From this perspective, consumer demands for more responsible forms of tourism and encouraging competition between suppliers to attract consumers are seen as a major mechanism to encourage improved industry behaviours (Hughes et al., 2008; Leonardo et al., 2011; Olson, 2011). However, the success of this approach in terms of behavioural change is debatable. For example, in the case of ecotourism, Stamou and Paraskevopoulos (2003) argued that rather than leading to fundamental shifts in the sustainability of tourism, it chiefly functions as a market mechanism through which consumers attenuate their environmental guilt.

A government decision to allow the market to act as a form of governance of supply and demand in tourism does not mean that government ceases to influence the market, particularly as the state retains the capacity to re-enter a vacated regulatory space. Instead of using regulatory mechanisms, government may seek to use other forms of encouragement to influence industry actions, such as financial incentives (subsidies or tax incentives), education and even the potential for future intervention as threat to encourage certain behaviours. Nevertheless, the failure to achieve desirable outcomes as a result of self-regulation, market failure and the limits of the market as a form of governance has in-creasingly become recognized, especially with respect to the failure to achieve more equitable policy outcomes (Schilcher, 2007) and the relationship of marketization with the different sets of property rights of stakeholders (Lapeyre, 2011), as well as a real reduction in the environmental impacts of tourism (Gössling et al., 2010, 2012).

Governance via Networks

Network approaches to governance, including public–private partnerships, are a significant contemporary focal point in tourism policy because of the way in which they may facilitate coordination of public and private interests and resources, thereby potentially reducing the costs of governance for the state (Bramwell, 2005; Dredge, 2006; Hall, 2008a; Scott et al., 2008; Beaumont and Dredge, 2010). None the less, policy networks vary widely with respect to their degree of cohesion, ranging from 'sub-governments', 'iron triangles' and coherent policy communities marked by a high degree of cohesion and common action and interest, through to issue specific coalitions that only coalesce on specific policy concerns and may be in opposition on others (Gais et al., 1984; Rhodes, 1997b; Thatcher, 1998).

Networks have been proposed as a means to potentially integrate the range of policy perspectives that may exist among stakeholders, although the capacity for integration depends on such factors as the inclusiveness of the planning process, the conditions influencing actors' perceived pay-offs from participation and the degree of perceived common interest among policy actors (Hovil and Stokke, 2007; Hall, 2011a). A major concern in the appropriateness of network governance approaches is the extent to which non-state leadership of networks as well as the networks themselves work towards the achievement of self-interests policies as opposed to those that may be in the public interest, or at least a notion of interest that transcends narrow corporate goals (Hall, 1999; Dredge, 2006). Such an issue is arguably especially important in the context of responsible tourism given the significance of community and environmental goals (Zeppel, 2011). Similarly, Erkuş-Öztürk and Eraydin (2010), in a study of the contribution that networks may make to sustainable tourism in a Turkish destination, suggest that while there was an increase in local collaboration, their findings show that environmental motivations fall far behind economic considerations in networking practices.

An additional dimension of the development of policy networks and the public–private partnerships that may surround responsible tourism is the extent to which their shared philosophical and/or value base may serve to exclude other perspectives on governance and the appropriateness of different approaches. For example, Duffy (2006) argued that the politics of ecotourism in Madagascar are ideologically informed by neo-liberal definitions of development which underpin global

governance as well as the interplay between different interest groups involved in it, including the World Bank and environmental NGOs. Duffy's (2006) findings not only reinforce the observation that 'new governance' structures have strengthened the position of some policy networks in determining the trajectories of policy change (Pierre and Peters, 2005), but also Hall's (1999) conclusion that policy communities may become solidified to such an extent that policy alternatives are closed off within a policy arena unless there is some radical change in the dominant policy paradigm (Hall, 2011d). However, such policy blockages may only be recognized if there is a shift in the government policy agenda, objectives, desired outcomes and/or underlying policy values. Where this occurs, the state may face a dilemma in that while it may want to utilize policy networks 'to bring societal actors into joint projects, it tends to see its policies obstructed by those networks' (Pierre and Peters, 2000, p. 20). In such situations, the response of the state may be to seek to influence and negotiate with dominant policy coalitions, seek to advance a new policy network, or utilize other means of governance to achieve its aims.

Community Approaches to Governance

The final approach to governance is that of the community. Elements of this approach have long been advanced in tourism, even if the underlying rationale in terms of governance has been relatively poorly articulated (Murphy, 1983). The community conceptualization of governance has been greatly influenced by communitarianism and demands for more direct citizen involvement in governance (Hall, 2011a). Communitarianism proposes that large-scale government should be replaced by smaller spatial units of governing that are closer to the 'community' (Etzioni, 1998). Arguably, the most influential dimensions of communitarianism have been with respect to the focus of the significance of social capital in community and economic development (Putnam, 2001), and the development of alternative forms of consumption based on localism and voluntary simplicity (Doherty and

Etzioni, 2003). In addition, Pierre and Peters (2000) suggest that the communities framework also builds on traditions of deliberative and direct democracy.

The significance of community attitudes and values towards tourism has long been a significant theme in responsible tourism (Richins, 2009). Many supporters of community-based tourism contend that in the less developed countries community-based tourism might not only reduce rural poverty and advance conservation by strengthening local economies and empowering communities, but also manage natural resources for long-term economic, sociocultural, and ecological benefits (Stone and Rogerson, 2012). However, the capacity of communities to manage tourism in an equitable and sustainable fashion has often been romanticized (Hall, 2008a). Nevertheless, the development of new governance approaches that emphasize the role of the local state in decision making has given renewed emphasis to community governance in tourism (Beaumont and Dredge, 2010).

The main issues that emerge with community governance and tourism are the extent to which democratic approaches may not only be followed but also to which they actually reinforce sustainable and responsible tourism development. Community governance is also bedevilled by the difficulties in defining what the community actually is and where its boundaries lie, as well as a range of institutional issues (Hall, 2008a). Such issues are highlighted in Stone and Rogerson's (2012) study of community-based resource management and tourism in Botswana, which found serious shortcomings in terms of the local community perceptions of the management, distributional benefits and project ownership. Similarly, a review of community tourism in Nicaragua found that it was important to distinguish between top-down community-based tourism usually established and funded by foreign NGOs and those that were developed by local initiatives (Zapata et al., 2011). The former was characterized by low economic impact in terms of jobs and income, low project life expectancy after external funding ends, the monopolization of benefits by local elites, and/or the lack of business skills to make it

operational. In contrast, bottom-up community-based tourism, resulting from local initiative, demonstrated longer life expectancy, faster growth and more positive impacts on the local economy (Zapata et al., 2011). The outcomes of such research are also significant as they highlight that while many tourism development projects utilize the moniker of being community based or community governed, the notion of community and the underlying power relationships in it that lead to certain decisions and actions being made may well be substantially different and need to be subject to a more considered critique.

Conclusion

This chapter has sought to emphasize that different forms of governance, both overtly and covertly, influence understandings of not only who is responsible for what in tourism but of how tourism should be managed. This applies both to tourism development in general and to the field of responsible tourism. Such issues are important because of the extent to which responsible tourism projects are subsumed within broader institutional arrangements and networks of policy actors with both overt and covert policy agendas, as well as associated sets of values (Duffy, 2006). However, many of the governance assumptions that are made or even promoted in responsible tourism policy are not adequately interrogated with respect to their effectiveness, implications and the underlying assumptions that are made with respect to participation, power and policy-making processes.

The approach has used Hall's (2011a) typology of governance, which utilizes the core public policy concepts of governance with respect to the relationship between state intervention/public authority and societal autonomy or self-regulation. This allows for the relative balance of the power relationships that exist between public and private policy actors and for steering modes that range from hierarchical top-down steering to non-hierarchical approaches. Importantly, different modes of governance have been identified with different sets of policy instruments. This is significant as 'the selection of policy indicators is not a neutral device' (Hall, 2011d, p. 660). 'Imposing the rules of the game, that is to say, the rules used to calculate decisions, by imposing the tools in which these rules are incorporated, is the starting point of relationships of domination' (Callon, 1998, p. 46), not only between institutions, but also of one policy paradigm over another. Similarly, Majone (1989, pp. 116–117) stressed that 'policy instruments are seldom ideologically neutral ... distributionally neutral ... [and] ... cannot be neatly separated from goals' and instead tend to reflect the values of the policy paradigms within which they are selected. 'The performance of instruments depends less on their formal properties than on the political and administrative context in which they operate' (Majone, 1989, p. 118). Indeed, Majone states that 'the choice of policy instruments is not a technical problem that can be safely left to experts. It raises institutional, social, and moral issues that must be clarified' (Majone, 1989, p. 143).

In the case of responsible tourism, it is arguably the situation that the nature of the underlying policy paradigms, in this case with respect to governance, need a far more critical examination than has hitherto been the case. Many governance approaches are taken as a given, with their underlying propositions and even notions of effectiveness not given adequate consideration. This is especially so considering the preponderance of international experts, institutions and networks in actually offering advice on governance matters as part of NGO, consulting and development aid services. Yet those networks are themselves embedded in some of the networks that may constrain capacities to see governance alternatives. This is an important concern because of the dominance of neo-liberal thinking with respect to the role of the state and governance (Hall, 2011c). This situation may well mean that many of the assumptions that underlie the perceived value of some forms of governance over others, including the supposed value of governance via market mechanisms over state intervention, are likely to be based more on political economic faith than on considered appreciation of their efficacy and their contribution to equity and the environment.

References

Beaumont, N. and Dredge, D. (2010) Local tourism governance: a comparison of three network approaches. *Journal of Sustainable Tourism* 18, 7–28.

Bramwell, B. (2005) Interventions and policy instruments for sustainable tourism. In: Theobold, W. (ed.) *Global Tourism*, 3rd edn. Elsevier, Oxford, UK, pp. 406–426.

Bramwell, B. and Lane, B. (eds) (2000) *Tourism Collaboration and Partnerships: Politics, Practice and Sustainability*. Channel View, Clevedon, UK.

Bramwell, B. and Lane, B. (2011) Critical research on the governance of tourism and sustainability. *Journal of Sustainable Tourism* 19, 411–421.

Bramwell, B. and Lane, B. (2012) Towards innovation in sustainable tourism research? *Journal of Sustainable Tourism* 20, 1–7.

Callon, M. (1998) Introduction: the embeddedness of economic markets in economics. In: Callon, M. (ed.) *The Laws of the Markets*. Blackwell, Oxford, UK, pp. 1–57.

Coles, T. and Hall, C.M. (2011) Rights and regulation of travel and tourism mobility. *Journal of Policy Research in Tourism, Leisure and Events* 3, 209–223.

Davis, G., Wanna, J., Warhurst, J. and Weller, P. (1993) *Public Policy in Australia*, 2nd edn. Allen and Unwin, St Leonards, New South Wales, Australia.

Dinica, V. (2009) Governance for sustainable tourism: a comparison of international and Dutch visions. *Journal of Sustainable Tourism* 17, 583–603.

Doherty, D. and Etzioni, A. (eds) (2003) *Voluntary Simplicity: Responding to Consumer Culture*. Rowman and Littlefield, Lanham, Maryland.

Dredge, D. (2006) Networks, conflict and collaborative communities. *Journal of Sustainable Tourism* 14, 562–581.

Duffy, R. (2006) Global environmental governance and the politics of ecotourism in Madagascar. *Journal of Ecotourism* 5, 128–144.

Duffy, R. and Moore, L. (2011) Global regulations and local practices: the politics and governance of animal welfare in elephant tourism. *Journal of Sustainable Tourism* 19, 589–604.

Erkuş-Öztürk, H. and Eraydin, A. (2010) Environmental governance for sustainable tourism development: collaborative networks and organisation building in the Antalya tourism region. *Tourism Management* 31, 113–124.

Etzioni, A. (ed.) (1998) *The Essential Communitarian Reader*. Rowman and Littlefield, Lanham, Maryland.

Frances, J., Levačić, R., Mitchell, J. and Thompson, G. (1991) Introduction. In: Thompson, G., Frances, J., Levačić, R. and Mitchell, J. (eds) *Markets, Hierarchies and Networks: The Coordination of Social Life*. Sage, London, pp. 1–19.

Gais, T.L., Peterson, M.A. and Walker, J.L. (1984) Interest groups, iron triangles and representative institutions in American national government. *British Journal of Political Science* 14, 161–185.

Gössling, S., Hall, C.M., Peeters, P. and Scott, D. (2010) The future of tourism: a climate change mitigation perspective. *Tourism Recreation Research* 35, 119–130.

Gössling, S., Scott, D., Hall, C.M., Ceron, J.-P. and Dubois, G. (2012) Consumer behaviour and demand response of tourists to climate change. *Annals of Tourism Research* 39, 36–58.

Hall, C.M. (1994) *Tourism and Politics: Policy, Power and Place*. John Wiley, Chichester, UK.

Hall, C.M. (1999) Rethinking collaboration and partnership: a public policy perspective. *Journal of Sustainable Tourism* 7, 274–289.

Hall, C.M. (2008a) *Tourism Planning: Policies, Processes and Relationships*, 2nd edn. Prentice Hall, Pearson Education, Harlow, UK.

Hall, C.M. (2008b) Regulating the international trade in tourism services. In: Coles, T. and Hall, C.M. (eds) *International Business and Tourism: Global Issues, Contemporary Interactions*. Routledge, London, pp. 33–54.

Hall, C.M. (2009) Archetypal approaches to implementation and their implications for tourism policy. *Tourism Recreation Research* 34, 235–245.

Hall, C.M. (2011a) A typology of governance and its implications for tourism policy analysis. *Journal of Sustainable Tourism* 19, 437–457.

Hall, C.M. (2011b) Biosecurity, tourism and mobility: institutional arrangements for managing biological invasions. *Journal of Policy Research in Tourism, Leisure and Events* 3, 209–223.

Hall, C.M. (2011c) Consumerism, tourism and voluntary simplicity: we all have to consume, but do we really have to travel so much to be happy? *Tourism Recreation Research* 36, 298–303.

Hall, C.M. (2011d) Policy learning and policy failure in sustainable tourism governance: from first and second to third order change? *Journal of Sustainable Tourism* 19, 649–671.

Hall, C.M. and Jenkins, J.M. (1995) *Tourism and Public Policy*. Routledge, London.

Harvey, D. (2005) *A Brief History of Neoliberalism*. Oxford University Press, Oxford, UK.

Hemingway, S. (2004) The impact of tourism on the human rights of women in South East Asia. *International Journal of Human Rights* 8, 275–304.

Hovil, S. and Stokke, K.B. (2007) Network governance and policy integration – the case of regional coastal zone planning in Norway. *European Planning Studies* 15, 927–944.

Hughes, A., Wrigley, N. and Buttle, M. (2008) Global production networks, ethical campaigning, and the embeddedness of responsible governance. *Journal of Economic Geography* 8, 345–367.

Kooiman, J. (2003) *Governing as Governance*. Sage, Los Angeles, California.

Lapeyre, R. (2011) Governance structures and the distribution of tourism income in Namibian communal lands: a new institutional framework. *Tijdschrift voor Economische en Sociale Geografie* 102, 302–315.

Leonardo, B., Federico, G. and Nazaria, S. (2011) What to do in globalised economies if global governance is missing? The vicarious role of competition in social responsibility. *International Review of Economics* 58, 185–211.

Litchfield, C. (2001) Responsible tourism with great apes in Uganda. In: McCool, S.F. and Moisey, R.N. (eds) *Tourism, Recreation, and Sustainability: Linking Culture and the Environment*. CAB International, Wallingford, UK, pp. 105–125.

Majone, G. (1989) *Evidence, Argument and Persuasion in the Policy Process*. Yale University, New Haven, Connecticut.

Milward, H.B. (1996) Symposium on the hollow state: capacity, control and performance in interorganizational settings. *Journal of Public Administration Research and Theory* 6, 193–195.

Murphy, P.E. (1983) Tourism as a community industry – an ecological model of tourism development. *Tourism Management* 4, 180–193.

Olson, E.A. (2011) Notions of rationality and value production in ecotourism: examples from a Mexican biosphere reserve. *Journal of Sustainable Tourism* 20, 215–233.

Peters, B.G. (2000) Governance and comparative politics. In: Pierre, J. (ed.) *Debating Governance: Authenticity, Steering and Democracy.* Oxford University Press, Oxford, UK, pp. 36–53.

Pforr, C. (2005) Three lenses of analysis for the study of tourism public policy: a case from Northern Australia. *Current Issues in Tourism* 9, 323–343.

Pierre, J. (2000) Introduction: understanding governance. In: Pierre, J. (ed.) *Debating Governance: Authenticity, Steering and Democracy.* Oxford University Press, Oxford, UK, pp. 1–12.

Pierre, J. and Peters, B.G. (2000) *Governance, Politics and the State.* Macmillan Press, Basingstoke, UK/St. Martin's Press, New York.

Pierre, J. and Peters, B.G. (2005) *Governing Complex Societies: Trajectories and Scenarios.* Palgrave Macmillan, Basingstoke, UK.

Putnam, R.D. (2001) *Bowling Alone: The Collapse and Revival of American Community.* Simon and Schuster, New York.

Rhodes, R.A.W. (1997a) From marketisation to diplomacy: it's the mix that matters. *Australian Journal of Public Administration* 56, 40–53.

Rhodes, R.A.W. (1997b) *Understanding Governance: Policy Networks, Governance, Reflexivity and Accountability.* Open University Press, Buckingham, UK.

Richens, H. (2009) Environmental, cultural, economic and socio-community sustainability: a framework for sustainable tourism in resort destinations. *Environment, Development and Sustainability* 11, 785–800.

Ruhanen, L., Scott, N., Ritchie, B. and Tkaczynski, A. (2010) Governance: a review and synthesis of the literature. *Tourism Review* 65(4), 4–16.

Saul, J.R. (1995) *The Unconscious Civilization.* Anansi, Concord, Ontario, Canada.

Schilcher, D. (2007) Growth versus equity: the continuum of pro-poor tourism and neoliberal governance. *Current Issues in Tourism* 10, 166–193.

Scott, N., Cooper, C. and Baggio, R. (2008) Destination networks: four Australian cases. *Annals of Tourism Research* 35, 169–188.

Stamou, A.G. and Paraskevopoulos, S. (2003) Ecotourism experiences in visitors' books of a Greek reserve: a critical discourse analysis perspective. *Sociologia Ruralis* 43, 34–55.

Steinberger, P.J. (1980) Typologies of public policy: meaning construction and the policy process. *Social Science Quarterly* 61, 185–197.

Stone, M.T. and Rogerson, C.M. (2012) Community-based natural resource management and tourism: Nata Bird Sanctuary, Botswana. *Tourism Review International* 15, 159–169.

Thatcher, M. (1998) The development of policy network analyses: from modest origins to overarching frameworks. *Journal of Theoretical Politics* 10, 389–416.

Tyler, D. and Dinan, C. (2001) The role of interested groups in England's emerging tourism policy network. *Current Issues in Tourism* 4, 210–252.

Wesley, A. and Pforr, C. (2010) The governance of coastal tourism: unravelling the layers of complexity at Smiths Beach, Western Australia. *Journal of Sustainable Tourism* 18, 773–792.

Yee, A.S. (2004) Cross-national concepts in supranational governance: state–society relations and EU-policy making. *Governance – An International Journal of Policy and Administration* 17, 487–524.

Yüksel, F., Bramwell, B. and Yüksel, A. (2005) Centralized and decentralized tourism governance in Turkey. *Annals of Tourism Research* 32, 859–886.

Zapata, M.J., Hall, C.M., Lindo, P. and Vanderschaeghen, M. (2011) Can community-based tourism contribute to development and poverty alleviation? *Current Issues in Tourism* 14, 725–749.

Zeppel, H. (2011) Collaborative governance for low-carbon tourism: climate change initiatives by Australian tourism agencies. *Current Issues in Tourism*, DOI: 10.1080/13683500.2011.615913. Available online 7 October 2011.

9 Adventure Tours: Responsible Tourism in Practice?

Jacqueline Holland
Northumbria University, UK

Introduction

Tour operators play a pivotal role in the distribution of tourism products, acting as intermediaries between principals and the consumers. They provide packages of products for tourists to purchase easily, which otherwise would be time-consuming and, in some cases, very difficult to arrange independently. An indication of the scale of this provision is that Mintel (2010) estimated that 14.4 million package holidays would be purchased in 2010. On such a basis, it is obvious that tour operators have an influential role in the development of a destination and its long-term success (see Leslie, Chapters 1 and 2). Recent changes in the market have seen a transformation from the very popular, standardized and rigidly packaged holidays into new products targeted at niche markets. This shift, to an extent, correlates with changes in consumption patterns 'towards healthier lifestyles, a heightened sensitivity to green issues and a more quality conscious consumer' (Swarbrooke et al., 2003, pp. 57–58), and in generating demand for special-interest-based niche products (Novelli, 2005), which are also seen to be active, environmentally sensitive and of high quality (see Leslie, Chapter 4). Adventure is one of these niche products.

Adventure tourism appeals to a wide market, though predominantly to middle-aged

groups, and the fastest growing market is the 'empty nesters' who have a higher disposable income and the time to take part in longer trips (Mintel, 2008). The majority of these trips are of short duration therefore companies tend to have tight itineraries and incorporate (pack) as much as possible into the programme, but often with some time to relax at the end. The inclusion of remote and challenging destinations on itineraries is one of the major attractions for tourists who want to see more; these 'new tourists' (Poon, 1993) are demanding authentic experiences and a chance to see the 'real' country.

This shift from the 'old tourist' (Poon, 1993) with fixed itineraries to the 'new tourist' in search of adventure, excitement and individualization of products has enabled niche sectors of the tour operation business to grow and, especially, to provide specialist interests in more diversified categories (Weiler and Hall, 1992; Spenceley and Rylance, Chapter 10). This has not only led to an increase in adventure- and activity-based tourism, but also opportunities for tour operators to create portfolios of products to meet those new markets which are demanding a more cultural product with increased contact with host societies (Gursoy et al., 2010). This increase in demand is affirmed by Mintel (2008), who noted that some operators, including Intrepid, Wild Frontiers and KE Adventures, have reported growth of up to 30% a year. Of particular note is that this appears contrary to the trend of consumers seeking to organize their own trips.

However, adventure tours, given their potential negative impacts on both the environment and communities, have not been without their detractors. UK trade organizations such as the Association of Independent Tour Operators (AITO) and the Tour Operators Initiative (Tour Operators Initiative, 2011) – a collection of tourism stakeholders from around the world that promote the development, operation and marketing of tourism in a sustainable way, and pressure groups such as Tourism Concern (Tourism Concern, 2011) and the Travel Foundation (2011), have all produced guidelines to aid tour operators on how to achieve the ideals of responsible tourism. AITO represents over 140 independent specialist operators, who it markets as having principles of fair trade and sound environmental policies (Curtin and Busby, 1999). The organization introduced a responsible tourism policy in 2000 to provide guidelines for its members, while allowing them to implement procedures in line with their own operations (AITO, 2011). In essence these are:

- Protect the environment – its flora, fauna and landscapes.
- Respect local cultures – traditions, religions and built heritage.
- Benefit local communities – both economically and socially.
- Conserve natural resources – from office to destination.
- Minimize pollution – arising from noise, waste disposal and congestion.

These guidelines, however, are imprecise in operational terms, and it is left to the operators to implement them using their own policies; they also do not encourage evaluation of the benefits. In 2008, AITO introduced a ratings system, and in order to achieve star ratings, companies need to fulfil a number of criteria of 'Responsible Tourism Policy', such as the implementation of sustainable office practice, communication with customers, environmental practice and practical destination activity, with

the latter two areas having the most points allocated to them (AITO, 2011).

As a result of the increasing advocacy of responsible tourism and at the same time the growth in demand, notably arising in the 1990s – especially for the more specialist culture- and community-orientated packages, many of the small-sized independent adventure tour operators were encouraged to engage with the tenets of responsible tourism. Owing to their comparatively small-scale operations they were able to implement the appropriate policy and procedures swiftly (Holden and Kealy, 1996) and, as Carey et al. (1997) identified, these niche tour operators are more orientated to the environment and to environmental protection than their mainstream counterparts. With the emphasis clearly on the operational issues in destinations, this raises concerns over whether the operator's claims of responsibility are justified and how they are implemented. Thus, this chapter aims first to examine the practices involved in their implementation, focusing on the overseas operational aspects of adventure tour operators and, in particular, examining their products, supply chain and impacts. The second section of the chapter reviews practices implemented by operators and the guidance by non-governmental organizations to improve operations and create responsible tourism products.

Adventure Tourism

The adventure sector is not a new tourism product, but stems back to the 1960s 'hippy trail' and the creation of companies such as Hann Overland and Penn World, who operated overland trips from the UK to Kathmandu, Nepal. It is from these roots that many of the UK adventure operators started – with ex-tour leaders and sometimes clients setting up their own companies (Mintel, 2005). As a result, the adventure tourism sector in the UK predominantly comprises companies that are small independent businesses, and sole traders who have turned their passion for the destinations and adventure into a business. As the range of independent operators increased so too did the interest of the vertically integrated, major tour operators, which led to many small independent operators being bought out by larger companies, e.g. First Choice created an Adventure Division after purchasing several operators including Exodus, Peregrine Adventures, The Adventure Company and The Imaginative Traveller, and is now part of TUI Travel PLC, which has meant a growth in purchasing power and a drive for economies of scale.

Product

The product offerings vary according to the specialist interest of the company, for example, a specific area (Journey Latin America), an activity (Ramblers) or a client group (Families Worldwide). In general, products offered within this field involve visits to predominantly cultural and nature-based destinations and are likely to incorporate popular attractions as well as more remote destinations e.g. Explore Worldwide offer trips to Morocco, staying in Marrakech, but also include a village house and an auberge in the desert. As responsible tourism aims to utilize the travel amenities created by the host population, it eschews international hotel chains in favour of properties owned and managed by locals. Where little or no accommodation is available, then home stays or camping may be used. Specialist UK adventure tour operators such as Exodus, The Adventure Company and Explore Worldwide identify the use of locally owned accommodation as a key component of their products. Although this can be seen as responsible, it is also very realistic as destinations that are so remote are unlikely to have international hotel chains. A variety of itineraries that include adventure but culture and nature are also invariably available. According to Mintel (2005) the average length of trip is 15 days and will vary between long weekends (Explore, Exodus) to overland trips of several months (Dragoman, Overlanding Africa). The tours are usually, but not always, composed of multi-destination itineraries, where the accommodation is changed every day or two; for example, if trekking, a new camp is fixed each night, whereas culture-based trips may involve daily changes as new cities, towns or villages are incorporated into the itineraries.

Overall, there is a wide range and diversity of trips available with companies such as Explore Worldwide, Exodus, the Adventure Company and Activities Abroad offering tours such as treks to Everest Base Camp, safaris, island hopping, sailing, dog sleighing and multi-activity based trips. The cost of such tours varies according to the destination, activities and flights, but they are certainly not a budget holiday purchase (Buckley, 2007). The tours include accommodation, transport and a tour manager/leader, as many of the destinations are hard to access or are 'off the beaten track'. Most of these tours are small in size, with 16–22 persons being the norm, although the group size is dependent on equipment or transportation availability, for example, trips on gullets in Turkey are limited by the boat capacity.

Supply chain management

The majority of the goods and services included in these adventure tours are provided by a supply chain of subcontracted companies, organizations and agents. Therefore tour companies are reliant on those suppliers for their quality and safety and, as a result, they are not always in direct control of the environmental and social impacts of their tours. Identifying these third-party suppliers, for instance the choice of ground agent, hospitality suppliers and transport providers, is critical and needs to be considered carefully. All the more so given that the customers increasingly appear to expect their tour operator not only to provide quality and value for money but also to seek to safeguard the environment and maintain social sustainability (see Leslie, Chapter 2; Spenceley and Rylance, Chapter 10). From the tourists' perspective, these suppliers are seen as one with the operator. Furthermore, the performance and operational activities of these third-party suppliers is the responsibility of the tour operator, including a legal responsibility through the EU (European Union) Package Travel Directive of 1990 (currently under review).

For small tour operators who offer itineraries mainly comprising contracted goods and services, this means that the effective implementation of responsible policies requires working closely with the suppliers to improve their input and performance in all the components of the holiday. It is not the case though that the ideal provision is always present, as noted in the case of accommodation. In such instances, the best practical option is sought. For example, the contracting of transport suppliers relies on local companies which must have available the appropriate vehicles suitable for the type of itinerary, e.g. jeeps or minibuses. Ideally, the use of public transport would be included, but as tours are of a limited duration, this often proves un-attainable.

Tour leaders

Tour guides, invariably known as tour managers or leaders, play a crucial role in adventure tours; not the least of which is being a role model to the clients (Cohen, 1985). Pond (1993, cited in Christie and Mason, 2003) suggests that they have five roles: leader, educator (to enhance understanding of the destinations; Ap and Wong, 2001), public relations representative, host and conduit between the tourist and the place/local community visited; in practice these are all interwoven. Indeed, Christie and Mason (2003) developed this theme by focusing on interaction, in which the guide is seen as telling, selling, participating and delegating in the activities. To this we should add the role of culture broker and mediator (Reisinger and Steiner, 2006). Nash (1989, p. 37) argued that the role of the cultural broker is the more significant in less developed countries because 'the tourist, like the trader, the employer, the conqueror, the governor, the educator, or the missionary, is seen as the agent of contact between cultures and, directly or indirectly, the cause of change particularly in the less developed regions of the world'. Thus, the role of the tour leader in providing information and education is not only about sites, but about behaviour and culture and an insight into the 'real' country. This is taken a step further by Weiler and Davis (1993, p. 97), who suggested that the guides are also promoters of responsible tourism, and

motivators and educators for 'long term behavioural change'.

The importance and value placed on the quality of these tour leaders is in little doubt. This is often demonstrated by the inclusion of their profiles in the tour literature. The larger providers of adventure tours (both independent and those brands within large companies, e.g. Exodus, The Adventure Company and Footprints) use their web pages and brochures to identify tour leaders and highlight their personal achievements. These leaders are usually from the tourists' home region, but tour operators also seek locally based staff for their operations, depending on the type of itinerary and availability of suitably qualified staff. For local leaders with passion and knowledge for their job, culture and heritage will enhance the tourists' experience; this strategy also provides employment opportunities. One tour operator's web site includes a 'hall of fame' which introduces tour leaders and their environmental and academic achievements and, notably, includes overseas tour leaders and information on their expertise and experience of working with the company.

Impacts on vulnerable destinations

It is acknowledged by adventure tour operators that there are many impacts on the social, environmental and economic systems within communities. While such impacts are in general well documented (see Buckley, 2009) they can, as Ewert and Jamieson (2003, p. 81) identified 'be exacerbated by the needs for adventure tourism to take place in remote, exotic locations'. For example, traditional livelihoods may be replaced by tourism-based activities and farmers may turn into guides or porters (Ewert and Jamieson, 2003). Income and economic benefits may go to individuals or companies who work with the operators (e.g. transport or excursion providers), but who may not be from the local community. Conversely, these tours do bring income to the area and opportunities for employment, and this may encourage entrepreneurship and further inward investment. These impacts further fuel the argument that the attraction of remote locations will diminish as the destination becomes more popular, and once these changes become more noticeable, then the operators will seek new, less visited, destinations. This may leave host communities with limited income and a damaged environment if they had previously become reliant on the tour operator's activity.

In regard to these impacts, it is important to recognize that they will vary according to the type of tour and activities involved. This can be illustrated by reference to one of the most popular activities offered, which is trekking. Considerable concerns have been raised (Nepal, 2000; Holden, 2010) about the impact this activity has on the destinations, in particular the number of tour groups completing the same circuits. For example, in Morocco, tours focusing on the ascent of Mount Toubkal have increased in numbers to the point that it was beginning to resemble a highway and, as a result, some operators are changing their routes to make the tour seem more remote and to avoid contact with other tour groups. On many treks, camping is integral, often taking the form of wild camps (i.e. not a permanent campsite), and this has become an increasing problem as groups operating in the same area grow in number. The selection of appropriate sites is critical to prevent pollution of watercourses; what tourists wash in may be someone else's drinking water downstream. Areas such as the Egyptian Nile riverbank have become renowned for the quantity of human waste, which does not decompose in desert conditions, while toilet paper is abundantly visible along the trekking circuits in Nepal, again largely owing to the climatic conditions.

Local porters and muleteers are frequently hired for tours to carry luggage and equipment. These are predominantly local staff that facilitate the tour and provide camp for the tourists. In the 1980s, concerns were raised about the porters in destinations such as Nepal, Peru and Morocco, who were working with minimal equipment while carrying excessive loads. This situation was highlighted in 1990 by Tourism Concern (Tourism Concern, 2011), and led to the establishment of guidelines by the International Porter Protection Group (2010), which was started in 1997. These require that porters carry loads

that are appropriate (relative to their physical abilities), that clothing is appropriate to season and altitude, and that suitable accommodation and adequate food and fuel are provided. The guidelines also call for medical support for porters, for fair pay and for a management plan for illness (some tour operators, such as Walks Worldwide, now provide insurance for the porters).

Opportunities for Improvement

This section of the chapter aims to illustrate some of the opportunities for improved practice within the adventure tourism sector. Owing to the limited academic research in this area, it draws on the author's extensive operational experience, and current research, in adventure tours.

Tour operators have a three-pronged role in the implementation of responsible tourism:

- developing, managing and marketing the operation responsibly;
- creating a product that has positive economic, social, cultural and physical impacts for the destinations; and
- operating responsibly in both the UK and overseas.

For a tour operator to strive to operate in a responsible manner does provide an opportunity for companies to compete on different levels. The production of this 'augmented' product provides opportunities for product differentiation, quality and value (Weedon, 2001).

Responsible planning

Where possible, tour operators need first to ensure that when designing a tour, the destination is able to support the projected visitor numbers, and so the sustainability of the destinations needs to be considered by determining first the appropriate number of tourists that is sustainable. This may mean the need for smaller groups that will minimize disruption to the people and wildlife. Secondly, Curtin and Busby (1999) and Sharpley (2005) have raised concerns that these new tourists and their demands for local interaction are more detrimental to destinations than mass tourism. They argue that these tours can intensify acculturalization and, as much of the adventure tourism product takes place in remote and underdeveloped destinations, leads to concern that these destinations are indeed more likely to be susceptible to such impacts. The wide variety of destinations visited by adventure tourism companies means that the impacts are spread on a wide geographical base.

Consideration should be given to the types of attractions that are included in the tours. Operators should be discouraged from including activities that rely on the exploitation of hosts, wildlife and the environment. For example, tours should not include shows where animals are expected to perform unnatural activities, or where the activities are illegal (e.g. snake charming in India), or include visits to turtle hatcheries which could be considered as exploitative (see Born Free Foundation, 2012).

Supply chain management

Many operators, such as Explore Worldwide, encourage the introduction of environmental management practices in their chosen accommodation operations and undertake checklist evaluations of environmental management practices in the hotels they use. But while these checklists are useful, in some destinations there is not the infrastructure to provide support for the desired practices. In reality, while recycling is seen as essential, this relies on facilities for collection and processing in the destination which is often not available. Attention is also given to the potential for alternative energy sources, such as the use of solar panels, but they are expensive to introduce and very unlikely to be found in accommodation in remote towns and villages. However, some operators have provided financial support to enable changes in operations, such as the popular African lodges in Botswana and Namibia which now utilize solar power for the provision of electricity and have low-energy bulbs.

Minimizing the impacts of accommodation operations is particularly problematic in rural

areas. Nepal (2000) identified that in Nepal deforestation has occurred in areas surrounding the local tea houses as a result of increased demand for fuel for cooking and heating, and also for building lodging houses for tourists. Along with this deforestation, litter and sanitation are also problematic, exacerbated by increasing pressures to accommodate more tourists, and are threatening the fauna, which is one of the main attractions. In response, operators – such as Explore Worldwide – are encouraging tea-house owners to use paraffin stoves and not to provide hot water showers for guests.

A major concern for local accommodation and transport providers is seasonality, so accommodation owners and transport providers will have little or no income during the off season. These peaks and troughs are controllable with planning; for example, Greek island hotel owners may return to the mainland for the winter. Responsible operators – such as Activities Abroad – work with suppliers to try to increase the length of the season or to design new tours to take advantage of seasonal variations.

An uncontrollable *force majeure*, such as when destinations are declared unsafe by the (UK) Foreign and Commonwealth Office and the tour operators have to withdraw, is less able to be managed. Any planned income is lost, thus highlighting the fragility of these tours and the risks involved in depending on tourism, especially in remote rural areas.

Training of staff and monitoring

In practice, most adventure operators train their tour leaders in responsible tourism and practice according to the company's policy and to respect this policy whether in situ or in the UK. Explore Worldwide, for example, insist that their tours ensure people who work for them are treated well and paid fairly, that tours respect local communities and ensure the communities benefit from tourism and respect the local environment by seeking to minimise negative impacts (Explore Worldwide, 2011). Therefore the role of the staff is to encourage all parts of the supply chain to implement responsible tourism policy and identify operational improvements that are specific to each destination.

Adventure tourism products incorporate some level of risk, challenge and uncertainty (Stanbury et al., 2005). The role of the tour leader is to be responsible for the health and safety of the tourists and to minimize these risks. Health and safety assessments, including Activity Risk Assessments are conducted to assess hazards. These assessments evaluate the level and frequency of potential hazards and risks, and decisions are made. If they continue to be promoted, such activities that are considered unacceptably risky are eliminated, and those activities which have some risk, result in plans being put in place to minimise the risk. So it is the role of the tour leader to identify potential risks and the company will then work with suppliers and tour leaders on a Threat and Risk Assessment and develop proactive and reactive control measures. For example, at Explore Worldwide, throughout tour leader training, tour leaders are regularly tested on their understanding of safety. Many companies have undertaken risk assessments for most elements of the tour, such as transport, hotels, and excursions.

Education

One of the key roles of tour leaders is the education and advice to passengers about how they can help minimise their use of resources, for example to encourage passengers to turn off fans, lights and televisions, in particular not leaving them on standby. Some countries do not have the same level of sewage disposal and guidance needs to be provided as to the appropriate way of disposal of such waste, for example the toilet bin or, when camping, the burial or burning of waste. If the environmental conditions do not support the disposal of waste then this needs to be removed from the area and carried out to a suitable disposal point. It is the role of education that is fundamental to acting responsibly and the wellbeing of the sites.

Water shortages are often problematic in many destinations, even if they seem to have abundance, and shortage can lead to a depletion of the water table and cause pollution. Guidance therefore needs to be provided on how to limit water usage. Whilst it is necessary to drink safe water, a reliance on bottle water should be discouraged, instead using filters or purification tablets and reusable bottles to reduce the plastic waste that may not be recyclable.

Responsible marketing

To examine further the adoption of the tenets of responsible tourism by tour operators, we should also consider how they promote their products. Brochures, both electronic and paper based, are still the main information distribution method for adventure tour operators. As well as the legal responsibility to include full information about the accommodation, itinerary, booking conditions and cost, brochures must provide an image of what can be expected at a local level and what can be expected on the tours. Britton (1979) noted that whatever the brochure portrays, there will be no representations of any poverty or issues that, however relevant, may disrupt the 'escape'. There is no room for negativity in a brochure as tourists do not imagine their paradise to be affected by poverty.

A study carried out by MacKay and Fesenmaier (1997) confirmed that the images portrayed by cultural brokers strongly affect the perceptions that tourists hold of a destination and its people. Thus, tourism marketers seek to match the promoted images with what they consider to be the perceptions of their potential customers (MacKay and Fesenmaier, 1997). As long as the reality is also concealed when they are in the resort, the tourists should be satisfied and there will be fewer gaps between their expectations and reality (Cloke and Perkins, 2002). The images so presented help to perpetuate stereotypes of places, people, and tourist–host interactions, for example images of the Karen tribe in Thailand, and of the Touareg in Morocco.

The images in the brochure provide the basis for the expectations of tourists, and how they perceive and, most importantly, how they treat their hosts (Selwyn, 1996). Therefore, they are an influential factor in tourist behaviour (see Hunter, 2008). In the same way, tourists may search out the iconic images of a destination as seen in the brochure and may replicate the tourist–host interaction shown in brochures. As such, then the images used in adventure tourism brochures need to demonstrate responsible behaviour and to resist the temptation to use stereotypical images.

Research by Pennington-Gray et al. (2005) found that very few operators were providing guidance for responsible behaviour in their marketing material, but of those that did, none explained why they were necessary. These authors go on to argue that operators may not see themselves as having the job of educating tourists. This is contrary to Tearfund's (2000) research, which suggested that tourists are prepared to accept a more responsible role in tourism and that over 50% of those that were surveyed wanted to receive more information about how to behave; also, that it is the responsibility of the tour operator and/or travel agent to provide such information.

Respecting the hosts

The tourist experience may be more enjoyable for tourists as a result of more meaningful connections with local people and a greater understanding of local cultural and environmental issues. But it is this interaction that is frequently seen as cause for concern as the much documented sociocultural impacts bear witness (see Wall and Mathieson, 2006). Contact between host populations and adventure tourists is frequently highlighted as a selling point for operators. Interacting with hosts is a key motivation for tourists and enables them to learn about the hosts' way of life and gain an authentic experience (Sharpley, 2005). The reality though is that these interactions are in fact brief owing to the nature of the packages, and superficial as a result of the language barriers (Budeanu, 2004) and the temporal limitations of the holiday (Wall and Mathieson, 2006), which often reduce such interactions to the servicing of the tour or a photo opportunity.

These encounters are typified by a lack of knowledge on the part of the tourist and it becomes the role of the tour leader to act as an intermediary (or broker) in order to provide access to the host population, while guiding and educating tourists to sensitive behaviour and cultural understanding. For example, tourists have complained about the role of women in the south of Morocco, e.g. women carrying goods on their backs while the men ride the donkeys, which seemed to upset many tourists; it then becomes the role of the guide to explain the cultural reasons for this. The guide must remind tourists not to criticise but to accept that this cultural gulf is actually one of the reasons for choosing the trip. This includes reminding them to ask before taking photos, and that sometimes the host may ask for money for the photograph. Although this may be seen as encouraging a begging culture, sometimes hosts may actually make most of their income from being photographed – such as the water sellers in Djemma el Fna in Marrakech, Morocco. Often tourists will take along gifts for the local community. The tour leader needs to provide guidance as to an appropriate time to give and for whom such gifts would be best, for example giving pens to school teachers who can give them to most needy, rather than giving them directly to children, which also may encourage begging.

A final point is that clear advice should be given to tourists about bargaining customs and guidelines established about acceptable prices, as bargaining aggressively may reduce the price of the goods but leave the seller too little income.

Corporate social responsibility (CSR)

The preceding discussion has already highlighted a number of examples that come within the context of CSR, but another area which merits attention is that of contributions to charities. Holden and Kealy (1996) identified, albeit over a decade ago, that almost two-thirds of the tour operators studied supported conservation activities, both global and locally specific campaigns. Later research (Tearfund, 2001) found that 75% of the operators interviewed made charitable donations, with the majority donating to charities in the destinations. The research also noted that the smaller companies gave comparatively more than the larger operators. More recently still, it has become increasingly popular for tour operators to highlight the charitable organizations that they work with in the destinations visited. In fact, this travel philanthropy has become a popular inclusion in the brochure. While one cannot criticise the generosity of the support, the problem comes from supporting one village/school and not others. This creates a have/have not culture in which resentment towards tourism can stem from those that do not have access to donations. Perhaps the most successful projects are those that support the national/international campaigns of conservation organizations which promote awareness and educate local communities in the value of the protection of species; for example, cheetahs and rhinoceros in Namibia, and tiger conservation in India and Nepal.

Conclusion

The primary role of tour operators is to sustain their businesses in an extremely competitive environment. The adoption of responsible practices in adventure tourism is evident from company documentation and NGO membership, but the actual benefits are mainly anecdotal. In general, the responsible operations lead to the development of good working relations with both suppliers and hosts. Reducing waste keeps costs down, and keeps costs of suppliers down which, in turn, improves operating margins.

While many potential customers do not ask about responsible tourism practices before their departure, specialist operators have found that tourists are more interested in such practices on their return from the holiday. This reinforces the educational aspects of the tours and the role and importance of the tour leader as an ambassador for positive change. Education of the tourist starts with company policy, but has to be consistently implemented by those representing the company in the field. Tour leaders can, at best, only encourage responsible behaviour, especially when one considers that the tourists are on holiday and may not wish to be told what to do. Indeed, it appears to be rather assumed that adventure tourists are responsible in their behaviour, which has yet to be proven.

While companies portray a responsibility for fair pay, contracts with accommodation suppliers, and with transportation and local employees are very competitive to maintain low operating costs. In destinations that do not sell, the tours are withdrawn or rearranged, denying those providers of an income, often without notification, as a tour operator's allegiance to any destination is tenuous.

What is evident from the research and marketing material is that many adventure tour operators are actively considering the tenets of responsible tourism while creating and operating their portfolios. While this is no guarantee of success, responsible tourism provides an opportunity for marketing differentiation and potentially a win–win situation for both operators and hosts.

References

AITO (2011) ST (Sustainable Tourism) Guidelines. Association of Independent Tour Operators, Twickenham, UK. Available at: http://www.aito.co.uk/corporate_RTGuidelines.asp (accessed 22 June 2011).

Ap, J. and Wong, K. (2001) Case study on tour guiding: professionalism, issues and problems. *Tourism Management* 12, 31–47.

Bornfree Foundation (2012) Animal Welfare and Tourism: Welfare advice from Bornfree. Available at: http://www.thetravelfoundation.org.uk/green_business_tools/animal_welfare_tourism/welfare_advice_from_bornfree/ (accessed 11 April 2012).

Britton, R.A. (1979) The image of the third world in tourism in marketing. *Annals of Tourism Research* 6, 318–329.

Buckley, R. (2007) Adventure tourism products: price, duration, size, skill, remoteness. *Tourism Management* 28, 1428–1433.

Buckley, R. (2009) *Ecotourism: Principles and Practices.* CAB International, Wallingford, UK.

Budeanu, A. (2004) Impacts and responsibilities for sustainable tourism: a tour operator's perspective. *Journal of Cleaner Production* 13, 89–97.

Carey, S., Gountas, Y. and Gilbert, D. (1997) Tour operators and destination sustainability. *Tourism Management* 18, 425–431.

Christie, M.F. and Mason, P.A. (2003) Transformative tour guiding: training tour guides to be critically reflective practitioners. *Journal of Ecotourism* 2, 1–16.

Cloke, P. and Perkins, H. (2002) Commodification and adventure in New Zealand tourism. *Current Issues in Tourism* 5, 521–549.

Cohen, E. (1985) The tourist guide: the origins, structure and dynamics of a role. *Annals of Tourism Research* 12, 5–29.

Curtin, S. and Busby, G. (1999) Sustainable destination development: the tour operator perspective. *International Journal of Tourism Research* 1, 135–147.

Ewert, A. and Jamieson, L. (2003) Current status and future directions in the adventure tourism industry. In: Wilks, J. and Page, S. (eds) *Managing Tourist Health and Safety in the New Millennium.* Pergamon, Oxford, UK, pp. 67–97.

Explore Worldwide (2011) Responsible Travel and Tourism. Available at: http://www.explore.co.uk/explore-formula/responsible-travel (accessed 28 June 2011).

Gursoy, D., Chi, C. and Dyer, P. (2010) Locals' attitudes toward mass and alternative tourism: the case of Sunshine Coast, Australia. *Journal of Travel Research* 49, 381–393.

Holden, A. (2010) Exploring stakeholders' perceptions of sustainable tourism development in the Annapurna Conservation Area: issues and challenge. *Tourism and Hospitality Planning and Development* 7, 337–351.

Holden, A. and Kealy, H. (1996) A profile of UK outbound 'environmentally friendly' tour operators. *Tourism Management* 11, 60–64.

Hunter, W.C. (2008) A typology of photographic representations for tourism: depictions of groomed spaces. *Tourism Management* 29, 354–365.

International Porter Protection Group (2010) Trekking Ethics. International Porter Protection Group, Bonville, New South Wales, Australia. Available at: http://ippg.net/trekking-ethics/ (accessed 11 April 2012).

MacKay, K.J. and Fesenmaier, D.R. (1997) Pictorial element of destination in image formation. *Annals of Tourism Research* 24, 537–565.

Mintel (2005) *Adventure Travel – Central and Eastern Europe – May 2005.* Reports, Travel and Tourism Analyst, Mintel, London, Chicago, New York, Sydney, Tokyo and Shanghai. Details and summary available at: http://academic.mintel.com/sinatra/oxygen_academic/my_reports/display/id=144790&anchor=atom/display/id=163303 (accessed 21 September 2011).

Mintel (2008) *Adventure Tourism – Europe –May 2008.* Reports, Travel and Tourism Analyst, Mintel, London, Chicago, New York, Sydney, Tokyo and Shanghai. Details and summary available at: http://academic.mintel.com/sinatra/oxygen_academic/search_results/show&/display/id=294937/display/id=335459#hit1 (accessed 21 September 2011).

Mintel (2010) *Package Holidays – UK – July 2010.* Reports, Travel and Tourism Analyst, Mintel, London, Chicago, New York, Sydney, Tokyo and Shanghai. Details and summary available at: http://store.mintel.com/package-holidays-uk-july-2010.html (accessed 11 April 2012).

Nash, D. (1989) Tourism as a form of imperialism. In: Smith, V. (ed.) *Hosts and Guests: The Anthropology of Tourism,* 2nd edn. University of Pennsylvania Press, Philadelphia, Pennsylvania, pp. 37–52.

Nepal, S. (2000) Tourism in protected areas: the Nepalese Himalaya. *Annals of Tourism Research* 27, 661–681.

Novelli, M. (2005) *Niche Tourism: Contemporary Issues, Trends and Cases.* Elsevier Butterworth-Heinemann, Oxford, UK.

Pennington-Gray, L., Reisinger, Y., Kim, J.E. and Thapa, B. (2005) Do US tour operators' brochures educate the tourist on culturally responsible behaviours? A case study for Kenya. *Journal of Vacation Marketing* 11, 265–284.

Poon, A. (1993) *Tourism, Technology and Competitive Strategies.* CAB International, Wallingford, UK.

Reisinger, Y. and Steiner, C. (2006) Reconceptualising interpretation: the role of tour guides in authentic tourism. *Current Issues in Tourism* 9, 481–498.

Selwyn, T. (1996). *The Tourist Image: Myths and Myth Making in Tourism.* John Wiley, Chichester, UK.

Sharpley, R. (2005) *Tourists, Tourism and Society,* 3rd edn. ELM Publications, Huntingdon, UK.

Stanbury, J., Pryer, M. and Roberts, A. (2005) Heroes and villains – tour operator and media response to crisis:

an exploration of press handling to strategies by UK adventure tour operators. *Current Issues in Tourism* 8, 394–423.

Swarbrooke, J., Beard, C., Leckie, S. and Pomfret, G. (2003) *Adventure Tourism: The New Frontier*. Elsevier Butterworth-Heinemann, Oxford, UK.

Tearfund (2000) *Tourism – An Ethical Issue: Market Research Report*. Tearfund, London.

Tearfund (2001) *Tourism – Putting Ethics into Practice: A Report on the Responsible Business Practices of 65 UK-Based Tour Operators*. Tearfund, London.

Tour Operators Initiative (2011) Tour Operators Initiative. Available at: http://www.toinitiative.org (accessed 28 December 2011).

Tourism Concern (2011) Tourism Concern. Available at: http://www.tourismconcern.org.uk (accessed 20 September 2011).

Travel Foundation (2011) The Travel Foundation. Available at: http://www.thetravelfoundation.org.uk (accessed 28 December 2011).

Wall, G. and Mathieson, A. (2006) *Tourism: Change, Impacts and Opportunities*. Prentice Hall-Pearson Education, Harlow, UK.

Weedon, C. (2001) Ethical tourism. *Journal of Vacation Marketing* 8, 141–153.

Weiler, B. and Davis, D. (1993) An exploratory investigation into the roles of the nature-based tour leader. *Tourism Management* 14, 91–98.

Weiler, B. and Hall, C. (eds) (1992) *Special Interest Tourism*. Belhaven Press, London.

10 Responsible Wildlife Tourism in Africa

Anna Spenceley[1] and Andrew Rylance[2]

University of Johannesburg and Spenceley Tourism And Development (STAND) cc, South Africa[1] and Deutsche Gesellschaft für Internationale Zusammenarbeit (GIZ), South Africa[2]

Introduction

Africa is a continent that is famed for its rich natural heritage and diverse wildlife. Travellers' anecdotes of 'wildlife in Africa' range from stampeding wildebeest crossing rivers inhabited by crocodiles in Tanzania's Serengeti; climbing the Virunga Volcanoes in Rwanda to catch a glimpse of the rare mountain gorillas; taking a cool drink at sundown overlooking the Sabie River in the Kruger National Park; and watching manta rays, dolphins and whale sharks in the warm Indian ocean of Mozambique. This is a continent rich in opportunity for tourism based on wildlife. However, it is essential in the development and delivery of such tourism products that this is undertaken responsibly.

Responsible tourism is about providing better holiday experiences for guests and good business opportunities for tourism enterprises. It is also about enabling local communities to enjoy a better quality of life through increased socio-economic benefits and improved natural resource management (Spenceley *et al.*, 2002). 'Wildlife tourism' is defined as a form of nature-based tourism that includes the consumptive and non-consumptive use of wild animals in natural areas (Roe *et al.*, 1997). Non-consumptive use may be undertaken through guided or self-drive excursions in vehicles, or through guided walks, where wildlife is not physically killed. In contrast, consumptive use involves wildlife either being killed (e.g. hunting, or extracted from its natural environment). Therefore, responsible wildlife tourism is simply wildlife tourism where the principles of responsible tourism are applied.

How do the policy makers in these destinations, and the tourism operators who work there, manage their enterprises in a way that does not destroy the wildlife resources that their businesses are based on? How do they balance the social and cultural needs of residents with the demands of tourists? How do protected areas generate sufficient revenues to equitably support local livelihoods and finance conservation management? To explore answers to these questions, this chapter first provides an overview of the concepts and principles surrounding responsible wildlife tourism. This is followed by sections that review the policy context, environmental, economic, and social and cultural implications of the sector.

Responsible Wildlife Tourism

When tourism is operated responsibly, operators take proactive action to minimize negative economic, environmental and social impacts, to enhance the well-being of host communities and to make positive contributions to the conservation of natural and cultural heritage. Responsible tourism also aims to provide more enjoyable experiences for tourists through more meaningful connections with local people, and a greater understanding of local cultural, social and environmental issues (Cape Town, 2002).

There is no clear or consistent way for tourists or tour operators to discern whether wildlife tourism is being operated responsibly or not. In some countries, tourism certification programmes have emerged which provide a mechanism through which enterprises can achieve voluntary standards of performance that meet or exceed baseline standards or legislation (Spenceley and Durbarry, 2010) (see also Roe et al., 2003). In 2010 there were 11 voluntary tourism certification programmes operating in Africa, and six in the process of development (Spenceley and Seif, 2010) (see Table 10.1). Some of these, such as eco awards Namibia, and the Eco-rating scheme in Kenya, particularly focus on wildlife tourism. However, only a minority of wildlife tourism enterprises participate in these certification programmes.

With less stringent criteria than certification programmes, there are a number of international awards that have recognized responsible wildlife tourism operations in Africa (see Table 10.2).

The risk of not operating wildlife tourism responsibly is that the natural environment will deteriorate and biodiversity will be lost. Irresponsibly managed tourism may influence changes in wildlife behaviour to such an extent that it may reduce the likelihood of survival of the individual animals and, potentially, also site-specific populations. In summary, wildlife tourism may destroy its very basis and become unsustainable.

Policy Context

The policy framework and political environment heavily influence the structure and delivery of responsible wildlife tourism in Africa. These can influence the management of wildlife areas by the state, by communities, or by the private sector (Spenceley, 2008). For example, South Africa has developed and adopted Responsible Tourism Guidelines and National Minimum Standards for Responsible Tourism (Spenceley, 2010a). These incorporate a series of environmental standards that address biodiversity conservation, wildlife and endangered species. The Seychelles has developed a comprehensive national ecotourism strategy for the 21st

Table 10.1. Tourism certification schemes in Africa (Spenceley and Seif, 2010).

Country	Name of programme
Botswana	Botswana Tourism Board
Egypt	Green Star Hotel Initiative
Kenya	Ecotourism Kenya Eco-rating scheme
Madagascar	Green Label
Morocco	Zakoura Microcredit Foundation Programme[a]
Namibia	eco awards Namibia
Seychelles	Seychelles Sustainability Label[a]
South Africa	Audubon Green Leaf
	Baobab Green Leaf Certification Programme
	Fair Trade in Tourism South Africa
	Green Flag Trails
	Green Leaf Environmental Standard
	Green Stay SA[a]
	Green Wilderness[a]
	Heritage Environmental Rating Programme
Zambia	South Luangwa Environmental Awards[a]

[a]Denotes scheme in development.

Table 10.2. International tourism awards for African enterprises and destinations (Spenceley and Durbarry, 2010).

Award programme	Beneficiary
World Travel and Tourism Council (WTTC) Tourism for Tomorrow Awards	Botswana Tourism Board – Winner, destination stewardship award, 2010
	Bushman's Kloof, South Africa – Finalist Conservation award, 2006
	CCAfrica – Finalist, Community Benefit award, 2005
	Damaraland Camp, Namibia (Wilderness Safaris) – Winner, conservation award, 2005
	Grootbos Nature Reserve, South Africa – Finalist Conservation award, 2008
	Manda Wilderness Project, Mozambique – Finalist Conservation award, 2005
	Namibia's Communal Conservancy Tourism Sector (NACSO) – Finalist, Community benefit award, 2010
	Singita Grumeti, Tanzania – Finalist, Conservation award, 2010
	Wilderness Safaris – Finalist global tourism business award 2007, 2010
Virgin Responsible Tourism Awards	Azafady, UK/Madagascar – Winner, Best Volunteering Organisation, 2007
	Gamewatchers Safaris and Porini Camps, Kenya – Best for conservation of wildlife and habitats, 2008
	Great Plains Conservation, South Africa – Winner, Best for conservation of wildlife and habitats, 2009
	Guludo Beach Lodge, Mozambique – Winner, Best for poverty reduction, 2009
	Nkwichi Lodge, Mozambique – Winner, best small hotel, 2008
	Ol Malo Lodge and Trust, Kenya – Overall joint winner

century called SETS-21 (Ministry of Tourism and Transport, 2003). SETS-21 includes the natural and marine environment, community-based tourism, cultural heritage, handicrafts, beaches and city redevelopment goals (Spenceley and Durbarry, 2010). The policies of agencies responsible for managing protected areas can be particularly influential, as has been demonstrated in South Africa and Namibia.

In South Africa, the parastatal responsible for national parks in the country, South African National Parks (SANParks) has developed two clear strategies that support the development of responsible wildlife tourism. These are a Responsible Tourism Strategy for the national parks and a strategy for private concessions within the national parks. The concessions programme was preceded by a change in policy that allowed the private sector to invest in, and operate, tourism within the national parks (a realm that had previously been reserved for government). The initiative was driven by the need to stimulate investment that was ecologically sensitive in protected areas. Prospective concessionaires not only submitted

financial bids, but also environmental and socio-economic proposals (Spenceley, 2004). Through the ongoing monitoring and evaluation of concessionaires' environmental and socio-economic performance, SANParks realized that the tourism operations that were state run were actually not as environmentally sensitive as the concessions. For example, the concessionaires were required to use no more than 350 litres water per person per day but the SANParks-run camps were not even monitoring the volumes of water used (Spenceley, 2004). The concessionaires were also required to encourage and report on the value of services and products procured from local communities, but the state-run camps did not. These contradictions led to the development of the new responsible tourism strategy for SANParks in order to consistently integrate the principles of the national Responsible Tourism Guidelines and the National Minimum Standards for Responsible Tourism into national parks operations (SANParks, 2009).

The Namibian government has devised a land-tenure system involving conservancies that gives communities the opportunity to generate revenue from responsibly using wildlife resources on their land. Legislation was passed that allowed communities living in communal lands to acquire common property rights to manage and use their wildlife. Tourism joint ventures in conservancies now represent 856 tourist beds, 789 full-time jobs and over 250 seasonal positions. In addition, the private sector has invested more than N$145 million (US$19 million) in tourism in conservancies since 1998 (MET, 2012). There are several noteworthy and exceptional factors regarding the concessions programme in Namibia. These include that it has worked from a top-down, policy-led approach, but has recognized the value of devolving responsibility for the management of wildlife to local people through a community-based natural resource management (CBNRM) approach. The policy has had strong participation and buy-in from communities and has provided them with stable land tenure. It has worked from the basis that the main threat to wild habitats and resources is not overuse, but actually the conversion of land for agriculture and livestock (SASUSG, 1996). This implies that biodiversity conservation depends on giving landowners the right incentives for sustainable land use (Spenceley, 2010b). The conservancy process has been successful in extending the protected areas to include 19% of the country (equivalent to the entire land area of Greece). Namibia has the world's largest population of black rhinos and this is managed through a custodianship programme with farmers. It is the only country in Africa where endangered black rhinos are being translocated out of national parks and into communal conservancies (MET, 2010). The success of the conservancy programme in Namibia demonstrates how a combination of economic incentives and proprietorship creates suitable conditions for sustainable wildlife use (Jones and Weaver, 2009).

From the perspective of the private sector, the success of wildlife concessions is underpinned by a number of factors, including: long-term commitment and relationships; credibility with communities and governments; and consistent and supportive regulations and a policy environment of good governance (Spenceley, 2010b). This means that providing

a stable and supportive enabling environment is critical for both government and private sector operations in the realization of responsible wildlife tourism.

Environmental Impacts

Wildlife tourism can have impacts on the environment in which the animals live, and also on the animals themselves. For example, using off-road vehicles to access unsealed roads can help visitors to get close to charismatic wildlife, such as lions or elephants, but it may cause damage to flora or soils if not done sensitively. Boats used for whale or dolphin watching can not only disturb wildlife behaviour but can also cause water pollution. Viewing wildlife may increase the chances of disease transmission, such as transmission of the influenza virus between humans and gorillas. Vehicle-based wildlife tourism may disrupt feeding, such as hunting cheetahs in the Maasai Mara (see Newsome et al., 2005). Responsible wildlife tourism ensures that guides are trained to minimize the negative impacts on the environment and wildlife. Where tourists are self-guided, rules or codes of conduct, coupled with fines to enforce them, can be used to manage visitor impacts.

Some tourism enterprises have achieved net positive contributions to wildlife from their activities. For example, Wilderness Safaris is luxury safari tourism operator and developer working in over 70 destinations in seven southern African countries. This company has an impressive track record of active conservation of habitats and species, and of sensitive infrastructure development in ecologically important destinations, while also ensuring local economic benefits to communities through employment, procurement, and joint-venture operations. The Wilderness Wildlife Trust (WWT) is an initiative of the company that channels donations into three target areas: research and conservation; community empowerment and education; and anti-poaching and management (WWT, 2010). In 2009, the Trust had 43 projects operating across sub-Saharan Africa, ranging from ecological studies of rhinos in Botswana, to an anti-poaching project in Zimbabwe (WWT,

2010). In 2010, Wilderness Safaris secured the Chelinda Concession in Nyika National Park, Malawi. This move expanded the wilderness biodiversity footprint from seven biomes to eight, incorporating an additional 90 bird species, 27 mammal species and 13 amphibian species (Wilderness Holdings Ltd, 2010, p. 18). The company has developed and reported on a series of indicators to demonstrate the sustainability of their practices, based on the Global Reporting Initiative (Spenceley, 2010b).

In the case of black rhino conservation, Phinda, a community-owned reserved operated by &Beyond in South Africa, has supported the expansion of the protected range of these rhinos. Phinda hosts four luxury lodges and a walking safari operation, with a capacity for a hundred guests. Starting in 1991, the company worked to rehabilitate degraded agricultural and pastoral land and also supplemented wildlife populations with over 1500 head of game, including white rhinos (Spenceley and Barnes, 2005). In 2004, Phinda became involved in a Rhino Range Expansion Project. As a 'seed' population, they received 15 black rhinos from KZN Wildlife, the provincial conservation authority. Phinda did not purchase the rhinos because rather than owning them, they are their custodians. KZN Wildlife retains ownership and management control over the animals. However, Phinda was obliged to pay for the ongoing monitoring of the rhinos in their care and to regularly report on their behaviour for a period of 25 years. The reserve is also obliged to maintain the quality of habitat, browse and water availability for the safe custody, survival and growth of the black rhino population (Anon., 2004). Although the presence of the black rhinos has not led to an increase in the profitability of tourism at Phinda, it offers a rhino-related product: white rhino darting safaris. Guests are provided with information on rhino tracking, darting and microchipping, and are allocated responsibilities such as measuring heart rate, watering the animal and so on. Under the supervision of experts, including a veterinary surgeon, the package includes participation in a rhino-darting operation (Spenceley and Barnes, 2005). Once the cost of darting the rhino has been deducted, these safaris cumulatively generated R2.8 million net profit between 1999 and 2004. This illustrates the use of tourism not only to finance conservation monitoring of rhinos but also to generate profit for tourism enterprises, despite the small number of tourists who participate. Clearly there is a limit to the frequency of this type of operation in relation to the management requirements and safety for the animals; more unobtrusive activities (e.g. rhino tracking) would provide a more stable income (Spenceley and Barnes, 2005). Phinda supports environmental education for local schoolchildren, which incorporates awareness raising of the black rhino and its conservation status (Spenceley and Barnes, 2005).

Away from the land, and towards the coast, responsible marine wildlife tourism attempts to educate tourists and the private sector on how to interact with wildlife in a sensitive way. Inhambane province in Mozambique is internationally renowned because of the potential to see manta rays and whale sharks. Two researchers studying the ecology of these charismatic megafauna have initiated outreach programmes and awareness raising for the tourism sector. For example, on Manta Reef there are consistently high sightings of manta rays because of the presence of cleaning stations. The rays visit these areas regularly to have dead skin, parasites and wounds cleaned or removed by several species of small fish. The cleaning stations are critical habitats, and require protection from both fishing and unrestricted dive practices. The researchers report that although conscientious divers appear to have minimal impacts on manta behaviour, the rays are easily disturbed by people not following simple guidelines. They work directly with local dive operators, and at a national level through a Mozambican diving association, to encourage best-practice conduct by all parties. The researchers are currently conducting research on the impacts of swimmer behaviour on whale sharks, and how effectively the introduction of a code of conduct on interaction mitigates any potential disruption. They are also working to educate dive operators and customers on how to maximize the enjoyment of swimmers while avoiding any negative responses by sharks (FPMM, 2009a,b).

On the south coast of South Africa, Gansbaai is an area that tourists flock to in order to view great white sharks. A cage is lowered into the water and tourists enter the cage wearing thick wet suits and dive masks. A sent trail is made using bloody water, and the tourists view the sharks as they swim past the cage, searching for seals. Dyer Island Cruises (2012) works closely with the provincial conservation authorities and scientists to support research and conservation efforts. They provide support for marine biologists, and in shark tagging and tracking projects, and have a dedicated research boat and a volunteer and intern programme. They are involved in helping injured birds and seals found in their operating areas as well as supporting the habitat of the penguins on Dyer island. The company has received a Fair Trade in Tourism South Africa award, and in 2006 won a First Choice Responsible Tourism commendation for 'Best in Marine Environment'.

Responsible wildlife tourism can achieve considerable conservation benefits. These include expansion of the conservation estate (as demonstrated by Wilderness Safaris) and the protection of populations of rare and endangered species (as illustrated by the black rhino translocations at Phinda). Castley (2010) suggests though that external forces, and factors that cannot be controlled, reduce the potential for conservation through tourism. These external factors include climate change, political instability and civil war.

Economic Impacts

Research on the economic impacts of wildlife tourism is patchy on a number of counts: in terms of geographical location, the (small) number of studies and the type of information that is reported. Reports indicate that the benefits accrued by employees and host communities vary widely between enterprises and destinations, dependent on the institutional structures, partnership arrangements, business viability of a particular venture and the indigenous wildlife (Spenceley, 2008).

Emerton (2001) argues that the livelihood benefits from wildlife tourism are not always sufficient to make up for the costs of living with

wildlife, particularly when the costs and benefits are unequally distributed between people. This means that generating broad development benefits for a whole community does not ensure that wildlife will produce net local economic gains; it is also not the same as providing economic incentives for conservation. For example, local people often suffer substantial costs from living with wildlife and close to protected areas. This may include crop raiding, damage to infrastructure and threats to their personal safety (Spenceley, 2008). As a result, if wildlife does not generate benefits or the benefits do not reach the rural population, then people are unlikely to appreciate and conserve it. The more livelihood benefits that are obtained, the more widely wildlife is appreciated by local people (Arntzen, 2003). Excluding local communities from the decision-making processes and preventing communities from benefiting from wildlife resources thus hinders responsible business practice.

Wildlife tourism offers a means for the conservation of wildlife resources and provides income-generating opportunities for communities. The survival of wildlife requires reconciling the needs of animals with the financial and social demands of the surrounding communities (Eltringham, 1994, p. 163). For economists, wildlife is perceived as an economic unit that imposes a cost to manage but that can potentially also generate revenue. Understanding and accurately determining the direct and indirect monetary value of an animal is critical for promoting the survival of animals. For example, the opportunity cost of hunting a rhino in the present is substituting the potential revenues from tourists paying to view the animal in the future. Hence, accurately determining its value informs decision making both within local communities and at a national policy making level.

The values of wildlife tourism can include consumptive value (hunting), non-consumptive value (photography), as well as non-use value (e.g. from an appreciation that rhinos may not become extinct). These are not mutually exclusive activities, and the same animal can be involved in more than one. For example, a buffalo can generate economic benefits for many years by being photographed and when it has passed its reproductive prime it can be hunted for a trophy. Although controversial, hunting potentially generates revenues for communities, meat for families, and additional business activities such as the tanning of animal hides and their sale. Moreover, the ecological carrying capacity of land deems that at some point the marginal benefit of an additional wildlife unit becomes zero. Too many animals in an area have a negative impact on biodiversity and the natural ecosystem. Understanding the components that constitute the total economic value of wildlife enables stakeholders to make informed decisions. In the absence of this appreciation, the economic value of wildlife is often undervalued (see Fig. 10.1).

As noted, detailed studies on this topic are very limited and so the following are particularly notable. Barnes (1996) determined the economic use value of elephants in Botswana during the period when the international trade of elephant products was banned. He estimated that during the ban the economic value was reduced by nearly half because legal hunting and the legal sale of ivory, in addition to the knock-on business opportunities, such as meat processing, hide tanning and ivory carving, all dramatically declined. This loss in revenue represents the financial burden incurred by the government to pay for continued wildlife management and

the required amount to be paid to communities as compensation for forgoing converting their land use from wildlife management to livestock farming. Therefore, without being able to efficiently exploit the total economic value of wildlife resources, competing land uses become more attractive to local communities. The economic value of wildlife tourism can be determined by using a travel cost method, which estimates a tourist's willingness to pay for the experience by using proxy indicators of time and money spent travelling to, from and within the destination (see Day, 2002). At the policy level, this kind of research has been used to justify public funding for protected areas by presenting the loss of welfare to surrounding communities if they are closed. In addition, it shows the monetary values of non-market recreational values of public expenditure at the reserves. Furthermore, a study by Brown and Henry (1990; cited in Swanson and Barbier, 1992), who used a mixture of the travel cost method and contingent valuation, estimated the viewing value of elephants at US$25 million (1990 prices), and as increasing by 10–15% each year. This provides important insights into the economic impact of wildlife tourism and how improper and irresponsible management of wildlife can have negative multiplier effects throughout the tourism sector.

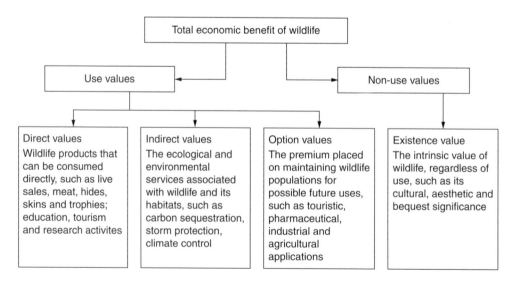

Fig. 10.1. Values of wildlife. Adapted from Emerton (2001, p. 210).

Accurately accounting for the total economic value of wildlife tourism, although extremely important, is redundant unless the revenues generated are allocated in an appropriate manner. The Communal Areas Management Programme for Indigenous Resources (CAMPFIRE) in Zimbabwe enabled communities to have 'co-ownership of local natural resources, which [would] generate income through leasing of trophy hunting concessions, harvesting natural resources, tourism, live animal sales, and meat cropping' (Fischer et al., 2011, p. 304) Between 1989 and 1996, revenue earned by rural district councils exceeded US$9.3 million. More than 90% of this amount was generated from the lease of sport-hunting rights to commercial safari operators (Bond, 2001, p. 231). Experiences from CAMPFIRE showed that although there was some reduction in poaching activities, this situation deteriorated when communities did not receive the benefits generated and rural district councils did not earn enough to afford the implementation of the anti-poaching units (Fischer et al., 2011, p. 317). Therefore, although the economic impacts, both through direct financial revenues and indirectly through business opportunities, may display a great potential for rural communities, this is not a result in itself. Ensuring that money reaches the communities, that contracts are negotiated on fair and equal terms, and that systems are in place to regulate and monitor the financial impact of wildlife on rural communities are all critical components of a wider system. Emerton (2001, p. 226) argues that 'providing communities with economic incentives to conserve wildlife means ensuring that they are better off in financial and livelihood terms with wildlife than they would be without it, at the same time as overcoming the root economic factors which cause them to engage in economic activities which threaten and deplete wildlife resources'.

Mitchell and Keane (2008) tracked the financial flows along the value chain for wildlife tourism in northern Tanzania. They estimated that the revenue impact to local communities and businesses totalled 19% of a typical safari tourist's expenditure. A breakdown of the value-chain components showed that 36% of the typical safari package was considered to be pro poor (Mitchell and Keane, 2008, pp. 50–51). However, despite the opportunities for wildlife tourism to create income-generating opportunities for local communities, Mitchell and Keane's (2008, p. 51) comparative analysis found that wildlife safaris were relatively less pro poor than other forms of tourism in Tanzania, such as mountain climbing. Another example, gorilla tourism in Rwanda, generates employment opportunities for communities surrounding the Virunga National Park. Since 2005, nearly US$428,248 has been directly invested in community projects, including building schools, tree planting and soil erosion measures, as well as the installation of over 30 water tanks that serve at least 1250 people (Spenceley et al., 2010). However, only 5% of tourism revenues are allocated directly to the local community and although direct jobs have been created for those who work inside the park, the communities outside do not receive the benefits of their sacrifice. Failing to realize the true total value of gorillas means they will be undervalued, and without strict enforced government interventions, such as are in place in Rwanda, communities will choose alternative livelihoods to conservation. Expecting communities living in protected areas not to hunt or farm to generate a livelihood while being unwilling to compensate them for their sacrifice is unsustainable. Responsible tourism promotes mutually beneficial relationships within wildlife conservation. Accurately capturing the economic value of wildlife – and also the services – that communities provide to wildlife conservation is critical, but can only be successful if agreements are negotiated in a fair and responsible manner. Furthermore, irresponsible tourism practice that depletes the wildlife stock can influence a tourist's decision to visit a different country with high wildlife stock, which has economic ramifications not only for tourism but for the wider economy.

Social and Cultural Impacts

The social and cultural impacts of wildlife tourism arise from three main sources: interactions with visitors, interactions with the private sector and interactions with wildlife.

Interactions with visitors, to varying degrees, are similar to those found in other areas of tourism. These are well documented in the preceding chapters and thus we will focus here on the latter two categories.

In their operations, responsible private sector enterprises often provide social and cultural benefits to local people that are above and beyond employment and the procurement of goods and services. Typically, enterprises may have corporate social responsibility (CSR) programmes where either donations or profits from tourism are used to support education or health care (see Zientara, Chapter 12). For example, the luxury safari operator &Beyond has a charitable foundation which channels donations into the communities that neighbour their lodges. &Beyond focuses on improving health care (building clinics, providing access to water, creating vegetable gardens), education (building classrooms, granting bursaries, donating school supplies), income generation (support of small businesses, buying produce from local farmers), community equity and assisting vulnerable children and orphans. Guests to &Beyond lodges are encouraged to visit the communities and to see the foundation's many projects in action (see Spenceley, 2010a). Environmental education, in particular, provides a win–win for wildlife tourism operators, because it educates the local youth on the benefits of conservation. For example, Wilderness Safaris has a 'Children in the Wilderness' (CITW) programme. The aim is to offer rural children a 6-day life skills and environmental educational experience. The programme combines leadership, environmental education, life skills and recreation in a unique and safe wilderness environment. It is designed to increase self-esteem, teach new skills and impart knowledge to children. In order to operate the CITW programme, Wilderness Safaris closes down some of its camps to full paying guests for a number of weeks each year and provides the children with exclusive use of these camps (Spenceley, 2010b).

Despite these proactive measures, in general the interactions of local people with wildlife in Africa are characterized by conflict. The challenge for responsible tourism operations is to ensure that there is a net benefit for local communities from tourism. If the conservation of wildlife is understood by local people, and if the threats and risks that it presents are more than offset by financial benefits, then wildlife is at less risk from poaching and from the conversion of its habitat to agriculture.

Conclusion

Responsible tourism focuses on the 'triple-bottom line' of environmental, economic and sociocultural responsibility. This chapter has demonstrated how responsible wildlife tourism in Africa has been utilized to promote conservation through practices that are environmentally and socially sustainable, and financially viable. However, how does the prospective customer know who is or who is not responsible in their management and practices? One way certainly is through appropriate certification systems, which can give an independent measure of responsibility and thus some degree of assurance. Linking conservation to a business objective has been one of the main strengths of responsible tourism legislation and certification schemes. Nevertheless, a representative of &Beyond once stated that the company's responsible and sustainable business practice does not necessarily attract new customers, although it does encourage repeat business.

The economic impact of wildlife tourism is substantial if the total economic value of the wildlife is captured and distributed to communities based on responsible principles. In order to expect communities to conserve wildlife it is required to provide economic benefits that outweigh those of alternative land uses. Expecting conservation without beneficiation is irresponsible and unsustainable. Considering wildlife economic units that generate both revenues and costs enables policy makers to place a value on wildlife and on the services provided by communities.

Improving the financial and employment benefits that reach the local community also improves the experience for the tourist and encourages repeat business. African communities have a deep cultural history that is of potential interest to tourists. Many responsible wildlife tourism enterprises offer cultural activities for their tourists in between game-viewing drives. These cultural activities add value to the tourist's holiday while also providing more financial opportunities for local communities to benefit from access to tourists. Working with these local businesses to improve their product and service quality as well as their marketing is a way that a responsible enterprise can pass on its experience of the needs of tourists to communities. Furthermore, wildlife tourism enterprises often operate within communal land or bordering communities. Therefore, supporting the community or society in which the tourism businesses operate is important for strengthening the efficiency of their supply chains for both employees and fresh produce, and for increasing the number of quality activities available to tourists, thereby enabling them to spend more locally, as well as improving the security of the tourism

enterprise. Social responsibility by the wildlife tourism sector is particularly strong in Africa. By channelling donations, a proportion of turnover, or in-kind support, the private sector is able to support education, health and water programmes in local rural communities.

The exemplars of trans-African companies involved in wildlife tourism described in this chapter provide valuable lessons in the adoption and promotion of responsible tourism, which are more widely applicable and can inform government policy and institutional practices. Embedding these lessons into national systems is critical to actively encouraging the many other tourism enterprises involved in wildlife tourism to become more responsible in their management practices. By providing an appropriate enabling environment for responsible wildlife tourism, governments and protected area agencies can encourage and support the tourism sector overall in developing sustainable economies.

References

Anon. (2004) *Custodianship agreement between the Kwa-Zulu Natal Nature Conservation Board and Mun-ya-wana Game Reserve, October 2004*. Publisher unknown. Cited in Spenceley, A. and Barnes, B. (2005) *Economic Analysis of Rhino Conservation in a Land-Use Context within the SADC Region*. SADC Regional Programme for Rhino Conservation, Report to IUCN–ROSA (World Conservation Union–Regional Office for Southern Africa), September 2005, SADC RPRC Task 6.3-1.2 (Phase II), Harare, Zimbabwe. Available at: http://anna.spenceley.co.uk/files/Spenceley%20&%20Barnes.pdf (accessed 13 April 2012).

Arntzen, J.W., Molokomme, D.L., Terry, E.M., Moleele, N., Tshosa, O. and Mazambani, D. (2003) *Final Report of the Review of Community-based Natural Resource Management in Botswana*. Centre for Applied Research for the National CBNRM Forum, Maun, Botswana.

Barnes, J. (1996) Changes in the economic use value of elephant in Botswana: the effect of international trade prohibition. *Ecological Economics* 15, 215–230.

Bond, I. (2001) CAMPFIRE and the incentives for institutional change. In: Hulme, D. and Murphree, M. (eds) *African Wildlife and Livelihoods: The Promise and Performance of Community Conservation*. Heinemann-James Curry, Oxford, UK/Portsmouth, New Hampshire, pp. 227–243.

Cape Town (2002) The Cape Town Declaration [of Responsible Tourism in Destinations], August 2002. Available at: http://www.responsibletourismpartnership.org/CapeTown.html (accessed 13 April 2012).

Castley, J.G. (2010) Southern and East Africa. In: Buckley, R. (ed.) *Conservation Tourism*. CAB International, Wallingford, UK, pp. 145–175.

Day, B. (2002) Valuing visits to game parks in South Africa. In: Pearce, D., Pearce, C. and Palmer, C. (eds) *Valuing the Environment in Development Countries: Case Studies*. Edward Elgar, Cheltenham, UK, pp. 236–273.

Dyer Island Cruises (2012) Dyer Island Cruises: Whale watching tours. Marine Dynamics: Shark cage diving. Gansbaai, South Africa. Available at: http://www.dyer-island-cruises.co.za/index.html (accessed 13 April 2012).

Eltringham, S. (1994) Can wildlife pay for itself? *Oryx* 28, 163–168.

Emerton, L. (2001) The nature of benefits and the benefits of nature: why wildlife conservation has not economically benefited communities in Africa. In: Hulme, D. and Murphree, M. (eds), *African Wildlife and Livelihoods: The Promise and Performance of Community Conservation*. Heinemann-James Currey, Oxford, UK/Portsmouth, New Hampshire, pp. 208–226.

Fischer, C., Muchapondwa, E. and Sterner, T. (2011) A bio-economic model of community incentives for wildlife management under CAMPFIRE. *Environmental Resource Economics* 48, 303–319.

FPMM (2009a) Sustainable Marine Tourism. Foundation for the Protection of Marine Megafauna, Inhambane, Mozambique. Available at: http://marinemegafauna.org/sustainable-marine-tourism/ (accessed 19 June 2011).

FPMM (2009b) Education. Foundation for the Protection of Marine Megafauna, Inhambane, Mozambique. Available at: http://marinemegafauna.org/education/ (accessed 19 June 2011).

Jones, B. and Weaver, C. (2009) CBNRM in Namibia: growth, trends, lessons and constraints. In: Suich, H., Child, B. and Spenceley, A. (eds) *Evolution and Innovation in Wildlife Conservation*. Earthscan, London/ Sterling, Virginia.

MET (2010) Statement by Hon. Netumbo Nandi-Ndaitwah, MP Minister regarding Namibia's communal conservancy tourism sector nomination for top international award on 24–26 May 2010, Beijing, China. Ministry of Environment and Tourism, Windhoek, Namibia. Available at: http://www.met.gov.na/ Documents/Speech%20for%20the%20Hon%20Minister%20PRESS%20CONFERENCE%20Beijing%20 19%20APRIL.pdf (accessed 13 April 2012).

MET (2012) Protected Areas. Ministry of Environment and Tourism, Windhoek, Namibia. Available at: http:// www.met.gov.na/Pages/Protectedareas.aspx (accessed 13 April 2012).

Ministry of Tourism and Transport (2003) *Towards an Ecotourism Strategy for the 21st Century (Sets-21)*. Ministry of Tourism and Transport, Victoria, Mahé, Seychelles. Available at: http://www.natureseychelles.org/index. php?option=com_docman&task=doc_download&gid=152&Itemid=89 (accessed 13 April 2012).

Mitchell, J. and Keane, J. (2008) *Tracing the Tourism Dollar in Northern Tanzania. Final Report to the Netherlands Development Organisation (SNV)*. Overseas Development Institute, London.

Newsome, D., Dowling, R. and Moore, S. (2005) *Wildlife Tourism*. Aspects of Tourism Series, Channel View, Clevedon, UK.

Roe, D., Leader-Williams, N. and Dalal-Clayton, B. (1997) *Take Only Photographs, Leave Only Footprints: The Environmental Impacts of Wildlife Tourism*. Wildlife and Development Series, No. 10, International Institute for Environment and Development, London.

Roe, D., Harris, C. and Andrade, J. de (2003) *Addressing Poverty Issues in Tourism Standards: A Review of Experience*. PPT Working Paper No. 14, February 2003, PPT Partnership, Overseas Development Institute/International Institute for Environment and Development/International Centre for Responsible Tourism London/Leeds, UK.

SANParks (2009) *Responsible Tourism Strategy and Implementation Plan, Draft, 18 May 2009*. South African National Parks, Pretoria, South Africa.

SASUSG (1996) *Sustainable Use Issues and Principles*. Southern Africa Sustainable Use Specialist Group, IUCN Species Survival Commission, Gland, Switzerland.

Spenceley, A. (2004) Responsible nature-based tourism planning in South Africa and the commercialisation of Kruger National park. In: Diamantis, D. (ed.) *Ecotourism: Management and Assessment*. Thomson Learning, London.

Spenceley, A. (2008) Impacts of wildlife tourism on rural livelihoods in Southern Africa. In: Spenceley, A. (ed.) *Responsible Tourism: Critical Issues for Conservation and Development*. Earthscan, London/ Sterling, Virginia, pp. 159–186.

Spenceley, A. (2010a) *Tourism Product Development Interventions and Best Practices in sub-Saharan Africa: Part 1: Synthesis Report*. Report to the World Bank, 27 December 2010. Available at: http://www.anna. spenceley.co.uk/files/Final%20Synthesis%20report%2024%20Dec%202010.pdf (accessed 13 April 2012).

Spenceley, A. (2010b) *Tourism Product Development Interventions and Best Practices in sub-Saharan Africa: Part 2: Case Studies*. Report to the World Bank, 27 December 2010. Available at: http://anna.spenceley. co.uk/files/Final%20Case%20study%20report%2024%20Dec%202010.pdf (accessed 13 April 2012).

Spenceley, A. and Barnes, J. (2005) *Economic Analysis of Rhino Conservation in a Land-Use Context within the SADC Region*. SADC Regional Programme for Rhino Conservation, Report to IUCN–ROSA (World Conservation Union–Regional Office for Southern Africa), September 2005, SADC RPRC Task 6.3-1.2 (Phase II), Harare, Zimbabwe. Available at: http://anna.spenceley.co.uk/files/Spenceley%20&%20 Barnes.pdf (accessed 13 April 2012).

Spenceley, A. and Durbarry, R. (2010) *Sustainable Tourism in Africa, Case Study Prepared for UNEP Green Economy Report.*

Spenceley, A. and Seif, J. (2010) Tourism sustainability in Africa, presentation at a consultative workshop on accreditation of sustainable tourism certification to support the establishment of the Tourism Sustainability Council, Johannesburg, 18–20 January 2010.

Spenceley, A., Relly, P., Keyser, H., Warmeant, P., McKenzie, M., Mataboge, A., Norton, P., Mahlangu, S. and Seif, J. (2002) *Responsible Tourism Manual for South Africa*, Department for Environmental Affairs and Tourism, July 2002. Available at: http://www.anna.spenceley.co.uk/files/Responsible%20Tourism%20Manual%20(Entire).pdf (accessed 13 April 2012).

Spenceley, A., Habyalimana, S., Tusabe, R. and Mariza, D. (2010) Benefits to the poor from gorilla tourism in Rwanda, *Development Southern Africa* 27, 647–662.

Swanson, T. and Barbier, E. (eds) (1992) *Economics for the Wilds: Wildlife, Wildlands, Diversity and Development.* Earthscan, London.

Wilderness Holdings Ltd (2010) *Annual Report 2010.* Maun, Botswana/Rivonia, South Africa. Available from: http://www.wilderness-group.com/system/assets/40/original/Annual_Report_2010.pdf?1306840219 (accessed 13 April 2012).

WWT (2010) 2010 *Annual Report.* Wilderness Wildlife Trust, Maun, Botswana/Rivonia, South Africa. Available from: http://www.wildernesstrust.com/about/annual-reports/wilderness-trust-annual-report-2010-pdf/pdf_download (accessed 13 April 2012).

11 Cultural Heritage: World Heritage Sites and Responsible Tourism in Argentina

Albina L. Lara and Alicia Gemelli

University of Buenos Aires, Argentina

Introduction

Cultural heritage refers to 'monuments, groups of buildings and sites with historical, aesthetic, archaeological, scientific, ethnological or anthropological value' and 'is our legacy from the past, what we live with today, and what we pass on to future generations. Our cultural and natural heritage is both irreplaceable sources of life and inspiration' (UNESCO, 2011) This condition of uniqueness makes it fragile. A 'packaged landscape', especially prepared to be sold to tourist, is not genuine. If people and their stories are not authentic, tourism cannot be responsible. Authenticity of cultural heritage allows the protection of cultural diversity, a basic condition for sustainable development.

Heritage tourism is based upon the concept that each community has a unique story to tell; this unique story is a tool for learning respect for others and a source of inspiration to others. The relationship between cultural heritage and responsible tourism is without doubt important, and this is particularly evident in the case of a World Heritage Site (WHS). Between 1999 and 2003, three outstanding features of the cultural heritage of Argentina were designated as WHSs. This period is also notable for the beginnings of a substantial increase in international and domestic tourism, which may well have been influenced by the international status awarded

to these sites. Between 2002 and 2009, international arrivals in Argentina increased by approximately 88% and accommodation operations increased by 57%, while domestic tourism rose only by approximately 30% (Ministerio de Turismo, 2009). Certainly in the early years, this increase is due to a combination of factors, not the least of which were an advantageous exchange rate following the devaluation of the local currency at the start of 2002, and more effective promotion and diversification in product offerings, which were supported by a national marketing campaign to position the country as one of South America's Best Destinations. In response to this, the Federal Government created the Ministry of Tourism in 2010.

In this chapter, we will explore the relationship between cultural heritage and responsible tourism primarily through an analysis of three of Argentina's WHSs, but complemented by two other case examples, with a focus on the early period of their establishment and an emphasis on community involvement. The latter in particular is important given that a key tenet of responsible tourism is that the local community should be at the very centre of tourism development interventions in terms of participation in the decision-making process and also in the sharing of benefits (see Timothy, Chapter 5; Pleumarom, Chapter 7). Through the analyses of these cases, it clearly emerges that such participation can be either a driver for, or an obstacle against, the implementation of responsible tourism.

World Heritage Sites

The United Nations Educational, Scientific and Cultural Organization (UNESCO) encourages the identification, protection and preservation of cultural and natural heritage considered to be of outstanding value to humanity. This is embodied in an international treaty, the 1972 Convention Concerning the Protection of the World Cultural and Natural Heritage. The Convention lays out the duties of state parties in identifying potential sites and their role in protecting and preserving them. By signing the Convention, each country pledges to conserve not only its WHSs but also to protect its national heritage in general. Additional to the sites based on the built or natural heritage, UNESCO has created a specific category for 'cultural landscape' which, compared with the other categories, is far more complex, as illustrated herein by the Quebrada de Humahuaca site in Argentina (see below).

Landscape is symbolic, meaning that it is the expression of the culture of a particular community. Different cultural landscapes are representative of diverse cultures and identities; they express a unique relationship between a community and its environment. Landscapes can be fragile and deteriorate, perhaps lost, if they are not appropriately cared for. A cultural landscape is the territorial expression of the past and present of a unique community, of its way of living, feeling and believing. Zukin (1991, p. 1) describes such landscapes 'as a fragile compromise between market and place' and as the major cultural product of our time. She also emphasized that market culture poses the most danger to the cultural values of place, and therefore to the landscape. This fragility is often expressed in the weakening of local distinctiveness as a result of globalization.

Many WHSs lack resources, experience and trained personnel to be able to manage tourism as a benefit to the long-term preservation of their World Heritage values. To meet these challenges, in 2001 the UNESCO World Heritage Committee (2003) launched the World Heritage Sustainable Tourism Programme, which identified seven main actions to enhance the ability of WHSs to preserve their resources:

- Building local management capacity for dealing with tourism
- Training local communities in tourism-related activities
- Helping to promote relevant community products
- Raising public awareness and building public pride in the local communities
- Encouraging local economic sustainability
- Sharing expertise and lessons learned with other sites
- Building an increased understanding of the need to protect WHSs.

In the process, we note the need for partnerships to be established with the tourism sector as a base for promoting responsible tourism. UNESCO has also published a practical manual for WHS managers (Pedersen, 2002).

The World Heritage Site Case Studies

The initial objective for our analysis was to identify whether WHS status is a prerequisite for responsible tourism development. Secondly, we aim to further our understanding of the relationship between heritage sites and responsible tourism and draw out, as appropriate, the lessons to be learnt which can then be applied to further the development of responsible tourism. Central to this is the role and place of the community. These case studies, the locations of which are shown in Figure 11.1, were chosen because of their differences both in complexity and in the issues involved. In each case, we seek to draw out a particular factor. Thus, the first case affirms the importance and role of an interpretation centre and the second serves to demonstrate the way in which the interrelated work of local and regional institutions is a strength. The final WHS is the most complex and draws out the difficulties of implementing responsible tourism in a living, indigenous cultural landscape. These differences lead to variations in the

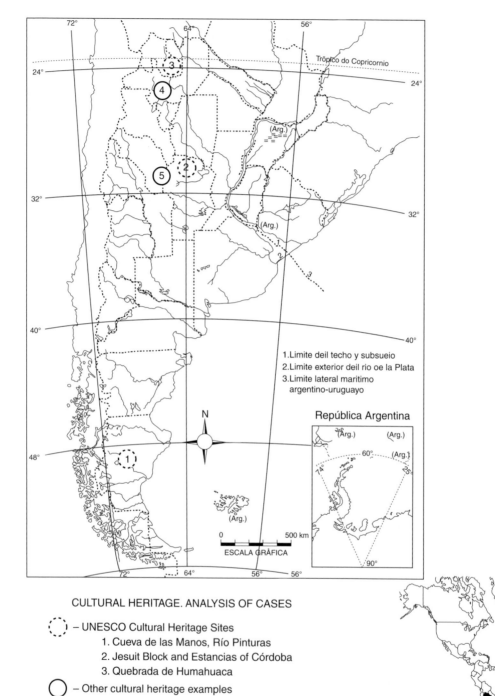

CULTURAL HERITAGE. ANALYSIS OF CASES

- UNESCO Cultural Heritage Sites
    1. Cueva de las Manos, Río Pinturas
    2. Jesuit Block and Estancias of Córdoba
    3. Quebrada de Humahuaca
- Other cultural heritage examples
    4. Valles Calchaquies. Heritage has Jobs.
    5. Mina Clavero. The Artisan's Road

Fig. 11.1. Map of the sites analysed.

presentation and structure of the cases, which also serve to highlight the different issues involved.

Cueva de las Manos (Cave of the Hands), Río Pinturas, province of Santa Cruz

The Cueva de las Manos Río, which has been managed by the National Institute of Anthropology and Latin American Thought (INAPL) since 1991, gained WHS status in 1999. The site contains an outstanding collection of prehistoric rock art which bears witness to the culture of the earliest societies in South America – perhaps the historic hunter–gatherer communities of Patagonia. This WHS is a very interesting institutional initiative and it was brought about with the participation of different organizations working together in the management of the site through a committee. This committee comprises representatives of national, provincial and local agencies, the government, and voluntary and private sectors.

Lessons learnt

The main advance in relation to responsible tourism was the design and implementation of an interpretative centre, which was initiated by the Asociación Identidad, Perito Moreno (a local non-governmental organization, or NGO), designed by Fundación Naturaleza para el Futuro (an environmental Argentine NGO) and supported by a grant from the Spanish Agency for International Development Co-operation (AECID). The interpretative centre displays, through billboards and replicas, the flora and fauna of the site, the work of archaeologists and researchers, the life of the hunter–gatherers and the different techniques with which they painted the rocky walls. Visitors' attention is also drawn to other places in the world where such rock art is to be found.

The establishment of interpretative centres is essential in promoting responsible tourism because this is a communication process designed to reveal the meaning and links between cultural and natural heritage through the relationship of objects, landscapes and sites. The aim of interpretation is to arouse curiosity, stimulate interest and captivate

attention. These centres encourage guests to deepen their knowledge and understanding of the values of place, through the translation of the characteristics and heritage of the site into plain language presented by staff, and also in appropriate guidelines, brochures, audiovisual interactive videos and exhibitions.

Manzana Jesuitica y Estancias de Córdoba (Jesuit Square and Estates)

This analysis of Jesuit Square is largely based on a synthesis kindly prepared for this chapter by the architect Edgardo Venturini, a member of the site's management committee.

The Jesuit Square – or Block – in the city and province of Córdoba, lies at the midpoint on the route used to transport Peruvian gold and silver to Spain, between Alto Peru and the port of Buenos Aires. In 1599, the Jesuits arrived in Córdoba and, over time, established a noviciate, Argentina's first university – founded in 1613, and a church which is one of the oldest buildings in South America. They also developed five indigenous Missions 'Reducciones' in the fertile valleys of the surroundings: Caroya, Jesús María, Santa Catalina, Alta Gracia and Candelaria. These Missions were developed as social and economic centres to bring the Roman Catholic religion to the indigenous populations, through spiritual instruction, education, commercial endeavours and trade. The promotion of creativity and art led to beautiful churches and chapels and architecture in the Missions. Overall, they comprise six different locations: the historic block in Córdoba and the five Missions in rural and urban areas of the province. It is in respect of the exceptional buildings in these locations and their cultural significance that WHS status was awarded.

The quest for WHS status

The initial idea of petitioning for WHS status was first formulated in 1998 by the Association of Friends of the National Museum and the 'House of the Viceroy Liniers' in Alta Gracia (a community where one of the farms is located). This gathered momentum and subsequently the support of provincial, municipal and national organizations. After due process and recommendations, including the need to establish buffer zones to protect the site compounds and to obtain clear commitments from the private consortium that owns the whole of the estate – 'Estancia de Santa Catalina', the site was granted WHS status in 2000.

In relation to community participation, the first systematized awareness and dissemination actions were carried out by the Friends of the Museum of Alta Gracia through the creation of Heritage Days and tourist guide training courses. The Department of Culture also carried out educational programmes with schools and the Ministry of Tourism for the province of Córdoba staged a number of training courses. In addition, the Jesuit estate 'Estancias of Córdoba' was included in the provincial plan for promoting tourism products at regional, national and international levels. As a result of these activities, the population of the city of Córdoba, and especially of Alta Gracia, gained greater awareness of the value and historical heritage of these sites.

Impact of WHS status

Once WHS status was confirmed, the Córdoba Tourism Agency started the dissemination and popularization of the whole Jesuit Square and estates – 'Estancias' as a tourist destination based on a cultural tourism plan approved by UNESCO at the time of the declaration. Promotional activities were carried out at regional, national and international levels. This led to a doubling of visitor numbers in the first 3 years, partly aided by local travel agencies which 'specialize' in the Jesuits (e.g. Native Stylo Travel and Tours) and other operators, which incorporated visits into their itineraries. Further, local schools became more interested, generating significant demand for visits as part of the development of teaching on the subject.

Lessons learnt

The primary lesson from this case study is that of participation. From the outset, local people and institutions have supported and participated 'with pride' in meetings, exhibitions and awareness-raising events. In effect, communities

seized the project and made it their own; notably supported by the Association of Friends of Alta Gracia. Quite remarkably, the municipalities of Alta Gracia and Jesús María modified their ordinances on urban affairs and architecture to formalize the conditions required to establish the buffer areas for the locations in their areas. Similarly, in the city of Córdoba, the Downtown Association (merchants in the central area and surroundings) and the civil association 'Córdoba Ours' supported the work of improving the urban surroundings adjacent to the Square.

Key problems

A range of significant issues has arisen since WHS status was granted, as follows. First, the institutional complexity of the Jesuit heritage site requires a framework for the management partnership involving the different categories of stakeholders: the Federal Government, the Provincial Government, the Municipality of Alta Gracia, the University of Córdoba, the Catholic Church and private owners. In recognition of the problems that could arise owing to the site as a whole involving more than one property owner, the Committee of Jesuit World Heritage Sites was established in 2002. The main problem is that this Committee has not yet been recognized as the authority. Also, there is no integrated and overall management plan for the site, but rather individual plans for each of six locations. This lack of a comprehensive management plan is certainly a priority problem to be solved.

Secondly, a major problem facing this Committee arises from the close proximity of the urban environment. Problems have arisen from pressures in the housing market as a result of increasing land values – an outcome of proximity to any one of the sites. This is manifest in Jesús María, Alta Gracia and, particularly so, in Cordóba. Here a major real estate project, including flats and a large shopping centre, has been proposed for the site of the historic Bank of Córdoba, one block away from the Jesuit Square. This proposal awaits approval and is being considered by the World Heritage Committee. Other issues arising from the urban situation include traffic, parking, commercial activities and advertising hoardings. Further, the Estancias La Candelaria and Santa Catalina, which are accessed by dirt roads that are not well maintained, cause a variety of problems, particularly in the rainy season. The Committee of Jesuit World Heritage Sites has been seeking to resolve this in discussion with the Provincial Road and Traffic Authority and local members of the consortium that manage the roads.

Thirdly, there is a lack of funding. Maintenance may be delayed and many projects take longer to complete because of funding issues. Before designation as a WHS this does not appear to have been much of an issue; however, since then, tensions have arisen, which partly explains why over the last 10 years there have been major intercessions (public and private) for the restoration, conservation and enhancement of buildings and their immediate surroundings.

Overall, the key problem is the lack of an integrated site management plan, which is not aided by members of the Committee of Jesuit World Heritage Sites, who are struggling to understand that the site is a single unit – integrated by a 'series of sets'. This is not helped by a lack of dedicated staff and the fact that there is no overall management authority recognized by the government (provincial and municipal). In the absence of such a plan, the Committee has acted in a reactive rather than proactive manner; for example, in respect of infrastructure projects that might impinge on the sites, as in the case of the construction of a new bridge in Jesús María, which the Committee belatedly managed to ensure was built outside the site's buffer zone.

Responsible tourism

From the outset, it was decided that tourist visits would be conducted in a controlled manner with specially trained guides for each location, thus pre-empting the possibility of problems arising from over demand (except for a few occasions in Alta Gracia, the most popular site). In all cases, graphic information systems were organized to support the task of the tour guides, and also for the management of waste generated by visitors. As a result of these measures, there has been no vandalism or cases of 'unsustainable' behaviour on the part of visitors.

Quebrada de Humahuaca, province of Jujuy

By way of background to discussion of the site of Quebrada de Humahuaca, it is important to note that an outcome of rising unemployment owing to decline in traditional sectors of the economy in the 1990s was that the provincial government of Jujuy was actively supporting and promoting the development of tourism (Troncoso, 2009). However, the increase in tourism activity in the province, especially after the location of the Quebrada de Humahuaca WHS was confirmed, generated a range of negative impacts.

This site is the setting of a major cultural route of some 155 km along the valley of the Río Grande, which is part of the 10,000-year-old Camino del Inca. Its distinctive pre-Hispanic and pre-Incan settlements and their associated field systems form a dramatic addition to the landscape; one that can certainly be called outstanding. The site was inscribed in the World Heritage List in 2003 in the category of Cultural Landscape, as a living landscape that maintains an active social role in contemporary society closely linked to the traditional way of life and cultures of native communities. One of the complexities of the site relates to the institutional aspects. The political organization of Argentina is as a federal country consisting of autonomous provinces, and local issues are dealt with directly by the municipal authorities. In combination with the complexity of this site, this poses problems of jurisdiction and dominion.

The site comes under three different departments in the province and involves nine municipalities. To add to the complexity, some matters pertaining to the site are in the sphere of the government. Also, the area is not all in public ownership and so the private sector is involved too. Thus a wide range of stakeholders has converged since the site's nomination for World Heritage status. This poses a major challenge for the integrated management of the site, with often conflicting visions, interests and values to be articulated.

Community participation

A number of substantive weaknesses in this WHS were evident from the outset. The provincial Department of Culture undertook the preliminary studies, which were then taken forward with the support of the government. When the procedure of nomination was started in 2000 (Provincia de Jujoy, 2001), not all stakeholders were included. Meetings staged to encourage participation were often criticised on the grounds that the decisions had already been made. Furthermore, the disparity between the actors, in terms of relative power in the process, was also an obstacle. This limited participation in the application process is a major cause of the conflict that exists today. Secondly, no comprehensive diagnosis of the starting situation was conducted, which would have been useful in planning and subsequent monitoring. Instrumental in the management of Quebrada de Humahuaca are local site committees, composed of six representatives from each of the nine municipalities within the heritage area (including representatives of indigenous communities). These committees were formed before the heritage designation and participated in workshops organized by the provincial government. Their participation in the asset management of the site continued after designation and they worked on developing the management plan for the area (Secretariá de Turismo y Cultura de Jujoy, 2006), a weakness within which was the evident failing to consider the different perceptions, needs and tensions between modernization and identity, globalization and diversity.

Impact of WHS status

Visitors to the villages of Quebrada between 1994 and 2006 increased from 7175 to 109,057, while visits to the province overall increased threefold (from approximately 115,000 in 1994 to approximately 373,000 in 2006). Based on the limited statistics available, we can identify that the number of accommodation operations doubled between 2002 and 2007, and notably so in Tilcara, Purmamarca and Humahuaca (Secretaría de Turismo y Cultura de la Pcia de Jujuy, 2008).

This growth in demand has had a range of negative consequences (see Bidaseca and Gigena, 2009; Troncoso, 2010), of which the main effects are as follows:

- alterations in the festive events calendar that are contrary to tradition, e.g. the dates of the Pachamama celebration were changed;
- the introduction of non-traditional musical instruments, damaging the authenticity of the site;
- signs of tension between tourists and local residents;
- risk of losing community identity;
- rising land values, which have generated disputes over ownership and, in some instances, has led to the eviction of families who have lived on the site for many years;
- the emergence of new players, from outside the region as well from within local communities, who have gained influence since WHS status and are promoting their own agendas, often orientated to patrimonial and tourist demands; and
- repositioning of the gorge as a place of international significance.

In effect, the site has become com-moditized. This has catalysed conflict over the land due to conflicting perceptions of the site itself, and of its value and relevance as a symbol and in cultural expression on the one hand and as a tourism commodity on the other. The attendant problems are primarily seen as a failure to ensure that the appropriate govern-ance and management planning and control were in place, and that these were suitably resourced to ensure effective implementation in the first instance (see Hall, Chapter 8). Tourism enterprise has gained at a cost to the local communities (Troncoso, 2008). This is neither an equitable balance nor demonstrates responsible tourism.

Key issues

The key issues arising from the site's status as a WHS were identified through an analysis of the Management Plan of 2009, and through various research studies (see Bidaseca et al., 2008, 2010; Borghini, 2010; Troncoso,

2008, 2010). On the basis of this analysis, it is clear that the Quebrada de Humahuaca site presents major challenges for the implementation of responsible tourism principles in this cultural landscape. A synthesis of the main issues, collated by categories correlating with the main facets of responsible tourism, is as follows.

ENVIRONMENT

- Global–local tension: difficulty in maintaining the fragile balance between heritage conservation and the strength of external global influences.
- Limited awareness and understanding of the fragility of the natural and cultural site.
- Demand is highly seasonal.
- Inadequate protection of archaeological sites.

COMMUNITY

- Some key players in the community have felt left out of the participatory process.
- Differences and tensions between different ideologies, world views and beliefs.
- Changes in the valuation of the land.
- Difference in perceived value of the land between the indigenous people (equity) and others (purely economic).
- Problems of land tenure and title holding.

CULTURE

- Change in habits and customs.
- Little differentiation of local crafts, locally produced, and similar products imported owing to absence of authenticity certification.
- Import of non-local crafts and related products which are produced elsewhere.

GOVERNANCE

- Little attention has been given to the basic infrastructure despite increasing levels of tourism activity.
- Lack of attempts to coordinate tourism supply and demand leading to weaknesses in the provision of quality services.
- Lack of due consideration to conservation

and preservation of the natural and social capital.
- Many stakeholders exhibit little or no social responsibility.

Of the themes and issues identified, we consider that global–local tension is the key issue to address. This is manifest in the inherent conflict between tourism development and Quebrada as a place in the cultural heritage of indigenous communities. It is much more than a touristic resource; it represents unity, identity and symbolizes the ties of the indigenes to the 'Pachamama' and to their ancestors. Cultural landscape is, in a certain way, intimate. The way in which this tension is addressed will define the sustainability of the site.

The key challenge

The 2009 management plan for Quebrada de Humahuaca was developed based on a methodological approach of participatory development workshops that brought together the main stakeholders from the public and private sectors, intermediary organizations and the community at large. The plan includes a Tourism Development and Heritage Enhancement Programme. However, it has no legal status and does not replace the legislative framework, nor does it supersede the responsibilities of the local community or of their organizations. It has yet to be fully implemented because this requires the formal establishment of the organization proposed to take on the management of the site – the Institute of Management of Quebrada de Humahuaca – which needs to be confirmed in provincial law. The key challenge is whether the implementation of the plan will help to rectify the mistakes made in the appointment process and during the early years of site management.

The Alternative Case Studies

A major factor of WHSs is that of their complexity, the tensions that arise and the inherent conflicts between promotion and conservation/preservation. To varying degrees, and on a smaller scale, such tensions are found in other initiatives based on cultural heritage, not the least of which are funding and the demands placed on initiators to ensure full and ongoing participation of the communities involved. We therefore present two alternative cases which evidence success in this, and illustrate what can be achieved through a responsible tourism approach. Furthermore, the two cases chosen illustrate well Leslie's point (see Chapter 2) that more consideration should be given by government to the possibility of alternative economic development options other than market-led tourism, options that are first resource based and in tune with sustainability and, secondly, evidence the central tenets of responsible tourism and thereby provide added value.

El Patrimonio tiene Oficio (Heritage has Jobs), Valles Calchaquíes, province of Salta

This case study draws on the work of the Fundación Naturaleza para el Futuro (2011) and on further research including discussions with personnel actively working on this project.

The Valles Calchaquíes connects several communities by the renowned Route 40. The local crafts particular to the area are knitting, pottery and architecture using natural materials, all of which are sustained by old traditions and a profound religious conviction. Many of the historic towns along this route have experienced a decline in traditional employment, leading to high unemployment among young people. Because of the generally low level of education, these young people often have few skills and, at best, the opportunities available to them in the locality are poorly paid. As a result, poverty becomes structural.

In response to this situation, the Fundación Naturaleza para el Futuro (FuNaFu), financed by the Mitsubishi corporation and supported by the provincial and municipal governments, introduced the environmental responsibility tourism promotion project 'Heritage Has Jobs' in order to promote sustainable development and create jobs while protecting the cultural and natural heritage in the Valles Calchaquíes. The project aims to generate jobs and promote training for the youth in local architecture,

handicrafts, traditional arts, preservation techniques and responsible tourism in the area. A secondary objective is to promote traditional ways of construction and artisanal activities through the development of schools of trades (learning by doing) to train youngsters in activities related to sustaining the area's cultural heritage. An interpretation and training centre has been established for the area's community which also provides an outlet for traditional crafts and guide services for tourists. The project, as part of the economic development programme, has restored a historic building in Molinos, on national route 40, which is now an interpretation centre and outlet for local artisanal products and a traditional activities workshop. This centre also includes hospitality facilities, which provide a setting for local events such as musical evenings.

El Camino de los Artesanos, Mina Clavero (Road of the Artisans), province of Córdoba

This case study is summarized from the *Catalogo de Prácticas sustentables en la Gestión Municipal* (Secretaría de Turismo de la Nación y Red Federal de Municipios Turísticos Sustentables, 2009).

The Artisan's (Craftsmen's) Road is located in the Traslasierra Valley. A group of families, who live by or near this road, initiated a project designed to preserve their traditional native craftwork in 1998. At the time, potters, owing to a lack of promotion and demand, had to leave their home-based workshops to market their products at fairs or craft shops located in the town. This was problematic for two reasons. First, due to the absence of public transport they had to personally carry their wares and, second, they gained lower prices. For these reasons, they gradually abandoned their crafts to work in the tourism sector during the season. In recognition of this, the Department of Tourism of the Municipality of Mina Clavero established the Camino de los Artesanos programme with the objective of preserving and strengthening the production of traditional handicrafts and, in the process, developing this activity in order to achieve a more secure economic footing, thereby better supporting the livelihood of local potters. In furtherance of this, the road/area has been designated as a tourist attraction.

The 'Tour of the Road of the Artisans' was launched in 2000. In 2003, a knitted crafts exhibition involving local weavers was established and a retail outlet was opened. In the following year, local potters and weavers initiated an educational campaign in the area's rural schools to foster the development of these traditional skills on the part of the children to help sustain these traditional techniques for the future. The project succeeded in bringing buyers to the production areas, thus further enabling the potters to continue in their home workplaces, so that families can maintain their traditional living environment while preserving the unique cultural value of Traslasierra Valley, based on the skills and crafts of the indigenous community.

Conclusion

Cultural heritage has to do with community history and geography, with what defines identity and with ways of doing and ways of feeling the territory, and with the distinctive circumstances in which human development is expressed in a given community. In those instances where some feature of a society's heritage is considered outstanding in some way(s) and of international significance, then steps may be taken to seek the designation of such a site as of World Heritage status. In adopting this approach, the process of application itself will help to promote awareness of the site and its key issues, among which, invariably, will be the need for increased resources. In this, designation as a WHS can prove particularly beneficial in attracting and gaining funding to help the preservation/ conservation, management and development of the site, although this is not necessarily guaranteed. However, WHS status serves to promote the site and plays a major role in increasing overall visitor numbers and thus tourism activity. As such, this will help in attracting resources to further support tourism development. In effect the designation of any outstanding heritage as a WHS serves two

masters: the preservation/conservation of the site; and visitor interest and demand. It can create an economic incentive to protect the WHS and its setting; but it can also consume the sites upon which it depends. It is therefore all the more important that the central tenets of responsible tourism are not only adopted but applied in all these areas.

The three sites discussed bear witness to the trials and tribulations of WHSs, the analysis of these has led to the following conclusions/ lessons to be learnt:

- An interpretative centre is essential to enhance the tourists' experience, create awareness, foster understanding of the local cultural values and promote responsible behaviour and consumption, which are all integral to responsible tourism.
- The participation of local communities must be promoted and guaranteed from the outset. This must be genuine as all too often distrust hinders true participation and may transform it into pseudo forms of participation that instead of reducing conflict actually increase it. This means that it is necessary that the state has the political will to ensure participation and that this takes place in an open and transparent way, which is just not the dissemination of information. Communication and provision of information is but the first step. Genuine participation, a prerequisite for sustainable development, means power sharing in the decision-making process and the continued involvement of the community. This is well illustrated by the alternative cases presented, which show what can be achieved when all stakeholders work together in the process of promoting responsible tourism initiatives. The purpose, functions, benefits and costs of the heritage sites should be discussed with the local community from the outset. Two of the cases also emphasize the need for ongoing education and capacity building to support and better able communities to protect their own heritage.
- The development of the site needs to be carefully considered; too much or too quickly can lead to conflict which may have a significant negative impact. Likewise, if an attempt is made to artificially freeze a

landscape, it can deteriorate and lose its community sense and authenticity.

- Cultural heritage is complex and fragile. Therefore, it is necessary to carefully assess proposed developments and to monitor change. This is all the more the case with cultural landscapes, which are fragile. The question is: how to protect them and for whom – for the world or for the community, and are these the same?
- Overarching all of these issues is the need to address from the outset the imperative of the organizational, economic and personnel resources that are essential to carry out effectively and efficiently the planning, management and development of heritage sites. These resources are crucial in managing tensions and conflicts between stakeholders and between internal factors and external forces. This aspect in particular merits further research in the context of management planning and, especially, into the effectiveness of administrative structures and with regard to developing responsible tourism.

When tourism is developed responsibly, it can be a tool for learning and an opening to other cultures and lifestyles that are different from those of the visitors, and this can engender respect for diversity in communities. For this to happen, it is necessary to promote both responsible production and consumption in tourism. Thus, instead of 'consuming' the heritage or the place, one can appreciate and enjoy it in such a way as to produce a unique and enriching experience. In this way, when the encounter between the tourist and cultural heritage, especially in a cultural landscape situation, takes place within the framework of responsible tourism which is necessarily respectful, the result is a profound effect of mutual enrichment.

Acknowledgments

The authors would like to acknowledge the contributions of Edgardo Venturini, a Committee Member from the Córdoba site, Juliana Burton and María Florencia Noya Dive from CONAPLU (Comisión Nacional Argentina de Cooperación con la UNESCO), Luis Castelli and Oscar Iriani from Fundación Naturaleza para el Futuro, Juan Francisco Otaño for the elaboration of the map (Fig. 11.1) and Sergio F. Otaño, who made the original translation into English.

References

Bidaseca, K. and Gigena, A. (2009) Occidente y las civilizaciones. Temporalidades arcaicas, culturas vivas: la alteridad indígena en las políticas hegemónicas Provinciales. Presentation to: VIII Reunión de Antropología del MERCOSUR (RAM), 'Diversidad y poder en América Latina', Buenos Aires, Argentina 29 September–4 October.
Bidaseca, K., González, M., Jaramillo, I., Paolucci, C. and Salleras, L. (2008) Voces quebradas. Tilcara, después de la Declaratoria de Patrimonio de la Humanidad. Ponencia en colaboración. Presentation to: IV Congreso Internacional Patrimonio Cultural, Centro Cultural Canadá Córdoba, Argentina.
Bidaseca, K., Borghini, N. and Salleras, L. (2010) Turismo, patrimonio y políticas de identidad en la Quebrada de Humahuaca. Presentation to: II Congreso Internacional De Desarrollo Local – I Jornadas Nacionales en Ciencias Sociales y Desarrollo Rural, Universidad Nacional de La Matanza, Argentina.
Borghini, N. (2010) Tenencia precaria de la tierra y políticas públicas en Jujuy. Un análisis de los vínculos entre provincia, nación y pueblos originarios. Apuntes 67, 129–155. Centro de Investigación de la Universidad del Pacífico, Peru. Available at: http://www.up.edu.pe/revista_apuntes/SiteAssets/ Natalia%20Borghini%20Apuntes%2067.pdf (accessed 12 April 2012).
Fundación Naturaleza para el Futuro (2011) Acerca de la Fundación Naturaleza para el Futuro [About the Nature Foundation for the Future]. Available at: http://www.naturalezaparaelfuturo.org/ (accessed 12 April 2012).
Ministerio de Turismo (2009) Anuario Estadístico de Turismo 2009. Ministerio de Turismo, Argentina.
Pedersen, A. (2002) Managing Tourism at World Heritage Sites: a Practical Manual for World Heritage Site

Managers. World Heritage Manuals (Series) No. 1, UNESCO World Heritage Centre, Paris. Available at: http://whc.unesco.org/uploads/activities/documents/activity-113-2.pdf (accessed 12 April 2012).

Provincia de Jujuy (2001) *Postulación de la Quebrada de Humahuaca.* Consejo Federal de Inversiones (CFI), Buenos Aires, Argentina.

Secretaría de Turismo de la Nación y Red Federal de Municipios Turísticos Sustentables (2009) *Catalogo de Prácticas sustentables en la Gestión Municipal.* Secretaría de Turismo de la Nación y Red Federal de Municipios Turísticos Sustentables, Argentina.

Secretaría de Turismo y Cultura de Jujuy (2006) *Plan de Desarrollo Turístico Sustentable.* Horwath Argentina, Provincia de Jujuy, Argentina.

Secretaría de Turismo y Cultura de la Pcia de Jujuy (2008) *Datos Estadísticos.* Secretaría de Turismo y Cultura de la Pcia de Jujuy, Provincia de Jujuy, Argentina.

Troncoso, C. (2008) Turismo, desarrollo y participación local. La experiencia de Quebrada de Humahuaca, Jujuy, Argentina. *Aportes y Transferencias* 12, 110–130. Universidad Nacional de Mar del Plata, Argentina.

Troncoso, C. (2009) Patrimonio y redefinición de un lugar turístico. La Quebrada de Humahuaca, Provincia de Jujuy, Argentina. *Estudios y Perspectivas en Turismo* 18, 144–160.

Troncoso, C. (2010) Patrimonio, turismo y lugar: selecciones, actores y lecturas en torno a La Quebrada de Humahuaca (Jujuy, Argentina) como Patrimonio de la Humanidad. *Cuadernos de Turismo* 25, 207–227.

UNESCO (2011) *Our World Heritage.* Available at: http://whc.unesco.org/uploads/activities/documents/activity-568-2.pdf (accessed 20 July 2011).

UNESCO World Heritage Committee (2003) *Decisions Adopted by the 27th Session of the World Heritage Committee,* Paris, 30 June–5 July 2003. Publication No. WHC-03/27.COM/24, UNESCO World Heritage Centre, Paris. Available at: http://whc.unesco.org/archive/2003/whc03-27com-24e.pdf (accessed 12 April 2012).

Zukin, S. (1991) *Landscapes of Power. From Detroit to Disney World.* University of California Press, Berkeley, California.

12 Hospitality Enterprise: A Key Influence

Piotr Zientara
University of Gdansk, Poland

Introduction

It is hardly in dispute that these days the tourism sector is one of the most important sectors of the modern economy (World Travel and Tourism Council, 2009; Agarin *et al.*, 2010). Indeed, it is a mainstay of local economic activity in several countries and regions all over the world (Egypt and Tunisia in Africa, Spain and Greece in Europe, Thailand and Cambodia in Asia, just to cite the best-known examples). Equally importantly, the entire sector (with aviation at the forefront) is thought to propel globalization and, at the same time, to benefit from the worldwide integration processes. Thus it can be seen to act as one of the major forces shaping today's socio-economic reality (Zientara, 2009). Yet, while accounting for a growing share of employment and income in developed and developing economies alike, the tourism and hospitality sector produces a variety of negative outcomes.

In particular, given the imperative to tackle climate change and to protect the planet's fragile biodiversity, much attention has been paid to the environmental impact of tourist activity in general and to the operation of hotels in particular (Zientara and Bohdanowicz, 2010; Bohdanowicz and Zientara, 2012). In point of fact, it is estimated that a typical hospitality facility that uses fossil fuel-generated electricity emits on average more than 40 kg of CO_2 equivalents per room per night and produces approximately 3 kg of waste per guest night (Chiesa and Gautam, 2009). This is of capital importance because an undamaged environment underpins, to a large degree, the attractiveness of most tourist destinations and, by implication, determines the future development of the industry. Furthermore, serious questions have been asked – from the human resource management (HRM) per-spective – about the quality of hotel jobs, especially in matters of remuneration, training provision and, crucially, the reconciliation of work and private life (Cullen and McLaughlin, 2006; Mulvaney *et al.*, 2006; Cleverland *et al.*, 2007; Karatepe and Uludag; 2007; Deery and Jago, 2009; Ioannides and Petridou, 2012).

Not surprisingly, the last two decades have seen the emergence and propagation of interrelated concepts and constructs – such as corporate social responsibility (CSR), sustain-able tourism or sustainable development – that provide theoretical underpinnings to the efforts undertaken with a view to mitigating the environmental effects of tourist activity and to improving the situation of hospitality business staff as well as those living in communities in which hotels are located (Devuyst and Hens, 2000; Hall and Richards, 2000; Sharpley, 2000; Moscardo, 2008). In this context, there needs to be a recognition that, in recent years, many international hotel companies have gone to great lengths – within their CSR programmes – to ameliorate working conditions and to enhance the quality of life of their employees, as well as to strengthen environmental protection in particular localities (Bohdanowicz and Zientara, 2009). In other words, what it comes down to is the broadly defined *responsibility* of the tourism industry. It is this responsibility – for employees, environment and local communities – that, while being the chief focus of the entire book, also takes centre stage in the present chapter.

The emphasis on responsibility is also important in the light of another aspect of this study. As is well known, owing to their *global* reach, top hotel chains – such as Marriott, Hilton Worldwide or Intercontinental – can be seen as representing or embodying global capital. But their day-to-day operations are essentially *local* in character. From a certain point of view, it is therefore possible to argue, drawing on the insights (and terminology) of the regional development literature, that these interactions constitute a particular case of 'glocalization' (Swyngedouw, 1992; Torrance, 2008). Hence, given that in the public discourse global capital is increasingly (and often unfairly) associated with abuse and – aptly – with irresponsibility, acting *responsibly* on the part of the industry assumes a particular significance and therefore merits special attention.

It is against such a background that the present chapter, in adopting a critical–positivist approach (Neuman, 2003; Walsh, 2003), provides a contextualization of the hospitality-enterprise influence. More specifically, it sets out to explore hospitality-related employment and community issues, placing them into the wider context of globalization, CSR and environmental sustainability. Building on these considerations, the chapter shows how hospitality enterprises, with international hotel companies to the fore, can improve the quality of employment and provide support to local communities (see Timothy, Chapter 5). Consequently, it argues that these enterprises are particularly well positioned to project a more positive image of both globalization and business, which – at a time of the crisis-induced

backlash against the corporate world (Zientara, 2009) – goes against mainstream thinking.

The structure of the chapter is as follows. The next section focuses on the tourism and hospitality industry and job creation in today's globalized reality. Subsequently, the nature and quality of hotel employment are discussed in the context of HRM, with special emphasis being placed on the concept of work–life balance. We then move on to explore the ramifications of the interrelatedness between CSR and HRM in the sector. The subsequent two sections of the chapter conceptualize the CSR-driven, sustainability-oriented initiatives of international hotel companies that are aimed to support communities in terms of global–local interactions. Eventually, we conclude by summarizing the argument, emphasizing the study's wider implications and suggesting further research directions.

The Hospitality Industry and Job Creation in a Globalized Reality

Nowadays, the tourism and hospitality sector is commonly regarded as one of the chief drivers of economic growth and societal progress (Wahab and Pigram, 1997; Bosselman *et al.*, 1999; Butler, 1999; World Travel and Tourism Council, 2009). It is, to reiterate, one of the most important sectors of the modern economy that generates much needed jobs in developed and emerging economies alike (Agarin *et al.*, 2010). Indeed, it is estimated that the entire industry accounts for approximately 10% of global gross domestic product (GDP) and 8% of employment worldwide (World Travel and Tourism Council, 2009). In many a country, it is by far the biggest contributor to the national GDP. Likewise, different forms of tourism are increasingly seen as a viable tool of regional development. For instance, it is often argued that some rural and remote communities marked by high unemployment and poverty rates should diversify from (inefficient) farming into agritourism. In fact, such thinking is in line with the European Union's (EU's) rural development policy for the 2007–2013 period (European Commission, 2011). There is evidence that at least in certain areas (in both rich and poor countries) tourism-based developmental strategies have proved successful. It follows that if it were not for tourist activity, millions of people all over the world would be worse off.

Equally importantly, it is fair to say that tourism and hospitality – in sharp contrast to manufacturing and certain office functions – are less vulnerable to the vagaries of global-ization. As is well known, such phenomena as offshoring and relocation of production – due to their (short-term) job-destroying effects – have recently become the focus of growing public concern (predominantly in North America and Western Europe). In effect, this is one of the reasons why there has been a serious backlash against globalization processes in general and closer economic integration in particular. Consequently, recent years have seen a revival of protectionist thinking in the West (Nonneman, 2007; Zientara, 2011). As high-skilled manufacturing and office jobs are increasingly transferred or outsourced to lower cost locations in eastern Europe or South-east Asia, Westerners fret about rising un-employment (a trend that has been magnified by the nefarious consequences of the 2008–2009 recession) and, accordingly, call on decision makers to resort to protectionist measures (Beddoes, 2008; Zientara, 2011). Unsurprisingly, nationalistic and anti-immigrant sentiment has been on the rise – foreigners are increasingly and – by and large, unjustifiably – seen to steal native inhabitants' jobs, to reduce their wages and to drive down labour standards (Nonneman, 2007; Somerville and Sumption, 2009).

In this context, tourism and hospitality stands out *favourably* among other sectors of the economy. One reason is that owing to their intrinsic characteristics, hospitality-generated jobs are unlikely to – or just cannot technically – be spirited away to other low-cost destinations. Thus in rich countries it is generally considered to be a sheltered sector. For another, it is due to globalization that tourism and hospitality are thriving all over the world. Certainly, for various interrelated reasons, globalization – which, by definition, is about the unimpeded circulation of capital, goods, services and people in the global space

(Harvey, 2006) – can be perceived as the moving force (as well as the effect) of cross-border tourist activity (Zientara, 2009). It propels economic growth (through trade and outsourcing) in previously poor countries (such as India, Thailand or China), which means that more and more people there, seeing their disposable income rise, can afford to pay a visit to Europe or America. Conversely, rich-country citizens – due to their considerable spending power and to the lower price of services in emerging economies – are still able to afford frequent holidays abroad.

The Quality of Hospitality Employment

Things, however, are not as unequivocally positive as the above picture might suggest. Above all, even though most jobs created in hospitality (or, more generally, thanks to tourist activity) cannot be transferred elsewhere; they are – because they fall under the category of low-end services – by and large of worse quality than traditional manufacturing employment. Specifically, most of these jobs, while requiring lesser skills, are usually worse paid and offer far less security than (traditional) jobs in manufacturing. This is because, among other things, jobs in hospitality are often part-time occupations (without perks), while those in manufacturing used to be full-time ones (with generous benefits). The implication is that, from a certain perspective, they are particularly suitable for younger people, with students to the fore (though of course, this is not to say that older workers cannot perform them well; in fact, there is evidence from the Scottish hospitality sector that seniors might even fare better than their younger counterparts; Magd, 2003). Because the vast majority of young adults have no families to maintain, for them, relatively low remuneration and lack of employment security do not constitute a big problem. This drawback is also outweighed by the opportunity to acquire professional experience, which for those at the beginning of their professional careers is priceless.

Nonetheless, there is no denying that – apart from relatively low remuneration – being employed in hospitality has other disadvantages. The relatively flat organizational structures of most hospitality facilities imply that staff are less likely to change positions (job rotation) and, critically, to be promoted (Furunes and Mykletun, 2005). Arguably, this not only makes it hard to retain and recruit talented and ambitious employees, but also might have a negative effect on job satisfaction and organizational commitment. That – given the existence of the service profit chain, which 'establishes relationships between profitability, customer loyalty, and employee satisfaction, loyalty, and productivity' (Heskett *et al.*, 1994, p. 164) – has far-reaching ramifications. Indeed, there is a link, *ceteris paribus*, between employee satisfaction and commitment and the level of service quality he or she extends to his/her guests (Worsfold, 1999; Kini and Hobson, 2002), which directly affects customer satisfaction (Crawford and Hubbard, 2008). This, in turn, affects customer loyalty and, by extension, revenue growth.

Another problem with hospitality-generated jobs relates to the issue of work–life balance (WLB). As is commonly acknowledged, the hospitality industry is characterized by certain specificities (Worsfold, 1999) that render it truly hard for employees (at all levels of corporate hierarchy) to reconcile work and private life (Cullen and McLaughlin, 2006; Mulvaney *et al.*, 2006; Cleverland *et al.*, 2007; Karatepe and Uludag; 2007; Deery and Jago, 2009). As hospitality establishments usually operate 24/7, the hours worked in the sector are not only long, but also unsocial (Mulvaney *et al.*, 2006). It follows that hotel staff have comparatively more difficulty (than other professional groups) in striking a balance between the spheres of work and family.

Matters are not helped by the prevalence of what Cullen and McLaughlin (2006, p. 510) call 'presenteeism', which connotes 'an overwhelming need to put in more hours or, at the very least, appear to be working very long hours'. In practice, that means that they stay at the premises far longer than is actually necessary or required of them. We may note in passing that the culture of presenteeism in hotels rests on three basic realizations. First, hotel managers tend to see themselves as having a duty to provide emotional support to their staff, which – in the eyes of many – entails staying at work for long hours. Secondly, most of them believe that they are the 'face' of the hotel and have to be continually present. Thirdly, it is the very nature of the industry – the fact that a hotel is open at all times – that makes managers assume that they need to be available for inordinately long hours. The implication is that hotel jobs are hardly appreciated by women, who generally attach greater importance to WLB than men. Relevantly, Doherty (2004, p. 448), while exploring the issue of WLB in the context of female hospitality employment, argues that 'a male model of a career based on commitment in the form of long hours persists'. She points out that what discourages women from seeking senior management positions is – alongside certain workplace inflexibilities – the prevalent culture of excessively long hours.

For all these reasons, it is often immigrants – rather than native inhabitants – that fill (especially, the low-level) hospitality jobs. For instance, in Ireland shortly before the economic crisis, the share of Irishmen employed in hotels and restaurants stood at only 3.2%, against 12.1% for foreigners (Barrett *at al.*, 2008, p. 20). As is commonly acknowledged, immigrants – whose position, on balance, is weaker than that of locals in the local labour market – can ill afford to be choosy in matters of employment (Somerville and Sumption, 2009). It follows that foreigners, in contrast to natives, are unlikely to sniff at jobs in hospitality (hence it is highly problematic to assume, as right-wing politicians often claim, that foreigners steal locals' jobs). In fact, there is evidence that after 2004, when the ex-communist countries from Eastern Europe joined the EU, many (often well-educated) Poles and Lithuanians found employment in British or Irish hotels, restaurants and guest houses (which, by the way, prompted talk of so-called brain waste). Admittedly, that does not mean that they were oblivious to the typical disadvantages related to hospitality jobs. Yet, faced with the prospect of unemployment (or very low remuneration) back home, they simply viewed the relatively high salary (by Eastern European standards) and the very fact of having *any* work, all things being relative, as attractive.

Corporate Social Responsibility and Human Resources Management in Hospitality

The difficulty with reconciliation of work and private life, coupled with other drawbacks, is thought to lie behind the high levels of staff turnover and increasingly acute labour shortages in the hospitality industry (Pratten and O'Leary, 2007). All this inevitably raises the question of HRM. Indeed, the fact that hotels are regarded as specific workplaces only emphasizes the significance of HRM. It is in this area that CSR could potentially play an important part. This is because there is a sort of conceptual overlap – or interrelatedness – between CSR and HRM (Bohdanowicz and Zientara, 2008, 2009). Although definitions and conceptualizations of CSR vary, there is broad consensus that it is about making 'a positive impact on society and the environment' through interactions with the main stakeholders – such as employees, customers, investors and suppliers (Business in the Community, 2009). It follows that CSR ought to help businesses to 'harness the market's potential for sustainability products and services while at the same time successfully reducing and avoiding sustainability costs and risks' (Dow Jones, 2009). In other words, businesses that wholeheartedly embrace CSR are supposed to behave ethically towards, among others, their employees and the environment.

Referring back to hospitality employment problems, a CSR-driven company might potentially show that it really *cares* for its employees not only by, for instance, offering relatively high wages or skill-upgrading training, but also by instituting an organizational culture facilitating WLB and enhancing motivation (also via well-designed career paths). In this context, Bohdanowicz and Zientara (2009) point to a CSR-inspired initiative – the Pause programme – implemented by Hotel Villa Magna-Park (Hyatt) in Madrid. In 2007, when 14-month redecoration works were initiated, the company decided to retain – rather than dismiss – most of the hotel's personnel (with salaries paid every month). More importantly, it engaged the employees in all sorts of activities focused on human capital development (English and computer classes, visits to

museums or trips to the countryside). But the chief idea was to reinforce their *esprit de corps* and, crucially, their organizational commitment, by showing that Villa Magna-Park really cares (*mimar* in Spanish) for its employees. For their part, the staff, who admitted that it was really unusual for a business to adopt such a caring attitude towards its employees, viewed the project very favourably. Thus one can reasonably expect that they would be genuinely committed to their employer; in this sense, the company simultaneously served its own interest, which implies a win–win outcome.

Yet organizational commitment – alongside job satisfaction – can also be strengthened in other ways. For instance, all Marriott and Starwood employees, regardless of their position in the corporate hierarchy, are called *associates*, while those working at Hilton and Scandic are called *team members* (Bohdanowicz at al., 2011). The idea is to reinforce the atmosphere of partnership and fair treatment, thereby indirectly enhancing employees' job satisfaction and organizational commitment. Furthermore, if a (prospective) employee is genuinely concerned about the state of the environment and believes that businesses should, as CSR proponents argue, take action against climate change and environmental degradation, he or she will naturally be more likely to gravitate towards (and identify themselves with) companies that attach weight to ecological issues; companies that, accordingly, introduce environment-friendly, energy-efficient technologies (Bohdanowicz and Zientara, 2008). Hence such firms – in line with the person–organization fit concept (Chapman, 1989) – are well positioned to recruit, retain and motivate ecologically minded individuals (Ramus, 2001). There is also evidence that certain categories of employees – in particular, well-educated managers and those living in Scandinavia – do prefer working for companies that are explicitly and authentically committed to environmental sustainability (Cacioppe et al., 2008).

It follows that by embracing CSR, companies might enhance their employees' job satisfaction and organizational commitment (Brammer et al., 2007; Valentine and

Fleischman, 2008); and these work-related attitudes, albeit of great importance to any organization, play a crucial role in the service sector and, by implication, in hospitality. This is because service quality, which is ensured mainly (but, of course, not only) by employees having direct contact with clients, is one of the major factors behind customer loyalty and organizational performance (Kini and Hobson, 2002). Because there is a positive association between how committed a hotel employee is and the level of service quality he or she extends to his/her guests (Worsfold, 1999), this is critical to the success of hospitality establishments (Crawford and Hubbard, 2008). In this sense, Baron (2001, p. 7) points out that CSR not only has 'a direct effect on the costs of the firm', but also has 'a strategic effect by altering the competitive positions of firms in an industry'. The implication is that companies embracing CSR are likely to enhance their competitiveness (see Leslie, Chapter 2; Buckley, Chapter 6).

Top Hotel Companies' CSR Initiatives Aimed to Support Local Communities

The interrelatedness between CSR-inspired HRM and environmentalism also has far-reaching implications for another reason. The tourism and hospitality sector, though generating much-needed jobs (notably so in remote and rural areas) makes assorted negative impacts on a location's human milieu and natural environment, which are well documented in the preceding chapters. This has led to a shift in focus to sustainable tourism and sustainable development. While the former is about minimizing the impact of tourist activity in a location's environment, the latter aims to ensure that humanity 'meets the needs of the present without compromising the ability of future generations to meet their own needs' (Kates et al., 2005, p. 10). Of late, the two concepts have become the focus of growing academic, public and corporate interest (see, inter alia, Devuyst and Hens, 2000; Hall and Richards, 2000; Bohdanowicz and Zientara, 2008; Moscardo, 2008; Dow Jones, 2009).

Once again it is in this domain that CSR – which, as mentioned above, emphasizes the need to help local communities as well as to act in a *sustainable* way – comes into play. This is of great significance, especially in view of the aforesaid government-led attempts to turn tourism into a tool for regional development. Symptomatically, in the last two decades, large hotel corporations have implemented various CSR-inspired programmes – such as 'Investors in People' (InterContinental), 'Hilton in the Community Foundation' (Hilton Worldwide), 'Regenerating Communities' (Whitbread), 'Omtanke' (Scandic) and 'Spirit to Serve Our Communities' (Marriott International) – that aimed to improve things in local communities. Although these initiatives differed, to some extent, in scope and execution, they were all meant to support either those communities in which their facilities were located or those situated all over the world which, for various reasons, were in need of help (Bohdanowicz and Zientara, 2009).

Scandic's initiative called 'Scandic in Society' – carried out within the framework of its CSR *Omtanke* programme – is a case in point (Bohdanowicz and Zientara, 2008). It was designed to contribute to the well-being of the local communities in which Scandic operates. The programme was implemented in two phases: first, staff in every hotel were invited to attend meetings, during which the question of how Scandic can help local societies was broached. Subsequently, managers in each hotel came up with a holistic programme tailor-made for a concrete community. Such a scheme usually included the following initiatives: (i) donating hotel linen and furniture to local charity organisations; (ii) serving lunch to the homeless; (iii) sponsoring local sports teams and cultural events; (iv) offering part-time jobs to people with disabilities (to stave off social exclusion); (v) donating blood to local hospitals; (vi) coaching troublemaking youths; (vii) organizing entertainment events for elderly inhabitants; and (viii) holding discussions with teenaged pupils about social problems.

Another exemplary initiative has been carried through by Marriott. The company has set up a special fund, which is administered jointly by the Amazonas Sustainable

P. Zientara

Foundation and Brazil's State of Amazonas (Marriott, 2012). The principal idea behind the scheme is to monitor and to enforce the protection of 1.4 million acres of endangered rainforest in the Juma Sustainable Development Reserve, with a view to reducing greenhouse gas emissions (resulting from avoided deforestation). Yet the programme goes far beyond rainforest protection. In fact, it attempts to ensure long-term sustainability by helping – and empowering – the residents of Juma. This is done, among other things, by distributing mosquito nets and *Bolsa Floresta* (The Forest Conservation Allowance Programme) stored value (special credit) cards to each of the local families for protecting the rainforest. The initiative is worth emphasizing because, while combining the ideal of environmental sustainability with help for local community, it involves local authorities, the private sector and inhabitants of a protected area (note that Marriott has entered into other partnerships such as Conservation International and the International Tourism Partnership). This, of course, bears on the philosophy of community-based tourism (of which more below).

Other hotel companies emphasize the significance of employee involvement in the life of local communities. Starwood, for instance, asks its hotel staff to devote at least 8 hours a year to activities that benefit local children. In a similar vein, employees at Polish Radisson SAS hotels are encouraged to do community work. The Radisson hotel in Wrocław, for instance, co-operates with – and supports – a children's home situated in the small (and poor) town of Kąty Wrocławskie. Furthermore, in 2006, employees from all Polish Radisson SAS hotels took part in the 'Clean up the World' campaign. Within its framework, they cleaned – working shoulder to shoulder with local residents – the city forests (Szczecin and Wrocław) on the right bank of the Oder river (Radisson, 2008).

Community Support as a Case of Global–Local Interactions

Yet there is far more to it than that. Top hospitality companies have global reach and thus might be seen as representing 'global capital' and, by implication, the global scale. Considering that establishments belonging to international chains are situated in concrete localities, their involvement – through, but *not only* through, various CSR-driven schemes – in the life of local communities (hence the local scale) contributes to the intensification of global–local interactions. Actually, globally funded and internationally devised CSR initiatives are locally implemented, and so have local-level impacts. All this suggests that, from a certain viewpoint, there is a 'glocal' dimension to hotels' activities, which therefore could be regarded as a form of glocalization (Swyngedouw, 1992; Graham and Marvin, 2001; Torrance, 2008).

In its broadest sense, 'glocal' is used to describe the space where globalization and localization meet, or 'the combined process of globalization and local territorial reconfiguration' (Swyngedouw, 1992, p. 61). More specifically, 'glocal' is often employed to refer to the situation whereby local infrastructure assets, while being owned by global entities, are controlled by (nation-state) public regulators (Torrance, 2008). In this way, residents living in a given place and using local infrastructure are connected to global circuits. But multinational corporations also co-fund local infrastructure projects (Zientara, 2009), create jobs for local residents and boost local-level economic activity through place-based supply chains and subcontracting (see below). It follows that globalization might a priori bring assorted benefits to local communities.

How then does all this bear on the hospitality industry? International hotel chains are – among other agents – an important driving force behind globalization. To reiterate, they embody the global scale. Yet, at the same time, their impact is in essence *local*. Given that their establishments are situated in concrete localities, their *very* presence – while contributing to the intensification of generally understood global–local interactions – affects local economies. After all (and irrespective of whether a given hospitality business embraces CSR or not!), local residents find employment in hotels and are often offered training that provides them with useful skills and competences (thereby enhancing their human capital and expanding the local skills base).

What is more, as hospitality is part of the service sector, jobs created in hotels, as already mentioned, are far less likely to be transferred elsewhere: most hotel employees just have to be *in situ* to perform their tasks. Likewise, hotels usually cooperate with local farmers/ food producers, which helps to sustain local jobs and, equally importantly, to protect the environment as *locally produced* food – that is, food produced as close as possible to the consumer – makes it possible to avoid carbon emissions due to transportation (though producing some products locally during the non-growing season requires much higher energy consumption than does importing them). Besides, tourists/hotel guests, constituting a customer base for niche agricultural and handicraft products as they do, often boost the revenues of tourism-related businesses such as restaurants, shops and vineyards (Hall and Mitchell, 2000).

For these reasons, large hospitality companies are particularly welcomed (foreign) investors. This implies that local authorities might be tempted to cut corners and bypass certain (formal and/or democratic) procedures to respond effectively to the needs of multi-nationals. So, for instance, it might occur that a location site for a future hotel will be selected with scant regard being paid to environmental and/or urban planning concerns, or that the voice of neighbourhood residents (who might object to living in the vicinity of such an establishment) will be dismissed. Of course, this problem, which also has far-reaching implications for the advancement of local-level democracy, takes community-based tourism centre stage, stressing the involvement of local stakeholders in the decision-making processes concerning the types and locations of proposed tourism developments and auxiliary infrastructures (Kirsten and Rogerson, 2002; Hall, 2005).

However, doubts have recently been cast over the *raison d'être* of this approach (Moscardo, 2008). It is argued that the rationale for the engagement of local residents in decision making is problematic as they often do not possess the necessary knowledge of their rights and the understanding of the nitty-gritty of the processes they are supposed to take part in. This implies that there is a danger that either they will take (potentially) mistaken developmental decisions or that the very decision making will be dominated by authorities (or external agents). Hence the need on the part of (hospitality-sector) investors to abide by high moral standards; and it is CSR that, by definition, is well placed to help to ensure that. Indeed, to repeat, compliance with ethical norms (which guarantee respect for the interests of broadly defined stakeholders, with local residents to the fore) is central to the idea of socially responsible behaviour.

It follows that a specific combination of global scope and local focus, coupled with adherence to CSR ideals, makes international hotel chains particularly well positioned to project a more positive image of globalization. Consequently, their CSR-inspired conduct – as exemplified by the above-mentioned initiatives – does substantiate the claim that not all corporations are ruthless organizations which, riding roughshod over the interests of employees, local residents and the environment, are fixatedly committed to maximizing profits at all costs. In this way, they perform an important public function by helping to shape (and sometimes change) societal attitudes towards modern-day capitalism in general and business in particular.

Conclusion

This chapter has made an attempt to provide a contextualization of the hospitality-enterprise influence. It has touched upon a wide array of employment-related problems, placing them in the wider context of globalization, corporate social responsibility, human resource management and sustainable development. In particular, it has conceptualized international hotel companies' CSR initiatives aimed to support communities in terms of global–local interactions. As is commonly acknowledged, the tourism and hospitality industry is a sheltered sector and, rather than being exposed to some negative consequences of globalization, it is one of its major drivers. It does generate much-needed jobs in rich and emerging economies alike, but the quality of this employment often leaves much to be desired. Serious problems with maintaining work–life balance, few promotion prospects, generally lower-than-average remuneration and the sensation of job insecurity all seem to lie behind low job satisfaction, insufficient organizational commitment and high turnover rates in hospitality businesses.

Conversely, the operations of hospitality enterprises (especially, hospitality facilities) produce various negative impacts, which, in turn, affect the environment and the socio-cultural milieu of a given locality. Related to this – and given that multinational hotel corporations are sometimes perceived as unaccountable and uncontrollable entities that threaten local-level democracy and well-being – worries can arise that these impacts can even be magnified. For instance, local authorities, eager to court foreign investment, might be tempted to disregard placed-based democratic procedures and pay scant regard to inhabitants' views on where exactly the construction of a new hospitality facility should take place. Hence, in line with the focus of the entire book, the recurring emphasis on the significance (and necessity) of responsibility (responsible behaviour) on the part of the industry.

Indeed, this chapter has argued, among other things, that CSR has a critical role to play in the above processes. Although social responsibility still amounts – in some cases – to little more than isolated public relations-oriented projects, in a growing number of hotel companies, as we have indicated, CSR goes deeper than that and comes closer to being embedded in the business model. Accordingly, the locally implemented, CSR-driven initiatives of hotels can, for one thing, reinforce the positive effects of their functioning in concrete places (not only in terms of job creation, but also environment protection and support for local inhabitants); for another thing, they can improve the quality of employment. It is fair to say therefore that such glocal interactions might produce win–win outcomes and, crucially, lend credence to the assumption that international hotel chains – representing global capital but being embedded in local communities – are particularly well positioned to highlight, by their *responsible* conduct, the 'human face' of globalization.

It is hoped that the present chapter will make an important contribution to the existing literature of the subject. It aims both to widen our understanding of the phenomena at hand and to provoke further discussion. Undoubtedly, in the near future, the questions analysed in this study are set to occupy a prominent position on the agenda of local-level policy makers and hospitality managers alike. For this reason, the significance of ongoing research into the complex relationship between tourism, employment, community involvement and globalization cannot be emphasized enough.

References

Agarin, T., Jetzkowitz, J. and Matzarakis, A. (2010) Climate change and tourism in the Eastern Baltic Sea region. In: Jafari, J. and Cai, L.A. (eds) *Tourism and the Implications of Climate Change: Issues and Actions.* Bridging Tourism Theory and Practice, Emerald, Bingley, UK, pp. 262–281.

Archer, B. and Cooper, C. (1998) The positive and negative impacts of tourism. In: Theobald, W.F. (ed.) *Global Tourism.* Butterworth-Heinemann, Oxford, UK, pp. 63–81.

Baron, D. (2001) Private politics, corporate social responsibility, and integrated strategy. *Journal of Economics and Management Strategy* 10, 7–45.

Barrett, A., McGuinness, S. and O'Brien, M. (2008) *The Immigrant Earnings Disadvantage across the Earnings and Skills Distributions: The Case of Immigrants from the EU's New Member States.* IZA Discussion Paper No. 3479, Institute for the Study of Labor (IZA), Bonn, Germany.

Beddoes, Z.M. (2008) When fortune frowned. *Economist,* No. 8601, pp. 3–34.

Bohdanowicz, P. and Zientara, P. (2008) Corporate social responsibility in hospitality: issues and implications. A case study of Scandic. *Scandinavian Journal of Hospitality and Tourism* 8, 271–293.

Bohdanowicz, P. and Zientara, P. (2009) Hotel companies' contribution to improving the quality of life of local communities and the well-being of their employees. *Tourism and Hospitality Research* 9, 147–158.

Bohdanowicz, P. and Zientara, P. (2012) CSR-inspired environmental initiatives in top hotel chains. In: Leslie, D. (ed.) *Tourism across Europe: Steps towards Sustainability – Tourism Enterprises and the Sustainability Agenda*. Ashgate, Farnham, UK, pp. 93–120.

Bohdanowicz, P., Zientara, P. and Novotna, E. (2011) International hotel chains and environmental protection: analysis of Hilton's *we care!* programme (Europe, 2006–2008). *Journal of Sustainable Tourism* 19, 797–816.

Bosselman, F.P., Peterson, C.A. and McCarthy, C. (1999) *Managing Tourism Growth: Issues and Applications*. Island Press, Washington, DC.

Brammer, S., Millington, A. and Rayton, B. (2007) The contribution of corporate social responsibility to organizational commitment. *International Journal of Human Resource Management* 18, 1701–1719.

Business in the Community (2009) Corporate Responsibility (CR). Available at: http://www.bitc.org.uk/resources/jargon_buster/cr.html (accessed 13 April 2012).

Butler, R.W. (1999) Problems and issues of integrating tourism development. In: Pearce, D.G. and Butler, R.W. (eds) *Contemporary Issues in Tourism Development*. Routledge, London, pp. 65–80.

Cacioppe, R., Forster, N. and Fox, M. (2008) A survey of managers' perceptions of corporate ethics and social responsibility and actions that may affect companies' success. *Journal of Business Ethics* 82, 681–700.

Chapman, J.A. (1989) Improving interactional organizational research: a model of person–organization fit. *Academy of Management Review* 14, 333–349.

Chiesa, T. and Gautam, A. (2009) *Travel and Tourism Climate Change Report: Working Towards a Low Carbon Travel and Tourism Sector*. United Nations Framework Convention on Climate Change, Copenhagen, Denmark.

Cleveland, J., O'Neil, J., Himelright, J., Harrison, M., Crouter, C. and Drago, R. (2007) Work and family issues in the hospitality industry: perspectives of entrants, managers and spouses. *Journal of Hospitality and Tourism Research* 31, 275–298.

Crawford, A. and Hubbard, S.S. (2008) The impact of work-related goals on hospitality industry employee variables. *Tourism and Hospitality Research* 8, 116–124.

Cullen, J. and McLaughlin, A. (2006) What drives the persistence of presenteeism as a managerial value in hotels?: Observations noted during an Irish work–life balance research project. *International Journal of Hospitality Management* 25, 510–516.

Deery, M. and Jago, L. (2009) A framework for work–life balance: addressing the needs of the tourism industry. *Tourism and Hospitality Research* 9, 97–108.

Devuyst, D. and Hens, L. (2000) Introducing and measuring sustainable development initiatives by local authorities in Canada and Flanders (Belgium): a comparative study. *Environment, Development and Sustainability* 2, 81–105.

Doherty, L. (2004) Work–life balance initiatives: implications for women. *Employee Relations* 26, 433–452.

Dow Jones (2009) Dow Jones Sustainability Indexes. Available at: http://www.sustainability-index.com/ (accessed 13 April 2012).

European Commission (2011) Rural Development policy 2007–2013. Available at: http://ec.europa.eu/agriculture/rurdev/index_en.htm (accessed 13 April 2012).

Furunes, T. and Mykletun, R.J. (2005) Age management in Norwegian hospitality business. *Scandinavian Journal of Hospitality and Tourism* 5(2), 1–19.

Graham, S. and Marvin, S. (2001) *Splintering Urbanism: Networked Infrastructures, Technological Mobilities and the Urban Condition*. Routledge, London.

Hall, C.M. (2005) *Tourism: Rethinking the Social Science of Mobility*. Prentice Hall, Harlow, UK.

Hall, C.M. and Mitchell, R. (2000) Wine tourism in the Mediterranean: a tool for restructuring and development. *Thunderbird International Business Review*, No. 42, pp. 445–447.

Hall, D. and Richards, G. (eds) (2000) *Tourism and Sustainable Community Development*. Routledge, London/New York.

Harvey, D. (2006) *Spaces of Global Capitalism*. Verso, New York.

Heskett, J.L., Jones, T.O., Loveman, G.W., Sasser, W.E. and Schlesinger, L.A. (1994) Putting the service-profit chain to work. *Harvard Business Review* 72, 164–174.

Ioannides, D. and Petridou, E. (2012) Tourism workers and the equity dimension of sustainability. In: Leslie, D. (ed.) *Tourism across Europe: Steps towards Sustainability – Tourism Enterprises and the Sustainability Agenda*. Ashgate, Farnham, UK, pp. 187–204.

Karatepe, O. and Uludag, O. (2007) Conflict, exhaustion, and motivation: a study of frontline employees in northern Cyprus hotels. *International Journal of Hospitality Management* 26, 645–665.

Kates, R.W., Parris, T.M. and Leiserowitz, A.A. (2005) What is sustainable development? goals, indicators, values, and practices, environment. *Science and Policy for Sustainable Development* 47(3), 8–21.

Kini, R.B. and Hobson, C.J. (2002) Motivational theories and successful total quality initiatives. *International Journal of Management* 19, 605–613.

Kirsten, M. and Rogerson, C. (2002) Tourism, business linkages and small enterprise development in South Africa. *Development Southern Africa* 19, 29–59.

Magd, H. (2003) Management attitudes and perceptions of older workers in hospitality management. *International Journal of Contemporary Hospitality Management* 15, 393–401.

Marriott (2012) Spirit to Preserve. Available at: http://www.marriott.com/green-brazilian-rainforest.mi (accessed 13 April 2012).

Moscardo, G. (2008) Sustainable tourism innovation: challenging basic assumptions. *Tourism and Hospitality Research* 8, 4–13.

Mulvaney, R., O'Neill, J., Cleveland, J. and Crouter, A. (2006) A model of work–family dynamics of hotel managers. *Annals of Tourism Research* 34, 66–87.

Neuman, W.L. (2003) *Social Research Methods: Qualitative and Quantitative Approaches.* Allyn and Bacon, Boston, Massachusetts.

Nonneman, W. (2007) *European Immigration and the Labor Market.* Migration Policy Institute/Bertelsmann Stiftung, Washington, DC.

Pratten, J. and O'Leary, B. (2007) Addressing the causes of chef shortages in the UK. *Journal of European Industrial Training* 31, 68–78.

Radisson SAS (2008) News Releases [in Polish]. Available at: http://www.sasgroup.pl/ (accessed 13 April 2012).

Ramus, C.A. (2001) Organizational support for employees: encouraging creative ideas for environmental sustainability. *California Management Review* 43, 85–105.

Sharpley, R. (2000) Tourism and sustainable development: exploring the theoretical divide. *Journal of Sustainable Tourism* 8(1), 1–19.

Somerville, W. and Sumption, M. (2009) *Immigration and the Labour Market: Theory, Evidence, Policy,* Migration Policy Institute/Equality and Human Rights Commission, Washington, DC.

Swyngedouw, E. (1992) The mammon quest: 'glocalization', interspatial competition and the monetary order – the construction of new scales. In: Dunford, M. and Kafkalas, G. (eds) *Cities and Regions in the New Europe.* Belhaven Press, New York, pp. 39–67.

Torrance, M.I. (2008) Urban infrastructure as networked financial products. *International Journal of Urban and Regional Research* 32, 1–21.

Valentine, S. and Fleischman, G. (2008) Ethics programs, perceived corporate social responsibility and job satisfaction. *Journal of Business Ethics* 77, 159–172.

Wahab, S. and Pigram, J.J. (eds) (1997) *Tourism Development and Growth.* Routledge, London.

Walsh, K. (2003) Qualitative research: advancing the science and practice of hospitality. *Cornell Hotel and Restaurant Administration Quarterly* 44(2), 66–74.

World Travel and Tourism Council (2009) *Leading the Challenge on Climate Change.* WTTC, London.

Worsfold, P. (1999) HRM, performance, commitment, and service quality in the hotel industry. *International Journal of Contemporary Hospitality Management* 11, 340–348.

Zientara, P. (2009) A few remarks on globalisation, democracy and spatiality. *Economic Affairs* 29(2), 56–61.

Zientara, P. (2011) International migration: a case against building ever higher fences. *Economic Affairs* 31(1), 66–72.

Zientara, P. and Bohdanowicz, P. (2010) The hospitality sector: corporate social responsibility and climate change. In: Jafari, J. and Cai, L.A. (eds) *Tourism and the Implications of Climate Change: Issues and Actions.* Bridging Tourism Theory and Practice, Emerald, Bingley, UK, pp. 91–111.

13 Conclusion

David Leslie
Freelance Researcher and Consultant

The promotion of responsible tourism (RT) and correlating initiatives bears witness to the widening scope of environmentalism over the last 25 years of the 20th century. This gained further impetus as a result of the advocacy of sustainable development and, over the last decade, because of the shifting emphasis on climate change and the need for appropriate, responsive action. Over the same period, we have witnessed the emergence of a variety of terms used to describe reputedly benign forms of tourism products; terms that, it may be argued, encapsulate a reawakening of 19th century notions of pristine landscapes, nature and romanticism. But, and dependent on the stance adopted, although these terms may be rather idealistic, nevertheless they demonstrate concern for a more responsible approach to the development of tourism and to better environmental management and practice. Thus we have 'responsible tourism', which conceptually means that everyone involved in the production, delivery and consumption of tourism has a responsibility to ensure that resource consumption and negative impacts are minimized and positive benefits maximised.

Responsibility in tourism though is not just about the more obvious connections with local people and with their environment, nor just about the environmental performance and policies of those involved in supply and demand; it is also about wider considerations, which have been accentuated by climate change and sustainability. This is perhaps nowhere more manifest than in the field of transport, which too often gains little attention in discussion of tourism development. Is this because it is taken for granted or due to the fact that so often the focus is on the destination? However, transport *is* integral to tourism – and primarily as a result of climate change issues gaining attention; as Somerville (Chapter 3) argues, tourism is not going to decline in the foreseeable future. His analysis of air transport and the supporting discourse on sea-based transport illuminates the past as well as presenting the main issues and actions being taken to address the inherent problems of pollution and greenhouse gas emissions. But a major concern is that in spite of progress towards cleaner, quieter engines and alternative fuel potential, the evidence all suggests that whatever gains are made will be cancelled by increasing demand. In spite of this, the transport sector also needs to be recognized for its contribution to national economies and to the generation of millions of jobs around the world – jobs that are predominantly dependent on leisure-based tourism. In destinations, it is also employment opportunities and revenues from tourist spending which are the oft-cited benefits of tourism development.

Equity in the sharing of benefits to the host community is a central tenet of RT, the realization of which is a function of not only their involvement but also of the degree of control they may (or may not) have. The involvement of the community is a pervasive theme throughout these pages and their empowerment is explored in depth by Timothy (Chapter 5). Of particular note are the indications that indigenous peoples are taking back control of their own cultures – a sign of progress, he argued, that is supported by the developing idea of 'geotourism'. This emphasizes the significance of the unique characteristics of a destination, which make it different and should therefore be appropriately maintained. Overall, this reaffirms that tourism development should be resource based and not market led. As Timothy establishes, and especially with regard to the ascribed benefits and indeed the sustainability, it is invariably more effective that control on tourism development is at grassroots level and so with the local community. This is well illustrated by Lara and Gemelli (Chapter 11), and particularly so through the two local case studies that are presented, which also show the value of the representative approach rather than just the participatory approach, which too often predominates. In contrast, the trials and tribulations of community participation (or the lack of it) were exemplified through the three case studies based on World Heritage Sites. As they note, such status brings with it a raft of potential problems, not the least of which is the requisite funding to respond effectively to increased visitor demand while at the same time seeking not to jeopardize the very heritage the accreditation was designed to protect. So World Heritage Status is not a panacea, especially as regards a cultural landscape. Many sites are plagued by a plethora of tourists and given the forecast growth in demand arising from fast developing economies such as India, China and Brazil, is not going to abate.

Tourism is very much based on a community's resources. It is these resources that are being consumed by the visitors and by those enterprises that seek to provide for, and meet, the needs/wants of tourists. Tourism enterprises, in whatever guise, are encouraged, and as appropriate facilitated, to reduce their demands on energy and water and more broadly to address, and take effective measures

to tackle, their overall environmental performance (EP), including, therefore, their social responsibility. Furthermore, and with attention to the wider context, tourism activity is a major consumer of food, which brings additional impacts, e.g. increased demand within the locality/area and food imports, and contributes further to water consumption; as is well known, the resources of both of these commodities are becoming global issues (WWF, 2010; Polman, 2011). Indeed, water scarcity is seen as a bigger risk to global companies than is access to energy in emerging economies (GlobeScan and SustainAbility, 2011). The EP of tourism enterprises, particularly in terms of reducing resource consumption, is thus all the more important. This tenet of RT is primarily explored by Buckley (Chapter 6), who well makes the point that the context – the environment – within which tourism enterprise operates, is a key influential factor on performance. As he highlights, it is not the case that there is a 'blueprint' which can be applied in all situations with equal success, thereby heralding a recurrent theme in the following chapters: that local conditions must be taken into consideration. EP and social responsibility are the specific focus of Zientara (Chapter 12) who addresses these issues in the context of international hotel operations and illustrates what can be done by major players.

Major players, both transnational and national companies, can have, through their financial resources, substantial influence on tourism development. Their primary concern may often be less about being responsible and socially sustainable than maintaining profit and growth; however, it is also evident that the control of local resources may lie in the hands of a few 'dominant' stakeholders. This kind of influence may often not be beneficial to host communities, as the foregoing pages, and notably Chapter 7, well demonstrate. There are though many examples of comparatively small tourism enterprises which do demonstrate best practices, whether this is in environmental management or social responsibility, as Holland (Chapter 9) and Spenceley and Rylance (Chapter 10) collectively attest through a range of cases. But what is happening, especially in the context of wildlife tours, just outside the 'picture'? Other operators, less responsible in their practices, seek to capitalize on manifest demand. It is inescapable that there are many enterprises that are not addressing the issue of responsibility and not adopting what is recognized as best responsible practice. Primary reasons for this include lack of interest or knowledge or resources.

Collectively the chapters mentioned so far serve to illustrate some of the complexity of tourism and the need for the adoption of an holistic approach within which tourism enterprises are not treated in isolation but within the context of the local economy, environment and community. However, it is not just those enterprises involved in supply that have a responsibility. There are many other stakeholders, especially international and national agencies and governmental organizations. Given their pronouncements on the way tourism should be developed to the benefit of local economies and communities, questions arise over how much of this is just rhetoric, and rather furthers the status quo as opposed to helping the very communities (and the less advantaged members of those communities) on whose resources tourism is so dependent. Questions such as these are very much at the core of Pleumarom's Chapter 7, a lively discourse on the theme of politics and poverty in the development of tourism. This whole matter of benefit to 'less advantaged' communities as an outcome of tourism development, particularly in the guise of pro-poor tourism, is extensively challenged. That many of the situations cited are in lesser developed countries does not negate the very issues she raises. Indeed, to varying degrees, these issues are far more widely applicable – whether this is community participation, or direct benefits to locals or migrants, for example, taking local jobs in hospitality. The voice of the disadvantaged is all too often absent. But it is also inescapable that tourism is not the provision of welfare. Far from it, it is private enterprise operating in a capitalist system fuelled by consumption. A key fault arguably therefore lies with those who seek to promote tourism development based on an agenda that stresses the benefit to local communities. Undoubtedly, this does happen, but where the real value lies is in those situations where this kind of

development is part of a more comprehensive and inclusive development plan.

Tourism development is not then an end in itself but should be part of an overall strategy for urban or rural development. In this the requisite is both for cross-sectoral cooperation and 'joined-up thinking'; for example between policies for different spheres, such as funding for community-based initiatives and project support for sustainability-orientated projects as exemplified by renewable energy sources. The key here is cross-sector integration and, overall, a holistic approach. This is hardly new, witness Crow (1956), who articulated the need for integrated development, including consideration of the landscape, with care to amenity value, quality of life and sustainability. Counter to this is the promotion of tourism, predominantly by major stakeholders and their professional agencies, as a 'global industry'. This agenda reinforces approaches to tourism development that are based on treating it in isolation, thereby failing to recognize the complexity of the tourism system and the interrelationships that extend well beyond the locality visited. The free market approach advocated to tourism development is short term and unlikely to generate much in the way of wider benefit for society, e.g. welfare and education. Furthermore, and accepting for a moment that tourism is the 'biggest industry', then logic suggests that it would be *the* player castigating any development or practice that damages its operational capacity, e.g. pollution of the air and bathing water, damage to coral reefs, oil spills, etc. Yet we do not hear the representatives of this 'industry' bewailing these types of issues. Where are the leaders arguing for effective measures to help address climate change and increasing consumption?

Tourism development thus may not be the best way forward. There are examples of destinations with a high dependency on tourism, which has displaced a 'cash crop' monoculture of earlier years, but the level of dependency on overseas markets may have changed little. Also, there are many examples from the past of declining tourism demand leading to economic problems. How many visitors to today's 'must go' destinations are the result of perceived over-commercialization of yesterday's resorts? In this sense, tourism in lesser developed countries is similar to Western manufacturers seeking cheaper labour. For example, from a distance tourism may be seen as benign compared with mineral extraction, but this is not so in the perceptions of the local community where it may take place. Even then, the property rights of locals may be overlooked in favour of foreign investment. But such potential alternatives are the domain of government. It is all too easy a failing to recognise that tourism takes place, and develops in destinations, within the context of the prevailing government policy and so whichever way a destination develops largely rests in the purview of the government.

Governance, as Hall (Chapter 8) articulates, is complex; there are variant forms, but central to all are the key elements of participation, power and policy making influenced by personal agendas and vested interests. This applies equally at any level of governance. However, at the national level, major criteria are what are the policy instruments to be applied and in what context? Further, how effective are they? All too often, it appears, as Hall argues, that too much is based on political economic faith; most likely with short-term horizons. That is, short-term economic imperatives underpin the development of tourism with often the environment and social dimensions, which are longer term, at best gaining second place. We should acknowledge that this situation is by no means only manifest in tourism planning and development; social dimensions of sustainability are often some way behind environmental issues, including in countries perceived as leaders in the field of sustainability (see Rowe and Fudge, 2003). But in this, we should pay heed to the effect of internationalization/globalization in potentially diminishing the influence of national players. In effect, capitalism combined with globalization, and the key facilitator – information communications technology, are increasingly undermining the national state; witness growth in supranational and international agencies etc. (see Thake, 2009). Indeed, it might be argued that tourism development legitimizes these power relations – that inequality is masked in terms of tourists wishing to experience other places and other cultures, which are often

commodified by national and international players to serve their markets. This commodification is the equivalent in tourism of what, to cite Lattas (for *capitalist employers* read post-industrial nations, for *labourers* read lesser developed countries) is 'the ideological way it conceals and rationalises the appropriation of surplus value so as to legitimise the power relations between capitalist employers and wage labourers' (Lattas, 1993, p. 108; cited in Hutnyk, 1996, p. 220). As Butcher (1997) says in his diatribe on the way we see tourists, this in effect masks the differences between north and south and echoes Nash's (1989) argument that tourism is a form of imperialism.

What also emerges from these pages overall is a manifest lack of progress in all areas of tourism; an outcome which reflects earlier studies (see Mowforth and Munt, 2005; Leslie, 2009). Yet the application of RT practices is not difficult, as a raft of exemplars herein attest. Certainly, addressing and the effective application of the tenets of RT relating to equity in access to resources and attributable benefits is more challenging, notably so in terms of governance and community empowerment. These fields require a more holistic approach, which necessarily involves careful deliberation, commitment and longer term objectives, which are often found to be lacking. Instead, the emphasis is on short-term macroeconomics at a cost to communities, as Pleumarom (Chapter 7) emphatically argues. Undoubtedly, in all facets of RT, the key is the commitment of all stakeholders, irrespective of level, position or the size of the enterprise, to the adoption and promotion of greater responsibility in the development and delivery of tourism products and services.

To achieve such change is difficult in itself, but all the more so given that the effectiveness of practices in furthering the tenets of RT, and so also of sustainability, are dependent on the situation and context. Potentially, further research into this area and subsequent effective dissemination could be influential. Also, there is a need for analytical models designed for these different situations. Further research into the efficacy of policy measures in achieving their defined objectives, and so too into the assessment of projects funded by government (or non-government) organizations in terms of their defined objectives, is very limited. The absence of this sort of evaluation serves to reinforce Hall's assessment that within the sphere of governance much is often based on political economic faith. But what is fundamental to all of this is the attitude and values of the very people involved. If they are orientated towards being responsible, towards sustainability, in their ways, then it is far more likely that these attitudes will materialize in whatever aspect of tourism in which they are involved.

    In this, as with much that has gone before, is the central figure of the tourist. As Leslie (Chapter 4) argued, tourists have a responsibility both for their actions and the consequences of their action, not only in terms of RT but also in the wider context of sustainability. It has been found though that, at best, this accounts for a small minority of tourists. Even then, the figure will be inflated by the assumption that those tourists on perceived RT packages variously labelled, for example as eco/nature/alternative, are all choosing them on the basis that they wish to be responsible. Albeit that surveys invariably find that respondents indicate they support responsibility on the part of suppliers and are willing to pay extra for these policies and related practices, such intentions evidently do not convert into purchases. As different suppliers confirm, the majority of tourists are not that interested in high-price purchases. What the marketing of these alternative products to conventional tourism achieves in many cases is that destinations become fashionable – the latest positional good of the moment (e.g. Buckley's 'ecochic') – but as demand increases then so their status as such wanes, and all the more quickly given the processes of globalization. The products have a shorter life cycle and therefore there is a need to develop new markets, in the process often leading to a changing dynamic in both the form and structure of the early touristic development, which is not necessarily to the benefit of the local economy and communities involved. This leads to the resource paradox in tourism: the need for a quality environment versus the requirements (and increasing expectations) of tourists in terms of the

superstructure and infrastructure. Furthermore, there are certainly expectations in some quarters, which are often implicit in commentaries, that tourists should not only be aware that, but also aware of the extent to which, their holiday expenditure goes to benefit local people in their chosen destinations, and so forth.

    People go on holiday for a variety of reasons, although for the most part it is to relax and enjoy themselves; irrespective of how this may be articulated. While they may seek to go to destinations new to them, their general pattern of touristic behaviour will change little. In this, and to a greater or lesser extent, their behaviour will not be dissimilar from that in the home environment. Their attitudes and values will not have changed, nor will their environmental behaviour and green purchasing. As one may well argue, why should they behave otherwise? Does the shopper in the High Street enquire as to the conditions of the workers who produced the goods they are inspecting or how their purchase might aid the poor in the society where the raw materials were sourced? Why then would one expect tourists to do so? Basically, tourists are interlopers, foreigners; as Krippendorf (1987, p. 42) argued 'The tourist is his own advocate and not an international ambassador; he is not there to aid development or protect the environment'. However, today this is not just a matter of how tourists behave. It is the issues of sustainability and climate change that provide the argument for their acceptance of responsibility for their actions and choices. It is, therefore, consumption that needs to be addressed, and thus the consumer.

    The way and the what we consume lies at the core of sustainable consumption and is an underlying factor of RT. Whether in society generally, or in the context of the development of RT, to achieve SPC requires behavioural change; the norms, values and attitudes of Western societies need to change. Despite first gaining prominence at the Earth Summit (1992) and subsequently a major impetus at the UN's World Summit on Sustainable Development at Johannesburg in 2002, there are few signs of real progress; as the subsequent Summit of 2012 attests. But herein also lies a dichotomy in sustainability between the 'north' and the 'south', which is especially applicable to tourism, For the north, sustainability is often translated in terms of 'reduce, reuse, recycle', and conservation of the environment is something societies therein can afford. It is no coincidence that environmental consciousness arose during the industrial revolution, the development of transportation and increasing affluence. In contrast, for the south, sustainability is more about access to resources, economic development, education, health and so forth. This debate is not dissimilar to nimbyism ('not in my backyard') on the part of the majority of society in these northern countries who see lesser developed parts of the world as their back garden – potentially places to visit and enjoy.

To achieve progress in sustainability requires incentives and supporting frameworks, knowledge of options and access to such, and exemplars in all facets to demonstrate how change can be achieved (see Jackson, 2005). In this wider context, there is need of fundamental change in consumerism, in the habits and lifestyles of the people in general in affluent societies. But behaviour is not easily changed. It is an outcome of society and institutions, and of personal relationships, and is as much influenced by 'others' as by personal choice, as well as by context. For instance, that in some societies people recycle more can be just a function of municipal authority action and not a change in attitude: a function of habit rather than an intrinsic attitude. As Lindholt stated (1998, p. 5): 'It is the personal introspection that drives one's commitment to environmentalism'. This makes it all the more imperative to address the lack of research into the outcomes of initiatives that aim to change behaviours (Souterton et al., 2011).

The quest for more sustainable forms of consumption brings into contention the question of why do people go on holiday? There is no obvious discernible answer that adequately explains this practice in the postindustrial nations of today, other than that it is part of societal conditioning: 'the norm'. Fundamentally, this is what needs to be addressed. It is inherent in the production and consumption of tourism that negative impacts will arise just as, to use a metaphor, there are

with the burning of coal. Equally, such is capitalism that as with coal, there will be those who benefit and those who do not. It is both the disparities in this process and the consumption involved that raise the issues that are being challenged in tourism. If tourism per se is to be more responsive to the issues of sustainability then so must the processes that underpin it (Leslie, 1994). In this, there is not just the need for shared meanings and definitions but also the need for shared values and therefore, as necessary, the need to change the values of all stakeholders. Evidently progress is limited. Yet, as these pages bear witness, these issues in tourism were very much to the fore in the late 1980s. However, change tends to be incremental and, thereby, is limited in effect. How much of this progress is largely due to the intrinsic attitudes and values of those involved rather than to any direct outcome of external factors, policy initiatives and so forth?

Ultimately, as Cairncross (1991) argued, no amount of action by consumers will ever achieve the substantial progress that is necessary to gain a major shift towards more responsible attitudes, behaviour and choice on the part of tourists. Indeed, 'anything today's green consumer may do will be swamped by the actions of millions of their counterparts in emerging markets' (Elkington, 2010). To make substantive progress will require actual and sustained change. To expand on Hutnyk's (1996, p. 223) argument, leading towards a transformation in the ways of tourism will in effect lead towards its own demise. Conceptually, this is the only sustainable outcome. But it is not going to occur in the foreseeable future. In the meantime, it is imperative that the central tenets of RT are widely applied and that every action that can be taken is taken and, as appropriate, in all facets of tourism production and consumption. This applies in no small measure and broadly to all tourism products and developments, irrespective of scale and context.

There is a raft of principles and many lessons and practical examples within these pages to draw on, the wider application of which will certainly contribute to more responsible approaches in, and the adoption of greater responsibility for, the development of tourism. In this, the approach propounded here is not to be confused with the packaging of products for tourists as, or otherwise labelled in some way as, 'alternative', i.e. alternative to what commentators invariably consider as mass tourism. Rather, the promotion of an agenda such as that which has been portrayed in this book can contribute to more sustainable forms of production and consumption in tourism. In the process, there is the prospect of more equitable involvement on the part of host communities and respect not only for their environment but for the wider environment overall.

References

Butcher, J. (1997) Sustainable development or Development? In: Stabler, M.J. (ed.) *Tourism and Sustainability: Principles to Practice.* CAB International, Wallingford, UK, pp. 27–39.

Cairncross, F. (1991) *Costing the Earth.* Harvard Business School Press, Boston, Massachusetts.

Crowe, S. (1956) *Tomorrow's Landscape.* Architectural Press, London.

Elkington, J. (2010) Can consumers save the climate? *Director,* January 2010, p. 26. Institute of Directors, London.

GlobeScan and SustainAbility (2011) The Sustainability Survey 2010. *Survey on Urbanization and Megacities: Emerging Economies.* GlobeScan, Toronto, Ontario/SustainAbility, London.

Hutnyk, J. (1996) *The Rumour of Calcutta: Tourism, Charity and the Poverty of Representation.* Zed, London.

Jackson, T. (2005) *Motivating Sustainable Consumption – A Review of Evidence on Consumer Behaviour and Behavioural Change.* Centre for Environmental Strategy. University of Surrey, Guildford, UK.

Krippendorf, J. (1987) *The Holidaymakers.* Butterworth-Heinemann, Oxford, UK.

Leslie, D. (1994) Sustainable tourism or developing sustainable approaches to lifestyle? *World Leisure and Recreation* 36(3), 30–36.

Leslie, D. (ed.) (2009) *Tourism Enterprise and Sustainable Development – International Perspectives on Responses to the Sustainability Agenda.* Advances in Tourism Series, Routledge, New York.

Lindholt, L. (1998) Writing from a sense of place. *Journal of Environmental Education* 30(4), 4–10.

Mowforth, M. and Munt, I. (2005) *Tourism and Sustainability: Development and New Tourism in the Third World.* Routledge, London.

Nash, D. (1989) Tourism as a form of imperialism. In: Smith, V. (ed.) *Hosts and Guests: The Anthropology of Tourism.* University of Pennsylvania Press, Philadelphia, Pennsylvania, pp. 37–54.

Polman, P. (2011) Food security in a changing climate. *Hospitality* 21, 20–25.

Rowe, J. and Fudge, C. (2003) Linking national sustainable developing strategy and local implementation: a case study in Sweden. *Local Environment* 8, 125–140.

Souterton, D., McMeekin, A. and Evans, S.D. (2011) *International Review of Behaviourism Change Initiating Climate Change Behaviours.* Research Programme, Scottish Government Social Research, Edinburgh, UK.

Thake, S. (2009) *Individualism and Consumerism: Reframing the Debate.* Joseph Rowntree Foundation, York, UK.

WWF (2010) *WWF Report INT 2010. Living Planet Report 2010: Biodiversity, Biocapacity and Development.* WWF International, Gland, Switzerland. Available at: http://assets.wwf.org.uk/downloads/wwf_lpr2010_lr_1_.pdf (accessed 12 April 2012).

Index

Page numbers in **bold** refer to illustrations and tables

access
    to company environmental performance data
        84–85, 87–88
    destination, transport infrastructure 31, 78,
        147
accommodation
    environmental impacts **85**
    quality demands, ecotourism destinations 24,
        31, 60
    in remote destinations 121, 124
adventure tours
    customer characteristics 119–120
    impacts on destinations 122–123
    product and provider characteristics 120–122
    responsible practices 11, 123–127
        policy guidelines 120
Africa, wildlife natural resources 130, 133–135
Agenda 21 (1995) 6, 23
air passenger duty (APD) 7, 19
air transport *see* aviation
aircraft design 44, 45, 46
    cabin air quality 87
airports
    expansion and improvement 31
    noise issues 44, 47, 50
    siting and capacity 46
airships 43–44
all-inclusive resorts 26, 27, 31, 62
alternative tourism (AT)
    definition 20–21
    World Bank support funding 94–95
Alternative Travel Group (ATG) 26
Angkor temples (Cambodia) 96–97
Argentina, cultural heritage sites 142, **144**
    Artisan's Road, Mina Clavero 150–151
    Cueva de las Manos, Río Pinturas 145

    Jesuit Block and Estancias of Córdoba
        145–147
    Quebrada de Humahuaca, Jujuy province
        147–149
    Valles Calchaquíes, Salta province 150
Association of Independent Tour Operators (AITO)
    120
auditors, environmental 84–85, 87
aviation
    climate impact control measures 48, 49–50,
        51–52
    environmental concerns 43, 47–48, 58
    history
        air flight, pioneering technologies 43–44
        commercial service development 44–45
        postwar aircraft design and airlines 45–46
    see also airports
awards 88, 90, 131, **132**

Balearic Islands (Spain) 26, 64
Bali (Indonesia) 4, 25, 31
'barefoot' approach 101–103
begging 126
Belize (Central America) 10, 30
'best practice' benchmarks 83–84
British Airways (BA) 7, 28, 46
brochures, quality of information 125–126
buildings
    heritage sites 12, 145–146
    restoration 147, 150
business enterprises
    competitive advantage of CSR standards 28–
        30, 127, 159
    environmental performance 8–9, 82–84,
        166–167
    ethics in business practices 21, 158

business enterprises – *Continued*
   image improvement opportunities 154–155, 161
   integration of independent operators 120–121
   responses to recession 55, 101
   sustainability and status quo 23
   see also small (/micro) enterprises

Cambodia, 'Stay Another Day' campaign 96–97
Camino de los Artesanos (Artisan's Road), Argentina 150–151
carbon dioxide emissions
   from aviation 47–48, 50, 51
   from hotels 154
   from shipping 48–49
carbon offsetting schemes 30, 57
carbon trading 7, 49–50
Caribbean islands 3, 76
carrying capacity studies 25, 136
certification schemes 27, 88, 131, **131**
charity donations 126–127, 138, 159
climate change
   aviation industry responses 7, 47–48
   international agreement challenges 50
   potential impact on water resources 30
   public attitudes and behaviour 64
   tourism industry impacts and attitudes 98–99
'clubbing' resorts 4, 62
codes of conduct 10, 28, 133, 134
communities (host)
   development programmes 100, 115, 147, 150–151
   local governance **111–112**, 114–115
   needs and values 33–34, 101–103, 148
   participation and ownership 21, 32–33, 73–74, 133, 166
   poverty and equity 9–10, 91–97
   tourism impacts and benefits 5, 8, 74–78
      contact with tourists, quality of 125–126, 152
      heritage awareness encouragement 146
      mediator role of tour leaders 122, 126
      support initiatives, hotel companies 159–161
      wildlife tourism revenue, access to 137
conservation
   funding support from private sector 126–127, 133, 134
   international conferences 3–4
   investment deficiency 31, 147
   local and state regulatory roles 109, 115
   movement (growth in awareness) 17, 56
   rainforest, with community support 159–160
   tourism as rationale for 5, 137
   working holidays (volunteers) 59

consumers
   access to corporate environmental performance data 87–88
   behaviour, effective influences on 63–65, 125–126, 127, 169
   green (environmental) concerns 54–56, 119
   opportunities for responsible tourism 58–61
   purchasing decisions 7–8, 56–58, 66
   see also tourists
contrails (aircraft condensation) 47, 48
Convention on Biological Diversity (CBD) 98
coral reefs, threats and damage 30
Cornwall (UK) 4, 29
corporate social responsibility (CSR) 13, 29, 126–127, 138, 158–162
   see also environmental performance
cost–benefit analysis, tourism 96, 135–137
costs
   air travel 44, 46, 48
   bargaining 126
   holidays, and destination choice 3, 57–58, 62, 121
   of tourism, to host communities 8, 135
   unexpected events and disasters 101
cruise altitude (flight) 45, 48
cruise shipping sector
   growth in demand 60
   negative impacts of major companies 27–28
   scale of CO_2 emissions 49
Cueva de las Manos (Cave of the Hands), Argentina 145
cultural heritage
   community pride in 74, 146
   definition 142
   exploitation and indigenous rights 75–76, 148
   interpretative centres 145, 150, 151
customers *see* consumers

democracy, models of 110, **111**, 115
destinations
   developing and established, compared 4
   global–local interactions, with hotel chains 160–161
   popularity and demand 2–3, 62–63, 167
   poverty in local communities 9–10, 95, 96
   remote areas, adventure tourism 121, 122–123
   responsibility for protection 56–57, 146–147
   tourism expansion control and planning 29–33, 72–73, 123–124, 151–152
   unique character, in place-based tourism 77, 143
Discovery Tours (American Museum of Natural History) 23, 26

Earth Summit (Rio, 1992) 6, 169
'ecochic' 9, 88–89, 169

ecolabelling 29, 60, 65
ecological awareness
    in consumers (tourists) 64–65
    in hotel companies' employees 158
    in local communities 33, 127, 136
    in society and politics 55–56
economic growth
    contributions of airline sector 7
    and recession, effects on responsible tourism
        55, 65, 101
    related to demand for tourism 6, 18, 26,
        155–156
    sharing of benefits 74, 77–78, 91–93,
        95–97
    small island states 9–10, 21
    value of wildlife 135–137, **136**
ecotourism (ET)
    definition and products 23–25, 58–59
    expansion and control 18, 30–32, 35
    long-term outcomes 10–11, 65
    market growth potential 57, 89
education
    cultural heritage site initiatives 146,
        150–151
    entrepreneurial training 78
    environmental
        influence on behaviour 64–65, 125
        provision for local children 134, 138
    as part of marketing package 59, 122
elephants, economic value analysis 136
emissions
    reduction targets 7, 47–48, 51
    sulfur dioxide, from shipping fuel 49, 50–51
    see also carbon dioxide emissions; carbon
        trading
employment opportunities
    adventure tour leaders 122
    hospitality sector 12–13, 155–156
    job creation by tourism, value misgivings 94,
        156–157, 161–162
    regional distribution 77–78, 137
    tourism working conditions 92–93, 123, 157,
        158–159
empowerment 73–74, 76, 114–115, 166
Endogenous Tourism Project (ETP) 100
energy consumption
    fuel efficiency, transport 7, 88
    and living standards 6
    for pollutant removal from fuels 49
    sustainability objectives 55, 124
environment
    management strategies 11–12, 83–84, 124
    tourism impacts **85, 86**
        damage from ecotourism 30–31, 98
        green and brown (/grey) components 82
        hotel operational activity 154, 158
        influencing factors 82–83

mass tourism 3
    positive contributions from wildlife tourism
        133–135
    see also ecological awareness; fragile
        environments
environmental performance (EP)
    assessment by auditors 84–85, 87, 88
    challenges, related to business size 8–9
    EMS (environmental management system)
        adoption 29, 30, 84
    measurement 9, 82, 132
        best practice benchmarks 83–84
        legal standards compliance 83
    policy and funding support 12
    shareholder/public access to data 87–88
ethical tourism (ET)
    consumer choices, ethics and morality 54–55
    definition 21
European Union (EU)
    EC Charter for Cultural Tourism (1989) 4
    Emissions Trading Scheme (ETS) 49–50
    rural development policy 155
    sustainability action plans 5

Faliraki (Greece) 4, 62
flying see aviation
food supplies (local and imported) 33–34, 97,
    161
foreign exchange earnings
    benefits for less developed countries 25,
        77–78
    leakage 9–10, 31, 72, 96
    as regional development driver 18, 161
fragile environments
    alternative tourism, negative impacts 21
    cultural heritage sites 142, 143, 152
    ecotourism projects, acclaimed 10
    risks from cruise sector 27–28
fuels
    domestic/cooking, supplies 8, 124
    transport, alternative types 7, 47–48, 49

GAP Adventures 59
General Agreement on Tariffs and Trade (GATT)
    19, 93
geotourism 77, 166
Global Code of Ethics for Tourism (GCET) 7
globalization
    effects of air transport 46, 51–52
    exemplified by cruise ships 28
    impacts on indigenous cultures 8, 149
    and speed of tourism development 2, 156
    state and international relationships 108,
        168
    trade liberalization consequences 95, 156
golf courses 4, 8, 11, 98
gorilla tourism (Rwanda) 130, 137

governance
    categories and definition 109, **110**
        characteristics, related to responsible tourism
            111–112
    changing government roles in tourism
        107–109
    community-based approaches 114–115
    hierarchical structures 109–110, 113
    market mechanisms 113
    partnerships and participation networks 10–11,
        91, 113–114
    political implications 115–116, 168
    problems of organizational authority 147, 149
Grand Tour (19th c. Europe) 2
green consumerism 54–56, 58, 170
green tourism (GT) 22, 56
greenhouse gases (GHGs)
    chemical interactions, climate effects 48
    linked with deforestation 160
    sources of emissions 55
        commercial flights 7, 47–48
'greenwashing' 60, 65

health and safety risk assessments 125
health care, public and private services 99
heritage see cultural heritage; World Heritage Sites
hierarchical governance 109–110, **111–112**,
    113
holidays, reasons for 61–63, 170
hospitality industry
    corporate social responsibility 158–162
    employment, scale and quality 12–13,
        155–157
    expansion of services, effects 31–32
hotel companies
    energy- and water-saving measures 88
    global–local interactions 155, 160–161, 162
    transnational, green transformation 9,
        159–160
human resources
    local availability 32, 122, 160–161
    migrant workers 101, 157
    staff quality and training 122, 124–125, 147,
        157
    young people/students 156
hunting (wildlife) 130, 135–136, 137

Inca trail see Quebrada de Humahuaca, Argentina
indigenous peoples (IPs)
    art and handicrafts 76, 150–151
    recognition of rights 32, 75–76, 98, 149
    resistance to tourism development 101
    socio-economic development 24, 33–34
    territorial land loss 97
industrial heritage sites 12
International Civil Aviation Organization (ICAO)
    emissions reduction targets 7, 49, 51

establishment (1947) 45
noise performance standards 47
International Council of Tourism Partners (ICTP) 7
International Maritime Organization (IMO) 48–49
International Union for the Conservation of Nature
    (IUCN) 3, 24
interpretative centres, heritage sites 145, 150, 151
Irresponsible Tourism Convention (Kerala, 2008)
    90–91

Jesuit Square and Estates (Manzana Jesuitica
    y Estancias de Córdoba), Argentina
    145–147
job creation see employment opportunities

Kerala Tourism Watch (KTW), protest action
    90–91, 101
Kyoto Protocol (1997) 49, 50, 51

land (property)
    acquisition for tourist complexes 97–98
    communal, community rights 132–133
    price inflation 32, 97, 146, 148
    use competition, wildlife and farming 135–136,
        138
landscapes, cultural 143, 149
Least Developed Countries (LDCs) 93, 96, 100
Leave No Trace (LNT) initiative 59
local people see communities (host)

Maasai communities (East Africa) 77, 101
management
    environmental 11–12, 83–84
    guidelines for World Heritage Sites 143
    human resources 154, 158–159
    natural (wildlife) resources 130, 133, 134, 136
    of risks, planning policies 101, 124
    site management plans 146, 147, 148–149
    supply chains 11, 27, 121–122, 124
marine wildlife watching 12, 28, 133, 134–135
market, as governance mechanism **111–112**, 113
marketing
    brochure information quality 125–126
    by destinations and tour operators 11
    ecotourism packages 25, 59–60
    promotion of World Heritage Sites 146, 148
mass tourism
    economic benefits 26, 72
    historical development 2–3, 46
    negative impacts 17, 18
    relationship to alternative tourism 19, 20–21,
        24
    responsible tourism opportunities 66
medical tourism 99
Mediterranean coast resorts 3
Millennium Development Goals (MDGs) 92, 98, 99
monitoring, environmental 87

National Geographic Society (US) 77, 79
national parks
    biodiversity and rare species 83, 87, 133
    development cycle 12
    private concessions, wildlife tourism 132, 134
    voluntary donation schemes 64
native peoples *see* indigenous peoples
nature, eco or adventure tourism (NEAT) 6, 11, 60
Nepal
    community involvement in tourism 32, 123
    'hippy trail' (1960s) 120
    trekking impacts 8, 124
networks, collaborative governance **111–112**,
        113–114
New Age movement 75
New Zealand, Maori heritage 32, 75–76
nitrogen oxides (NO$_x$) 48
noise
    aircraft, public reactions to 44, 47, 50
    impacts from tourist accommodation and
        transport **85**, **86**
non-governmental organizations (NGOs) 20, 78,
        113, 114, 115

outsourcing (jobs) 156

package holidays 3, 27
    age group targeted products 62
    high-cost niche products 31, 66, 119–120,
        121
participation
    degrees of involvement 73, 90–91
    power balance and pre-formed decisions 102,
        148, 151
planning, policies and regulations 18, 31,
        123–124
poaching (wildlife) 133, 137, 138
policy context
    methods for influencing behaviour 63–65
    public and private sector roles 4, 108–109,
        131–133
    solidification in governance networks 114, 116
    sustainability and economic growth 5–6, 107
    translation into action 100–101, 168–169
politics
    changing role and nature of the state 108–109,
        168
    developing countries, tourism sector recognition
        93
    empowerment of resident communities 74, 79,
        114–115, 161
    grassroots protest actions 90–91, 102
    influence and diversion of profits 94, 95, 97
    neoliberal approaches in tourism sector
        100–101, 110, 113, 167
    reaction against globalization 156
    regional autonomy 147

pollution 8, **85**, **86**
    aviation and shipping fuel components 48, 49
    of coastal/river waters by sewage 88, 123
poverty
    aggravation, from tourism developments
        97–99
    alleviation initiatives 10, 93, 100
    services provision, tourism linkages 92, 97
    understanding realities of 95–97, 102
prices, holiday *see* costs
privatization, political rationale 110
pro-poor tourism 22, 74, 77, 137, 167
    supporting organizations and projects 92–93,
        100
public–private partnerships 12, 76, 113–114, 146

quality, public perceptions and standards 47
Quebrada de Humahuaca, Argentina 147–149

recycling
    aircraft cabin air 87
    waste, at home and on holiday 61, 63, 124,
        125, 170
regulations
    government actions, methods and aims 63–64,
        109–110
    implementation and enforcement 50
    laws and standards, variation between countries
        83
    reliance on voluntary initiatives 100–101
resources
    consumption, global inequalities 6
    economic value of wildlife 135–137, **136**
    overuse by tourists 8, 166
    tourism-induced land use changes 97–98
    see also water resources
responsible tourism (RT)
    aims and effective practices 26, 29, 72, 115
    definition and scope 1, 8, 20, 34, 165
    historical emergence of term 4
    policy instruments (governance) 108–109,
        111–112
retrofitting (environmental improvements) 84
rhino conservation 133, 134, 135
risk management planning 101, 125
routes (travel)
    adventure tour itineraries 121, 123
    cultural heritage trails 76, 147, 150–151
    flight paths 46, 47

'Scandic in Society' community support initiative
        159
seaside resorts 2, 32
seasonality, tourism demand 124
sewage disposal 88, 123, 125
sex tourism 54, 99
shark viewing and marine conservation 134–135

shipping
    history of growth 43
    polluting emissions 48–49, 50–51
    regulations and climate impact trade-offs
        49–51, 52
    see also cruise shipping sector
small (/micro) enterprises
    charitable donations 126–127
    environmental performance 9, 29–30
    financial support sources 78
    responsible tourism implementation 120, 166
social empowerment 73–74
socio-cultural impacts of tourism
    development opportunities 77–78, 137–138
    growth of concerns over 4–5, 93–94
    on indigenous peoples 24, 33–34
    risks of tourism dependence 122–123
    visitor preconceptions and understanding
        125–126
South Africa
    Fair Trade in Tourism (FTTSA) scheme 27, 135
    tourism standards and policy initiatives 131,
        132
    wildlife tourism and conservation 134, 135
staff training see human resources
sulfur dioxide (SO$_2$) 49, 50–51
'sun, sand and sea' (3S) tourism 3, 76
supply chain management
    best and worst practice 27
    integration and links 11, 139, 160–161
    responsibility for third-party suppliers 121–122
    seasonality planning 124
sustainability
    business performance criteria 29
    commitment to, hospitality sector 12–13,
        159–161
    holistic approach 5, 61, 170
    policy output and actual impacts 107, 167
    understanding, global differences 169–170
sustainable tourism (ST), scope of concept 22–23

taxation
    'green' (environmental) taxes 7
    incentive and penalty approaches 63–64, 113
    revenue spending on public services 94
terminology, interpretations and values 19–20, 25
theme parks 3, 27
tokenism 57, 73
tour leaders (adventure tours) 122, 124–125, 126
tour operators (TOs)
    adoption of responsible tourism practices 27,
        29–30, 123–127
    business growth and mergers 120–121
    market influence 11, 26
    responsibilities, consumer perception of 56–57,
        121–122, 126
    visitor management practices 28, 97

tourists
    alternative/independent travellers 21,
        119–120
    categories of ethical behaviour 58
    motivation and attitudes 7–8, 57, 61–63, 65,
        169
traditional livelihoods
    artisan craft production 149, 150–151
    change and development 33–34, 77, 94,
        97–98, 122–123
trains, electrification 7
transport
    energy efficiency 6–7
    environmental impacts **86**, 133, 165
    local/public transport suppliers 122, 150
    long-haul
        aviation industry growth 51–52
        commercial airlines, history of development
            44–46
    'slow travel' 25, 58
    traffic increase, tourist sites 146–147
Travel Foundation, the 57, 120
trekking holidays, impacts 8, 123
TUI Travel (Dutch tour operator) 11, 29, 56, 121
Turkey, tourist developments 17, 18, 26

United Nations
    Commission on Sustainable Development
        (UNCSD) 9, 18, 98
    Conference on Trade and Development
        (UNCTAD) 22
    designation of World Heritage Sites (UNESCO)
        143
    Environment Programme (UNEP) 4, 18,
        24–25, 93
    Framework Convention on Climate Change 50
    promotion of tourism growth 5–6, 93, 98
    support for community participation 32
    see also World Tourism Organization

Valles Calchaquíes, Argentina 150
Voluntary Service Overseas (VSO) 59

water resources 8, 30, 98, 125, 166
whale-watching 12, 28, 133
Wilderness Safaris (tour operator) 133–134, 138
wildlife tourism
    economic value 135–137, 136
    environmental impacts 133–135
    over-commercialization risks 28
    public access to wildlife data 87
    public and private policy setting, Africa
        131–133
    responsible practices 12, 130–131, 138–139
    social and cultural impacts 137–138
women, tourism working conditions 93, 99, 157
work–life balance, hospitality industry 157, 158

World Bank, tourism support projects 94–95
World Conservation Union (WCU) *see* International
  Union for the Conservation of Nature
World Heritage Sites (WHS)
 growth in tourist demand 12, 142, 146, 148
 management guidelines 143
 persistence of local poverty 96–97
 quest for WHS status 145–146, 151
 tourism impacts and challenges 143, 146–147,
  148–149, 151–152, 166

World Tourism Organization (UNWTO)
 Global Code of Ethics for Tourism 7
 policies on tourism development 3, 4, 19, 92,
  93
 stance on women's opportunities 99
World Travel and Tourism Council (WTTC) 10,
  18–19
 strategic frameworks 92
 Tourism for Tomorrow awards 90, **132**
World Travel Market (WTM) 6